new york

a virgin guide

First published in 1999
Virgin Publishing Ltd, London w6 9HT
Copyright 1999 © Virgin Publishing Ltd, London
All rights reserved

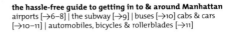

transport
[→6–11]

the hassle-free guide to getting in to & around Manhattan
airports [→6–8] | the subway [→9] | buses [→10] cabs & cars
[→10–11] | automobiles, bicycles & rollerblades [→11]

⚲ getting your bearings
[→12–13]

mapping new york's key areas

virgin new york

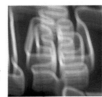

lower east side & chinatown
[→14–17]

eastern delights
edgy | colourful | hip

tribeca
[→18–20]

hollywood east
quiet | cool | professional

soho
[→21–26]

soho, so chic
glamorous | expensive | busy

nolita & noho
[→27–31]

in the no
young | hip | cute

east village
[→32–37]

village people
wild | funky | creative

west village
[→38–42]

west side story
quaint | literary | gay

Written by 20 contributors in-the-know, this guide gives the inside take on New York. The focus is on having fun; where to hang out, shop, eat, relax, enjoy and spoil yourself. And there's a selection of the top cultural hot spots...

contents

chelsea & the meatpacking district [→43–47]

go west
gay | clubby | friendly

gramercy park & the flatiron district [→48–51]

all square
pretty | rarefied | calm

midtown
[→52–57]

middle ground
full on | workaday | vertical

upper east side
[→58–61]

the gold coast
wealthy | gracious | exclusive

upper west side
[→62–64]

western hemisphere
affluent | residential | laid-back

harlem
[→65–67]

take the a train
urban | vibrant | historic

brooklyn
[→68–71]

over the east river
diverse | authentic | emerging

the lowdown on the best shops, restaurants, cafés & bars in each area

getting your bearings

mapping new york's top sights, museums & galleries

[→72–73]

sights, museums & galleries

[→74–88]

big apple higlights
a selection of the best on offer

Manhattan landmarks [→74–76]
one offs [→77–78]
take five [→79–81]
historic houses [→82–83]
melting pot [→83–84]
in the mix [→85–86]
in the picture [→86–88]

spectator sports [→89]
a piece of the action

parks & beaches [→90–91]
turf 'n' surf

children [→92–93]
kids' corner

body & soul [→94–95]
feelgood factor

games & activities [→96–97]
have a blast

getting your bearings

mapping new york's top shopping zones

[→98–99]

shops

[→100–115]

retail therapy
the pick of new york's shops

department stores [→100]
fashion [→101–105]
shoes [→106]
vintage & secondhand [→106–107]
discount stores [→107]
accessories [→108]
sports gear [→108]
theme stores [→108]
beauty [→109]
interiors [→110–111]
gift & museum stores [→111–112]
books [→112]
electronics [→113]
CDs, records & tapes [→113–114]
food stores [→114–115]
markets [→115]

getting your bearings
mapping new york's night-time hot spots
[→116–117]

restaurants & cafés
[→118–138]

what's where [→118–119]

dine out
70 plus restaurants & cafés to cross town for

talk of the town [→120–121]
big bucks [→122–124]
eat-in delis [→123] timeless
classics [→124–125] diners [→126]
bargain gourmet [→126–127]
ethnic spice [→127–128]
romantic rendezvous [→129–131]
burgers [→129] brunch [→131]
veg out [→131] neighbourhood
standouts [→132–133] 24-hours [→133]

bars
[→134–138]

drink up
60 plus bars/pubs to cross town for

club mode [→134] live sounds
[→135] cigar bars [→135] live it up
[→135–136] the status quo [→136]
sports bars [→136] great dives
[→137] quiet retreats [→137]
themes & schemes [→137–138]
gay thirst [→138]

entertainment
[→139–154]

that's entertainment
how to get a slice of the action

theatre [→139–140] cabaret [→140–141]
comedy [→141] cinema [→142–143]
opera & classical music [→143–144]
dance [→144–145] poetry [→145–146]
music [→146–147] media [→148]
directory [→149] clubs [→150–152]
events [→153–154]

hotels
[→155–163]

what's where [→155]

sleep easy
50 of New York's best hotels from the
last word in luxury to budget beds

dead famous [→156] last word in
luxury [→156–157] designer label
[→157–158] chic boutiques
[→158–159] themes & variations
[→159–160] city b & b's [→160–161]
home from home [→161–162]
budget beds [→162–163]

practical information [→164–167]
a–z of essential things you need to know

**index &
acknowledgements** [→168–175]

symbols & key to maps [→176]

subway map [→back cover]

↓ arrivals

Two international airports serve New York: JFK is the larger, although Newark is actually busier. La Guardia, the closest to Manhattan, is used for domestic flights only.

transport

John F Kennedy [JFK]

JFK, in the borough of Queens, covers an area equal to the lower half of Manhattan: annually, around 31 million people pass through this chaotic 'perpetual construction site', with 353,000 flights in and out out of the nine terminals.

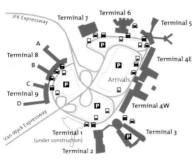

☎ useful numbers:

Enquiries: 1-718-244-4444
Lost and found:
1-718-244-4225/4226
Parking: 1-718-656-5344
Ground Transportation:
w www.jfk-airport.com
1-800-247-7433
☞ **Ramada Plaza**
1-718-995-9000
☞ **Holiday Inn**
1-718-659 0200
General enquiries on transport to/from NYC's airports:
1-800-247-7433 (Port Authority)
w www.panynj.gov

↓ transport options

🚇 Public Transportation

60–75 min to/from Howard Beach on Rockaway A train.

⏱ 24 hours daily, every 10–15 min at peak times 7.30–9.30am, 4.30–7pm, every 15–30 min offpeak.

💷 $1.50

Connects with free bus service (yellow, white and blue bus) to all terminals, every 15 min, approx 30-min ride.

⚲ The cheapest option and not dependent on traffic.

⚠ **1|** Avoid late at night.
2| The journey can feel arduous with heavy bags.

❶ **1|** Make sure you get trains going to Rockaways and not Ozone Park-Lefferts Blvd.
2| Howard Beach is not the last stop on the line.
3| Allow enough time a) for both parts of the journey and b) delays on the subway.

☎ 1-718-330-1234

🚌 Shuttle Buses

New York Airport Service

60–75 min to/from Grand Central Station, Port Authority and Penn Station.

⏱ 6.05am–1pm every 30 min, and 1–11.40pm every 15 min, daily.

💷 $13

⚲ Set schedule and well-marked bus stops.

⚠ Travel times are dependent on traffic.

☎ 867-2816/1-718-706-9658.

❶ Formerly Carey Airport Express.

Gray Line Airport Shuttle

60–75 min to any Midtown hotel.

⏱ 6am–11pm, daily.

💷 $14

⚲ Door-to-door service.

⚠ Up to a 20-min wait for the shuttle bus.

☎ 315-3006/1-800-451-0455 allow an hour if booking to go to the airport, or order service from Ground Transportation.

Super Shuttle

60–75 min to/from Midtown.

⏱ 24 hours, daily.

💷 $14–17 to east/west Manhattan (serves Downtown to 110th St Manhattan).

⚲ Service through the night.

⚠ **1|** Allow a 30-min wait at the airport.
2| Buses accomodate up to seven people – drivers wait until enough people want to go to the same part of town before departing.

☎ 258-3826 or order service from Ground Transportation.

🚗 Taxis, limos & cars

Taxis

45–65 min journey

⏱ 24 hours, daily.

💷 $33 flat rate, plus tolls ($3.50) and tip.

⚲ Most convenient.

⚠ Relatively expensive.

❶ **1|** At the airport, only accept a cab from an official taxi dispatcher.
2| If you decide to share a cab to split the cost, note that after the first stop the meter starts running.

Limos & Cars

45–65 min to/from Manhattan.

⏱ 24 hours, daily.

$30–$35 for cars (minicabs). $70–$80 for limos. Plus tolls ($3.50) and tip.

⚑ Travel in style.

❧ Most expensive option.

❶ 1| If you call a Manhattan company, ensure they already have a car at the airport.
2| It is illegal for cars to make pick-ups without being formally dispatched.
3| Make sure you know which terminal you are at when you give the pick-up details.
☎ Some companies have direct phones located at terminal exits, or call:

Town Cars Anywhere: 1-800-532-3730

Carmel: 1-800-924-9954

Classic Limousine: 1-800-666-4949

Tel Aviv: 1-800-222-9888

Newark [EWR]

Passenger traffic figures at Newark – New York's second largest international airport, based in New Jersey – now exceed JFK's, with over 32 million people using the 56 airlines flying from its three terminals each year.

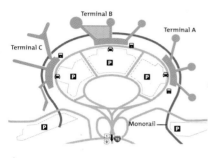

transport

☎ **useful numbers**

Enquiries: 1-973-961-6000
Lost and found: 1-973-961-6633
Ground transportation:
w www.panynj.gov
1-800-247-7433
✆ **Concordia Hotel:** 1-973-824-4700
✆ **Days Inn:** 1-973-242-0900

↓ transport options

⊞ Public Transportation

Airlink Bus & PATH/New Jersey Transit Trains [→9]

1| Airlink Bus: 15–30 min to/from Penn Station.

🕓 6.15–1.45am daily, every 20 min.

💳 $4, exact fare only.

☎ 1-800-626-7433

2| Connecting with either:
a) PATH train, 15–25 min ride, via Christopher St; 9th & Sixth Ave; 14th St & Sixth Ave; 23rd St & Sixth Ave and 33rd St & Sixth Ave.

🕓 24 hours daily, every 15 min.

💳 $1

☎ 1-800-234-7284

or b) NJT train, 20 min to/from 34th St (bet. Seventh & Eighth Aves).

🕓 24 hours daily, every 15–20 min.

💳 $2.50

☎ 1-800-626-7433

⚑ Cheapest way to get to the city.

❧ Unreliable scheduling and connection times.

❶ 1| Have small bills and change for your fares.
2| Connections with the subway involve quite a walk.
3| Trains run 24 hours, but the bus link does not.

⊟ Shuttle Buses

Olympia Trails Bus Company

30–40 min to/from Grand Central Station or Penn Station to Newark.

🕓 5am–11pm daily, every 20–30 min.

💳 $10

⚑ Very convenient and there are always places available.

❧ Allow a 20-min wait at the airport.

❶ For an additional fare (💳 $5), there is a hotel connection bus (8am–9pm) to/from Grand Central Station.

☎ 964-6233 or order minibus from Ground Transportation.

Gray Line Airport Shuttle

30–60 min to/from any Midtown hotel.

🕓 6am–11pm, daily.

💳 $14 ($19 return)

❧ Allow a 20-min wait at the airport.

☎ 315-3006/1-800-451-0455 or order minibus from Ground Transportation.

Super Shuttle

60–90 min to/from Midtown.

🕓 24 hours daily.

💳 $17

⚑ Door-to-door drop off throughout the night.

❧ Up to a 30-min wait at the airport.

❶ 1| Up to a 30-min wait at the airport.
2| Buses take up to seven people and drivers wait until enough people want to go to the same part of town before departing.

☎ 258-3826 or order from Ground Transportation.

⊟ Taxis, limos and cars

50–60 min to/from Midtown.

🕓 24 hours daily.

💳 $40 and up, plus tolls ($5.70) and tip.

☎ Some cab companies have direct phones near the terminal exits, or call:
Route 22: 1-800-680-3334
Airport Express: 1-877-546-6332
Carmel: 1-800-924-9954
Tel Aviv: 1-800-222-9888

⚑ The luxury way to travel.

❧ Most expensive option.

❶ 1| Be sure you know which terminal you are at when you give the pick up details.
2| If you take a car from the rank, check the price of your exact destination before you set out.

La Guardia [LGA]

La Guardia sees 22 million people and 355,000 planes come and go each year. Twenty-three airlines, serving destinations all over the US, fly from this convenient Queens base with four terminals.

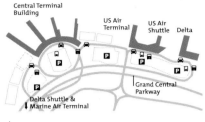

Central Terminal Building

US Air Terminal

US Air Shuttle Delta

Grand Central Parkway

Delta Shuttle & Marine Air Terminal

☎ useful numbers:

Flight enquiries:
1-800-555-1212
General enquiries:
1-718-533-3400
Emergencies:
1-718-533 3900
Lost and found:
1-718-533-3988
w www.panynj.gov
☞**Marriott:**
1-718-565-8900

↓ transport options

⊞ Public Transportation

Subway/Bus

1| To/from 74th St-Roosevelt Ave on E•F•G•R•7 trains. (approx 30-min ride to/from Midtown) ⏰ 24 hours daily, every 10–15 min. ⊞ $1.50

Connecting with Q33 bus – a 10-min ride to/from the central terminal building. ⊞ $1.50 (or free subway transfer).

2| Around 30 min to/from Astoria Blvd on N train; 125th St on A•B•C•D•2•3•4•5•6 trains; 116th St-Columbia University on 1•9 trains ⏰ 24 hours daily, every 10–15 min. ⊞ $1.50

Connecting with M60 bus, a 20–60-min ride to/from La Guardia with bus stops outside each terminal. ⊞ $1.50 ⏰ approx 5–1am daily, every 15–30 min.

❶ Ask the driver for a transfer so you can hook up with another bus route.

☎ 1-718-330-1234

⊟ Shuttle Bus

New York Airport Service
45–50 min to/from Grand Central Station or the Port Authority bus terminal.
⏰ 5.30am–11.30pm daily, every 15–30 min. ⊞ $10

✎ **1|** Grand Central Station is convenient for Midtown hotels.
2| Set schedule.

✎ **1|** Travel times are dependent on traffic.
2| Port Authority has lots of escalators and stairs to reach street and subway levels.

☎ 1-718-706-9658

New York Airport Express Connection

Bus (approx 20-min ride) to/from Jamaica station (Queens).
⏰ 7am–10pm daily, hourly from outside each terminal. ⊞ $5

Connect with LIRR [→9] to Penn Station, approx a 20-min ride. ⏰ 24 hours daily, every 10–15 min. ⊞ $5.50 (7.30–9.30am & 4.30–7pm), $3.75 (off-peak).

✎ The cheapest option.

✎ **1|** Making connections with luggage is difficult.
2| The LIRR is often busy.

☎ 1-718-205-7825

⊟ Taxis, limos and cars

30–45 min to/from Midtown. ⏰ 24 hours daily. ⊞$22 and up, plus tolls ($3.50) and tip.

✎ Contact Ground transportation, or call:
Carmel: 1-800-924-9954
Tel Aviv: 1-800-222-9888

✎ The luxury way to travel.

✎ Most expensive option.

⚓ Ferry

Delta Water Shuttle
30–45 min to/from E 62nd St pier, E 34th St pier, or Pier 11 (Wall Street). ⏰ every hour, 6.30am–5.30pm to La Guardia; 7.45am–6.45pm to Manhattan. ⊞ $15 ($25 round trip)

✎ fun, quick and easy.

✎ essentially only runs during office hours.

☎ 1-800-533-3779

↓ general info

⊟ metrocards

These come in a variety of denominations. The pay-per-ride card allows you to put money on your card in whatever increment you choose ($3–$80). For refills of more than $15, there is a bonus ride – that's 11 for the price of 10. You can get cards valid for seven days ($17) or 30 days ($63). The Fun Card offers unlimited rides on buses and subways for a whole day ($4).

With all MetroCards™, you can make a free transfer within two hours subway-to-bus, bus-to-subway and bus-to-bus (the ticket machines

will display 'Xfer' for transfer). As well as in stations, $3, $6 and $15 MetroCards™ are sold in delis and supermarkets. For up-to-date information on where to buy MetroCards™ call ☎ 638-7622.

❶ Fun Cards are sold at Grand Central Station at the transit museum store; Times Square Visitors' Centre; some pharmacies and cheque agencies.

⊟ kids

Children under 44 inches high ride free on subways and buses.

♿ disabled travellers

Access for the disabled in New York is good; buses are the best option, as they are all fully equipped for wheelchairs and the drivers are good-hearted folk. For bus and subway travel enquiries ☎ 1-718-596-8585. *Accessible Travel* is a free guide with a Braille subway map, available from the MTA New York City Transit.

For private car hire, Upward Mobility Limousines have roll-in wheelchair-accessible cars.
☎ 1-718-645-7774

❶ the disabled travel at half-fare on public transportation.

↓ going underground

The subway is as chaotic as the city and people it serves – on average it carries 3.8 million customers a day.

subway map [→back cover]

Maps are available free upon request from all stations. They are the definitive user's guide – the one drawback is that they are huge.

↓ using the subway

• There are 25 routes, all colour-coded and identified by a number or letter. Local trains stop at all stations; express trains only stop at stations marked with a black-ringed white circle.

• Transfers are possible when two or more lines serve one station. On maps, two stations connected with a line shows a transfer point.

☎ **useful numbers:**

Information: 1-718-330-1234
Transit police: 1-718-330-3330
Lost and found: 1-718-625-6200

❶ subway essentials

⏲ 24 hours daily, every 2–5 min (6.30–9.30am & 3.30–8pm, Mon–Fri), every 10–15 min at other times. Reduced service after midnight – check official subway map as some stations close.

🎫 $1.50 flat fare. You must buy a MetroCard™ or a token to pass through the turnstiles.

👍 1| Cheap and handy.
2| Much cleaner and less intimidating than anything you may be expecting.

👎 1| Not ideal for crosstown journeys.
2| If you are not used to the subway system, it is easy to miss your stop, get on the wrong train or go in the wrong direction – some trains go for miles between stops.
3| The idiosyncratic service can be a nuisance if you

don't know which lines and stations to avoid.

❶ Some stations have different entrances for Downtown or Uptown platforms – usually on opposite sides of the street. Check on a map before going through the turnstile.

do
1| Double-check to see if you are on the local/express or Uptown/Downtown platform.
2| Stand in the designated area, or wait near the manned ticket booth after peak hours or at empty stations.
3| Be aware of your belongings.
4| Ask fellow passengers if you're unsure as not all subway cars have line route maps inside.

don't
1| Smoke anywhere on the subway.
2| Jump the turnstiles: police

will give you an on-the-spot fine or even arrest you.

MUNY (Music Under New York)

Performing arts are making subway travel more attractive thanks to MUNY – a creative arts programme funded by the Metropolitan Transportation Authority. Call for details of performances (Cajun, blue-grass, African, South American and jazz) scheduled in subway and commuter rail stations.

☎ 362-3830

transport

suburban trains

▥ Long Island Rail Road (LIRR)

The LIRR network stretches from the eastern tip of Montauk, Long Island to Penn Station (at 33rd St & Seventh Ave) nearly 120 miles away. Tickets purchased on trains when ticket offices are open cost more, so buy before you board. Most stations now have ticket-vending machines. Travelling offpeak saves you about 30%; rush-hour times are 6–10am and 4–7pm. These trains are good for getting to the beaches [→88].

☎ 1-718-217-5477

▥ New Jersey Transit

NJ Transit operates trains and buses throughout New Jersey. Commuter trains have two terminals: Hoboken, in northern NJ where

passengers can transfer to the PATH trains, ferries or buses to continue to NYC; and Newark Penn Station, which has services to NY Penn Station. There is a $3 penalty for purchasing a ticket on the train when the station's ticket office is open.

☎ 1-973-762-5100

▥ PATH

PATH (Port Authority Trans-Hudson) rapid trains run between New Jersey and NYC Newark, Harrison and Hoboken Stations 24 hours a day, seven days a week.

☎ 1-800-234-7284

▥ Metro-North Railroad

Serves lower New York State and SW Connecticut out of Grand Central Station (Lexington Ave at 42nd St).

☎ 532-4900

long-distance travel

▥ Amtrak

All long-distance rail services operate out of Penn Station.
☎ 1-800-872-7245

🚌 **Long distance bus travel**

These services operate out of Port Authority Bus Terminal, 40th–42nd Sts (bet. Eighth & Ninth Aves).

☎ 564-8484

➲ more buses | cabs | cars | automobiles | bicycles | rollerblades

↓ on the buses

NYC's buses carry 1.5 million people daily – and it feels like it. Because of their plodding progress, buses carry a certain kind of New Yorker – late-night workers, families and kids going to and from school. They tend to be neighbourhood-oriented, with many passengers and drivers on first-name terms.

bus map

Free from all subway stations, the bus map is easy to read and doubles as a tourist guide, with major sights clearly marked.

↓ using the buses

• Bus stops are located every two or three blocks, marked by route signs and yellow-painted curbs. Abbreviated route maps (occasionally) appear at bus stops, showing the buses that run along that avenue or street. The printed times are highly unreliable.

• The driver will stop if he sees you, but to make sure, hold out your arm and wave. After 11pm drivers will pick up and drop off between official stops.

• To indicate that you want to get off at the next stop, press any part of the 'strip' that runs in between and above the windows.

• The back doors take a bit of getting used to. Push on the yellow strip and the doors will slowly open – follow up with a firm shove. You can also get off at the front.

• There are two types of buses: regular, making all stops, and Limited (an LED sign with the word 'Limited'

is displayed in the front window). Limited buses stop only at major cross streets and transfer points.

❶ bus essentials

☺ 24 hours daily, but run less frequently after midnight.

💷 $1.50 flat fare.
Paying by MetroCard™: insert card as you get on. This entitles you to a free ride when connecting with the subway or another bus within two hours.
Paying by coins: drop into slot in front of the driver. Exact fare only, but you can also use subway tokens.

♵ 1| Buses run along all avenues and on major cross-streets; generally they are the best public transport option for cross-town travel.
2| Free sightseeing tour of the city.

❶ Even when paying for your ride with coins or a token, you can ask for a transfer ticket, which allows you to catch another bus for free (within two hours); ie after a cross-town bus ride, you can also hop on an uptown or downtown bus and vice versa.

♵ Don't go anywhere near a bus if you're in a hurry.

do
1| Have your exact fare, token or MetroCard™ ready.
2| Shout if the driver forgets to open the back doors.

don't
Smoke on buses.

☎ **useful numbers:**

Travel info (6am–9pm, daily):
1-718-330-1234
Customer service:
1-718-330-3322
Lost and found:
1-718-625-6200

↓ catch a cab

cab spiel

In case you forget to 'belt up, take all of your belongings and get a receipt', an automated celebrity voiceover will remind you. Everyone from Dr Ruth, the sex columnist, to Pavarotti has given their two-cents worth.

The yellow cab is synonymous with Manhattan. Careering madly through traffic, cabs seem able to move in even the thickest of jams; nevertheless in gridlocks the predominant colour is always yellow.

↓ using yellow cabs

• You can stop a cab if the middle panel only on the cab is lit. During rush hours, the competition is fierce.

• It is a good idea to have at least a vague notion of how to get where you want to go. 'Politely' suggest your favoured route and keep an eye open for unnecessarily long detours.

• As a rule, yellow cabs only take four people.

☎ **useful numbers:**

Lost property: 302-8294
Taxi Limousine Commission: 676-1000 (for complaints)

❶ cab essentials

Taxis are metered: the fare starts at $2 and rises 30¢ per 1/5 mile, or 25¢ per 75 seconds in slow traffic or when stationary.

Having successfully hailed a cab, get in quickly. The driver is likely to start moving before you've even told him where you want to go.

Tip 15–20% – or else!

Most drivers don't like to change anything bigger than a $20 note.

Pay the driver while still seated in the back of the cab.

♵ There are lots and lots!

♵ 1| Although plentiful at all other times, in bad weather conditions – forgeddaboutit.
2| Get in before you ask to go to Brooklyn or the Bronx, as legally they cannot then refuse you, but most drivers have threadbare knowledge of the outer boroughs.

do
Use them – taking a cab is not considered a luxury in NY.

don't
1| Argue with the driver: in yellow cabs the customer is never right.
2| Smoke – the driver could lose his licence.

car services

Generally referred to as 'cars', not 'minicabs', and suitable for longer journeys. For instance, if you need to go to/from Brooklyn, the company should supply a driver who is familiar with the neighbourhood.

❶ 1| When they say they'll be there in '5 minutes', they mean it!
2| You must look out for them – drivers never ring the bell.
3| Check the price of the ride before you set off or, better

still, with the controller when you order the car.

☍ 1| Convenient if you are not near a busy main street, or if it is late or raining.
2| You can specify what kind of car (eg 'station wagon' for more than four of you).
☍☍ Poor language skills, bad driving and no sense of direction ... only the worst-case scenario.

do
Only call when you are ready to leave.

don't
Get in a gypsy cab (unlicensed, unmarked cars) – they will rip you off.

☎ useful numbers:

Downtown Delancey Car Service: 228-3301
Brooklyn Evelyn Car Service: 1-718-230-7800/8244
Random Carmel: 1-800-924-9954/666-6666
Tel Aviv: 1-800-222-9888/777-7777

↓ freewheeling

Since New York's public transport system is both relatively efficient and inexpensive, the only reason to rent a car is to get out of town. Driving and parking in the city gives new meaning to the word nightmare, and only the most foolhardy would want to share the road with New York's army of yellow cab maniacs.

↓ rules of the road in NYC

• Drive on the right.
• You cannot make a right turn on a red light.
• Seatbelts are compulsory in front and rear seats.
• School buses are sacred and the fines for passing one which has stopped are huge.
• Do not park within 50 ft of a fire hydrant.
• Speed limit is 30 mph.
• Vandalism and car theft are rife.

At the wheel

Nowhere do the rules of supply and demand apply more than in New York's car rental business – prices rocket on a holiday weekend. If you call one of the major rental agencies, be prepared: know from what location you want to rent, how long for and the exact dates – all of these factors affect cost and availability (average $50–60 per day). You must have a major credit card, a passport and a valid driver's licence (foreign licences are accepted). Large companies have a minimum age of 25, but for an extra $10–30 per day, they'll bend the rules.

❶ 1| Always get the most comprehensive insurance.
2| It's cheaper to rent from outside the city. Ask the big companies for their regional office locations.

☎ Car hire:

A-1 Rent a Car: 348-5151
Avis: 1-800-831-2847
Budget: 1-800-527-0700
Enterprise: 1-800-325-8007

Hertz: 1-800-654-3131
Rent-a-Wreck: 1-718-784-3302
They will pick you up at the station.

gas

Gas stations in Manhattan are few and far between. These two are reliable and open 24 hours:
Uptown: Atlas Garage 303 W 96th St (bet. West End Drive & Riverside Drive).
Downtown: Amoco 610 Broadway (at Houston Street).

Parking meters and lots

Meters: depending on the neighbourhood and the time of day, it will cost you anything from 25¢ (for 20 min) to 25¢ (for 1 hr). If you are towed, call the helpline (Mon–Fri) and expect a fine of around $150. ☎ 477-4430

Lots: private parking lots are more expensive but at least you are guaranteed to find your car in one piece.

do
Note signs on opposite side of street, indicating which days the street cleaners come.

don't
Park anywhere a sign says 'no stopping' or 'no standing'; in a bus stop; or by a fire hydrant.

Bicycles

Most cycle routes are in city parks, but if you've got the guts, cycling is an excellent way to see the city. Though not illegal, it would be unwise to ride without a helmet or lights.

Bike riders must follow the same road rules as car drivers and fines for running red lights or riding without a

bell (!) in Midtown are commonplace.

Bike rental: A security deposit of $150 held on a credit card is usually required:

☎ Bike hire:

Bikes in the Park, Loeb Boathouse, Central Park (summer only)
☍ $8–$10 per hr (5 or 10 speed bikes) ☎ 861-4137
Bicycles Plus, Second Ave (bet. 87th & 88th Sts). ☍ $7.50 per hr/$25 per day ☎ 722-2201
Metro Bike .
☍ $6 per hr; $25 per day.
14th St (bet. First & Second Aves) ☎ 228-4344
1311 Lexington Ave (at 88th Street) ☎ 427-4450
Sixth Avenue (at 15th Street) ☎ 255-5100
417 Canal Street ☎ 334-8000

Roller Blades

So, you really want to get around in a hurry, while looking cool. Try blading it [→97]. Only for the very proficient.

☎ Roller Blade hire:

Blades East & West
☍ $16 per day, Mon–Fri; $27 per weekend (Sat–Sun)
❶ hire includes free protective gear.
160 E 86th St (bet. Lexington & Third Aves) ☎ 996-1644
105 W 72nd St (bet. Columbus Ave & Broadway) ☎ 787-3911
Second Ave (at 74th St) ☎ 249-3178
Village Wheels
63–73 E 8th St (at Broadway) ☎ 505-6753
☍ $10 for three hours.

new york's key areas

directory

Alphabet city ⌕B5
Named after Avenues A, B, C, and D, which march from First Avenue to the East River. The mainly Puerto Rican community has been supplemented by an influx of students and yuppies – though the area has always had its artsy-types (like Allen Ginsburg and Iggy Pop).

Brooklyn Heights ⌕B6
This is 'Cosby-country'. With its majestic brownstones, poetically named (Orange, Pineapple, Cranberry etc) tree-lined streets, and the Promenade overlooking the river, the Heights is what the term 'des-res' was invented for.

DUMBO ⌕B6
Down Under the Manhattan Bridge Overpass, the cobbled alleyways are lined with warehouses, which are rapidly being appropriated by escaping Manhattanites. Spectacular skyline views and a thriving art scene herald the area's revival.

Garment District ⌕A4
Delivery trucks and men wheeling racks of cheap clothing clog the streets around Seventh (Fashion) Avenue and 34th Street. Fashion Avenue is a sad misnomer; there is nothing fashionable to be had along the stretch of sweat-shop produced designer rip-offs.

Hell's Kitchen ⌕A4
Once a poor, down-and-out neighbourhood, the area west of the Port Authority Bus terminal is about to 'blow up' according to realtors. Meanwhile, the Cubans have transformed the former Irish enclave around 10th avenue in the 40's with a taste of the homeland. Although the area was rechristened 'Clinton' in 59, the name never really stuck.

Little Italy ⌕B5
With the ever-expanding China-town eating up this tiny neighbourhood, 'little' is an apt description. The tacky restaurants are over-priced, but the cafés are excellent for coffee and desserts; traditional Italian food stores can't fail to please either.

Lower Manhattan ⌕B5–B6
Bustling by day; ghost town by night, the tapered end of the island of Manhattan is home to City Hall [→74], Wall Street and the NY Stock Exchange. New housing developments in Battery Park City [→91] house the movers and shakers living in the shadow of the World Trade Center [→76].

Murray Hill ⌕B4
The constant traffic to and from the Queens–Midtown tunnel has taken something from this once toney neighbourhood south of 42nd Street. But elegant houses and the Pierpont Morgan Library [→83] raise the zip code's ratings and it's still considered a fashionable address to have.

Museum Mile ⌕B3–B4
Museums abound along Fifth Avenue, from the Frick Collection [→82] on 70th St all the way up to ICP Uptown [→87] on 96th, with the Met [→75], Solomon R Guggenheim [→80] and the Cooper-Hewitt [→82] to mention but a few, in between.

Navy Yard ⌕C6
During World War II, 70,000 employees worked here, where the motto was 'Can do'. Today, Navy Yard is still an industrial park but many of its unused buildings are in deep decay, lending it a strange, otherworldly feel. Rumoured to be the location for NY's answer to Hollywood, a plan masterminded by De Niro and co.

Red Hook ⌕B6
Cut off from the rest of Brooklyn by the Brooklyn–Queens Expressway, Red Hook is rather isolated, with Civil War-era warehouses, clapboard cottages, and some of the city's most notorious housing projects. (Red Hook was the setting for Hubert Selby Jr's Last Exit to Brooklyn.) Blessed with extraordinary light, the area is very popular with artists.

Roosevelt Island ⌕B3
Situated in the middle of the East River, the island that used to house a lunatic asylum and a smallpox hospital is now home to a community of 8000. The cable cars across to the island offer some of the best views in town [→76].

Spanish Harlem ⌕B2
East of Fifth Avenue and above 100th Street is a colourful and music-filled neighbourhood (also known as El Barrio), though quite desolate by night. Local landmarks are La Marqueta (the food market on Park Avenue from 110th to 116th Streets), or the Graffitti Hall of Fame at 106th Street between Park and Madison Avenues.

Theater District ⌕A4
Broadway wends its way through Times Square, lined with a profusion of theatres. In New York's sleazy past this was also home to the porn industry – now it's squeaky clean, and Disney has moved in.

Upper Manhattan ⌕A1
With an amazing view of the Hudson River to the west and the Harlem River to the east, the island's narrowest point is an odd mixture of inner city and wilderness. Location of The Cloisters Museum [→85], and Inwood Hill Park, which holds the last traces of the island's ancient forest.

Yorkville ⌕B3
Home to the 'old money' of NY: beautiful townhouses, doormen and expensive restaurants define the area from the 70's to 96th Street east of Lexington Avenue. Gracie Mansion – the mayor's official residence, is set in the area's lush Carl Shultz Park.

Bronx ⌕B1
The only NY borough that is not an island. Recent renovations and investment mean it is losing its reputation as a no-go zone and there are several attractions (Bronx Zoo [→92], Botanical Gardens [→81] Yankee stadium [→89]). For the curious, the elevated subway lines provide a safe view of the erstwhile battlegrounds of the South Bronx and will take you through New York's most ethnically diverse communities.

Queens ⌕C3
Visitors to New York will probably only see Queens when journeying to or from its two airports, and truth be told the same can be said for most New Yorkers. But delve deeper and the borough's multicultural makeup has lots to offer. Long Island City houses PS1 – the super-cool studio space and gallery [→88]. Then there's the Greek neighbourhood of Astoria, Irish Woodside, and Indian and South American Jackson Heights. The huge steel 'Unisphere' globe (as seen in Men in Black), is a left-over from the 1964 world fair held in Corona Park.

Staten Island ⌕see locator
The relationship between Staten Islanders and their neighbours is a love-hate one, with talk of secession bandied about over the last few years. Non residents mostly know it for being the site of the largest landfill in the world. But the free ferry service between Manhattan and Staten Island gives one of the best views of Manhattan, and a short trolley ride from the port takes you to the Snug Harbour Cultural Center where there's a gallery, a butterfly house and Opera performances.

getting your bearings

eastern delights

lower east side & chinatown

Nowadays, the tenement buildings of the Lower East Side (LES), New York's one-time Jewish ghetto, are more likely to be occupied by Hispanics and Koreans than bearded men in black hats. You'll still find some evidence of the district's ancestry: look for its die-hard delis and crumbling synagogues. Recently, a new generation of dream-seekers has moved in – boutique-keepers, bar owners, trust-fund anarchists, and latter-day bohos – migrating from the neighbouring East Village in search of lower rents. As a result, real estate prices here have rocketed, and the LES has been reborn as Hipster Central.

Chinatown, meanwhile, remains irrepressibly oriental. Bolstered by a continuous stream of Chinese immigration, the area teems with authentic markets, stalls, restaurants and teahouses (as well as those ubiquitous neon signs). However, with its proximity to ritzier areas, will it be victim to Downtown's rampant gentrification? It's hard to imagine that Chinatown's booming, energetic stronghold will ever be entirely repressed.

day

🛍 A mix of bargain shops and cool boutiques (which tend to open and stay open late), and the discount stores and stalls of Chinatown.

👁 Battery Park [→91]; Brooklyn Bridge [→74]; City Hall [→74]; Ellis Island [→77]; Lower East Side Gardens [→91]; Lower East Side Tenement Museum [→82]; National Museum of the American Indian [→84]; Statue of Liberty [→76]; Woolworth Building [→77]; World Trade Center [→76].

night

☆ An eclectic array of groovy bars and live music venues (especially on Ludlow and Orchard Streets).

🍽 Chinatown's excellent restaurants are as busy by night as they are by day.

Ⓜ B•D•Q to Grand St; F to 2nd Ave, E Broadway or Delancey-Essex Sts; J•M•Z to Canal St, Bowery or Delancey-Essex Sts; A•C•E•N•R•6 to Canal St.

🚌 M9 ⟶ E Broadway via Essex St & Ave B; M14 ⇕Essex St via Grand St; M15 ⇕St James Pl via Allen St, 1st & 2nd Aves; M21 ⟶ Houston St via Ave C; M103 ⇕Bowery via 3rd & Lexington Aves.

shopping

fashion & accessories

With its Sunday market on Orchard Street and discount stores on Delancey Street, the LES has always been a bit of a bargain-hunter's bazaar. But it's no longer just the place to pick up some *schmutter*. New stores open regularly in settings where the aesthetic screams minimalist chic, and the designs are definitely edgy and fresh. **Mary Adams** and ***Amy Downs** ✔ are the fashion pioneers of the LES. Mary is mistress of distinctive, feminine party dresses; Amy's forte is hats – always whimsical and themed (like those inspired by famous NYC locations). But the store that really made the LES happen is ***TG-170**, thanks to Terri Gillis's gift for finding brilliant new designers. It has ultra-girlie styles at (relatively) affordable prices. Check out United Bamboo, Rubin-chappelle and the house label (for basics), along with must-have bags from Pixie Yates and Karen Zoebe. At **Patch 155**, designer Cal Patch's treasure trove of quirky clothes – urban and funky-pretty – includes exclusive labels such as 'It's an Exciting Time to Be Me!'. Another tiny shop filled with brilliance is **Xuly Bet**, showcase of Parisian-based designer La Min, whose inspiring pieces often feature the signature multi-textured and multi-coloured patchwork made from recycled materials. Don't confuse him with **Min Lee**, who specializes in classic clothes

with a little twist – chic numbers that can be worn all day and into the night when teamed with tiny, fabulous evening bags. At **MIKS**, a spartan, light store is filled with simple, refined and remarkably inexpensive streetwear by the eponymous Japanese design collective. Local designer, Eun Joo Sohn, has space here too.

Alternatively, **DDC Lab** is an all-white style palace, radiating sophistication and big price tags. Lots of cashmere, but ultimate hedonism can be obtained in the form of limited-edition Reeboks at a mere $2500! Making quite a splash at the epicentre of the LES, minimal ***Nova**

USA ∆, surrounded by a haze of bright lights, carries the basics that make life worth living. For yet another version of sleek, urban sportswear, there's **Juan Anon**, where the colour palette is mostly neutral to match the low-key vibe.

Recon, on the other hand, is all camouflage paint and razor wire, selling T-shirts and hi-tech toys – a place where testosterone rules. Down the street is **Vinnie's Tampon Case**, which oozes oestrogen: devoted to selling the consummate carry-all for your tampons, Vinnie is so immersed in his products, he's even created a performance piece about them. Satisfy your need for more fun and groovy accessories in **Lucky Wang**. If the *tchotchkes* here don't turn you on, stop in at **Toys in Babeland**, a hip sex shop with naughty lingerie and toys like the Pocket Rocket for girls home alone.

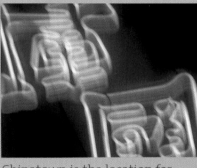

Chinatown is the location for designer knock-offs along with lots of real chinoiserie.

chinese emporiums

Discount stalls line Broadway and Canal Street selling fake fashion items. You might get a bargain or you might get ripped off. In the thick of it, the ***Pearl River Mart** – a longtime favourite with beauty editors and stylists – has elegant Chinese clothes at realistic prices. The top floor stocks a vast assortment of kimonos, silk and embroidered pyjamas and underwear, slippers, cheongsam dresses, and padded jackets. On other floors are kitschy home furnishings, trinkets, Chin- ese music, videos and food, and you're bound to see some celebrity picking through

the treasures. A tip – avoid the rickety elevator and take the stairs! **Oriental Gifts** also has a nice (though smaller) variety of Chinese goods, from vases to fans, lanterns and woks. If you want your cheongsam custom-made for a fraction of what it would cost you to buy the Dolce & Gabbana version (and it will be nearly as amazing), drop by the **Oriental Dress Company**. You can choose from the shop's own luxurious silks (in a wide variety of colours), or provide your own fabric. Orders take about three weeks, long dresses cost $280, short $250.

vintage & home furnishings

The LES is a good area for vintage gear, especially home furnishings. **Las Venus** deals in 20th-century pop culture, focusing on the 50's, 60's and 70's, including a few items of clothing that are very *Valley of the Dolls*. Neighbouring **Timtoum** acts as a magnet for those who attend the owners' club night. Clothing by local designers, used garb, and an eclectic selection of vinyl are the lure. **Cherry** has top quality 60's collectables and some really fun clothes (heavy on glamorous dresses), while **Shine** is a more understated vintage jewel box, with its small collection of clothes – mostly feminine and very fashionable.

lower east side & chinatown

restaurants & cafés | bars & clubs | directory & map

eating & drinking

restaurants & cafés

The LES has played host to waves of immigrants from around the world, which is reflected in the choice of restaurants on offer. Only a handful of Jewish eateries remain including *Katz's Deli. Although a bit frayed at the edges, it is still popular with locals and American presidents alike (look for proudly displayed letters from Reagan and Clinton). The countermen slap together glorious pastrami sandwiches thick enough for two. Yonah Schimmel's Knishery, founded in 1910, is a rather decrepit hole-in-the-wall, still beloved for dumpling-like potato knishes as well as homemade bagels. For more of a DIY snack, check out Russ & Daughters (known locally as the Herring Kings). Among the tasty treats on offer are lox, scallion cream cheese, superb chopped liver and chewy bagels to go. The rather shabby El Sombrero (aka The Hat) is frequented mostly by actors and musicians after performances. The Mexican food is cheap and pretty basic: its real appeal is the potent Margaritas. *Bereket is another cheap bet, a bright beacon dispensing fresh Turkish fast food, 24 hours a day.

The new, mod LES is epitomized by Torch, a swanky lounge and 40's-style supper club. Nightly cabaret acts can be enjoyed along with great cocktails and French/South American-inspired cuisine. For a daytime, bohemian hangout, Lotus Club provides healthy sandwiches and arty magazines, which you can peruse or purchase.

Undeniably, most of the best places to eat in this area are in Chinatown. The most celebrated is *Joe's Shanghai [→128], a fragrant, bustling spectacle with a line outside every night. During the day, the Chinese parade to the cavernous Jing Fong for dim sum carts loaded with a variety of sumptuous tidbits. It's noisy and service might be brusque, but it's the real McCoy. For a sweet snack, it's hard to beat the Hong Kong Egg Cake Co ♦, aka the Egg Cake Lady. Look for her fading red shack tucked down a side street (11am–5pm Wed–Thu & Sat–Sun), and slip her $1 for a sack of a dozen hot cakes with custard filling. Still hungry? Try Grand Sichuan, a bare-bones, spicy Szechuan restaurant. As well as Chinese standards, they serve ethnic specialties you won't find elsewhere. Roasted ducks hang in the window at New York Noodle Town, a bright and lively magnet for both Chinese and Westerners. Pan-fried noodles are tossed with an abundant variety of poultry, seafood, and vegetables.

Vegetarians are particularly well-served by Vegetarian Paradise 3, a friendly, pastel-hued cafeteria, with lots of tasty numbers. New Wonton Garden, with lights bright enough to cause sunburn, is good for cheap, quick, quality eats. Great Shanghai has a more sleek, dimly-lit ambience, and the sweet-and-sour fish and sauteed baby shrimp are excellent. The title for best Vietnamese is held by Nha Trang, a rather charmless abode that nevertheless pulls in crowds for its gorgeous, glossy platters of sauteed beef, seafood, and delicate vegetables. It's the ultimate for cheap dates. Another good bet for Southeast Asian fare is the Thailand Restaurant, a favoured lunch spot – although the somewhat tacky, wood-panelled room looks better at night. The aroma from these classic dishes is incredible. To perfectly cap off any meal, stop by the Chinatown Ice Cream Factory to try exotic flavours like lychee, and red bean.

bars & clubs

A star on the Ludlow Street nightlife trail is *Max Fish, a long-time hang-out for indie bands that attracts a young mixed crowd. Don't be put off by its large size or bright lighting. For fans of drum 'n' bass and electronica, *Orchard Bar (with decor inspired by natural history dioramas) is a required stop. Experimental music collectives regularly spin sounds in this dark, sexy space. Equally mellow is the beautiful *Kush, one of NY's many neo-Moroccan lounges. On a different theme, Welcome to the Johnsons' is a bar fitted out to resemble the typical mid-70's living room, complete with plastic-covered furniture. Or, if you're more in the mood for alternative comedy or theatre, head for *Tonic. Like *Baby Jupiter – with a restaurant, performance space and bar – it's one of a new breed of one-stop hybrid venues.

Retro swing parties and bottomless designer Martinis can be enjoyed at the ever-popular *Lansky Lounge, a once-clandestine bar located at the end of an alley. Meanwhile, upbeat hip-hop and funk is delivered in style at club-like Sapphire. Just around the corner, and with a lounge uncannily like an airplane's interior, is **Idlewild**, which boasts an eclectic array of parties. A less hetero scene is on offer at ***Meow Mix**, a hard-core lesbian dive that features fierce live-music performances. Neighbouring Chinatown's bars remain resolutely Chinese, but for a mix of local flavour and an English-speaking crowd, the only place to visit is ***Winnie's**, named best karaoke bar by a number of local mags.

✍ directory

Amy Downs *C1*
103 Stanton Street
598-4189

Baby Jupiter *C1*
170 Orchard Street
982-2229 ♪ $$

Bereket *A1*
187 E Houston Street
475-7700 $

Cherry *C1*
185 Orchard Street
358-7131

Chinatown Ice Cream Factory *B3*
65 Bayard Street
608-4170 $

DDC Lab *C1*
180 Orchard Street
375-1647

El Sombrero *C1*
108 Stanton Street
254-4188 $

Grand Sichuan *B3*
125 Canal Street
625-9212 $-$$

Great Shanghai *B3*
27 Division Street
966-7663 $-$$

Hong Kong Egg Cake Co *B3*
Mott & Mosco Sts $

Idlewild *B1*
145 East Houston St
477-5005

Jing Fong *B3*
20 Elizabeth Street
964-5256 $-$$

Joe's Shanghai *B3*
9 Pell Street
233-8888 $-$$$

Juan Anon *C1*
193 Orchard Street
529-7795

Katz's Deli *C1*
205 E Houston Street
254-2246 $

Kush *C1*
183 Orchard Street
677-7328

Lansky Lounge *C1*
104 Norfolk Street
677-9489

Las Venus *C1*
163 Ludlow Street
982-0608

Lotus Club *C1*
35 Clinton Street
253-1144 $

Lucky Wang *C1*
100 Stanton Street
353-2850

Mary Adams *C1*
159 Ludlow Street
473-0237

Max Fish *C1*
178 Ludlow Street
253-1922

Meow Mix *C1*
269 E Houston Street
254-0688 ♪

MIKS *C1*
100 Stanton Street
505-1982

Min Lee *C1*
105 Stanton Street
375-0304

New Wonton Garden *B3*
56 Mott Street
966-4886 $

New York Noodle Town *B3*
28 Bowery
349-0923 $-$$

Nha Trang *A3*
87 Baxter Street
233-5948 $

Nova USA *C1*
100 Stanton Street
228-6844

Orchard Bar *C1*
200 Orchard Street
673-5350

Oriental Dress Co *B3*
38 Mott Street
349-0818

Oriental Gifts *B3*
96 Bayard Street
608-6670

Patch 155 *C1*
155 Rivington Street
533-9995

Pearl River Mart *A3*
277 Canal Street
431-4770

Recon *B1*
237 Eldridge Street
614-8502

Russ & Daughters *B1*
179 E Houston Street
475-4880

Sapphire *B1*
249 Eldridge Street
777-5153

Shine *C1*
159 Ludlow Street
539-1761

TG-170 *C1*
170 Ludlow Street
995-8660

Thailand Restaurant *B3*
106 Bayard Street
349-3132 $

Timtoum *C1*
167 Orchard Street
780-0456

Tonic *C1*
107 Norfolk Street
358-7504 ♪ $

Torch *C1*
137 Ludlow Street
228-5151 $$

Toys in Babeland *C1*
94 Rivington Street
375-1701

Vegetarian Paradise 3 *B3*
33 Mott Street
406-6988 $-$$

Vinnie's Tampon Case *B1*
245 Eldridge Street
228-2273

Winnie's *B3*
104 Bayard Street
732-2384 ♪

Welcome to the Johnsons' *B1*
123 Rivington Street
420-9911

Xuly Bet *C1*
189 Orchard Street
982-5473

Yonah Schimmel's Knishery *B1*
137 E Houston Street
477-2858 $

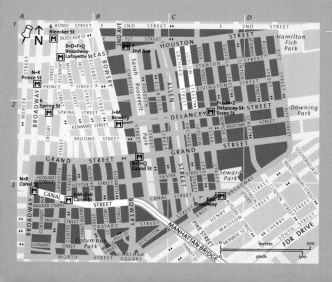

hollywood east

tribeca

Tribeca (the Triangle Below Canal Street) is fashionable Downtown's most south-westerly outpost. In spite of a prevalence of chic eateries and bars, and a smattering of interesting stores, the area feels positively residential. It's not hard to see why Tribeca, with its availability of cavernous factory and warehouse space, has emerged as the Hollywood of the East Coast – both Robert De Niro's Tribeca Films and Miramax are based here. Starry residents include Bobby himself, Harvey Keitel and John F Kennedy Jr, who, if you believe the gossip pages, can be seen regularly chowing down in the trendy diners. In reality, you're more likely to encounter bankers and brokers from the neigh-bouring Financial District, who have also made Tribeca home.

day

🛍 The majority of shops are along West Broadway and its adjacent streets. They sell mostly home furnishings, with a few notable fashion exceptions. Places open late morning and close early evening.

◉ Battery Park [→91]; City Hall [→74]; Ellis Island [→77]; National Museum of the American Indian [→84]; Statue of Liberty [→77]; Woolworth Building [→76]; World Trade Center [→76].

night

☆ Great music venues like the Knitting Factory [→146] and Wetlands [→147], as well as the Screening Room [→142] movie house.

🌙 The streets of Tribeca are fairly quiet after dark as the scene is focused on the neighbourhood's restaurants. Bars tend to be calmer than elsewhere in town.

Ⓜ A•C•E•N•R to Canal St; A•C•1•2•3•9 to Chambers St; 1•9 to Franklin St.

🚌 M6 ↑Church St via 6th Ave; M6 ↓Broadway; M10 ↑West St via Harrison St, Hudson St & 8th Ave; M10 ↓Varick St via 7th Ave; M22 ←Chambers St via Madison St.

shopping

home furnishings

Modern, sleek and distinctive defines *TOTEM ✔ (The Objects That Evoke Meaning). From the most fabulous sofas and rugs to loads of frosted plastic accessories, you'll want it all. **Amaranth** offers a more eclectic selection of must-

haves, from brightly-hued fur pillows, rocket lamps, sparkly swirl paintings, hand-blown glass *objets*, or groovy furniture for kids. At *Wyeth*, choose from a huge array of flawless 20th-century collectables, mostly from the 40's and

50's. In the same vein, **Antik** has a smaller collection, including lots of wood pieces. If Hawaiian bamboo furniture is more up your alley, then you will love **Oser**, where you can sip coffee at the bar, watch an old surf movie and

fashion & beauty

admire the giant shark you've bought to hang on your wall. In the name of over-the-top, quirky glamour, **Anandamali** features bureaux, tables and mirrors decorated (mosaic-style) with antique china. Visit **Orange Chicken** for a more traditional take on furnishing your home.

If you're only going to buy one pair of leather trousers in your life, make sure they're from ◄ **Behrle**. And for fetish-inspired pieces that will turn anybody into a sex goddess, check out her label, World Domination. **J Morgan Puett Studio**, as much an art gallery as a shop, features ethereal, romantic clothes, all hand-made and hand-dyed in situ. Linda St John, the designer behind ***D/L Cerney**, freely admits to being obsessed with the 40's, 50's and early 60's, which is reflected in her

'new vintage' clothes – tailored shirts, simple skirts, trousers (for men and women) – and all at reasonable prices. **Working Class** has elevated workwear to a new level of elegance, seen in their vintage jeans with leather pockets, handmade clogs and workboots, and schoolboy satchels – all in bright shades. If you'd rather be an exhbitionist or a glamour princess, head up to **Manic Panic** (owned by wild girls Tish and Snooky), purveyors of vibrant hair colours.

eating & drinking

restaurants

Dark streets, loading docks, lofts and lots of groovy restaurants define Tribeca. Mr Cool himself, De Niro, is part-owner of ***Nobu** [→124] and **Next Door Nobu**, both beautifully designed, innovative Japanese restaurants that regularly attract celebs. Next Door distinguishes itself by offering a range of noodle dishes and a no-reservations policy. Mega-restaurateur Drew Nieporent, De Niro's partner, started out in Tribeca with the three-star **Montrachet**, a minimalist bistro serving ravishing nouvelle French cuisine. Then came **Tribeca Grill**, a warehouse-sized restaurant with cross-cultural American food, an award-winning wine list, and paintings by De Niro's late father. **Layla** is also part of the empire, an opulent Middle Eastern palace (with bellydancers), featuring mezze, *tajines*, kebabs and couscous fit for a sultan.

But ***Odeon** [→125] continues to be the preferred upscale canteen for the fashion and art scene. Even if you can't get a table, it's fun to observe the action, while sipping a martini at the bar. Loungey, seductive

2 Seven 7 attracts an eye-catching crowd, and offers a global menu with an emphasis on seafood. For a spot of sangria and paella, **Flor de Sol**, reminiscent of a Spanish parador, is an appealing option and its long bar serves tapas. **The Independent** is another local hangout in warm, rustic surroundings. The American menu is inspired and moderately priced. ***Spartina** [→130] has all the ingredients for success – superb Mediterranean cuisine in a romantic setting. Perhaps one of the most unusual dining choices in Tribeca is the retro-style ***Screening Room** [→130], which provides the perfect one-stop venue for that movie-followed-by-dinner date. The movies are independents and the food is creative New American.

It is not without good reason that **Chanterelle** is one of NY's top-rated restaurants – creative French cooking in an austere yet friendly environment. Another gem is ***Bouley Bakery** [→122], which serves exquisite seasonal new French cuisine, while its bakery holds a myriad of delights.

Old-guard French food is served in the remote loft of ***Capsouto Frères** [→129]. Big names go there, not only for the elegant food, but also because they're left alone. Even more secluded is ***Rosemarie's** [→130], a posh Italian, specializing in robust-flavoured dishes.

cafés & diners

For a cheap pit stop, the tiny **Soup Pot** serves satisfying breakfasts, wonderful soups and rich, homespun desserts (closes 5pm). The same owners are behind **Kitchenette** ▲, a sweet American roadside stop with hearty country cooking (open 'til 10pm). **Bodega** is a neighbourhood joint that glows with good cheer. Specialties include meat loaf, fish and chips and big burritos. And **Walker's** is a friendly watering hole, serving burgers with beer on tap. Settle in and enjoy the live jazz.

bars & clubs

This area's bars have all the glamour of neighbouring Soho's but without the suffocating crowds. Adding a touch of luxe to Tribeca's up-and-coming Federal District is **Lush**, a quietly swank champagne bar, where you can also indulge in caviar. If you'd rather pop your cork in a crowd, head for ***Bubble Lounge**, located in a considerably more fashionable chunk of the neighbourhood. For a more casual, pub-like atmosphere, **S J South & Sons** serves classic British/Irish fare like beef stew and pints of Guinness. **Liquor Store**, another friendly local, features wall-to-wall windows overlooking the street – perfect for people-watching or just settling in with a pint and the paper. For a more rough-and-tumble experience, join the retired utility workers, hacks and shuffleboard aficionados at the ***Nancy Whiskey Pub**, an authentic dive that has steadfastly resisted gentrification. A younger scene can be found at the **Knitting Factory's Tap Bar**, where 18 beers are offered on tap. Free, live music ranges from funk to bizarre, experimental acts (11pm– 2am nightly). Meanwhile, renowned DJs spin hip-hop, funk and soul at actor Michael Rapaport's dark and atmospheric bar and club, **The Front**. It was a brave entry into the fledgling Fed District and, with its two new underground floors attracting larger, promoter-driven parties, the club has a secure future.

⌂ directory

Amaranth *C2*
77 Franklin Street
625-1246

Anandamali *B2*
35 North Moore Street
343-8964

Antik *B2*
104 Franklin Street
343-0471

Behrle *C2*
89 Franklin Street
334-5522

Bodega *B2*
136 West Broadway
285-1155 $

Bouley Bakery *C2*
120 West Broadway
964-2525 $$$

Bubble Lounge *C2*
228 West Broadway
431-3433

Capsouto Frères *A1*
451 Washington Street
966-4900 $$$

Chanterelle *B2*
2 Harrison Street
966-6960 $$$

D/L Cerney *C2*
222 West Broadway
941-0530

Flor de Sol *B2*
361 Greenwich Street
334-6411 $$

The Front *C2*
16 Warren Street
766-1070 ℂ

The Independent *C2*
179 West Broadway
219-2010 $$$

J Morgan Puett Studio *C2*
137 West Broadway
267-8004

Kitchenette *B3*
80 West Broadway
267-6740 $

Knitting Factory's Tap Bar *C2*
74 Leonard Street
219-3055

Layla *C2*
211 West Broadway
431-0700 $$$

Liquor Store *C2*
235 White Street
226-7121 ℂ

Lush *C3*
110 Duane Street
766-1275 $$

Manic Panic *C2*
4th floor,
64 White Street
941-0656

Montrachet *C2*
239 West Broadway
219-2777 $$$

Nancy Whiskey Pub *B1*
1 Lispenard Street
226-9943

Next Door Nobu *B2*
105 Hudson Street
334-4445 $$$

Nobu *B2*
105 Hudson Street
219-0500 $$$

Odeon *C2*
145 West Broadway
233-0507 $$$

Orange Chicken *B2*
152 Franklin Street
431-0037

Oser *C3*
148 Duane Street
571-6737

Rosemarie's *C2*
145 Duane Street
285-2610 $$$

Screening Room *B1*
54 Varick Street
334-2100 $$

S J South & Sons *C2*
273 Church Street
219-0640 ℂ $$

Soup Pot *B3*
78 West Broadway
962-7687 $

Spartina *B2*
355 Greenwich Street
274-9310 $$$

TOTEM *C2*
71 Franklin Street
925-5506

Tribeca Grill *C2*
375 Greenwich Street
941-3900 $$$

2 Seven 7 *C2*
277 Church Street
625-0505 $$$

Walker's *B2*
16 North Moore Street
941-0412

Working Class *B3*
168 Duane Street
941-1199

Wyeth *B2*
151 Franklin Street
925-5278

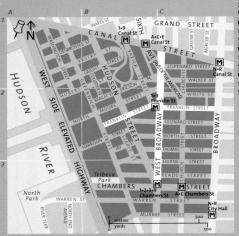

soho, so chic

soho

New York's most conspicuously fashionable neighbourhood is compact to a fault – every big-name designer has a store somewhere in this tiny pocket of intersecting streets. Such a cluster of important shopping venues – alongside swanky commercial art galleries, elegant restaurants and exclusive bars – could only act as a magnet for fashion and media types. Even if you don't run into Gwyneth Paltrow in Prada, catching sight of some impossibly thin beauty dashing to a shoot at one of the neighbourhood's many photo studios is an everyday occurrence. Despite so many manifest distractions, Soho's magnificent architecture is hard to ignore. The monumental 19th-century buildings are some of the finest and most varied examples of cast iron architecture in the US.

The days when Soho was the epicentre of NY's artistic life have gone, and while there are still plenty of highbrow art galleries (and long-time resident artists, who are blessed with favourable rents), the cutting-edge art scene has shifted to Chelsea, causing many to predict that Soho's reign as the coolest neighbourhood in NYC could well be over.

day

🏬 Soho is packed with upscale designer boutiques and one-off stores, which tend to open from late morning to 7–8pm – even on Sundays. Swanky galleries are great for browsing.

👁 Soho Guggenheim [→80–81], the Museum for African Art [→84], the New Museum of Contemporary Art [→87–88], New York Earth Room and Broken Kilometer (part of the Dia Center for Arts) [→86–87] are all close by.

night

☆ NY's premier arthouse cinema, The Angelika [→42], plus Performing Garage theatre [→140], and club-music venue Shine [→150] are all nearby.

🍸 This area is known for its super-stylish restaurants and bars, loungey bar-clubs with strict door policies.

Ⓜ B•D•F•Q to Broadway-Layfayette St; C•E to Spring St; N•R to Prince St; A•C•E•1•9 to Canal St; 1•9 to Housto n St.

🚌 M6 ↑6th Ave, ↓Broadway; M10 ↑Hudson St, ↓Varick St; M21 ⟷ Houston St.

→ more shopping

shopping

women's fashion

*Betsey Johnson ✔, one of the first designers in Soho when it was Nowheresville, makes crazy clothes, and has a dramatic flagship store to match. An eccentric American girl, Betsey's aesthetic is feminine and frilly with a rock 'n' roll edge. Another designer who con-sistently whips up the prettiest party dresses and accessories is ***Cynthia Rowley**. In her homey shop, the racks are filled with

rich fabrics and plenty of beads and embroidery. Another local lady, **Nicole Miller** has made a name for herself designing wearable evening dresses and chic separates. **Vivienne Tam**'s sleek, exotic clothes – form-fitting, beaded dresses; saucy suits; handbags and loungewear with an oriental flair – have become a staple of fashionable gals, including Julia Roberts. Another store with an Asian flavour, **Dosa**, has grown into a cult favourite with the It girls. Using classic shapes, it's the special fabrics and interesting details that give these elegant pieces their appeal. For designer **Atsuro Tayama**, however, it's all in the cut: check out his boldly asymetric, deconstructed garments, but only if you're feeling confident.

Always the Queen of hippy-inspired glamour, *Anna Sui's purple palace is a haven for the young and fabulous. Her leathers are divine and her accessories – based on vintage designs – adorable. Emerging as America's biggest fashion star is *Marc Jacobs, whose airy, minimalist shop is an important stop, even if you can only afford to look. Everything here is the height of sophistication and luxury. Fashion addicts from all over flock to get their fix of *Miu Miu. This more youthful (and less expensive) line from Miuccia Prada is always on the cutting edge of fashion, especially the undeniably fabulous and inventive shoes and bags. While the clothes vary wildly from season to season, the mood is always seductive in a Lolita sort of way. Ethereal and romantic is the theme at *Morgan Le Fay, where dresses resembling origami creations conjure up that urban-gypsy look. And at *Issey Miyake Pleats Please, there's more designer wizardry with every piece of clothing folding up like an accordion for a sexy fit with a Far Eastern essence; the store's window glass trickery is equally intriguing.

If you want a mix of styles under one roof, *Steven-Alan has the best of NYC's up-and-coming designers as well as accessories and watches. *Scoop is an equally important destination if you're looking for well-selected separates by young names. Another fashion pioneer is **Louie**, who also showcases the talents of a small group of burgeoning style-stars, with a unique collection of accessories. In a similar vein, **Big Drop** houses a colourful collection of clothing, including lots of little sweaters and items from Daryl K's 189 collection and '6' by Martin Margiela. A branch of the Spanish chain, **Zara** is also worth investigating for reasonably priced and stylish separates and shoes. A new addition to the scene, *Catherine ⅄, is all about creating a lifestyle rather than just getting dressed – sharp, girly clothes, lots of the designer's signature cowboy hats, and home furnishings all in a shop that looks more like an apartment than a store. Meanwhile, at *Vivienne Westwood, every customer is a star when they step out of their dressing room on to a 'stage' in one of her theatrical creations. More genius clothes (almost upstaged by the architecture) are to be found at **Alberta Ferretti**.

Soho's airy spaces vacated by the art world make ideal showcases for swelegant clothes and furnishings.

men's & women's fashion

Creating luxurious, brightly hued, modern clothes (for both sexes) with bold, graphic shapes is what **Alpana Bawa**, born in New Delhi, does best. Men love her filmy, embroidered shirts in muted hues. If expensive avant-garde is what you crave, *If Soho New York has an inspired collection from the fashion stars of today and tomorrow (Dries Van Noten, Veronique Branquino et al). Check out the Johnny Farah bags – très chic, and surprisingly affordable. Artsy but tailored shapes, unexpected fabrics and fascinating details are responsible for *Costume National's icon status. They also make distinctive, covetable shoes. At *Helmut Lang, the futuristic 'communications obelisk' is as entrancing as the geometric clothes, while everything in *Yohji Yamamoto's amazing gallery-like store is almost too beautiful to wear. How to look fabulous when you're actually doing something more than posing? *Prada Sport has filled the obvious gap in the market with its utilitarian designs. For men only, the *Yves St Laurent Rive Gauche boutique provides daring clothing in that proverbial St Laurent kind of way.

Edgy, trendy and occasionally kitschy clothes and accessories from around the world are to be found at *Hotel Venus (the Soho branch of Patricia Field, Downtown's trend-setting, leading lady for 20 years). This is still the only place in town to get the hugely desirable Courrèges collection and there's even an in-store wig salon. If you're looking for super-cheap clothes more on the casual side, there is plenty to choose from all along Broadway, where discount sportswear stores dominate, including good sneaker outlets. In their midst is *Canal Jeans, a kind of a New York institution filled with almost every kind of vintage and new jeans, and cheap T-shirts. Stussy is still the epicentre for upscale skatewear, meant for men but worn by everybody. Definitely for men only is *Sean, a welcome addition to the men's clothing scene, with a mix of well-priced separates by various designers that are smart without ever being stuffy.

beauty

Soho is a real oasis for beauty seekers. *Bliss Spa is a celebrity favourite: it's in-spa boutique has an amazing array of products from the world over. *Aveda is a more low-key, but very beautiful place to get natural products that really work. Parisian transplant *Sephora, a make-up superstore, offers an astonishing (even overwhelming) choice of perfume, make-up and bath products, from all the best lines. *M.A.C., an institution championed by make-up artists, is filled with the newest colours and products. *Shu Uemera has an equally high-end collection of potions in a fashionably minimal setting. For bargains, however, try *Ricky's, a pharmacy mini-chain where the goods are cheap and plentiful.

accessories & shoes

In the quest to finish your look, start at *Fragments, a showcase for 30 or so great new jewellery designers working in a range of styles. *Selima Optique ↘ has the most fabulous eyewear in town, plus an interesting array of hats, scarves and scents. Her nearby lingerie shop, Le Corset, is crammed with frilly items from around the world, including some vintage pieces. Everything in Louis Vuitton is a heart-stopper, especially the price tags! The tradiional LV accessories and luggage are still covetable design classics. On the other end of the price scale, *Steve Madden is famous for creating on-the-edge and over-the-top shoes and boots. For something more sleek, sharp footwear by an international posse of designers is on offer at *Tootsi Plohound. The new *Rockport 'concept' store is a kind of Niketown for the comfy shoe set, where it's possible to get a pair custom-made.

It's impossible to go anywhere these days without spotting one of *Kate Spade's bags on somebody's arm. She makes them saucy, serious, and sublime. Her store also carries cute accessories, like her date books or very fem stationery. And, to pull your whole outfit together, get yourself a Casio Baby G-Shock watch from the store that is devoted to the super-trendy timepieces.

food

The corner of Broadway and Prince sees a stream of folk ducking into the airy *Dean & Deluca. Recalling Milan's Peck & Peck, there's a bounty of flawless produce, appealing prepared foods and racks packed with goods that are great for gift-giving. *Gourmet Garage is more Woodstock than Milan, with organic fruits and vegetables and other delicacies. More cheap, less chic.

home furnishings

*Moss has the ultimate in modern, industrial design, and sets the tone for cool furnishings in NYC. All the big names are carried here, displayed museum-style in glass cases. Nearby *Troy is becoming increasingly influential: expect bold and interesting small furniture and accessories by new designers. *Shabby Chic offers furnishings with a softer edge – their comfortable sofas and 'T-shirt' sheets are legendary. *Zona bears a striking resemblance to a lived-in, country home. Vintage and new furniture, jewellery and other objets are here, but everybody's favourites are the gorgeous, colour-saturated, hand-dipped candles. *Jonathan Adler, known for his entertaining striped pottery (with a 50's accent) has a shop crammed full of treasures, including his own flea market finds he's willing to pass along to his devoted customers.

Portico Bed & Bath are lifestyle pioneers in Soho. They offer the finest, most elegant linens and other accessories that will make your home positively scream 'good taste'. *Ad-Hoc Software has a wackier edge with great tchotchkes for bathrooms, bedrooms and kitchens plus elegant tablewares and bed linens. For the ultimate in cheap and cheerful yet well-designed home furnishings, take the stairs up to Dom (above Hotel Venus), where you can get colourful home accessories for a song, along with whimsical lighting and inflatable furniture that's easy to store.

galleries

With its super-high rents, Soho's gallery scene is dominated by power dealers. **Larry Gagosian** alternates museum-quality shows of high moderns like Andy Warhol with the newest works of established contemporaries like Anselm Kiefer, while **Deitch Projects** exhibits a wide range of hot young artists from around the world. Yet more avant-garde is to be had at **American Fine Arts**, specializing in 'institutional critique' by young artists. For photos, visit **Janet Borden** – the wares range from the sharp-focus landscapes of Lee Friedlander to surreal post-apocalyptic visions by Oliver Wasow.

No visit to Soho would be complete without looking in at **Phyllis Kind**, the veteran Chicago dealer who specializes in Outsider art. Nearby is the **Tony Shafrazi Gallery**, centring on graffiti art by Jean-Michel Basquiat, and work by Keith Haring and Kenny Scharf. More on the area's fringes is **Ace Gallery**, easily New York's grandest gallery space. Look for monolithic minimalism, mural-sized painting and anything else that's massive in scale.

eating & drinking

restaurants

Expensive Soho rents mean many restaurants in the historic district are overpriced, catering to tourists, celebrities, and brash Wall Streeters with million-dollar bonuses to blow. The place to check out what the rich-and-famous are eating is *Mercer Kitchen [→121], where celebrity chef Jean-Georges Vongerichten excels at his unique American-Provençal cooking. The brick-walled, subterranean space in the Mercer Hotel [→157] is the height of glamour. Katy Sparks at *Quilty's [→130] is another much-honoured chef, creating highly innovative seafood, poultry and meat dishes for a sophisticated clientele. The creamy dining room is more homey than intimidating. In contrast is the rather more austere **Honmura An**, which has been esteemed for years as one of the city's top Asian restaurants. It's hard to imagine more artful noodle concoctions, and equally hard to imagine paying higher prices.

Places that are big on atmosphere rather than bucks include **Penang**, a Malaysian outpost that combines an industrial design with hut-like booths and a waterfall. The exotic dishes are flavourful – feast on roti canai and seafood. Coloured lights welcome you into the tiny interior of the **Country Café**, which is filled to the brim with charming knick-knacks. The French and Moroccan food is richly prepared and served by an affable staff. **Harmony**, whose entrance is dominated by neon liquor bottles, has an interior that is pure pop. A loungey crowd, reclining on banquettes, digs into eclectic New York cuisine, like seafood creole pie. Up front is a quick-service bar area offering shellfish and pizzas. *Alison on Dominick Street [→129] is pure romance, a small, out-of-the-way place with straightforward French and new American food. You go there to kiss and share bites, not to be blown away by innovative cuisine. More passion is almost sure to follow after a night at **Casa La Femme**, a candlelit Middle Eastern casbah, with tented booths and an incredible belly dancer. The food is good but not the point – especially for all the skinny models who slink in.

To savour what Soho used to be like, push through the etched-glass doors of **Fanelli**, a dark-wood corner tavern that opened in 1847. The crowd is interesting, dressed-down and boisterous, and it's a safe bet for burgers, chilli and chicken pot pie. Further west, the intimate *Blue Ribbon [→132] is popular for its wide-ranging menu and cocktails, and dispenses both until 4am, while **Lucky Strike** is a rollicking bistro that also serves competent (if unexciting) food into the wee hours. It's the ideal place to nibble and drink your way closer to solving the world's problems – or at least your vacation agenda; it's also one of Manhattan's smokers' havens.

Meeting friends for dinner, or looking for new ones? Consider **Aquagrill**, where singles gather in the brightly decorated front lounge, or at the bar while waiting for a table at this perpetually jammed seafood restaurant. The piscatorially-inclined can also try **Ideya** ▲, which features a culinary tour of the Caribbean, Central and South America, and a range of potent tropical drinks. Homemade plantain chips and fresh

salsa adorn every table at this warm and casual Latin American bistro. Seating is tight at both **Jean Claude** (classic French cuisine) and **Soho Steak** (you guessed it), rendering conversation with your neighbour effortless. The simply designed pair are owned by respected restaurateur Jean-Claude Iacovelli, who prides himself on serving quality bistro fare at affordable prices.

cafés & diners

If you'd rather splurge on lavish niceties than costly meals, several affordable possibilities await. The cheap **Brisas del Caribe** ✔ is a ramshackle Cuban luncheonette, which attracts a mixed bag of ragamuffins and cool Sohoites. Basic breakfasts, rice and beans, and sandwiches provide quick fixes. Every day the **Soup Kiosk** ladles out six steamy seasonal soups to slurp on the move. **Once upon a Tart** is more upscale, offering terrific baked goods, crusty sandwiches and salads in a relaxed café atmosphere. Take a table, spread your newspaper and ease those tired feet. **Pepe Rosso** is also fantastic for scrumptious focaccia and low-priced pastas. Seating is cramped, so it's prime for take-out. Or there's **Kelley & Ping**, an Asian grocery and noodle shop, and a trendy, modestly priced spot best for the buzz at lunchtimes. The bustling open kitchen, healthy stir-fries and vast tea selection are the appeal. Off the

beaten track, but worth seeking out, is **Herban Kitchen**, a dimly lit, engaging café, serving uncommonly tasty organic specialties. **Moondance Diner** is a friendly shack heavy on bygone charm. Satisfy your appetite with hearty soups, big sandwiches and piles of fries. Soho's idea of a modern diner, however, is ***Jerry's** [→124], frequented by rakish arty types and locals. At any time of day or night, the American-Mediterranean fare is appealing, but pricier than any old-school diner.

bars & clubs

Soho's once-cosy neighbourhood bar scene has alas, in recent years, fallen prey to velvet ropes and guest lists. As one of the first swank bars to move in, ***Bar 89** set the standard: its high ceilings, bottomless cosmopolitans and co-ed bathrooms with see-through doors (they turn opaque at the flip of a latch) have yet to be rivalled. Less grand in scale but equally intimidating is ***Magnum**, a lounge bar which has both a rope and a list, and all the right ingredients to perk you up after a hard day. Speaking of tough, the

door policy at super-trendy **Veruka** may be the area's strictest, though women dressed in Gucci and Prada fare well, and models are a shoo-in. Arrive early in **Sway**, a hot Moroccan lounge frequented by musicians and mannequins. Thursday nights are best, but avoid weekends, when the crowd pressing the door is impenetrable. If you can't abandon your posse, head to nearby **Denial**, a dark, sensual sake bar where your social pedigree is irrelevant.

For a taste of Soho's edgier side, pay a visit to ***Void**, a semi-secluded cyber bar that features tables-cum-web browsers, cult-film screenings and cocktails. Another good option for the attitude-weary is **Café Noir**, a sexy, smoker-friendly, Moroccan bar-restaurant.

*Raoul's is one of Soho's remaining old-guard bar-restaurants. Reserve for the dining room, but nothing beats their bar-steak special enjoyed with a glass of cabernet. Jimmy the barman is one of the best in the business. Now that the celebs have permanently abandoned ship, the **Merc Bar** has become not much more than a tolerable weekday cocktail lounge (weekends can get very crowded). And if all you want is a swift drink before bed, you can hardly do better than the elegant and relaxing ***Grand Bar** in the Soho Grand Hotel [→158].

directory

Ace Gallery ☐ A2
275 Hudson Street
255-5599

Ad-Hoc Software ☐ B2
410 W Broadway
925-2652

Alberta Ferretti ☐ C2
452 W Broadway
460-5500

Alison on Dominick Street ☐ A2
38 Dominick Street
727-1188 $$$

Alpana Bawa ☐ B2
41 Grand Street
965-0559

American Fine Arts ☐ B3
22 Wooster Street
941-0401

Anna Sui ☐ C2
113 Greene Street
941-8406

Aquagrill ☐ B2
210 Spring Street
274-0505 $$-$$$

Atsuro Tayama ☐ C2
120 Wooster Street
334-6002

Aveda ☐ B1
456 W Broadway
473-0280

Bar 89 ☐ C2
89 Mercer Street
274-0989 ☐

Betsey Johnson ☐ C1
138 Wooster Street
995-5048

Big Drop ☐ B2
174 Spring Street
966-4299

Bliss Spa ☐ C2
2nd floor
568 Broadway,
219-8970

Blue Ribbon ☐ B2
97 Sullivan Street
274-0826 $$-$$$

Brisas del Caribe ☐ C3
489 Broadway $

Café Noir ☐ B2
32 Grand Street
431-7910 ☐ $$

Canal Jeans ☐ B3
504 Broadway
226-1130

Casa La Femme ☐ C1
150 Wooster Street
505-0005 $$-$$$

Casio Baby G-Shock ☐ C2
458 W Broadway
260-4570

Catherine ✂B2
468 Broome Street
927-6765

Costume National ✂B2
108 Wooster Street
431-1530

Country Café ✂B2
69 Thompson Street
966-5417 $$

Cynthia Rowley ✂B2
112 Wooster Street
334-1144

Dean & Deluca ✂C2
560 Broadway
226-6800

Deitch Projects ✂B3
76 Grand Street
343-7300

Denial ✂B2
46 Grand Street
925-9449

Dom ✂B2
382 W Broadway
334-5580

Dosa ✂B2
107 Thompson Street
431-1733

Fanelli ✂C2
94 Prince Street
226-9412 $

Fragments ✂C2
107 Greene Street
334-9588

Grand Bar ✂B3
Soho Grand Hotel
310 W Broadway
965-3000

Gourmet Garage ✂B3
453 Broome Street
941-5850

Harmony ✂C1
100 W Houston Street
254-7000 $$

Helmut Lang ✂B2
80 Greene Street
925-7214

Herban Kitchen ✂A2
290 Hudson Street
627-2257 $-$$

Honmura An ✂C2
170 Mercer Street
334-5253 $$$

Hotel Venus ✂B2
382 W Broadway
966-4066

Ideya ✂B2
349 W Broadway
625-1441 $$-$$$

If Soho New York ✂B3
94 Grand Street
334-4964

**Issey Miyake Pleats
Please** ✂B2
128 Wooster Street
226-3600

Janet Borden ✂C2
560 Broadway
431-0166

Jean Claude ✂B1
137 Sullivan Street
475-9232 $$

Jerry's ✂C2
101 Prince Street
966-9464 $$

Jonathan Adler ✂B2
465 Broome Street
941-8950

Kate Spade ✂B2
454 Broome Street
274-1991

Kelley & Ping ✂C2
127 Greene Street
228-1212 $-$$

Larry Gagosian ✂C1
136 Wooster Street
228-2828

Le Corset ✂B2
80 Thompson Street
334-4936

Louie ✂B2
68 Thompson Street
274-1599

Louis Vuitton ✂C2
116 Greene Street
274-9090

Lucky Strike ✂B3
59 Grand Street
941-0479 $-$$

M.A.C ✂B2
113 Spring Street
334-4641

Marc Jacobs ✂C2
163 Mercer Street
343-1490

Merc Bar ✂C2
151 Mercer Street
966-2727

Mercer Kitchen ✂C2
Mercer Hotel,
147 Mercer Street
966-5454 $$$

Miu Miu ✂B2
100 Prince Street
334-5156

Moondance Diner
✂A2
80 Sixth Avenue
226-1191 $

Morgan LeFay ✂B2
151 Spring Street
925-0144

Moss ✂C1
146 Greene Street
226-2190

Nicole Miller ✂B2
130 Prince Street
343-1362

Once upon a Tart ✂B1
135 Sullivan Street
387-8869 $

Penang ✂C2
109 Spring Street
274-8883 $$

Pepe Rosso ✂B1
149 Sullivan Street
677-4555 $

Phyllis Kind ✂C2
136 Greene Street
925-1200

Portico Bed & Bath
✂B2
139 Spring Street
941-7722

Prada Sport ✂B2
116 Wooster Street
925-2221

Quilty's ✂B1
177 Prince Street
254-1260 $$$

Raoul's ✂B1
180 Prince Street
966-3518 ◐ $$-$$

Ricky's ✂C2
590 Broadway
625-1309

Rockport ✂B1
465 W Broadway
529-0209

Scoop ✂B2
532 Broadway
925-2886

Selima Optique ✂B2
59 Wooster Street
343-9490

Sephora ✂C2
555 Broadway
625-1309

Sean ✂B1
132 Thompson Street
598-5980

Shabby Chic ✂C2
93 Greene Street
274-9842

Shu Uemera ✂C2
121 Greene Street
979-5500

Soho Steak ✂B2
90 Thompson Street
226-0602 $$

Soup Kiosk ✂C2
Corner of Prince &
Mercer Sts $

Steve Madden ✂C2
540 Broadway
343-1800

Steven-Alan ✂B2
60 Wooster Street
334-6354

Stussy ✂C2
104 Prince Street
274-8855

Sway ✂A1
305 Spring Street
620-5220

357 ✂B2
357 W Broadway
965-1491 ◐ Thu–Sun
$$-$$$

**Tony Shafrazi
Gallery** ✂B2
119 Wooster Street
274-9300

Tootsi Plohound ✂B2
413 W Broadway
925-8931

Troy ✂C2
138 Greene Street
941-4777

Veruka ✂B2
525 Broome Street
625-1717

Vivienne Tam ✂C2
99 Greene Street
966-2398

Vivienne Westwood
✂B2
71 Greene Street
334-1500

Void ✂B3
16 Mercer Street
941-6492

Yohji Yamamoto ✂B3
103 Grand Street
966-9066

**Yves Saint Laurent
Rive Gauche** ✂B2
88 Wooster Street
274-0522

Zara ✂C2
580 Broadway
343-1725

Zona ✂C2
97 Greene Street
925-6750

in the no

Nolita (north of Little Italy) is another of New York's neighbourhood acronyms created by sharp real estators. It is not just the name that has changed however – over the last few years, the area, formerly known simply as Little Italy, has become so gentrified that it's hard to imagine these were once the mean streets on which Scorsese grew up and Coppola filmed *The Godfather*. Apart from the occasional Italian deli or restaurant along the area's fringes, evidence of the old Little Italy is in extremely short supply. Instead, the characteristic red brick buildings hung with fire escapes are now home to some of the moment's coolest boutiques, cafés and bars (as well as some of the very knowing crowd that frequent them).

Next door Noho (north of Houston) is a tiny enclave which is basically an extension of adjacent Soho. Altogether less populated and more laid-back than its glamorous neighbours, Noho nevertheless holds a smattering of chic attractions, including a few of Downtown's hottest names, in both fashion and food.

day

🎁 Nolita's and Noho's trendy one-of-a-kind boutiques are open from around midday to early evening.

👁 The Children's Museum of the Arts [→92] is in this area.

night

☆ The main entertainment spot here is the Public Theater [→140] and Joe's Pub [→141] but there's also live music at Fez [→147] and poetry readings at Poets House [→145].

🍸 This part of town is packed with ultra-hip bars, restaurants and diners; the occasional lounge for cocktails plus a couple of dive bars.

Ⓜ B•D•F•Q to Broadway-Lafayette St; J•M to Bowery; N•R to Prince St; 6 to Spring St.

🚌 M5 & M6 ↕Broadway; M21 ⟷ Houston St; M103 ↕Bowery.

shopping

fashion

Right on the edge of Noho, ***Antique Boutique**, once a vintage store, now mostly carries cutting-edge pieces from locals Kitty Boots and Stephen Sprouse, and also plays host to the innovative Britpack and other hard- to-

find European designers. More British designers are favoured at futuristic-looking **Nylon Squid** ✓, where the interesting selection of (men's and women's) streetwear couldn't be any more up-to-date if it tried.

Local artists have decorated the walls of the lofty space at **A Détacher**, filled with spare city clothes and housewares to match. Sophisticated urban clothes are also the order of the day at **Zero**.

No shopping neighbourhood is trendier than Nolita which has exploded into a crush of groovy, cosmopolitan, cutting-edge shops.

A recent addition, **Built By Wendy/Cake**, showcases the considerable talents of designers Sarah Kozlowski and Wendy Mullen, who offer a fresh approach to the decidedly downtown (ie stylish and sleek) look – all at fairly affordable prices. Another member of fashion's younger generation, **Margie Tsai**, consistently creates bright, adorable, fun clothes with matching accessories. **Dressing Room** positively shines with its affordable, edgy, very 90's section of young designers, and also boasts a good vintage department. In the same vein, **Phare**, the brainchild of two former models, features an eclectic selection of retro-inspired clothes for women, beautifully-tailored clothes for men, plus some unique accessories mixed in with real vintage finds.

In a cavernous space on trendy Bond Street, *Daryl K – one of fashion's current stars – does polished rock 'n' roll womenswear, including her much-beloved, low-slung hipster trousers, and also her less expensive K189 line. **Tracey Feith**, popular with fashionistas (and lots of celebrities), has plenty of space to show off his delectable,

sexy dresses, a line of menswear, and also Raj, his less expensive and colourful collection of gypsy-hippy clothes for women. **Language** has a rich and unusual line in higher-priced designer clothes and accessories (including pashmina shawls), while *Calypso St Barths, one of the first outlets to set up shop in Nolita, stocks flirty, feminine, flattering clothes made from fine fabrics. It seems that not a single issue of *Vogue* goes by without a mention of this store.

Dishing out more fashion fabulousness, **Hotel of the Rising Star** caters for men looking for an eminently wearable, minimalist look. In a more decorative mode, designer Martin Keehn fills his store, **Wearmart**, with gorgeous, custom-made shirts worn by celebs as diverse as David Bowie and John Kennedy Jr – along with men's essentials inspired by workwear. For the apogee in luxury, **Lucien Pellat-Finet**, known as the Cashmere King, creates ultra-hedonistic four-ply cashmere sweaters and separates (for both sexes) that, unsurprisingly, don't come cheap. At the other end of the seasonal

spectrum, **Malia Mills** stocks the latest and best swimwear – a whimsical collection of bikinis and maillots – which practically guarantee you'll look hot on the beach. If skating is more your thing, then **Supreme** has all the necessary hats, baggy pants, T-shirts and other neat stuff that boarders hoard, while **X-Large** is all about easy and refined streetwear for skate kids who've grown up a bit.

vintage clothes

Vintage is always the rage, and this neighbourhood has a fine selection of shops. The star of the vintage pack is *Resurrection. Though expensive, it's worth it for pristine examples of Gucci, Courrèges and Hermès (including some gorgeous Kelly Bags). Lots of famous designers shop here for inspiration. Ditto at *Screaming Mimi's, a NY institution, where there is never a shortage of genius clothes (for men and women), mostly from the 60's, 70's and beyond.

accessories, shoes, & one-offs

Modish, elegant shoes, both classic and trendy, have made *Sigerson-Morrison a stop for the terminally fashionable. Selima, owner of *Bond 07, has unerringly excellent taste and carries a focused collection of desirable accessories (especially the sunglasses), plus a few pieces of distinctive clothing that will make you drool. Exquisite, hand-crafted and totally-happening handbags and shoes from Paris in luxe fabrics, with beading, embroidery and other treats makes *Jamin Puech ✔ pure heaven for style devotees.

With more of a graphic spin, everthing at the **Pop Shop**, from T-shirts to key chains and plenty of other novelty merchandise, is decorated with the vibrant work of the late, great artist, Keith Haring.

So you wanna be a fireman, or just look like one? Then stop in at **Firefighter's Friend**, the outlet for authorized (and very snappy) NY Fire Dept merchandise, including standard-issue firemen's coats. Far more Zen is the merchandise at *Shi, from the tiny, distinc-

tive tea lights to an engaging collection of ceramics. At the other extreme, the mood at **Liquid Sky** (check out the waterfall in the window) is much more ravey. Upstairs has clever unisex clubwear, along with practical and stylish canvas shoulder bags. And, at the back of the store, there's a unique selection of music, heavy on ambient, jungle and other hybrid sounds.

eating & drinking

restaurants

Little Italy proper is over: the creeping tentacles of Chinatown have strangled the majority of Italian restaurants, essentially leaving tacky tourist spots with gruff service. Say *grazie* then to *Lombardi's [→126] for sticking to its roots, a lovable Italian place with checked tablecloths and delicious pizzas baked (since 1905 – when it served America's first) in a coal-fired oven.

Nolita and Noho are now peppered with a wider, more multicultural choice of eateries. **Mexican Radio** has tasty and inventive south-of-the-border dishes as well as potent Margaritas. Both the bar and dining area are tiny, lit by a myriad of candles and littered with Day of the Dead *tchotchkes*. The intimate **Rice** ✓, true to its name, stirs up a medley of different grains with Asian and Mediterranean toppings. Still in oriental territory, **Clay** is a stylish Korean spot, with steel-wrapped pillars and dramatic lighting. The seafood pancakes are sublime, as are the handmade vegetable dumplings and eggplant-stuffed tofu. There's also **MeKong**: its sultry dining room is always filled with the delicious aroma of flavourful Vietnamese soups, pork and seafood dishes; its bar is part of the cool neighbourhood scene. For Malaysian cooking, visit the lively **Nyonya** for a wonderful hodgepodge of fried noodles, exotic casseroles and aromatic seafood preparations – it's cheap too!

But the biggest draw in the area continues to be the pricier *Balthazar [→120], often flanked by a queue of purring limos. This beautiful French bistro actually lives up to its hype, serving dynamically flavoured *brandade* and duck shepherd's pie, as well as an extensive and reasonably priced French wine list. *Bond St [→120], a minimalist dream, has the ultra-chic flocking into the restaurant and snazzy basement lounge. The Japanese cuisine is extraordinary and exquisitely designed, with an equally impressive sake list. The eternally cool **Indochine** attracts a faithful cadre of raffish musicians and their model girlfriends, who pick at delicate Vietnamese dishes in a tropical setting. *B-Bar [→120], once thought too hot for its own good, has mellowed, enhanced by good American food and an outdoor patio.

*Rialto also has a fantastic back garden, plus a sexy lounge and a good vibe at the bar. Its bistro-style steak and pastas are fine, but nothing's as pleasing as the hamburger (or veggie burger) and fries. Serene, sophisticated parties gather at *Il Buco [→121], which is furnished with antiques, vintage toys and tools. In the afternoon it serves as a wine bar with light meals and snacks, and at night there's a full menu of superb Mediterranean tapas, pasta and meat dishes. It doesn't get any more charming than this. Il Buco's former manager has opened a restaurant of his own nearby, *Acquario [→132], with a similar menu of interesting tapas and Southern European fare (Portuguese fish stew is a highlight). You won't be surrounded by antiques, but it's snug and less costly.

The **Astor Restaurant & Lounge**, an art deco brasserie that bears a passing resemblance to Balthazar, attracts a young clientele. The American-Mediterranean menu is superb (crawfish corn chowder, braised lamb with pistachio couscous), providing ballast for when you retire to the Moroccan-style downstairs lounge for just another cocktail. **Time Café** has its own sensual and popular Moroccan lounge, Fez. The trendy restaurant also offers creative American food, such as pecan-pesto crusted tuna with roasted fennel risotto cake. Terrific sandwiches and chilli-dusted fries reign at lunch. But be warned, it's a bit overpriced and service can be patchy. The **Kitchen Club**, however, is very well run and civilized, with big draped curtains, and lamps on every table. The food is French with a hint of Asian and they do magical things with mushrooms. Check out, too, their adjoining sake bar. **Savoy** is a romantic haven, but perhaps their menu – salt-crust baked duck with braised kale, blood oranges and black olives – is a bit too ambitious. On the other hand, nothing disappoints at *Le Jardin Bistrot, [→130] from rich cassoulet to bouillabaisse. The Parisian ambience is engaging and the back garden a treasure.

cafés & diners

Old New York is epitomized by **Buffa's Delicatessen**, a no-frills hangout, staffed by smart alecks slapping down cheap breakfasts and honest lunch items for its regular actor and director customers (Mon–Fri, closes at 4pm). **Jones Diner** (the genuine free-standing variety) is another favourite for budget breakfasts and cheeseburgers, but shouldn't be confused with **Great Jones Café**, which has also been around for ages – a cramped roadhouse serving Cajun specialities. Rambunctious customers throng the bar, downing cold beers, spicy jalapeño Martinis and Bloody Marys, while honky tonk and country plays on the jukebox. **Bread & Butter** is a take-out shop offering utterly delicious sandwiches and baked goods at higher prices, while **Café Habana** is a spiffy paean to a Latin luncheonette – the grilled corn-on-the-cob coated in chilli powder and cheese is irresistible. **Café Gitane** is also immensely popular, with a super-cool crowd often spilling onto the pavement. They come here to smoke, drink coffee, chat, read and occasionally eat low-priced, healthy salads and sandwiches.

bars & clubs

Even on off nights, most of Nolita's watering holes are brimming with boozehounds: Ranging from beer-soaked dives to the hottest hipster lounges, Nolita's bars may be the perfect barometer of the area's recent demographic shift. For a taste of the old neighbourhood, visit **Milano's**, a shoebox-sized den where old men start nodding off at 3pm and Jimmy Rosselli tunes remain a jukebox favourite. **Spring Street Lounge** (aka The Shark Bar) is larger, cleaner and considerably more gentrified, but a few older locals still call it home. ***Mare Chiaro ✔**, on the other hand, clings tenaciously to its past. Photos of visiting celebrities – including Madonna and Ronald Reagan – proudly line the walls, and sawdust is strewn across the floor.

Nolita's younger dive denizens prefer **288** (aka Tom & Jerry's) – great for beer but a Martini might disappoint. ***Botanica** is a cosy basement bar especially prized for its DJs who spin drum 'n' bass, dub, and jungle. Excellent DJs are also a fixture at **Double Happiness**, a former Mafia-controlled gay social club transformed into a sleek subterranean lounge. When Double Happiness is packed to the gills, swing by neighbouring ***Sweet & Vicious**, a popular, roomy, local hangout where Turkish raki is the beverage of choice and a sweet garden beckons. If you need space, head straight to **Velvet**, where business has yet to boom and it's easy to get a drink in the restaurant's romantic, antique-furnished lounge bar. Room to move is not an option at **Ñ**, a sexy slip of a tapas bar with potent sangria and at least two people waiting for each seat at the bar. For a slightly less sardine-like experience, head to **M&R**, a neighbourhood staple, and mellow alternative to nearby **Rialto**. This joint is ground-zero for Nolita hipsters. Superb Margaritas served in two-and-a-half glass-sized shakers are a big draw.

Keith McNally's **Pravda** seems decidedly less glamorous since the famed restaurateur opened Balthazar [→120]. But if superb vodka (70 different varieties), fancy cocktails and caviar served in a retro-decadent Soviet atmosphere is your thing, you could hardly do better than this underground Russian speakeasy. Cocktails and clientele are equally swank at the spacious ***B-Bar**.

Noho's nightlife is also thriving, thanks to the addition of **Bond St** and ***Joe's Pub** [→141]. Opened by the owners of Indochine [→35], Bond St's sleek and minimalist basement lounge offers a modified version of the restaurant's menu, saketinis (both sweet and dry) and young, gorgeous girleens nibbling sushi – if only to have enough strength to continue on to Joe's Pub. Serge Becker's hot new bar is built into one end of the Joseph Papp Public Theater, and has a strangely 80's feel. But if you're in no mood to scream, 'I'm on the guest list!' stop by neighbouring **Fez** – a fun Moroccan-inspired lounge under the Time Café, where drag acts, and an eclectic roster of musicians (including the Mingus Big Band) perform regularly [→147].

⚘ directory

Acquario ♿C2
5 Bleecker Street
260-4666 $–$$

A Détacher ♿B3
262 Mott Street
625-3380

Antique Boutique ♿C1
712 Broadway
469-8830

Astor Restaurant & Lounge ♿C2
316 Bowery
253-8644 $$

Balthazar ♿A3
80 Spring Street
965-1414 $$–$$$

B-Bar ♿C1
40 E 4th Street
475-2220 $$

Bond 07 ♿C2
7 Bond Street
677-8487

Bond St ♿B2
6 Bond Street
777-2500 $$–$$$

Botanica ♿B2
47 E Houston St
343-7251

Bread & Butter ♿B3
229 Elizabeth Street
925-7600 $

Buffa's Delicatessen ♿B3
54 Prince Street
226-0211 $

Built By Wendy/ Cake ♿B4
7 Centre Market Place
925-6538

Café Gitane ♿B3
242 Mott Street
334-9552 $

Café Habana ♿B3
17 Prince Street
625-2001 $

Calypso St Barths ♿B3
280 Mott Street
274-0449

Clay ♿B4
202 Mott Street
625-1105 $$

Daryl K ♿C2
21 Bond Street
777-0713

Double Happiness ♿B4
173 Mott Street
941-1282

Dressing Room ♿B3
49 Prince Street
431-6658

Fez ♿C1
380 Lafayette Street
533-2680

Firefighter's Friend ♿B3
263 Lafayette Street
226-3142

Great Jones Café ♿C2
54 Great Jones Street
674-9304 $

Hotel of the Rising Star ♿B3
13 Prince Street
625-9659

Il Buco ♿C2
47 Bond Street
533-1932 $–$$$

Indochine ♿C1
430 Lafayette Street
505-5111 $$

Jamin Puech ♿B3
252 Mott Street
334-9730

Joe's Pub ♿C1
425 Lafayette Street
539-8770

Jones Diner ♿C2
371 Lafayette Street
673-3577 $

Kitchen Club ♿B3
30 Prince Street
274-0025 $$

Language ♿B3
238 Mulberry Street
431-5566

Le Jardin Bistrot ♿B3
25 Cleveland Place
343-9599 $$

Liquid Sky ♿B3
241 Lafayette Street
343-0532

Lombardi's ♿B3
32 Spring Street
941-7994 $$

Lucien Pellat-Finet ♿C3
226 Elizabeth Street
343-7033

Malia Mills ♿B3
199 Mulberry Street
625-2311

Mare Chiaro ♿B4
176 Mulberry Street
226-9345 ⊄

Margie Tsai ♿C3
4 Prince Street
334-2540

MeKong ♿B3
44 Prince Street
343-8169 $–$$

Mexican Radio ♿B3
250 Mulberry Street
343-0140 $$

Milano's ♿B2
51 East Houston St ⊄

M&R ♿C3
264 Elizabeth Street
226-0559

Ñ ♿A3
33 Crosby Street
219-8856 $

Nylon Squid ♿B3
222 Lafayette Street
334-6554

Nyonya ♿B4
194 Grand Street
334-3669 $

Phare ♿B3
252 Mulberry Street
625-0406

Pop Shop ♿B2
292 Lafayette Street
219-2784

Pravda ♿B3
281 Lafayette Street
226-4696 $$

Resurrection ♿B3
217 Mott Street
625-1374

Rialto ♿C3
265 Elizabeth Street
334-7900 $$

Rice ♿B3
227 Mott Street
226-5775 $

Savoy ♿B3
70 Prince Street
219-8570 $$$

Screaming Mimi's ♿C1
382 Lafayette Street
677-6464

Shi ♿B3
233 Elizabeth Street
334-4330

Sigerson-Morrison ♿B3
242 Mott Street
219-3893

Spring Street Lounge ♿B3
48 Spring Street
965-1774 ⊄

Supreme ♿B3
274 Lafayette Street
966-7799

Sweet & Vicious ♿B3
5 Spring Street
334-7915

Time Café ♿C2
380 Lafayette Street
533-7000 $$

Tracey Feith ♿B3
209 Mulberry Street
334-3097

288 ♿B2
288 Elizabeth Street
334-8429

Velvet ♿B3
223 Mulberry Street
965-0439 $–$$

Wearmart ♿B3
229 Elizabeth Street
334-5365

X-Large ♿B3
265 Lafayette Street
334-4480

Zero ♿B3
225 Mott Street
925-3849

ETTES

nolita & noho

village people

east village

Altogether edgier than its West Village neighbour, the East Village has long served as a refuge for the disenchanted and dispossessed. In the early 20th-century, it was Eastern European immigrants who set up shop here; in the 50's, the Beats (including leading light Allen Ginsberg) moved in; in the 60's hippies and free thinkers; then punk rockers in the 70's; and experimental artists and performers during the 80's.

These days, while die-hard bohemians claim the area has lost much of its maverick feel, the East Village still boasts a vibrant energy all of its own. Down-home Eastern European restaurants and the Hispanic hangouts of Alphabet City sit next to funky bistros, trendy boutiques, record stores and thrift shops. Street culture is really what counts here: in spite of the influx of young professionals and the bridge-and-tunnel crowd at weekends, it is possible to pass time ogling the non-stop parade of colourful folk and free spirits who still call East Village home.

day

🏛 East Village is busy with a myriad of funky boutiques – everything opens (and stays open) late.

👁 There are no sights per se, but the Lower East Side Gardens [→81] are a quiet retreat.

night

☆ Lots of Off-Off Broadway theatres [→140] around Third Avenue, the indie Anthology Film Archives [→142], live music venues [→146], plenty of clubs [→150–152] and poetry readings at joints like the Nuyorican Poet's Café [→145].

🍸 After dark the streets buzz with folks heading for one of the area's diverse restaurants, and hopping from one fun bar to the next.

Ⓜ L•N•R•4•5•6 to 14th St–Union Sq; L to 1st or 3rd Aves; 6 to Astor Pl.

🚌 M8 →St Mark's Pl, ←9 St; M9 ↕E Broadway, Ave B & Essex St; M14 ←→14 St; M15 ↑1st Ave ↓2nd Ave; M21 ↓Ave C.

shopping

beauty & accessories

*Kiehl's, the cult beauty brand loved by men, women and supermodels alike, has its one-and-only store in East Village. This former pharmacy, on the block since 1851, carries the full range of high-quality

Kiehl's products in its signature no-frills packaging. It's busy at weekends but, thankfully, the staff are old-fashioned and friendly, and the balms, lotions and potions work wonders on skin and hair.

Of the neighbourhood's accessory mavens, **Jutta Neumann** ↓ stands out. Her artful leather designs are favoured by Seventh Avenue designers like Marc Jacobs and Anna Sui (who use her handmade bags,

shoes and sandals in their catwalk shows). For jewellery, don't overlook **Greg Wolf**, whose excellent silver cufflinks, rings and chains are mainly for men. **Sarah Samiloff** is another talented local – her chunky silver pieces have a sweet, whimsical edge. Altogether less genteel are the toys, trinkets and T-shirts to be found at **Sears & Robot**, a wacky store specializing in Japanese imports and other kitschery.

fashion

Many of New York's designers started out in the tiny storefronts of the East Village before going on to bigger and better things. You'll see ***Daryl K**'s first store, which now offers up seriously reduced seconds and sale items, including her famous hipster, boot-cut pants. **Eileen Fisher** also keeps a boutique on in the East Village – her loose-fitting lines in quiet colours are popular with women who want fashion without ostentation. At ***Steven-Alan**'s **Outlet** store, the immaculate collection of young designer names carried at his Soho branch is sent here for quick clearance.

The East Village is still a breeding ground for up-and-comers touting edgy fashion. A new addition is **Red Tape**, a showcase for brilliant designer Rebecca Danenberg's bold, graphic pieces for women. For hardcore avant-garde style, **Horn** has Brit stars like Alexander McQueen, as well as the house line of strange-yet-tailored clothing for both sexes. A block away, **Jill Anderson** has altogether less serious garb for women – fun dresses and separates in interesting fabrics. On a more experimental note, **Anna** showcases the work of designers Claire Blaydon and Kathy Kemp, who deconstruct vintage clothing to create unique silhouettes. **Air Market** is a repository of all things Japanese including clubby asymmetric clothing and Hello Kitty backpacks.

vintage

Given the neighbourhood's bohemian edge, it's perhaps not surprising that the East Village is replete with vintage and thrift stores. For barely-worn, designer labels hit ***Tokio 7** and **Tokyo Joe**, two consignment stores offering up last year's Gaultier and Karan at considerably reduced prices. **Metropolis**, a favourite with the NYU set, sells new and used clothing with a funky feel, including never-before-worn utilitarian gear. **Apartment 141** has plenty of interesting

pieces for men and women, especially well priced antique frocks. For the highest calibre antique clothing, with price-tags to match, seek out ***Resurrection**, where the frocks date from the 1890's. Nearby **Fab 208** is home to a colourful mix of kooky vintage and brand new duds for both sexes. You'll have to look hard to find something worth taking home at **Filthmart**, a no-frills thrift store, but when you do, it'll definitely be a bargain.

Although they are still far from conventional, you will find designers here whose work appeals to the dressed-up set. On an entirely feminine trip, **Mark Montana**'s 'couture' suits and frocks are always colourful and amusing for a special party. For the total made-to-measure experience, however, head to **Blue**, presided over by the brilliant Christina Karas. Karas can rustle up a thoroughly modern wedding gown or cocktail dress in a matter of weeks. Nearby **Selia Yang** has supremely pretty party frocks in diaphanous fabrics – the handiwork of local designer Selia Yang. Send your male escort to **Savoia** for a suit, either off the rack or made-to-measure. This tailor continues to serve up the classic 40's look which has made him a favourite with a new generation of swing enthusiasts.

home furnishings

East Village is also a mecca for folks looking for flea market-style finds to dot around an apartment.

Ninth Street in particular is clogged with antique and vintage stores including **Cobblestones**, a tiny boutique brimful with *tchotchkes* as well as a small selection of accessories. **Quilted Corner** also plunders granma's attic – this time for stacks of vintage fabric, bedding and linens. **It's a Mod, Mod World** doesn't have vintage per se, but it does carry lamps and clocks recycled from such disposables as cereal boxes. **H**, meanwhile, is home to 90's lamps and furniture as pared down as the store's name.

books & records

The East Village is a haven for bibliophiles who prefer their paperbacks a little dog-eared. The biggest used bookstore in the world, *The Strand, is here, with three floors and eight miles of books at prices ranging from mere cents to hundreds of dollars. Of the other numerous used bookstores in the neighbourhood, Tompkins Square Books is a local favourite thanks to its cosy chaotic feel and late opening hours – there's a good selection

of vinyl here too. Fans of comics and sci-fi books, meanwhile, make tracks to *Forbidden Planet, where the selection of new and used collectibles is vast.

St Mark's Place (between Second and Third Avenues) is overrun with decent record stores selling new and used CDs at fair prices. *Kim's Video & Music is the biggest and brightest. This massive, yellow-painted place also sells and rents a huge range of videos.

Those in search of dance music have options – Throb carries the latest techno, house and electronica, likewise the excellent Temple Records. *Dancetracks is a neighbourhood institution – most DJs in the city stop here. Alternatively Etherea has a great selection of alternative, indie and experimental sounds. Finyl Vinyl is an endearing place that still refuses to carry CDs, while *Footlight Records is where to find showtunes and old movie soundtracks .

eating & drinking

THE ELEPHANT

restaurants

The East Village has gotten so hot as an eating destination that on weekends you'd better have a reservation or expect an hour's wait, especially at *Il Bagatto [→121], a dark and jovial Italian trattoria with low-priced, robust dishes. For a table here, patrons endure being packed in at the downstairs bar or else spill out onto the street. *First [→132] is also worth a wait, a fabulous lair with commodious booths, stellar new American cuisine, and expert cocktails. The Elephant ✓ is another neighbourhood magnet, with zesty Asian fusion creations, quirky decor and a constant hubbub at the door of those clamouring to get in.

To get into Lucien, a tiny popular French bistro, go early or very late to avoid the crush. Classic dishes are richly seasoned and excellent value, with a smart wine list to match. Chez Es Saada, a fashionable upscale casbah, has a

cramped dining-room, but there are roomier, candlelit lounges downstairs, reached bya staircase strewn with rose petals. Dazzling cocktails and savoury Moroccan-inspired food like chicken bisteeyah with saffron lemon sauce come at a price. Another ethnic favourite is Dok Suni's, a dimly-lit Korean joint, which is usually packed with a noisy, young crowd. Marinated beef, ribs and chicken dishes are high on the spiceometer, and are really wholesome and skillfully made.

Radio Perfecto is a hopping new place, filled with illuminated Bakelite radios, and there's a charming garden at the rear. The wide-ranging menu mixes up Argentine empanadas and rotisserie chicken with a delicious pesto dipping sauce on the side. Le Tableau offers lovely, innovative bistro renditions of wild mushroom casserole, calamari tagine with houmous, and bacon-wrapped

monkfish. Live combos make it festive, and sometimes overly loud. A more traditional French bistro is Jules, with nightly live jazz in a cosy, very Parisian setting. Salade niçoise, cheesy onion soup and steak frites are ace. A former Jules manager has recently opened Casimir, a very stylish bar-bistro on Avenue B with a French-accented menu and crowd to match. Creative, first-rate seafood is the draw at nautically-themed *Pisces [→133] – Avenue A's first upscale restaurant – always busy at dinner and also recommended for brunch on the weekends. Or there's Danal, one of the neighbourhood's sweetest, most romantic restaurants, which has a daily-changing but always tantalizing American-Mediterranean menu. It is open all day.

At the other end of the scale, Two Boots is a boisterous, child-friendly Italian-Cajun-Creole hangout with big red booths. Pizza is tops

– especially the spicy tomato sauce and cornmeal crust. **Mekka** is another comfortable, sociable place, with soulful southern Caribbean dishes (you can't beat the fried chicken). The bar scene is happening, with music-industry types, and great tunes always spinning.

Accomplished yet 'trashy' Southern fixins, like catfish and country ham, are featured at *Old Devil Moon [→126], along with an unusual wine and beer list; while Irish expats hang out at St Dymphna's, an affable pub, serving beef and Guinness casserole. Its low-key informality has attracted the likes of anti-scenesters Daniel Day Lewis and Ralph Fiennes.

A wave of young Asians has moved into the East Village, leading to a profusion of oriental eateries. One of the best – and most crowded – is *Takahachi [→128], serving both creative and homey Japanese specialties. **Soba-ya** is a clean, stylish environment, with exceptional *udon* and *soba* noodles combined with various meat and vegetarian morsels. Service is polished, prices are low and the sake list is noteworthy. For a trip back into the 80's, step into the clubby, ink-black **Avenue A Sushi**. Have faith: even though you can't see what you're eating, the Japanese fare is great, and the DJ spins a fun mix nightly. **Holy Basil** is a fine, similarly dark Thai restaurant where it's easier to hold a conversation. Their squid rings are the best, the seafood in general is superb, and the varied wine list is remarkable for a Thai place. **Lucky Cheng**'s [→97] is a colourful pan-Asian mecca for a mix of gay boys and suits. The food is theatrically served by cross-dressing waiters, and raunchy drag shows provide nightly entertainment. **Haveli** retains its crown as the king of 6th Street's Indian restaurants. It's a spacious duplex with courtly service and uniformly superior dishes; they even have topnotch, though distinctly un-Indian, Belgian beers to cut the spice.

cafés & diners

Probably the best brunch in the neighbourhood (weekends only) belongs to *7A, boho central 24 hours a day. For under $10 you get a judiciously prepared egg dish, crisp roasted potatoes, a juice and endless coffee refills. At other times it's good for burgers and passable Tex-Mex platters. *Yaffa Café ✓ is another 24-hour dive, whose big plus is its vast back garden. Inside, the screwball decor is diverting, and the fusion food (much of it vegetarian) reasonably healthy. The Italian **Three of Cups**, where Quentin Tarantino once got into a tussle, is great for big salads, hearty pastas and wood-fired pizza. Brunch is under $10 and includes unlimited Bloody Marys. **Dojo**'s proximity to NYU makes it a student fixture, and in all kinds of weather they'll take sidewalk tables so they can smoke in between courses of wholesome soy burgers, tofu salads and brown rice stir-fries. The hippy spirit of San Francisco is also alive and well at pretty *Angelica Kitchen, whose stimulating and nourishing organic veggie dishes prove that macrobiotic fare doesn't have to be boring.

Totally unhealthy and absolutely addictive is a little nook called **Pommes Frites**, dedicated to paper cones of golden Belgian-style fries. Dozens of inventive sauces are at hand for dipping, and although there are a couple of benches to sit on, most customers just eat on the hoof. Yummy street food is also available at **Habib's Place**, where Habib serves up fresh, cheap and abundant falafels to the sound of Louis Armstrong. If you want to avoid a sartorial mishap, try to nab one of the half-dozen little tables.

People of all ages love *Second Avenue Deli, an old Jewish kosher favourite. Their *matzoh* ball soup, corned beef and pastrami are legendary – as are the wise-cracking staff. Portions are huge and sharing costs extra, so give up and pig out. **Teresa's**, an authentic Polish diner, may have a new look but still serves the same old-fashioned *pierogis*, *kielbasa*, stuffed cabbage and blintzes. Breakfast is cheap and quick, and their chicken noodle soup is good for whatever ails you. **Veniero's** pasticceria has also been around for ever, fabled for towering cakes, rich cheesecake and Italian cookies. It's a sweet place to retire to at the end of a date, and a confectionery dream for children – and the sweet-toothed.

bars & clubs

The East Village's friendly, local bars tend to overrun with out-of-towners and college kids at the weekends, but if you're looking for down-to-earth boozy fun, few neighbourhoods can compare. Even the swank, newly-opened lounges have a laid-back feel, and the old-school dives can't be beat. **Sophie's** and **Mars** remain two of the finest. Each offers the requisite cheap drinks, video games and an excellent chance of scoring a one-night stand. Sophie's also has a competitive pool table and, to be honest, considerably fewer borderline personalities than Mars, so proceed according to your taste.

Indie-rock stars and rocka-billy kids love **2A**, a bi-level bar with views onto Avenue A, and a mish-mash of comfy sofas upstairs. The same crowd often frequents **Lei Bar**, a comparatively new addition to the basement of Niagara. Decorated like a tiki bar and no bigger than the average East Village studio, Lei Bar serves a delectable array of frozen tropical cocktails, while DJs spin mambo nightly. For live music, head to **Lakeside Lounge**, where local bands play regularly and the jukebox fills in beautifully when they don't.

Block for block, the East Village may very well boast Manhattan's densest concentrations of bars.

Gay bars are also well-represented in the East Village. **Dick's** is one of the diviest, with dirt-cheap shots, gay porn projected over the entrance, and a serious cruising scene – not to mention a killer jukebox brimming with classic punk and new-wave hits. **The Cock**, rivalled only by The Manhole bar in subtle nomenclature, attracts both rock 'n' roll gays and drag queens with its fierce parties, top-notch DJs and hot go-go dancers. The once notoriously sleazy **Wonder Bar** has managed to clean up its act without losing its edge, and is one of the city's best bars for groups of gay guys and their female friends.

Groups – either straight or gay – also do well at **Odessa**, a former Eastern European diner that was transformed into a bar when the owners relocated the diner to a larger space next door. (The bar kitchen still turns out diner fare 'til midnight.) If

you're intent on avoiding crowds, **Angel's Share** is the place to be. Accessed via a second-floor sushi bar, it strictly enforces a limit on parties of more than four. It's a perfect place for a tryst and, what's more, the cocktails are superb – everyone raves about the lychee daiquiris. **Decibel** is a better bet for those who want both their drink and their friends.

Literary types can find plenty of kinship at **KGB**, where the walls are lined with commie propaganda and the author readings are top-notch. Country and western aficionados should proceed directly to **Joe's Bar**. No live music here, but the jukebox could have easily been stolen from a Texas roadhouse. While both Joe's and KGB are

loosely thematic, nightlife doyenne Deb Parker takes it all the way. Parker's **Barmacy** and **Beauty Bar** are theme bars for a downtown crowd, with the former decorated like a 50's pharmacy, and the latter dolled-up to resemble a 50's beauty parlour. Both feature DJs each night.

DJs define the atmosphere at several East Village bars. **Baraza's** Latin nights are always packed thanks, in part, to excellent margaritas, and barbecues in summer. **Drinkland** is a favourite destination for fans of electronica and breakbeats. And Serge Becker's **B-Bar** – once a white-hot nightspot – has settled into quiet reliability. The parties here vary, but a perennial pleaser is Tuesday night's Beige, catering to fashionistas.

🔖 directory

Air Market ⌂B1
97 Third Avenue
995-5888

Angelica Kitchen ⌂B1
300 E 12th Street
228-2909 $–$$

Angel's Share ⌂B2
8 Stuyvesant Street
777-5415

Anna ⌂C3
150 E 3rd Street
358-0195

Apartment 141 ⌂B1
141 E 13th Street
358-0795

Avenue A Sushi ⌂C2
103 Avenue A
982-8109 $–$$

Baraza ⌂E2
133 Avenue C
539-0811

Barmacy ⌂D1
538 E 14th Street
228-2240

B-Bar ⌂B3
40 E 4th Street
475-2220 ◖

Beauty Bar ⌂B1
231 E 14th Street
539-1389

Blue ⌂B2
125 St Mark's Place
228-7744

Casimir ⌂D2
105 Avenue B
358-9683 $–$$

Chez Es Saada ⌂B3
42 E 1st Street
777-5617 $$

Cobblestones ⌂C2
314 E 9th Street
673-5372

The Cock ⌂C1
188 Avenue A
777-6254

Danal ⌂A1
90 E 10th Street
982-6930 $$

Dancetracks ⌂B3
91 E 3rd Street
260-8729

Daryl K ⌂B2
208 E 6th Street
475-1255

Decibel ⌂B2
240 E 9th Street
979-2733

Dick's ⌂B1
192 Second Avenue
475-2071

east village

Dojo *B2*
24 St Mark's Place
674-9821 $

Dok Suni's *C2*
119 First Avenue
477-9506 $–$$

Drinkland *D1*
339 E 10th Street
228-2435

Eileen Fisher *C2*
314 E 9th Street
529-5715

The Elephant *B3*
58 E 1st Street
505-7739 $$

Etherea *C2*
66 Avenue A
358-1126

FAB 208 *B2*
77 E 7th Street
673-7851

Finyl Vinyl *B2*
204 E 6th Street
533-8007

First *C2*
87 First Avenue
674-3823 $$

Footlight Records *B1*
113 E 12th Street
533-1572

**Forbidden
Planet** *A1*
840 Broadway
473-1576

Greg Wolf *C2*
346 E 9th Street
529-1784

H *C2*
335 E 9th Street
477-2631

**Habib's
Place** *C2*
438 E 9th Street
979-2243 $

Haveli *B2*
100 Second Avenue
982-0533 $–$$

Holy Basil *B1*
149 Second Avenue
460-5557 $–$$

Horn *C2*
328 E 9th Street
358-0213

Il Bagatto *D3*
192 E 2nd Street
228-0977 $

Indochine *A2*
430 Lafayette Street
505-5111 $$

**It's a Mod, Mod
World** *C2*
85 First Avenue
460-8004

Jill Anderson *C2*
331 E 9th Street
253-1747

Joe's Bar *D2*
520 E 6th Street
no phone

Jules *C2*
65 St Mark's Place
477-5560 $$

Jutta Neumann *C2*
317 E 9th Street
982-7048

KGB *B2*
85 E 4th Street
505-3360

Kiehl's *B1*
109 Third Avenue
677-3171

**Kim's Video &
Music** *B2*
6 St Mark's Place
598-9985

Lakeside Lounge *D1*
162–164 Avenue B
529-8463

Lei Bar *C2*
112 Avenue A
420-9517

Le Tableau *D2*
511 E 5th Street
260-1333 $$

Lucien *C3*
14 First Avenue
260-6481 $$

Lucky Cheng's *C3*
24 First Avenue
473-0516 $$

Mark Montana *C2*
439 E 9th Street
505-0325

Mars Bar *B3*
25 E 1st Street
473-9842

Mekka *C3*
14 Avenue A
475-8500 $–$$

Metropolis *B1*
43 Third Avenue
358-0795

Odessa *C2*
117 Avenue A
253-1470 $–$$

**Old Devil
Moon** *D2*
511 E 12th Street
475-4357 $–$$

Pisces *C2*
95 Avenue A
260-6660 $–$$

Pommes Frites *C2*
123 Second Avenue
674-1234 $

Quilted Corner *A1*
120 Fourth Avenue
505-6568

Radio Perfecto *D1*
190 Avenue B
477-3366 $

Red Tape *B2*
E 9th Street
529-8483

Resurrection *C2*
123 E 7th Street
228-0063

St Dymphna's *C2*
118 St Mark's Place
254-6636 $–$$

Sarah Samiloff *C1*
149 Avenue A
460-5392

Savoia *B2*
125 E 7th Street
358-1892

Sears & Robot *B2*
120 E 7th Street
253-8719

**Second Avenue
Deli** *B1*
156 Second Avenue
677-0606 $–$$

Selia Yang *C2*
324 E 9th Street
777-9776 $

7A *C2*
109 Avenue A
673-6583 $

Soba-ya *B2*
229 E 9th Street
533-6966 $

Sophie's *D2*
507 E 5th Street

Steven-Alan Outlet *C1*
330 E 11th Street
982-2881

The Strand *A1*
828 Broadway
473-1452

Takahachi *C2*
85 Avenue A
505-6524 $–$$

Temple Records *D3*
29a Avenue B
475-7552

Teresa's *C2*
103 First Avenue
228-0604 $

Three of Cups *C2*
83 First Avenue
388-0059 $

Throb *C1*
211 E 14th Street
533-2328

Tokio 7 *B1*
64 E 7th Street
353-8443

Tokyo Joe *C2*
334 E 11th Street
473-0724

**Tompkins Square
Books** *C2*
111 E 7th Street
979-8958

2A *C3*
25 Avenue A

Two Boots *C3*
37 Avenue A
505-2276 $–$$

Veniero's *C1*
342 E 11th Street
674-7070 $

Wonder Bar *D2*
505 E 6th Street
777-9105

Yaffa Café *C2*
97 St Mark's Place
674-9302 $

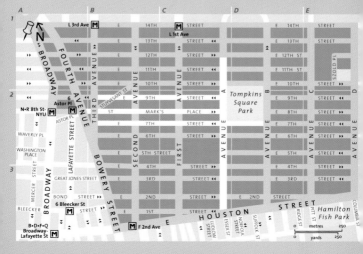

west side story

When Bob Dylan and Joan Baez busked for dimes in Washington Square in the heady days of the early 60's, Greenwich Village must have seemed the centre of the bohemian universe. And, while associations still persist, the image of the neighbourhood as a haven for musicians, writers, and artists became outdated a good 20 years ago. Today the term West Village has fallen into common use, and although initially a ruse for real estators to extend the neighbourhood boundaries, the moniker now also denotes the blocks of tacky, tourist-geared shops and bars in the area's eastern reaches.

The further west you go, the more Manhattan's rigid grid breaks down and you'll find the ineffably pretty tree-lined streets and beautiful brownstones of legend. Needless to say, this part of town is now home to the well-to-do who can afford to live in such elegant abodes. The neighbourhood's strong gay identity is still key, although the edgier gay scene has moved to Chelsea. For some residual bohemia, make for Washington Square Park, in the shadow of the NYU buildings, a hangout for students, skate kids and, to this day, busking Dylan wannabes.

day

🛍 There's a scattered selection of one-off boutiques and some big-name chain stores along Sixth Avenue. Hours vary, but most places are open till early evening and on Sundays.

👁 There are no sights per se in the West Village but plenty of picturesque streets like Washington Mews (just north of Washington Square).

night

☆ West Village entertainment is all about cosy Off-Off Broadway theatres [→139–140], lots of smoky jazz clubs and laid-back live music joints like the Bottom Line [→146–147]. For cinema goers there's always the Film Forum and the Angelika Film Center [→142].

🎷 This area is jammed with excellent restaurants of all descriptions as well as diverse bars and lounges, some with a gay slant.

Ⓜ A·C·E·B·D·F·Q to W 4th St-Washington Sq; 1·9 to Houston St or Christopher St-Sheridan Sq.

🚌 M5 →W Houston St, ↑6th Ave; M6 ↑6th Ave, ↓Broadway; M8 ↔9th & Christopher Sts, →10th & 8th Sts; M10 ↑Hudson St, ↓7th Ave; M21 ↔W Houston St.

shopping

men's & women's fashion & shoes

While those in search of designer names and cutting-edge fashion should look elsewhere, the West Village does boast a few stand-out boutiques.

Eighth Street (between Broadway and Sixth Avenue) is home to a slew of outlandish clothing and shoe stores. **Patricia Field** ✓ is the best-known of the

bunch, catering to clubkids and drag queens who subscribe to her taste in clingy clothing, 6-inch stilettos and colourful accessories (there's also a wig salon). **L'Impasse** ↖ has an equally wild collection of look-at-me garb for women. At their store next door, **Beau Gosse**, men can get into the act with tight T-shirts and sharp separates. For something a little more sophisticated, make for *Untitled, where the racks yield Martin Margiela and other hard-to-find designers for men and women. Elsewhere, **Veronica Bond**, a former Karl Lagerfield protégée, makes precious, handmade clothing for women with the emphasis on evening wear. Good quality, well-priced vintage frocks, meanwhile, are the specialty at *Stella Dallas – Catherine Deneuve shops here when she's in town.

home furnishings

For excellent home furnishings with a modern feel and moderate price tags look no further than Christopher Street, where the owners of the Amalgamated company have no fewer than three stores. **Amalgamated Home** is the place for furniture, lamps and home accessories. Aesthetic perfectionists make for **Amalgamated Hardware** (just along the block) selling interesting drawer pulls, door handles, hooks and other finishing touches. The third store (also called Amalgamated Home) has more accessories – clocks, vases and other unique pieces to dot around the apartment. For funkier flea market-style finds the **Lively Set** has an immaculate collection of furniture, pottery and lamps from the 40's through to the 70's.

Don't expect any bargains when shopping for antiques in Manhattan. The stretch of Broadway just below 14th Street has a row of antique stores selling furniture with price tags that frequently hit six figures. Many of these are trade-only, but **Howard Kaplan Antiques** is an exception; ditto **Pall Mall Antiques** on University Place. Both specialize in 18th- and 19th-century furniture.

Eighth Street is also New York's shoe central. There are upwards of 20 shoe stores here, touting everything from cowboy boots to platform sneakers. **Le Petit Peton** stands out

from the crowd thanks to a good range of European imports and the store's own line. Prices here, as with other stores on the block, are generally reasonable.

The boho 'village' of old can still be found in the neighbourhood's quaint side streets and specialty stores.

accessories & beauty supplies

Christopher Street's main drag has long been New York's Rainbow Row, and in spite of the Mayor's on-going clean-up campaign, you still find a residual number of stores selling sex toys, leather gear, tight T-shirts and sleazy underwear. These places tend to be on the tacky side, so for more up-scale erotica (this is New York, yes, there is such a thing!) make for **Pink Pussycat Boutique**, a neighbourhood institution that's so unintimidating, the staff might as well be selling candy bars. The **Pleasure Chest**, another erotic boutique, is as sleek as can be – prices here are reassuringly expensive and the window displays are often wildly imaginative.

Altogether less shocking is *Bigelow Pharmacy, one of the oldest in New York. Friendly staffers are happy to make recommendations from the excellent array of health and beauty products including homeo-

pathic remedies, top-notch cosmetics, European imports and the store's own brand of make-up, Alchemy.

one-offs

The **Village Chess Shop** has been in business since 72. Folks of all ages come here for the huge selection of boards and pieces, or to pick up a game at one of the store's small café tables. Another unique specialty store is **Kate's Paperie**, which holds no fewer than 5000 different kinds of paper, many of them handmade. Beautiful journals, pens and greeting cards are also carried. Just as enticing is **Alphaville**, which yields an amusing selection of market-style collectibles including tin toys, pop novelties and vintage movie posters in an all-white setting.

food

Less of a deli, more of a gastronomic event, legendary *Balducci's holds a mesmerizing selection of foodstuffs from all over the world. Even if you can't justify the high prices, it's worth a visit just for the spectacle of glistening fruits and vegetables, delectable pastries and mouthwatering prepared foods. Expect total sensory overload. Just down the block is another neighbourhood fixture, **Jefferson Market**; the selection is enormous and prices affordable, and the people who work here are without the attitude found in other more elitist foody venues (like Balducci's).

records & books

Sadly Bleecker Street – once New York's Record Row – has little to recommend to the avid CD shopper. Most of the old stores have closed now, so scoot around to Carmine Street, where a cluster of decent places have opened. **Vinylmania,** with its broad ranging collection of techno and electronica, stands out. Elsewhere, look out for *Fat Beats, New York's premier hip-hop record outlet, which also has a fine selection of reggae and jazz. For jazz and jazz alone, the **Village Jazz Shop** is an old-fashioned joint with a small but intelligent range of CDs and posters.

Despite its rarefied atmosphere, the West Village has only a small number of bookstores, the best loved of which is *Three Lives & Company. This charming place, with its unmistakable red-painted door, mixes new and used books in an intimate, erudite environment where the regular author readings are always impressive. Nearby, the **Oscar Wilde Memorial Bookstore**, America's first gay bookshop, has an excellent, if small selection of tomes dedicated to alternative lifestyles.

eating & drinking

restaurants

Throughout the West Village's charming tangle of streets are dozens of reasonably-priced restaurants. It is definitely a good place for daytime stops or, if you want an intimate evening, dine in one of its many invitingly romantic haunts.

One of the most striking exteriors is the one that harbours *Grange Hall [→132]. Organic chicken and cranberry-glazed pork chops are typical of the American heartland menu, and the bar is great for whimsical cocktails. The owners behind **Home** and **Drovers Tap Room** are from the Midwest and proud of it, presenting comfort food, along with alcohol-spiked lemonade. There's a bit more space in the tavern-like Drovers, though tiny Home, whose motto is 'fine wines, fine ketchup', has a garden.

For a more sophisticated experience, the hotshot

Italian chef, Mario Batali, at *Babbo ✓ [→120] tosses together magical pastas, such as mint 'love letters' with spicy lamb sausage. He first gained fame at nearby *Pó, [→133] serving earthy yet elevated Italian dishes. Loyal disciples have not abandoned Pó, despite Babbo eclipsing its brilliance. *Bar Pitti [→132] is perennially popular for rustic Italian favourites, like mozzarella and tomato salad; the simple dining room is always lively, and fashionistas fill the alfresco tables on warm nights. The Belgian-inspired *Waterloo [→121] is just as hot a ticket, with a good-looking crowd, and magnificent pots of mussels and beer-braised seafood.

*French Roast stays open 24 hours, 365 days a year, and is good for strong coffee, red wine and a repertoire of well-prepared French classics. The casual

milieu is pure Parisian flea market. At **Bar Six**, French-Moroccan fare is satisfactory for late-night noshing (until 2am), although the noise can be ear-splitting.

Eating in the intimate, Mediterranean-inspired 'cottage', **The Place**, is more rewarding than its name implies. Treats such as leek and butternut squash risotto, and curry-crusted leg of lamb are nicely prepared, and 10% of sales go to charity. The sweet appearance of **Casa**, an animated and appealing Brazilian spot, could be used as a movie location. The *empanadas* and *feijoada* (meaty stew with black beans) are homey, and the crowd arresting enough for celluloid. **Titou's** charms, however, are three-dimensional rather than skin deep: beautiful, leafy venue; French specialties; and a good deal on wine.

*Gotham Bar & Grill [→123] impresses on all fronts, with a high-ceilinged, high energy, modern room that suits its imaginatively structured American food. Also stylish is *Surya [→128] specializing in innovative, spicy seafood dishes based on southern Indian cuisine. It has a happening little lounge, exotic cocktails and a bewitching courtyard. Café Spice is part of the contemporary Indian trend as well: a colourful bistro with vividly flavoured regional specialties. Meanwhile, for Japanese food, you can't go wrong with *Japonica [→127]. The dining room is bustling yet peaceful, with the windowed café area prime for people-watching. Noodle hot pots, sushi, sashimi and tempura are all of unimpeachable quality. The sushi at Taka is also superb. What makes this unpretentious townhouse truly unusual is the fact that a woman is the chef/owner (sushi chefs being overwhelmingly male).

The creativity at Liam is significant without being showy. The simple ambience (exposed brick and wood flooring) belies the depth of dishes, like roasted sweetbreads and cod with portobello mushrooms. The food at Indigo, another unassuming neighbourhood bistro, is pure poetry. Service is professional, prices modest and the eclectic American cuisine exceptional – especially the wild mushroom strudel.

cafés & diners

Since so many West Village places are miniscule, seating is tight at night. That's why it's pleasant to visit adorable *`Ino [→126] in the afternoon, a licensed Italian bruschetta and panini stop. The eccentric *Tea & Sympathy ⏷[→127] is a delightful place to spend a few hours in the day, sampling authentic English fare and various brewed teas. The engaging Pearl Oyster Bar is also twice as nice in daytime when there's more space. Crisp Caesar salad and clam chowder with smoked bacon are an ideal combination.

Later on, join the night owls at the *Corner Bistro, a dark, old mahogany-stained pub with a television broadcasting sports. During and after drinking bouts, there's nothing like their cheap, messy burgers. If you've got a hankering for Mexican food, Taqueria de Mexico is recommended for roasted tomato and tortilla soup with chipotle chilli, delicious fiery sandwiches, and uncomplicated soft tacos and burritos. It's convenient for take-out but the cheerful dining room is perfectly agreeable.

The diminutive Chez Brigitte seats only 11 people at a time. Open for 40 years, Brigitte herself is long gone, but her spirit lives on in hearty, low-priced stews, light omelettes and heavy desserts. Moustache is another tiny treasure, serving tasty Middle Eastern pitzas. Snug little *Joe Jr's gets no points for epicurean talents, yet it's a genuine treat to huddle in one of its booths for diner staples like bagels with a cream cheese 'schmear' or grilled tuna melt.

bars & clubs

The area's winding, tree-lined streets and cosy brownstones are home to numerous bars. While still teeming with genial gay and lesbian watering holes, the West Village is now seeing its share of hipster hot-spots and impenetrable guest lists.

The owners of Spy, one of Soho's most notoriously exclusive bars, have also launched a second bar – *Moomba – which boasted near-daily mention in gossip columns for months after its opening. Celebs can still be spotted sipping martinis in the second-floor lounge, but their numbers are steadily dwindling. Henrietta Hudson, a neighbourhood girl bar, is also more about cruising than boozing, though there's still plenty of the latter.

A few notable names also hang out in the West Village institution, Marylou's. This beloved old bar-cum-restaurant serves a free midnight buffet every Sunday (booze must be purchased). This joint is always packed with regulars, and everyone seems to know everyone else.

For a dose of gay glam, head to *Bar d'O, a sexy little bôite where drag legends Joey Arias and Raven-O perform for a mixed crowd of fashionistas and local luminaries, as well as the occasional bona fide bold-faced name. Those looking for the company of pre- or post-op transsexuals, or even transvestites, need only to visit NowBar, where Gloria Wholesome hosts her popular Trannie Chaser party [→152].

Quiet drinks for two are the m.o. at Junno's, an intimate Korean-French bar that serves excellent sushi alongside creative house cocktails. If you're out with a group, a more swank vibe can be found at Clementine – resplendent cocktails (and inventive American fusion dishes) are available in the art deco lounge until 3am. For those who'd prefer a decent selection of beer and room to sit with friends, the former speakeasy, *Chumley's, is the answer. As a reminder of its past, there is still no sign posted on either of the two 'clandestine' entrances.

➔ map & directory

✑ directory

Alphaville ♫C3
226 W Houston Street
675-6850

Amalgamated Home & Hardware ♫C2
9, 13 & 19 Christopher Street
255-4161 (no.9)
989-6538 (no. 13)
691-8695 (no. 19)

Babbo ♫C2
110 Waverly Place
777-0303 $$–$$$

Balducci's ♫C1
426 Sixth Avenue
673-2600

Bar d'O ♫C3
29 Bedford Street
627-1580

Bar Pitti ♫C3
268 Sixth Avenue
982-3300 $$

Bar Six ♫C1
502 Sixth Avenue
691-1363 $$

Beau Gosse ♫D1
27 W 8th Street
598-0314

Bigelow Pharmacy ♫C1
414 Sixth Avenue
533-2700

Café Spice ♫D1
72 University Place
253-6999 $$

Casa ♫B2
72 Bedford Street
366-9410 $$

Chez Brigitte ♫B1
77 Greenwich Avenue
929-6736 $

Chumley's ♫B2
86 Bedford Street
675-4449

Clementine ♫D1
1 Fifth Avenue
253-0003 $$–$$$

Corner Bistro ♫B1
331 W 4th Street
242-9502 $

Drovers Tap Room ♫C2
9 Jones Street
627-1233 $$

Fat Beats ♫C2
406 Sixth Avenue
673-3883

French Roast ♫C1
78 W 11th Street
533-2233 $–$$

Gotham Bar & Grill ♫D1
12 E 12th Street
620-4020 $$$

Grange Hall ♫B2
50 Commerce Street
924-5246 $$–$$$

Henrietta Hudson ♫B3
438 Hudson St
924-3347

Home ♫C1
20 Cornelia Street
243-9579 $$

Howard Kaplan Antiques ♫E1
827 Broadway
674-1000

Indigo ♫C1
142 W 10th Street
691-7757 $$

˜Ino ♫C3
21 Bedford Street
989-5769 $

Japonica ♫D1
100 University Place
243-7752 $$

Jefferson Market ♫C1
450 Sixth Avenue
533-3377 $

Joe Jr's ♫C1
482 Sixth Avenue
924-5220 $

Junno's ♫C3
64 Downing Street
627-7995 $$

Kate's Paperie ♫D1
8 W 13th Street
633-0570

Le Petit Peton ♫D1
29 W 8th Street
677-8730

Liam ♫D3
170 Thompson Street
387-0666 $$

L'Impasse ♫D1
29 W 8th Street
533-3255

Lively Set ♫C3
33 Bedford Street
807-8417

Marylou's ♫D1
21 W 9th Street
533-0012 $$–$$$

Moomba ♫C1
133 Seventh Avenue S
989-1414

Moustache ♫B2
90 Bedford Street
229-2220 $

NowBar ♫C3
22 Seventh Avenue S
293-0323 ₵

Oscar Wilde Memorial Bookstore ♫C2
15 Christopher Street
255-8097

Pall Mall Antiques ♫D1
99 University Place
677-5544

Patricia Field ♫D1
10 E 8th Street
254-1699

Pearl Oyster Bar ♫C2
18 Cornelia Street
691-8211 $–$$

Pink Pussycat Boutique ♫C1
167 W 4th Street
243-0077

The Place ♫B1
310 W 4th Street
924-2711 $$

Pleasure Chest ♫B1
156 Seventh Avenue S
242-2158

Pó ♫C2
31 Cornelia Street
645-2189 $$

Stella Dallas ♫D2
218 Thompson Street
674-0447

Surya ♫B2
302 Bleecker Street
807-7770 $–$$

Taka ♫B2
61 Grove Street
242-3699 $$

Taqueria de Mexico ♫B1
93 Greenwich Avenue
255-5212 $–$$

Tea & Sympathy ♫B1
108 Greenwich Ave
807-8329 $–$$

Three Lives & Company ♫C1
154 W 10th Street
741-2069

Titou ♫B1
259 W 4th Street
691-9359 $$

Untitled ♫D1
26 W 8th Street
505-9725

Veronica Bond ♫D3
171 Sullivan Street
254-5676

Village Chess Shop ♫D2
230 Thompson Street
475-8130

Village Jazz Shop ♫D1
163 W 10th Street
741-2635

Vinylmania ♫C3
60 Carmine Street
924-7223

Waterloo ♫A2
145 Charles Street
352-1119 $$$

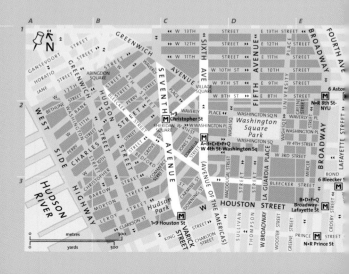

go west

Chelsea's concentration of tenements, warehouses and brownstones has experienced a major regeneration over the last decade. Thanks largely to the defection of Manhattan's gay scene from West Village, and the relocation of influential art dealers from Soho, Chelsea has exploded with cute cafés, fab boutiques, hip bars and restaurants, and major contemporary art spaces. These places, along with a cluster of big-deal nightclubs, means Chelsea is a magnet for the city's cool and queer crowd, especially at its southernmost edges.

Here, in the former factories of the Meatpacking District, white-hot art galleries and hang outs are opening at a great pace, making this as good a place as any to witness a cutting-edge scene in its nascent stages. But Chelsea's new image still has a place for the enduring Chelsea Hotel – where Sid Vicious killed his girlfriend Nancy Spungen in '78 – adding to the area's somewhat seedy, artsy fascination.

day

🛍 Big-name chain stores along Sixth Avenue, trendy one-off boutiques and the weekend flea market.

👁 Dia Center for the Arts [→86]; numerous commercial galleries, especially west of Tenth Avenue. ☎ 769-8100 for details on the free Art shuttlebus that runs between Soho & Chelsea.

night

🍴 Lots of bustling restaurants and gay-slanted bars on Seventh and Eighth Aves.

☆ The megaclubs of the far west side (sometimes called WeChe), and the Meatpacking District. A few Off-Off Broadway theatres like The Irish Rep [→140].

Ⓜ A•C•E•F•1•2•3•9 to 14th St; C•E•F to 23rd St; 1•9 to 18th, 23rd or 28th Sts; L to 6th Ave.

🚌 M5, M6 & M7 6th Ave; M10 18th Ave; M10 17th Ave; M11 ←15th St via 10th Ave; M11 19th Ave; M14 ←14th St; M23 ←23rd St.

chelsea & the meatpacking district

lifestyle stores | markets | galleries | restaurants

shopping

fashion & accessories

The shopping opportunities here are nothing short of diverse. One-off boutiques keep company with trendy sportswear outlets, major chain stores hog the main drag of Sixth Avenue, the city's biggest flea market

brings out the weekend hordes, and that's before you've taken in some art at one of the many commercial art galleries.

The opening of **Commes des Garçons** ✓ gave Chelsea

its first blast of 'serious' (and expensive) fashion – its avant garde creations wouldn't look out of place in one of the nearby art spaces. Besides Commes, the look on offer at the area's many boutiques

tends towards the clubby, sportswear-inspired gear favoured by Chelsea's gay male residents (affectionately known as 'Chelsea boys'). **Tom of Finland** is just one such place, offering a smarter take on the theme, with fashion forward clothes for men who aren't afraid to stand out in the crowd. **Raymond Dragon**

goes all-out with stretchy, second-skin numbers and swimwear for men that requires regular trips to the gym. The truly outrageous, however, head to **Lee's Mardi Gras** for the large-size dresses, beard-covering make-up, costume-jewellery and size-15 pumps beloved of drag queens and trannies.

There are plenty of stores on a grand scale in the area. The brainchild of the former shoe buyer at Barney's, ***Jeffrey** is a brand-new fashion department store, which will give this area its second shot of serious fashion chic. Meanwhile, on Sixth Avenue, big-name chains include

Old Navy, a kind of poor man's Gap, which specializes in inexpensive, basic clothing and accessories for all. More basic basics can be snapped up at **Dave's**, a tiny, 30-year old jeans outlet with a great selection of utilitarian workwear (Levis, Hanes, Schott, Carhartt) at excellent prices. The staff really know their stuff, making this a good alternative to the massive Canal Jeans in Soho. For a more conservative look, make for ***Loehmann's**, the giant discount store. Women's everyday separates are sold at ridiculously reduced prices – best bets are shoes and accessories.

lifestyle stores

Maison Moderne, a tiny, cluttered shop, has plenty of precious accessories, such as vintage silver knives and beaded lampshades. The latter would look equally at home in **Apartment 48**, a store laid out to resemble the pad of some clever interior decorator. The overall feel is traditional-casual chic, with a mixture of flea market finds, designer knick-knacks and useful kitchen implements. The ***Housing Works Thrift Shop** (all proceeds go to homeless people living with HIV) receives a constant stream of donations, which means the inventory of clothes, furniture, ceramics and paintings is vast. This is one of the few thrift stores in town where you're likely to get a real bargain. You can also spend with a good conscience at **And Bob's Your Uncle**, where most of the kitschy gifts and home furnishings are made from recycled materials. In contrast, **Eclectic Home** ✔, offers a sleek, post-modern aesthetic; its lamps, clocks and other accessories have a colourful, kooky edge. In a similar mode, the store that nobody can pronounce, **Mxyplyzyk**, carries lots of highly designed items to make every aspect of your home utterly groovy.

The **Chelsea Garden Store** (next door to the green oasis

of the Chelsea Garden Center) specializes in essential tools and interesting gifts for the green-fingered.

Of the chain stores, **Hold Everything** does just that – stocking containers, dividers and racks for all your wordly possessions. ***Williams-Sonoma**, a division of the popular Pottery Barn chain, is slightly more upscale than its sister stores with the focus on snazzy kitchen items and stylish tablewear.

Not surprisingly, the city's biggest gay, lesbian and trans-gender book and record store, ***A Different Light**, is located in Chelsea. This multi-storey outlet holds books on all aspects of gay interest, plus CDs, as well as a café and gift store. Nightly readings, meetings and events have turned this place into a veritable community centre. Home-from-home for vinyl jazz buffs is the ***Jazz Record Center**, whose collection (including Blue Note label treats) just can't be beat.

markets

The ***Annex Flea Market** is a quintessential New York experience. Every weekend, over 500 vendors set up around 26th Street. Precious antique pieces and outright junk can be found in equal measure, but don't expect any real bargains. Also clustered around 26th Street are several indoor antique 'malls' which hold higher-end furniture, jewellery and unusual objects. Nearby, along 28th Street, the weekday Flower District offers the chance to snag big bunches of blossoms at prices that can't be bettered – come early.

For a bit of DIY foodery, the ***Chelsea Market**, a mini-mall open daily for gourmets, offers a mouth-watering array of international delicacies: Amy's Bread, Thai and Italian import goods, an exclusive wine store and incredible ice-cream from Ronnybrook Farm Dairy.

galleries

A burgeoning commerical gallery scene has emerged west of Tenth Avenue, concentrated on 22nd and 24th Streets. These blocks are home to a complex known as 'MGM' – **Metro Pictures**, **Barbara Gladstone** and **Matthew Marks Gallery** – a compulsory stop for viewing what's new and what's hot. Metro grew famous for showing feminist postmodernists such as Cindy Sherman, while next door at Gladstone you can find works by Richard Prince who first made his mark with rephotographed images of the Marlboro Man. The suave young newcomer,

Matthew Marks, has two galleries where he shows mature blue chips such as Ellsworth Kelly and Brice Marden, while also establishing a market for fashionable and collectable new artists like Gary Hume and Katharina Fritsch.

Of note among the 22nd Street galleries are **Pat Hearn**, who specializes in poetic paintings filled with colour and light, and **303 Gallery**, a video gallery showing work by – among others – Doug Aitken and angry feminist painter Sue Williams.

Two veteran dealers who have set up shop in the area include **Paula Cooper**, whose grand space brings out the most of Cooper's eclectic stable ranging from minimalist sculptor Sol LeWitt to transgressive photographer Andres Serrano. **John Weber**, who made a name for himself in the 70's as the home of process-oriented art, now has a gallery on the second floor of a 10-storey building housing more than a dozen galleries large and small, and is still very strong on conceptual art.

Hot on the heels of art galleries relocating to the neighbourhood came scores of restaurants and bars catering to all, especially the local gay crowd.

eating & drinking

restaurants

The opening of the 24-hour ultra-mod ***Cafeteria** [→121] was so explosive that the food and service suffered under the crush of young style experts begging to be seen. Proceedings are now more under control, and American favourites like fried chicken and macaroni cheese score every time. Red firehouse doors conceal the formerly super-hot **Restaurant 147 ✓**. The fire may have burnt itself out, but it's still a groovy setting for caviar, crab cakes – and a spot of live jazz. **Bottino** is a spare, attractive Tuscan restaurant with a wonderful back garden, luring a cool art and publishing crowd. Pasta dishes and fish are straightforward, and the adjacent take-out shop sells panini and other prepared foods during the day. **The Tonic** is another

fashionable (read: pricey) enterprise, featuring sumptuous new American cuisine. If you want to say you've been there but don't want to pay top dollar, their handsome bar next door (the Tavern) serves a full menu including Yankee pot roast and fish and chips.

Date-places abound for gays and straights alike. Promising an illicit evening, is the speakeasy entrance to **Alley's End**. The candlelit dining room facing a picture-perfect garden is sure to seduce and the American bistro menu and boutique wine list crackle with creativity. **La Lunchonette** feels like a French version of a frontier saloon, a lively, red-hued affair with richly-flavoured Gallic classics. **El Rey del Sol**, a dark, below-

stairs hideaway, entices with an excess of tacky Mexican souvenirs and a back garden dappled with multi-coloured lights. Sangria and margaritas by the pitcher are the prelude to respectable *enchiladas*, *fajitas* and the like. Much sangria is also consumed in **El Cid**, a frumpy yet cherished tapas joint attracting vivacious groups. For a quick bite or a (relatively) quiet drink, stop by ***Florent** [→124]. This French diner is infamous for its annual Bastille Day celebration (complete with guillotine) and message-board advertising the best parties in the neighbourhood. At weekends, it hits peak traffic around 4am – just when all the clubs begin to close and its tables are quickly claimed by ravenous nightcrawlers.

more restaurants | cafés | bars & clubs | directory & map

Feast to a reggae beat on Jamaican chicken and roti bread at **Negril**. Swaying plants, beachside murals and an aquarium behind the bar give you that island feel. **Bistro at Candy Bar**'s humorous bar scene and cherry-red booths mislead some into thinking that the Austro-European food isn't serious. It is, and quite delicious. And there is no mistaking that **Siena** is just as serious when it comes to vital Italian dishes like *linguine vongole* and Barolo-braised pork. This unpretentious neighbourhood trattoria offers few distractions, correctly placing the focus on well-priced, lovely food and ravishing wines.

The Meatpacking District's **Markt** gained an immediate following upon opening. A bona fide reproduction of a stylish Belgian brasserie, its kettles of mussels and beer-braised seafood are superb – especially when washed down with world-class Belgian brews.

cafés

The old, authentically retro ***Empire Diner**, once home to late-night clubbers and drag queens, has become a haven for artists (paint-stained clothes and grubby fingernails), as well as gallery-goers (spotless attire and manicures). Updated comfort food and blue-plate specials are dished up 24 hours a day. **Le Gamin**, in a charming brick townhouse, also attracts an artsy crowd, serving French crepes, interesting salads and big bowls of coffee. Service is leisurely and the atmosphere especially magnetic at weekend brunch. While Le Gamin is languid, the Belgian **Petite Abeille** is brisk and cheerful, and adorned with Tintin posters. Omelettes, gourmet sandwiches and beefy carbonade offer sturdy daytime refuelling.

*O Padeiro [→132], lined with painted tiles and tempting baked goodies, exudes the spirit of Portugal. Their Portuguese loaves build exceptional sandwiches, as well as providing the base for the curious *açorda*, thick bread soup.

One of the homiest cafés along Eighth Avenue is **Cookie's Fine Foods**, a spick-and-span diner where meatloaf, burgers and milkshakes are served with a smile, and the check is sweetened by a free cookie. Southwestern cooking meets the Far East at **Bright Food Shop**, a cute spot open all day. The staff are welcoming and the prices pocket-friendly. **Rocking Horse Café Mexicano** ▲ is perpetually jammed with a varied crowd, who sup ambrosial libations and eat very fresh Mexican *comidas* in colourful, contemporary surroundings. Day and night, **Big Cup** is a fundamentally gay hangout, serving (yes) big cups of coffee along with muffins, pastries and sandwiches. The decor is droll and the atmosphere conducive to comfortable – and sober – cruising.

bars & clubs

Many of Chelsea's most welcoming nightspots are its gay bars. Once ground-zero for trannie clubs and prostitution, the Meatpacking District is seeing more suits and ties than ever before. The result? A schizophrenic bar and club scene equally dominated by late-night joints and ultra-trendy hangouts.

G is the place for serious gay cruising. The lounge's circular bar aids mass flirtation, and DJs spin sounds several nights a week. Plus, boys on the wagon can take advantage of the fully-stocked juice bar. ***Hell** attracts gay and straight alike. Lively parties and nightly DJs inspire some dancing, but most simply lounge around the bar, or table-hop. A resolutely straight meat market, good for late-night boozing, is **Hogs & Heifers**. Ostensibly

a biker bar with men in leather vests arriving on Harley-Davidsons, the scene is more kitsch than threatening, and it also attracts a fair number of bright young media moguls. The bar is most notorious for its collection of bras displayed behind the bar – Drew Barrymore once whipped off her brassiere here. A wild, raucous night is guaranteed.

If you're looking more for a bar to call home, swing by the **Village Idiot**. With a jukebox that plays Country &Western music, patrons who spontaneously two-step and some of the cheapest beer in town, it feels more like Nashville than 14th Street. Alternatively, ***Ciel Rouge**'s yards of red velvet and chiffon is sure to bring out the romantic in you. Ponder the extensive and

exceptional drinks list while being soothed by the torch singers crooning at the piano. **Bistro at Candy Bar** boasts a rivalling (though less traditional) drinks menu, including some wicked cocktails – 'shagadelic Martini', 'pink pussycat' and 'vampire's kiss'. **Restaurant 147**'s new basement lounge (designed by Christopher Ciccone, Madonna's brother) has returned some of the heat to this former hot-spot – another place to go for a pretty cocktail. **Lot 61** has certainly helped boost nightlife in West Chelsea. Located in a giant converted industrial space, it serves an array of cocktails and international tapas. Visit after gallery openings when local artists stop by to toast their new opuses.

🐾 directory

A Different Light ⬩ _D2_
151 W 19th Street
989-4850

Alley's End ⬩ _C3_
311 W 17th Street
627-8899 $$–$$$

And Bob's Your Uncle ⬩ _D2_
137 W 22nd Street
627-7702

Annex Flea Market ⬩ _E1_
Sixth Ave at 26th St

Apartment 48 ⬩ _E3_
48 W 17th Street
807-1391

Barbara Gladstone ⬩ _B1_
515 W 24th Street
206-9300

Big Cup ⬩ _C2_
228 Eighth Ave
206-0059 $

Bistro at Candy Bar ⬩ _C3_
131 Eighth Avenue
229-9702 $$

Bottino ⬩ _B1_
246 Tenth Avenue
206-6766 $$

Bright Food Shop ⬩ _C2_
216 Eighth Avenue
243-4433 $–$$

Cafeteria ⬩ _D3_
119 Seventh Avenue
414-1717 $–$$

Chelsea Garden Store ⬩ _C3_
207 Ninth Avenue
741-6052

Chelsea Market ⬩ _C3_
75 Ninth Avenue
243-5678

Ciel Rouge ⬩ _D2_
176 Seventh Avenue
929-5542

Commes des Garçons ⬩ _B2_
520 W 22nd Street
604-9200

Cookie's Fine Foods ⬩ _C3_
104 Eighth Avenue
989-7692 $–$$

Dave's Army & Navy ⬩ _E1_
779 Sixth Avenue
989-6444

Eclectic Home ⬩ _C2_
214 Eighth Avenue
255-2373

El Cid ⬩ _C3_
322 W 15th Street
929-9332 $–$$

El Rey del Sol ⬩ _D3_
232 W 14th Street
229-0733 $–$$

Empire Diner ⬩ _B2_
210 Tenth Avenue
243-2736 $–$$

Florent ⬩ _C4_
69 Gansevoort Street
989-5779 $–$$

G ⬩ _D2_
233 W 19th Street
929-1085

Hell ⬩ _C4_
59 Gansevoort Street
727-1666

Hogs & Heifers ⬩ _B3_
859 Washington Street
929-0655

Hold Everything ⬩ _D3_
104 Seventh Avenue
633-1674

Housing Works Thrift Shop ⬩ _D3_
143 W 17th Street
366-0820

Jazz Record Center ⬩ _D1_
8th flr, 236 W 26th St
675-4480

Jeffrey ⬩ _C2_
449 W 14th Street

John Weber ⬩ _B2_
529 W 20th Street
691-5711

La Lunchonette ⬩ _B3_
130 Tenth Avenue
675-0342 $$

Lee's Mardi Gras ⬩ _C3_
400 W 14th Street
645-1888

Le Gamin ⬩ _C2_
183 Ninth Avenue
243-8864 $–$$

Loehmann's ⬩ _C3_
101 Seventh Avenue
352-0856

Lot 61 ⬩ _B2_
550 W 21st Street
243-6555

Maison Moderne ⬩ _D2_
144 W 19th Street
691-9603

Markt ⬩ _C3_
401 W 14th Street
727-3314 $$–$$$

Matthew Marks Gallery ⬩ _B2 & B1_
522 W 22nd Street
523 W 24th Street
243 1650/243-0200

Metro Pictures ⬩ _B1_
519 W 24th Street
206-7100

Mxyplyzyk ⬩ _C4_
124 Greenwich Avenue
989-4300

Negril ⬩ _C2_
362 W 23rd Street
807-6411 $–$$

Old Navy ⬩ _E3_
610 Sixth Avenue
645-0663

O Padeiro ⬩ _E2_
641 Sixth Avenue
414-9661 $–$$

Pat Hearn ⬩ _B2_
530 W 22nd Street
727-7366

Paula Cooper ⬩ _B2_
534 W 21st Street
255-1105

Petite Abeille ⬩ _E3_
107 W 18th Street
604-9350 $

Raymond Dragon ⬩ _D3_
126 Seventh Avenue
727-0368

Restaurant 147 ⬩ _D3_
147 W 15th Street
929-5000 $$–$$$

Rocking Horse Café Mexicano ⬩ _C2_
182 Eighth Avenue
463-9511 $$

Siena ⬩ _C3_
200 Ninth Avenue
633-8033 $$

303 Gallery ⬩ _B2_
525 W 22nd Street
255-1121

Tom of Finland ⬩ _C2_
261 W 19th Street
229-1375

The Tonic ⬩ _E3_
108–110 W 18th Street
929-9755 $$–$$$

Village Idiot ⬩ _C3_
355 W 14th Street
989-7334 ⬩

Williams-Sonoma ⬩ _D3_
110 Seventh Avenue
633-2203

chelsea & the meatpacking district

all square

Straddling eternally hip Downtown and bustling, workaday Midtown, the section of Manhattan encompassing Gramercy Park, Union Square, the Flatiron District and Madison Square Park has experienced a reversal of fortune in recent years. The height of fashion in the 19th century, when it was home to the likes of Edith Wharton and the Roosevelts, the area was gradually abandoned by the rich who migrated uptown, leaving its buildings to fall into disrepair and its pretty parks to become squalid.

Now, city clean-ups, renovations and the arrival of publishing, new media and advertising companies, have rejuvenated the area, which holds manifest treats for those in search of fine dining (especially around Union Square and Gramercy Park) and historic architecture. Shoppers also fare well, particularly for home furnishings around the Flatiron District with its striking namesake which appears to sail up Fifth Avenue.

day

🛍 There are plenty of big-names and big-name chains all long Fifth Avenue, and home furnishing stores in the Flatiron District.

👁 All the Midtown sights are within walking distance, and the Flatiron Building [→74] is central to the area.

night

☆ Top bands play at Madison Square Gardens and Irving Plaza [→146]. There are a few cinemas in the area too.

🍴 There are superb and often expensive restaurants in Gramercy Park, all around Union Square and on Park Avenue, but good bars are few and far between.

Ⓜ F to 14th or 23rd Sts; L•4•5•6 to 14 St-Union Sq; 6 to 23rd or 28th Sts; N•R to 14 St-Union Sq, 23rd or 28th Sts.

🚌 M1 & M2 ↑Park Ave S; M1 ↓Park Ave, M2 & M3 15th Ave; M14 ⟷14th St; M15 ↑1st Ave, ↓2nd Ave; M101, M102 ↑3rd Ave; M101, M102 ↓ Lexington Ave .

shopping

fashion, shoes & accessories

A retail wasteland not that long ago, lower Fifth Avenue has turned itself into quite a stylish shopping zone. At *Paul Smith, expect men's classics (suits, shirts); fancy underwear and socks; accessories; and stylish objects for the home – all with a little English eccentricity.

Further North, *Emporio Armani offers sleek and glossy Italian fashion (less pricey than the Armani Collection Uptown) and there's even an in-store café for a classy pit stop. Isabel Toledo Lab overlooks the city from its fifth-floor vantage point, and is the showcase for the Cuban-

born designer. Check out her feminine yet architectural clothes for women; her capsule collection for men; pieces for the home, and pen-and-ink drawings by her artist husband, Ruben. Still in fabulous mode? Intermix, which offers innovative clothes from a group of rarely-found international designers, could be your next stop. For a similar look on the cheap, try **Club Monaco**. Once the well-kept secret of fashion editors, now everybody has found out that this great chain does the trendiest sportswear, in interesting fabrics and edgy colours, at excellent prices. Another chain that is bringing high fashion to the younger crowd is **Bebe**. You can find lots of suits, dresses, separates and coats here in current styles and hues: the accent is always on sexy. **J Crew** (a more expensive and conservative version of Gap) remains the perfect outpost for locating just the right T-shirt, sweater or plain chinos, while **Banana Republic** (with separate stores for men and women) is a bit more upscale – their home furnishings (in the women's store) follow suit.

Serious bargain-hunters can hit the jackpot at ?**Daffy's** discount superstore.

However, be prepared to pick through a lot of dross to find what you want; best bets are children's clothes, sleepwear and men's suits. The women's department can be very hit or miss, but the deeper you dig, the better the chance of lucking out. If you're stuck on the styles of yesteryear, hotfoot it to 19th Street, where **The Fan Club**, has OTT glamorous garb (some of it donated by celebrities) from the 20's to the 90's. All proceeds go to charity. At *****Darrow Vintage** ✓, the accent is more focused on the 40's, 50's and 60's, though with everything in such pristine condition, you'll find it hard to believe anything here was pre-owned. On a mission to outdo Imelda Marcos? Stop by **Kenneth Cole**, who has made his fortune by offering derivative versions of expensive, designer footwear for men and women at fairly affordable prices. He's also branched out into slick, mainly black, separates, bags, leather clothing and accessories.

lifestyle stores

Whether you're buying or browsing, don't miss the utterly unique *****ABC Carpet & Home** – a gigantic, six-storey palace (on both sides of the street), crammed with a fantastic selection of housewares. On the same street, you can let loose the purse strings at *****Fishs Eddy**, which features all sorts of cute, vintage crockery. Campagna, one of city's chic Italian restaurants, has spawned its own **Campagna Home** shop, which is full of imported painted porcelain, pots and pans too gorgeous to actually cook with, and other snazzy objects to make your house a little more like home.

*****Paragon** has been providing the best in sportsgear for nearly 100 years. Good for quality but no real bargains unlike **Circuit City**, which is filled with great deals on everything you've ever wanted that plugs in, has an on button or takes a picture.

For book buyers and browsers *****Barnes & Noble**'s flagship store is on Fifth Avenue: you can't beat this chain for selection and value. But those after a bargain should head for *****Academy Books & Records**: one store sells used books, the other mainly used classical CDs.

eating & drinking

more restaurants | cafés & diners | bars | directory & map

restaurants

The visionary restaurateur Danny Meyer first dared to take a chance on the emerging Union Square area in 85, opening the polished and hospitable *****Union Square Café** [→125]. Chef Michael Romano's resourceful American dishes with a melting pot of accents employ nearby Greenmarket produce, and the wine list is extraordinary. Meyer next helped revitalize Gramercy Park with *****Gramercy Tavern** [→125], a gently lit, active spot, whose eclectic American menu is likewise matched by an interesting assortment of wines. The tavern takes walk-ins (no reservation necessary). Meyer has since opened two more exciting restaurants, side-by-side in the same art deco building: *****Eleven Madison Park** [→121] – New York cuisine with a French slant – and *****Tabla** [→128] – contemporary American with Indian spices. Both are beautiful, dramatically designed showplaces that have lured back the upper-echelon types who used to populate Madison Park 100 years ago.

Another pioneer in the area was Bobby Flay, who opened *****Mesa Grill** [→128] in 91. The pop-style, dynamic atmosphere is the right setting for bold Southwestern flavours and topnotch margaritas. Around the corner, the **Blue Water Grill** is a sophisticated seafood

gramercy park & the flatiron district

restaurant with a great raw bar, fresh lobster, and grilled wild striped bass, plus a fab outdoor terrace overlooking Union Square.

Douglas Rodriguez's Nuevo Latino cooking (he invented the genre) at *Patria [→128] positively thrills, and the high energy in the Gaudi-inspired dining room is infectious. At *Union Pacific [→131] the daring global creations, such as sauteed foie gras with green papaya and tamarind, give jaded palates a seismic jolt, and the dining room is just as breathtaking. Hands down, Periyali features the most stupendous Greek seafood in town, served in a peaceful, civilized atmosphere, while Puglia's cuisine gets top billing at I Trulli, a gracious, exquisite spot with an enchanting little *enoteca* (wine bar) attached. Joanie's, with bordello-red walls and whimsical décor, is also prime for romance. The food is expensive but worth it for originality and flavour, such as blue crab chowder, and apple-curry pasta with seafood.

Hidden in the basement of a picturesque townhouse is Yama, which dishes up plentiful sushi at decent prices served in the ambi-ence of a Japanese living room. Another gorgeous townhouse holds *Verbena, [→131] run by owner/chef Diane Forley, one of New York's few women restaurateurs who has risen to the top. She offers a riveting organic take on American cuisine like wild Colum- bia River sturgeon with celery root, leek and chard. The garden is beautiful.

Fronting modern Union Square, *Zen Palate [→131] is cherished for its creative Asian vegan dishes and serene décor. Downstairs is cheaper and more casual, and upstairs more meditative (and expensive). Also on the pricey side is *Veritas [→133] known for its showy dishes and awesome wine list. Singles hang out at Candela, as dark and gothic as a medieval castle. Along with a hyper bar scene is surprisingly thoughtful food, such as an abundant seafood platter, and asparagus, goats' cheese and basil purée. Lola possesses a more assured sexiness, serving an inventive mix of American, Mediterranean and Asian cuisines; the live gospel music at Sunday brunch is especially rousing. If you're into jazz, head for 27 Standard (performances downstairs). The cavernous dining room offers superb eclectic dishes like pecan-crusted pork, and tuna sashimi wrapped in *nori*.

cafés & diners

Keeping pace with the wide number of local businesses, efficient lunchtime stops have multiplied. The slick City Bakery has huge cookies and other mouth-watering sweets, plus a line-up of fresh soups, sandwiches and prepared foods – to go or eat-in at several small tables (closes 6pm). Flavors, an illustrious catering company, has a market/café outpost selling assorted breakfast and lunch items, as well as a fantastic salad bar and beautiful desserts (closes 6.30pm). For the ultimate salad fix, head for Tossed ✓ where you can choose from eight types of lettuce, and vegetable toss-ins with dressings such as champagne-raspberry, and black peppercorn *asiago* (closes 10pm).

If you've maxed out on shopping, take a tranquil break at ABC Parlour at the back of this magical furniture store. Or, the Coffee Shop is a stylish canteen, with an amazing S-shaped bar, that pulses until 6am. What it lacks in service it makes up for in robust Brazilian dishes including a *feijoada* brunch, big enough to share. Republic is the consummate Pan-Asian cafeteria: minimalist, capacious and ultra-cool. Brothy noodle soups, grilled Japanese eggplant, and curried duck noodles are tasty and modestly priced.

The airy diner Mayrose is popular for turkey burgers, milkshakes and big breakfasts (served at any time). The food isn't amazing but it's abundant and popular with pre- and post-cinema goers. Curry in a Hurry in the part of Lexington Avenue known as Little India resembles an Indian McDonald's. *Masala dosa* – vegetarian pancakes stuffed with potatoes and peas – are the best item, and it's BYOB which makes it super-cheap. The rather dowdy Eisenberg Sandwich Shop (closes at 5pm) has been open since 29, and one hopes it'll last forever. Thank the counterman for your chocolate shake and cheap, thick tuna sandwich and he'll respond, 'My pleasure, darling.' How often do you hear that in New York?

bars

While both Gramercy Park and the Flatiron District boast a slew of restaurants, neither offers much in the way of a bar scene. **The Galaxy** is a bar and a fusion restaurant. The house cocktails – much like its planetarium-chic decor – are both imaginative and palatable, and it makes an ideal stop en route to or from a concert at Irving Plaza [→146].

For a more down-to-earth experience head to **Pete's Tavern**. Boasting original tin ceilings, an ancient oak bar and, in some cases, what look like original bartenders, this friendly neighbourhood institution is still going strong after a century of business. Expect old-fashioned cocktails and classic pub grub.

The boy-bar scene is considerably more lively in nearby Chelsea, but if you just can't get there, stop by **Splash**, which offers two floors of boozing and cruising, as well as DJs and dancing, It's one of the few spots in the neighbourhood that proves you haven't left sin city – and that it still exists.

🔔 directory

ABC Carpet & Home ♟B2–B3
888 Broadway
473-3000

ABC Parlour Café ♟B2
38 E 19th Street
677-2233 $–$$

Academy Books & Records ♟A3
10 W 18th Street
242-4848

Banana Republic ♟A3 & ♟A3
89 Fifth Avenue
366-4630
128 Fifth Ave (men's)
366-4691

Barnes & Noble ♟A3
105 Fifth Avenue
807-0099

Bebe ♟A3
100 Fifth Avenue
675-2323

Blue Water Grill ♟B3
31 Union Square W
675-9500 $$–$$$

Campagna Home ♟B3
29 E 21st Street
420-1600

Candela ♟B3
116 E 16th Street
254-1600 $$

Circuit City ♟B3
52 E 14th Street
387-0730

City Bakery ♟A3
22 E 17th Street
366-1414 $

Club Monaco ♟A2
160 Fifth Avenue
352-0936

Coffee Shop ♟B3
29 Union Square W
243-7969 $–$$

Curry in a Hurry ♟B1
119 Lexington Avenue
683-0900 $

Daffy's ♟A2
111 Fifth Avenue
529-4477

Darrow Vintage ♟A2
7 W 19th Street
255-1550

Eisenberg Sandwich Shop ♟A2
174 Fifth Avenue
675-5096 $

Eleven Madison Park ♟B2
11 Madison Avenue
889-0905 $$–$$$

Emporio Armani ♟A3
110 Fifth Avenue
727-3240

The Fan Club ♟A2
22 W 19th Street
929-3349

Fishs Eddy ♟B2
889 Broadway
420-9020

Flavors ♟A3
8 W 18th Street
647-1234 $

The Galaxy ♟B3
15 Irving Place
777-3631 ◖ $

Gramercy Tavern ♟B2
42 E 20th Street
477-0777 $$$

I Trulli ♟B1
122 E 27th Street
481-7372 $$$

Intermix ♟A3
125 Fifth Avenue
533-9720

Isabel Toledo Lab ♟A1
277 Fifth Avenue
685-0948

J Crew ♟A3
91 Fifth Avenue
255-4848

Joanie's ♟B1
126 E 28th Street
689-5656 $$$

Kenneth Cole ♟A3
95 Fifth Avenue
675-2550

Lola ♟A2
30 W 22nd Street
675-6700 $$$

Mayrose ♟A3
920 Broadway
533-3663 $

Mesa Grill ♟A3
102 Fifth Avenue
807-7400 $$–$$$

Paragon ♟B3
867 Broadway
255-8036

Patria ♟B2
250 Park Avenue S
777-6211 $$$

Paul Smith ♟A3
108 Fifth Avenue
627-9770

Periyali ♟A2
35 W 20th Street
463-7890 $$$

Pete's Tavern ♟B3
129 E 18th Street
473-7676 ◖ $–$$$

Republic ♟B3
37 Union Square W
627-7172 $

Splash ♟A3
50 W 17th Street
691-0073

Tabla ♟B1
11 Madison Avenue
889-0667 $$$

Tossed ♟B2
295 Park Avenue S
674-6700 $

27 Standard ♟B1
116 E 27th Street
447-7733 $$$

Union Pacific ♟B2
111 E 22nd Street
995-8500 $$$

Union Square Café ♟B3
21 E 16th Street
243-4020 $$$

Verbena ♟B3
53 Irving Place
260-5454 $$$

Veritas ♟B2
43 E 20th Street
353-3700 $$$

Yama ♟B3
122 East 17th Street
475-0969 $$

Zen Palate ♟B3
34 Union Square E
614-9291 $–$$

middle ground

midtown

For many New Yorkers office-heavy Midtown means one thing: work. But to the visitor, Manhattan's central segment is as exciting and intense as any place on earth. This is where you'll find vertigo-inducing skyscrapers, world-famous hotels, fancy stores, and some of NYC's most expensive restaurants.

Midtown's dramatic hub is Times Square [→76]. The stretch of Broadway which cuts through this dazzling neon morass is of course, *the* Broadway, with its slew of legendary venues in the Theater District. Also cutting through Times Square is 42nd Street, the city's former red light district. Theme stores and renovated theatres have now replaced most of the sex shops.

West of Times Square, Hell's Kitchen – formerly the stamping ground of Irish and Hispanic immigrants – is a fully gentrified neighbourhood. Directly south is the busy, work-a-day Garment District, home to clothing manu-facturers and textile wholesalers. Glamorous Fifth Avenue, which, to many, epitomises New York, lies directly east, and its vista of histo-ric skyscrapers and landmarks can truly take the breath away.

day

🏛 After ogling the skyscapers, check out the theme and flagship stores, and historic shops all along Fifth Avenue.

👁 American Craft Museum [→85]; Bryant Park [→91]; Chrysler Building [→74]; Empire State Building [→78]; Grand Central Station [→78]; ICP (Mid-town) [→87]; Intrepid Sea Air Space Museum [→93]; MetLife Building [→75]; MoMA [→80]; NY Public Library [→77]; Pierpont Morgan Library [→83]; Radio City Music Hall [→75]; Rockefeller Center [→75]; St Patrick's Cathedral [→75]; Trump Tower [→76]; UN Building [→76].

night

☆ Make for the bright lights of the Broadway theatres and Times Square.

🍽 Dine out in the Theater District and along Ninth Avenue.

Ⓜ Nearly all lines stop at various Midtown stations: major hubs are Times Sq-42nd St, 34th St-Herald Square, Grand Central-42nd St & 47–50th Sts-Rockefeller Ctr.

🚌 Similarly, several buses travel along 5th, 6th, & 7th Aves, Madison & Broadway; there are regular cross-street services too.

shopping

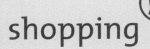

department stores

Midtown is a busy hive of shopping activity. The famous, superlative stretch of Fifth Avenue is home to a host of glossy shops, includ-ing several of the city's leg-endary department stores,

which attract the kind of high-class consumer who wants to part with lots of cash. The venerable ***Bergdorf Goodman** is a hedonistic shopping expe-rience for those with one

eye on the cutting edge. While it still has old-world elegance, it is also trendy Fashion Central, offering the top designers, excel-lent accessories and unique homewares. Across

the street, Bergdorf Men is a newer addition. *Saks Fifth Avenue is another NY institution – an old-fashioned department store (with excellent service) that also carries the top designers (for more designer-label street cred), while *Macy's, the 'biggest department store in the world', has just about everything and then some. Henri Bendel is a real jewel of a store filled with good things, especially if you're after a sweater (with a myriad colour options), or fabulous make-up brands with staff on hand to give you some top tips.

*Takashimaya (from Japan) and *Felissimo ➚ are two quasi-department stores which sell gorgeous clothes, accessories and homewares – all displayed and package-wrapped with great aesthetic flair.

megastores

The theme stores have arrived, packed with tempting licensed merchandise. There's plenty to see at *Sony Style ►, including a glimpse of entertainment 21st-century style, high-tech toys and music machines – all of which keep the cash tills whirring. Few people leave New York without a visit to the ultimate megastore, *Niketown. Five floors of gear with the 'swoosh' in a suitably futuristic interior, and a huge screen showing polished Nike commercials. *Warner Bros Studio Store is also good fun, with some imaginative toys, while at the NBA store, which holds a full-range of merchandise from every NBA basketball team, you can get kitted out just like Shaq. If Mickey, Minnie and Co are more

up your street, swing by the *Disney Store. *FAO Schwarz is just plain toy nirvana [→93].

Right on Times Square, the giant *Virgin Megastore must surely have the biggest selection of music in town (plus great quantities of videos and books): *HMV (with very helpful and knowledgeable staff) and *Tower Records are not as cavernous, but offer more of the same.

flagship stores

Flagship super-emporiums are a dime a dozen in this area. On one block of 57th Street (heading east from Fifth Avenue), the luxury stores abound – Versace, Chanel, Hermès, Burberry, and more. If hard-core fashion is what you crave, get your fix at the most recently-opened *Prada store. Behind the glass and marble storefront are Muiccia's genius clothes for men and women. Nearby is *Gucci, a stop for career fashion (and shoe) lovers. Along with high fashion for men and women, check out Tom Ford's beautiful handbags and inspired housewares. More perfect tailoring comes in the shape of Christian Dior.

There is nothing more essentially American than Gap, and the biggest and best of them all can be found here, offering affordable sportswear with a few extra, upscale surprises, like the baby cashmere boutique.

accessories & shoes

British-based *Manolo Blahník displays his fabulous footwear in a townhouse store. No price tags here – but if you need to ask... Another Brit import, *Jimmy Choo, has made a real splash with his unusual and very luxe collection, giving new meaning to well-heeled. For a bag on the cheap, sneak into Suarez ◢ which manufactures look-alike Hermès, Chanel and more. Or take a look at the edgy, of-the-moment bags by Karl Lagerfeld at *Fendi, where the clothes are also wonderful.

There is no better place for fine jewellery and fancy housewares than Tiffany's. The famous blue boxes decadently scream 'I've just spent a pile of money and don't give a damn!'. Nearby Cartier, purveyor of movie star jewellery offers equally extravagant retail therapy.

home furnishings, books & food

The famous Chicago home furnishings outpost, Crate & Barrel, has recently opened a beautiful and spacious NY store. On offer are high quality yet functional and chic furniture, dishwares, and other home accessories – all at affordable prices. To add to your book collection, it's worth visiting Coliseum Books, which has an enormous selection with lots of discounts. *Rizzoli has an equally impressive selection, particularly on art, design and architecture, displayed in a historic and utterly beautiful store.

All shopped out and need something sweet to give you a boost? Don't settle for anything less than the very best chocolate. Empyreal French delicacies almost too exquisite to eat can be found at Richart, while Godiva Chocolatier from Belgium and Teuscher from Switzerland are two other divine choices to keep you going.

galleries

In the upper floors of the buildings lining 57th Street are some of NY's toniest galleries. **PaceWildenstein** is one of the city's most successful contemporary spaces. Look for work by Photorealist Chuck Close, Minimalist Agnes Martin, feminist body artist Kiki Smith, Neoexpressionist superstar Julian Schnabel, and sculptor Henry Moore – to name just a few. The **Kennedy Galleries** have dozens of contemporary artists' work, as well as a huge collection of exclusively American paintings and prints dating from the 18th century, while the international **Marlborough Gallery** specializes in 'pop figuration' and has recently taken on neon artist Keith Sonnier.

It is a while since **Mary Boone** fled the boutiquification of Soho and moved Uptown – but the queen of the 80's art boom is still making new art stars. New talent also abounds in the dozen or so galleries located in the glorious art deco Fuller Building. Of particular note is **Robert Miller**, who features an eclectic assortment of modernist photography, classic Modernist painters (like David Hockney) and cutting-edge Contemporaries (such as Walter Niedermayr).

eating
& drinking

restaurants

In Midtown's asphalt jungle, it's easy to feel confounded when it's time to eat. Mediocre tourist traps abound but you won't feel cheated at any of these...

Surrounded by glitzy new high-rises, a little piece of New York's cultural history is still alive at the **'21' Club** [→125], marked by a line of colourful, miniature jockeys. It's outrageously expensive but incredibly charming and old-world, and the American classics are genuinely good. **Keens Steakhouse** has been around since 1885. The bygone tavern decor is glorious and the dry-aged steaks and mutton chops legendary. Prices are steep and the brief bar menu is more affordable (closed Sun). Red-checked tablecloths and a quaint French bistro ambience have made ***La Bonne Soupe** ✓ [→129] appealing for decades. Besides hearty Gallic classics, the soups are meals in themselves and the price includes a salad, dessert and glass of wine.

The restored and at times bustling ***Oyster Bar** ► [→125] in Grand Central Station is a lark for its antiquated setting, and serves well-nigh every type of fish in the sea – and of course oysters. Sit at the counter for chowder and beer, or choose the dark saloon for a more leisurely affair.

Upstairs, overlooking the main concourse, basketball superstar Michael Jordan's **The Steakhouse NYC** offers an awe-inspiring panorama of the commuter hubbub below and a canopy of illuminated stars above. The tables are ringed around the mezzanine and the steak-oriented menu is superb. Another impressive backdrop is beautiful Bryant Park [→91] (behind the Public Library) where **Bryant Park Grill & Café** offers a retreat from the hustle of Midtown. The Café wins hands down in the summer with an ample supply of alfresco seating (singles flock here on Thursday evenings), while the classy Grill serves topnotch New American food and has huge windows affording a great view. The ***Trattoria dell'Arte** [→125], near Carnegie Hall, also possesses an attractive grandeur. Big-name publishing and movie personalities frequent it, not only for the scene but also for its splendid Italian cuisine.

The trendy, attitude-heavy scene at **Asia de Cuba** can be over the top, so it's not for everybody. If, however, you want to lounge in a creamy boudoir, share punchbowl-sized tropical drinks and sample exotic, expensive Asian-Latin fusion dishes, step right up. Pretensions are wonderfully absent at **Don Giovanni**, a Theater District favourite adorned with vintage actors' photos and straw-covered Chianti bottles. The terrific brick-oven pizzas are better than the pastas. At **Virgil's Real BBQ**, goodwill towards all – even children – reigns. It's big, fun and rambunctious.

An unusual pre-theatre choice is **Lakruwana**, an opulent Sri Lankan restaurant embellished with brass, crushed velvet curtains and wooden sculptures. Dishes are spicy, there's a good vegetarian selection, and it's BYOB. Exceptional vegetarian choices are found at two of Koreatown's best restaurants: ***Cho Dang Gol** [→127] are the tofu specialists, though carnivores will also be happy with their barbecued prime beef ribs. The other is **Hangawi**, an enchanting, serene temple devoted exclusively to vegetarianism. Wear good socks as shoes are left at the door.

For something truly international, book a table at the **UN Delegates' Dining Room**. Expect an extravagant buffet and a room full of dignitaries with stunning river vistas (11.30am–2.30pm Mon–Fri). Allow 15 minutes to pass security (photo ID and jackets required).

The city's top Scandinavian restaurant is ***Aquavit** [→122], occupying the ground level of a mansion formerly owned by the Rockefellers. The tranquil main dining room offers an innovative menu while the upstairs, less formal café serves traditional herring, gravlax and Swedish meatballs. For the most fabulous French seafood creations in an elegant setting, ***Le Bernardin** [→123] is a

heavenly experience. You'll pay through the nose but not regret it. ***Lespinasse** [→123] evokes the Palace of Versailles, with prices ($35 appetizers) that could start a revolution. If money is no object, the French cuisine is breathtaking and memorable, the service faultless.

cafés

Midtown eateries dish it out to the lunchtime work crowd, early evening theatre-going set and night owls alike.

Don't let the varnished panelling and tacky chandeliers dissuade you from stopping in at ***Ess-a-Bagel** for arguably the best and biggest bagels in town. There are also smoked fish platters and a range of calorie-laden desserts. Service might be slow and prices rather high, but the soups at **Soup Kitchen International** (from which the famous 'Soup Nazi' *Seinfeld* episode was derived) are celestial (12–6pm Mon– Fri).

Within the Rockefeller Center [→75] is a busy Italian marketplace called **Tuscan Square**. The downstairs self-service café serves tasty prepared foods, delicious soups and has a great salad bar (closes at 8pm). Takashimaya, the fancy Japanese department store, has a calming, minimalist café, **The Tea Box**, which serves bite-sized finger sandwiches, elegant bento boxes and lovely afternoon tea (11am–6pm). Another fine spot is **Mezze**, a sunny, casual Mediterranean café near Grand Central

Station. Breakfast coffee can be savoured with rich pastries, and at lunch there are quality, pre-cooked meat, seafood and vegetable selections with fresh seasonings (closes at 5pm).

If you want something good and fast before a Broadway show, bypass the traditional options on 48th Street's 'Restaurant Row' and head for Ninth Avenue, which has recently been rejuvenated by an influx of new restaurants. **Vynl Diner** in Hell's Kitchen is super-friendly, with mosaic tabletops and camp decor. In addition to American staples like grilled cheese and meatloaf, there are Thai-accented curries and stir-fries. Great burgers and milkshakes (but no fries) are

found at ***Island Burgers & Shakes**, a relaxed, crowded nook that's especially popular at lunchtimes. They also make bang-up grilled chicken sandwiches with lots of toppings. **Los Dos Rancheros Mexicanos** has some of the most authentic Mexican *moles*, *tamales* and *chiles rellenos* in New York. It's a funky cafeteria with few gringos so you know it must be the real thing.

bars

While Midtown proper is dominated by tourist traps and theme restaurants, Hell's Kitchen is home to a number of fantastic dive bars. **Rudy's Bar & Grill** is one of the few original to survive the Mayor's current efforts to sanitize the neighbourhood. Free hot dogs at the bar, a great happy hour and heaps of authenticity add to its appeal. Several newer bars also offer a taste of that bygone scene. Two blocks away from the Port Authority, **Drag** is a good place to fortify yourself with a beer. Its subterranean sister bar *Siberia is another favourite. Tucked in a corner of the Downtown 1•9 subway station, it never fails to entertain – especially if you've sampled a few shots of chilled Soomskaya vodka. Vodka is just about the only thing you can drink at *The Russian Samovar ✓, a swank Theater District bar and restaurant boasting dozens of house vodkas infused with everything from plums to horseradish.

After the show, head to **Xth Ave Lounge** and mix with budding thespians, writers and other rent-challenged types. Don't

miss Saturday nights, when DJ Lady 'Miss' Bunny and Honey Dijon alternate at the turntables. *Swine on Nine, a new watering hole billing itself as Manhattan's only theme dive bar, could easily lay claim to the nation's largest assemblage of porcine paraphernalia. To jump-start their own collections, ladies get a free piggy bank as a souvenir.

If being so close to Broadway makes you want to belt out a few tunes of your own, head to **Japas 55**. Part bar, part sushi restaurant, Japas features private karaoke booths where you can humiliate yourself in front of up to 20 friends, or do a duet in a space for two. Singing around a piano is still a lively tradition at *Regents. An older, mostly gay clientele regularly gathers at this casually elegant brownstone for drinks, dinner and a few rounds of standards. Singers of a different stripe meet at **O'Reilley's Pub**, where young Irish expats – and anyone fond of whiskey and beer – sing along with the jukebox, seduce local lasses and generally have a raucous good time.

Too much whiskey is a phrase that could aptly describe Rande Gerber, Cindy Crawford's husband. The latest NY annexes to the bar impresario's empire are **Whiskey Blue** and **Whiskey Park**. The latter is housed in the Trump Parc building, and that is all you need to know. The former, located in the W New York Hotel [→158], attracts more of a bar-to-boudoir crowd, (especially on Thursdays when the crowd spills into the lobby), along with plenty of Hamptons-haunting ladies and wealthy sugar daddies. If you're looking for an old New York hotel bar, the *Blue Bar is a quiet retreat, while *Top of The Tower, a 26th-floor art deco gem, offers breathtaking views of Manhattan, a tinkling piano, and dapper old waiters serving classic cocktails.

directory

Aquavit ℓ E2
13 W 54th Street
307-7311 $$$

Asia de Cuba ℓ F6
Morgans Hotel,
237 Madison Avenue
726-7755 $$$

Bergdorf Goodman ℓ E1
754 Fifth Avenue
753-7300

Bryant Park Grill & Café ℓ E6
25 W 40th Street
840-6500 $$–$$$

Blue Bar ℓ E5
59 W 44th Street
840-6800 ◐

Burberry ℓ E7
9 E 57th Street
371-5010

Cartier ℓ E3
653 Fifth Avenue
753-0111

Chanel ℓ E2
15 E 57th Street
355-5050

Cho Dang Gol ℓ E7
55 W 35th Street
695-8222 $–$$

Christian Dior ℓ E2
703 Fifth Avenue
223-4646

Coliseum Books ℓ C2
1771 Broadway
757-8381

Crate & Barrel ℓ F1
650 Madison Avenue
308-0011

Disney Store ℓ E2
711 Fifth Avenue
702-0702

Don Giovanni ℓ B5
358 W 44th Street
581-4939 $–$$

Drag ℓ B6
538 Ninth Avenue
695-5507 ◐

Ess-a-Bagel ℓ G3
831 Third Avenue
980-1010 $

FAO Schwarz ℓ E1
767 Fifth Avenue
644-9400

Felissimo ℓ E2
10 W 56th Street
247-5656

Fendi ℓ E2
720 Fifth Avenue
767-0100

Gap ℓ D7
60 34th Street
643-8960

Godiva Chocolatier ℓ E2
701 Fifth Avenue
593-2845

Gucci ℓ E2
10 W 57th Street
826-2600

Hangawi ℓ E8
12 E 32nd Street
213-0077 $$–$$$

Henri Bendel ℓ X2
712 Fifth Avenue
247-1100

Hermès ℓ E1
11 E 57th Street
751-9339

HMV ℓ D7
57 W 34th Street
629-0900

Island Burgers & Shakes ℓ E2
766 Ninth Avenue
307-7934 $

Japas 55 ℓ B2
253 W 55th Street
765-1210 $–$$

Jimmy Choo ℓ E3
645 Fifth Avenue
593-0800

Keens Steakhouse ℓ E7
72 W 36th Street
947-3636 $$$

Kennedy Galleries ℓ E2
2nd flr, 730 Fifth Ave
541-9600

La Bonne Soupe ℓ E2
48 W 55th Street
586-7650 $–$$

Lakruwana ℓ B5
358 W 44th Street
957-4480 $$

Le Bernardin ℓ D3
155 W 51st Street
489-1515 $$$

Lespinasse ♪E2
St Regis Hotel
2 E 55th Street
339-6719 $$$

Los Dos Rancheros Mexicanos ♪A6
507 Ninth Avenue
868-7780 $

Macy's ♪D7
151 W 34th Street
695-4400

Manolo Blahnik ♪E2
31 W 54th Street
582-3007

Marlborough Gallery ♪E2
40 W 57th Street
541-4900

Mary Boone ♪E1
745 Fifth Avenue
752-2929

Mezze ♪E5
10 E 44th Street
697-6644 $-$$

Michael Jordan's The Steakhouse NYC ♪F5
Grand Central Station
42nd Street
655-2300 $$-$$$

NBA Store ♪E3
666 Fifth Avenue
515-6221

Niketown ♪E2
6 E 57th Street
891-6453

O'Reilley's Pub ♪D8
56 W 31st Street
684-4244 ♪

Oyster Bar ♪F5
lower level, Grand Central Station,
42nd Street
490-6650 $-$$$

PaceWildenstein ♪F2
32 E 57th Street
421-3292

Prada ♪E2
724 Fifth Avenue
664-0010

Regents ♪H3
317 E 53rd Street
593-3091 ♪ $$

Richart ♪E2
7 E 55th Street
371-9369

Rizzoli ♪D2
31 W 57th Street
759-2424

Robert Miller ♪F1
41 E 57th Street
980-5454

Rudy's Bar & Grill ♪A5
627 Ninth Avenue
974-9169 ♪

The Russian Samovar ♪C3
56 W 52nd Street
757-0168 ♪

Saks Fifth Avenue ♪E4
611 Fifth Avenue
753-4000

Siberia ♪C3
Downtown 1·9 subway station,
1627 Broadway
333-4141 ♪

Sony Style ♪E2
550 Madison Avenue
833-8800

Soup Kitchen International ♪C2
259a W 55th Street
757-7730 $-$$

Suarez ♪F2
450 Park Avenue
753-3758

Swine on Nine ♪A4
693 Ninth Avenue
397-8356 ♪

Takashimaya ♪E2
693 Fifth Avenue
350-0100

The Tea Box ♪E2
693 Fifth Avenue
350-0180 $-$$

Teuscher ♪E3
620 Fifth Avenue
246-4416

Tiffany's ♪E2
727 Fifth Avenue
755-8000

Top of the Tower ♪J4
Beekman Tower Hotel
3 Mitchell Place
355-7300

Tower Records ♪E4
Garden level, Trump Tower, Fifth Avenue
838-8110

Trattoria dell'Arte ♪C2
900 Seventh Avenue
245-9800 $$-$$$

Tuscan Square ♪E3
16 W 51st Street
977-7777 $-$$

'21' Club ♪E3
21 W 52nd Street
582-7200 $$$

UN Delegates' Dining Room ♪J4
45th Street (at First Avenue)
963-7626 $$

Versace ♪E3
645 Fifth Avenue
317-0224

Virgil's Real BBQ ♪D5
152 W 44th Street
921-9494 $$

Virgin Megastore ♪C5
1540 Broadway
921-1020

Vynl Diner ♪B2
824 Ninth Avenue
974-2003 $

Warner Bros Studio Store ♪E2
1 E 57th Street
754-0305

Whiskey Blue ♪F4
W New York Hotel
541 Lexington Ave
407-2947

Whiskey Park ♪D1
Trump Parc
100 Central Park S
307-9222

Xth Ave Lounge ♪A5
642 Tenth Avenue
245-9088

midtown

↓

the gold coast

upper east side

The UES is the stomping ground of New York's financial aristocracy, and every inch of this privileged enclave, from the designer stores of Madison Avenue to the magnificent museums along the edge of Central Park, screams big money. Fifth Avenue is punctuated by 19th-century mansion houses built by some of America's legendary millionaires, and now home to the city's premier museums. The magnificent townhouses, apartments and exclusive clubs of New York's fabulously rich line the adjacent streets of Fifth, Madison and Park Avenues. Madison Avenue is, of course, New York's most important shopping address, with its flagship stores and commerical art galleries. East of Lexington Avenue, the prevailing atmosphere becomes more neighbourly and family oriented but is still far from edgy.

day

🏛 Madison Avenue is the only address that counts for designer shopping.

👁 Central Park [→90]; Cooper-Hewitt, National Design Museum [→82]; El Museo del Barrio [→84]; Frick Collection [→82]; International Center of Photography (Uptown) [→87]; Jewish Museum [→83]; Metropolitan Museum of Art [→79]; Solomon R Guggenheim Museum [→80]; Whitney Museum of American Art [→81].

night

☆ The area is distinctly lacking in attractions after dark.

🍽 Dining out at one of the neighbourhood's many upscale restaurants is the main event.

Ⓜ 6 to 77th, 86th, 96th, 103rd or 110th Sts; 4•5 to 86th St.

🚌 M1, M2, M3, M4 ↑Madison Ave, ↓5th Ave; M15 ↑1st Ave, ↓2nd Ave; M31 ↓York Ave; M66 ←67th St, →68th St; M72 ↔72nd St; M79 ↔79th St; M86 ↔86th St; M96 ↔96th St; M101, M102, M103 ↑3rd Ave, ↓Lexington Ave.

shopping

fashion

If you're off to shop on the UES, chances are you're heading for Madison Avenue. Every inch of this strip is devoted to selling luxuries: expect to pay high prices, encounter snooty staff, and rub shoulders with the fake-tan-and-fur-coat brigade.

There are a couple of top department stores in the area: ***Bloomingdale's** [→100] is a revered NY institution, and much more old school than ***Barney's** [→100] – every upwardly-mobile New Yorker's style barometer. Its fantastically talented

buyers consistently discover the most exciting, unique and interesting designs. Across the street, ***Shanghai Tang** ↓ is an altogether wackier affair. The art deco-style space is filled with owner Alan Tang's modern take on the traditional Chinese aesthetic: coolie jackets in acid colours and beautifully tailored cheongsams.

The fashion heavyweights are all shoulder to shoulder on Madison Avenue, and the fashion-hungry flock here for the lastest creations. American über-designer *Calvin Klein's five-floor flagship is filled with the entire range of Klein's signature understatements, from evening wear to underwear. Opposite is the city's first *DKNY store, filled with the designer's rather glamorous take on streetwear. A few blocks north you'll find Giorgio Armani's more reserved flagship, *Emporio Armani, showcasing every aspect of the designer's work, including his cheaper diffusion lines, all against a minimalist backdrop. In contrast, the *Versace store is out-and-out exuberant. Although the late designer's flagship is located in Midtown, this smaller store is just a little less intimidating (and, of course, replete with Donnatella's wild designs). Whimsical and pricey fashion (for men and women) is the order of the day at Moschino, although there is a cheaper line for those who can't afford the four-figure price tags. Vying with Moschino for the most irreverent designer is Brit-star Alexander McQueen, who reigns at Givenchy. His genius couture is a marvel

of tailoring and innovation. Chlöe has recently opened its first American store on Madison to house the feminine womenswear by another British star, Stella McCartney.

The list of big names continues with Valentino. His elegant emporium is beloved of the neighbourhood's fur-coat-brigade. Few stores can rival the magnificent *Ralph Lauren flagship. Housed in a former mansion, and decked out to resemble an English stately home, it's filled with the designer's collection of classically influenced clothing. Across the street is the Polo Sport store, which carries Lauren's sportier creations.

Italians *Dolce & Gabbana have two enormous stores on Madison, one to house their less expensive D & G line. Fabulous sweaters and leather goods from Italy can also be found at Etro, or pop into Emilio Pucci, for clothing, swimwear, undies and home accessories featuring retro-style psychedelic swirls. *Prada's also in the nabe – its biggest outlet, stocking a large range of menswear, while *Diesel's trendy superstore has jeans and stylish sporty clothes that don't cost a bundle.

British favourite Joseph has two stores on Madison, one

for his perfect-fit pants and the other for luscious knitwear. The British invasion continues at Nicole Farhi, who has opened a store (across the road from Barney's) for her elegant easy-to-wear clothing.

Searle is an exclusive UES affair, which has no fewer than four stores on Madison. They specialize in clean-lined coats, sportswear and covetable knitwear. Cashmere is the raison d'être at TSE, where brilliant designer Hussein Chalayan spins the soft stuff into coats and sweaters. Missoni also excels in unusual and sensuous knits in gem-like colours.

beauty, shoes & accessories

Fresh is a welcome addition to the New York beauty scene. Imported cosmetics, as well as the store's own line, are displayed in an all-white setting. If you want to join the ranks of Madison's well-heeled, make straight for *Stephane Kélian ▲. The French shoemaker creates luxe and inventive fashion-forward footwear. Dropping down a little in price, Patrick Cox's 50's-style store carries the full complement of his signature Wannabes as well as a capsule collection of clothing for men and women. The popularity of shoemaker *Tod's shows no sign of abating. His version of the driving shoe (part loafer, part moccasin) is the slipper of choice for celebrity summers. Hair stylist Frédéric Fekkai has seen his fair share of famous clients. Drop by his in-salon boutique to pick up polished hair accessories and treatment products as well as bags and purses.

one-offs

Although most of the neighbourhood's street-level real estate is given over to designer stores, there are still a few unique and unusual places to be discovered. Chrome Hearts, a mecca for leather fans, is hidden away in an unmarked brownstone. The look here is biker-chic-meets -rock-star. More sedate fare is to be found at Nocturne, which, as the name might suggest, specializes in sleep wear. It's also one of the only places in town to stock up on cult favourite Lily Pulitzer's flowered frocks and separates. Hard to believe, but one of the

biggest thrift stores, Out of the Closet, is on the UES. The merchandise is pristine and varied and thanks to wealthy neighbourhood types who regularly donate their unwanted treasures, bargains are likely.

There are plenty of chichi home furnishing stores on the UES, but the enormous *Gracious Home, which takes up nearly two blocks, can't be beat in terms of price, range or service. Get a key cut, spend hundreds of dollars on linens, or shop for state-of-the art kitchen equipment: this place covers all the bases.

upper east side

galleries

Madison Avenue is home to some of the oldest and best galleries in the city. **Wildenstein & Co**, founded in Paris over 120 years ago, has assembled an inventory of old masters and impressionists which is the envy of the international art world. **C & M Gallery**, meanwhile, specializes in museum-quality exhibitions of classic moderns – sculpture by Maillol and portraits by Picasso. **Gagosian Gallery** houses an assortment of works from the stars of the 80's art boom, including Eric Fischl and David Salle. At **Hirschl & Adler**, Impressionists and American Modernists are kept downstairs and the contemporary artists upstairs. Next door is **Knoedler & Company**, which specializes in sturdy Modernists like Frank Stella and Helen Frankenthaler. **Salander-O'Reilly**, however, mixes shows of contemporary artists like Elaine de Kooning with retrospectives of work by Courbet and Ralph Albert Blakelock.

eating & drinking

restaurants

Epicentre of the social register, UES is filled with chic, clubby restaurants which, not surprisingly, are run by some of the most celebrated chefs in New York. The affable, well-known Daniel Boulud is at the stove at ***Daniel** [→122], a supremely grand Renaissance-style restaurant with seasonal French cuisine. His smaller and more informal (but still expensive) ***Café Boulud** [→122] serves global cuisine alongside traditional and seasonal Gallic classics. The room is comfortable and inviting, the clientele cultured and service impeccable. As if Boulud doesn't have enough on his plate, he also co-owns the dreamy ***Payard Patisserie & Bistro** [→133]. Rapturous desserts and savoury items are featured in the patisserie; at the back is a deluxe French bistro on two floors.

Another titan of the food world, Jean-Georges Vongerichten, is behind JoJo, a jewel box of a townhouse restaurant. The crowd is refined, the staff unfailingly pleasant, with inventive French cooking the speciality – the $28 prix-fixe lunch is a bargain. **Lenox Room** is another genteel option, with a great raw bar and exceptional new American food. The polished dining room attracts affluent, mature types until 9pm, when a younger crowd arrives for drinks and elevated snacks.

A more homey neighbourhood place is **Miss Saigon**, serving tasty, delicately prepared Vietnamese dishes at pocket-friendly prices. The whimsical architecture evokes a village hut, its walls adorned with Asian artefacts. For old-fashioned Sicilian food (veal parmigiana, chicken marsala) in a charming, bygone atmosphere, **Carino** will warm your heart – especially knowing that octogenarian Mama Carino is in the kitchen.

cafés & diners

The welcome mat is always out at ***Comfort Diner** ▲ [→126]: classic American favourites at affordable prices in an atmosphere to match, complete with a gleaming soda fountain. You'll feel like you're in an episode of *Friends* at DT-UT (DownTown-UpTown), a mellow coffeehouse (they have beer and wine too) with comfy chairs for reading. Bolt into the uptown branch of **Jackson Hole** for an energy-enhancing hamburger or one of their blue-plate specials. But for the best hot dog/shake combo around try **Papaya King**: the hot dogs are delicious and the shakes freshly made (unsurprisingly papaya is the specialty here). For good quality fare and fast service, the ultra-clean **First Wok** scores pretty high. The Chinese dishes are ample, but the real incentive is their free, unlimited house wine.

bars

This simply isn't the neighbourhood to visit for a wild night on the town. But for a taste of New York's toniest bars, look no further. Of all the UES institutions, ***Elaine's** may be the most famous. Frequented by literati, glitterati and anyone who aspires to socializing with them, it can be intimidating. Act like you belong and you'll do just fine. Understated designer clothing and a generous credit line are also boons at ***Harry Cipriani**, the

New York relative of Harry's Bar in Venice, and home of the famous Bellini, made of *prosecco* and peach purée.

Cabaret queens won't want to miss *Café Carlyle [→140], where Eartha Kitt

and other legends perform regularly. Just down the hall, another Carlyle Hotel classic, **Bemelman's Bar** offers all the swank of Café Carlyle without the steep tab. Hotel guests tend to prefer Bemelman's, where

piano players perform nightly. If you can't muster the energy to put on a tie, head to **Subway Inn**, easily one of UES's most beloved theme bars. The booze is cheap and everybody is welcome.

directory

Barney's ∅A7
660 Madison Avenue
826-8900

Bemelman's Bar ∅A4
Carlyle Hotel
981 Madison Avenue
744-1600 ◊

Bloomingdale's ∅B7
1000 Third Ave
705-2000

C & M Gallery ∅A4
45 E 78th Street
861-0020

Café Boulud ∅B4
20 E 76th Street
772-2600 $$$

Café Carlyle ∅A4
Carlyle Hotel
981 Madison Avenue
744-1600 $$$

Calvin Klein ∅A7
654 Madison Avenue
292-9000

Carino ∅C2
1710 Second Avenue
860-0566 $$

Chlöe ∅A5
840 Madison Avenue
717-8220

Chrome Hearts ∅B6
159 E 64th Street
327-0707

Comfort Diner ∅B2
142 E 86th Street
369-8628 $–$$

Daniel ∅B6
60 E 65th Street
288-0033 $$$

Diesel ∅B7
770 Lexington Avenue
308-0055

DKNY ∅A7
665 Madison Avenue
768 5800

Dolce & Gabbana ∅A5
825 Madison Avenue
249-4100

DT-UT ∅C2
1626 Second Avenue
327-1327 $

Elaine's ∅C2
1703 Second Avenue
534-8103 $$$

Emilio Pucci ∅A6
24 E 64th Street
752-4777

Emporio Armani ∅A6
760 Madison Avenue
988-9191

Etro ∅A6
720 Madison Avenue
317-9090

First Wok ∅B2
1570 Third Avenue
410-7747 $

Frédéric Fekkai ∅A5
874 Madison Avenue
583-3300

Fresh ∅A3
1061 Madison Avenue
396-0344

Gagosian Gallery ∅A4
980 Madison Avenue
744-2313

Givenchy ∅A4
954 Madison Avenue
772-1040

Gracious Home ∅B5
1217 & 1220 Third Ave
517-6300

Harry Cipriani ∅A7
781 Fifth Avenue
753-5566 ◊

Hirschl & Adler Galleries ∅A5
21 E 70th Street
535-8810

Jackson Hole ∅A1
1270 Madison Avenue
427-2820 $

JoJo ∅B6
160 E 64th Street
223-5656 $$$

Joseph ∅A6
804 Madison Avenue
570-0077

Knoedler & Co ∅A5
19 E 70th Street
794-0550

Lenox Room ∅B4
1278 Third Avenue
772-0404 $$$

Missoni ∅A5
836 Madison Avenue
987-9260 $$

Miss Saigon ∅C3
1425 Third Avenue
988-8828 $–$$

Moschino ∅A6
803 Madison Avenue
639-9600

Nicole Farhi ∅A7
14 E 60th Street
421-7720

Nocturne ∅A6
698 Madison Avenue
750-2951

Out of the Closet ∅B3
220 E 81st Street
472-3573

Papaya King ∅B2
179 E 86th Street
369-0648 $

Patrick Cox ∅A7
702 Madison Avenue
759-3910

Payard Patisserie & Bistro ∅B4
1032 Lexington Ave
717-5252 $–$$$

Polo Sport ∅A5
888 Madison Avenue
434-8000

Prada ∅A5
841 Madison Avenue
327-4200

Ralph Lauren ∅A5
867 Madison Avenue
606-2100

Salander-O'Reilly ∅A3
20 E 79th Street
879-6606

Searle ∅A3
1035 Madison Avenue
717-4022

Shanghai Tang ∅A7
667 Madison Avenue
888-0111

Stephane Kélian ∅A6
717 Madison Avenue
980-1919

Subway Inn ∅B7
143 E 60th Street
223-8929 ◊

Tod's ∅A7
650 Madison Avenue
223-2466

TSE ∅A5
827 Madison Avenue
472-7790

Valentino ∅A5
747 Madison Avenue
772-6969

Versace ∅A5
815 Madison Avenue
744-6868

Wildenstein & Co ∅A6
19 E 64th Street
879-0500

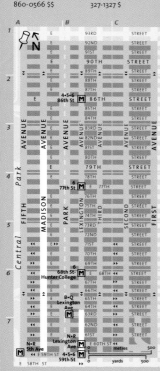

western hemisphere

upper west side

Characterized by its spacious avenues, landmark apartment buildings and proximity to Central Park, the UWS has the feel of a genuine, residential neighbourhood, albeit a very rarefied one. Celebrity sightings are plentiful and if you're lucky, you might even run into Upper West Siders like Woody Allen at Zabar's deli or Jerry Seinfeld at the Reebok gym. More likely you'll just stumble over the baby strollers of the many well-to-do families who live here. Without the distraction of happening nightspots or cutting-edge stores, residents take pride in two of the city's most important cultural institutions – the Lincoln Center and the American Museum of Natural History – plus a healthy sprinkling of dining options.

day

🏛 Big-name chains, one-off boutiques, great deli's & sidewalk cafés along Broadway, Columbus and Amsterdam Avenues.

👁 American Museum of Natural History [→79]; Central Park [→90]; Children's Museum of Manhattan [→92]; Dakota Building [→75]; Museum of American Folk Art [→85]; New-York Historical Society [→86]; Strawberry Fields [→75].

night

☆ Nightly performances at the Lincoln Center's various halls [→139–149].

🌙 Night-time activities are restricted to dining out at restaurants – bars are scarce and clubs non-existent.

Ⓜ A•B•C•D•1•9 to Columbus Circle-59th St; 1•9 to 66th St-Lincoln Center; B•C•1•2•3•9 to 72nd or 96th Sts; 1•9 to 79th, 86th or 103rd Sts; B•C to 81st St-Museum of Natural History.

🚌 M7 ↑via Sixth & Amsterdam Aves, ↓via Columbus Ave & Broadway; M11 ↑via 10th St & Amsterdam Ave, ↓via Columbus & 9th Ave; M104 ↑via Broadway & 8th Ave; M66 ←via E 67th & W 66th Sts, →via W 65th & E 68th Sts; M72 ←→via 72nd St & 65th St transverse; M79 ←→79th St; M86 ←→86th St; M96 ←→96th St.

shopping

fashion, beauty & accessories

The UWS has always been something of a shopping wasteland, so unless your preference is limited to the preppy staples offered up by The Gap and Banana Republic, you'll need to look elsewhere. There are some boutiques worth making a detour for, however. ***Olive & Bette's** continues to bring downtown style Uptown. This entirely girlish boutique carries hot young designers like Daryl K and Vivienne Tam, as well as fun T-shirts, cute bags and witty jewellery. Another neighbourhood duo, **Allan & Suzi ✔**, fill their racks with a riot of barely-worn and vintage couture. Versace and Gaultier are the designers of preference, and although you can find jeans, they'll probably be studded with rhinestones. With a less ostentatious vibe, **Only Hearts** showcases the store's own line of dreamy cotton-lycra lingerie. The rest of the store is replete with great PJs, dressing gowns and gift-items, most of which are heart-shaped. **Naughty & Nice**, on the other hand, is the neighbourhood's friendly sex store – the sign outside says 'Romance Boutique'. Inside are sex toys, naughty lingerie and erotic videos. This being the Upper West Side, it is only slightly tacky.

*Face Stockholm's largest NY store offers a new look at a reasonable price. A favourite with make-up artists and those in-the-know, it offers an intoxicating array of all-natural beauty products, cosmetics in unique and seductive colours as well as cool make-up bags. And for looking good when you work out, the members-only *Reebok Sports Club, New York's most prestigious gym, carries requisite sweats and cycle shorts at the in-house store.

food

*Zabar's is a New York legend with good reason. This marvellous deli has been supplying locals with bagels, freshly ground coffee and cold-cuts since 43. The upstairs kitchen supply store is a superb resource for culinary equipment. Fairways is another UWS deli that wows foodies, and is open 24 hours.

one-offs

The question most regularly asked at Maxilla & Mandible is 'are they real?'. 'They' refers to the human bones for sale at this extraordinary place, and the answer is 'yes'. If dem bones aren't your thing, the store also has fascinating fossils, seashells, bugs, butterflies and other natural history-related phenomena.

eating & drinking

restaurants

Until recently the UWS was disparaged for its scarcity of fine or trendy establishments but that is rapidly changing. Jean-Georges Vongerichten's signature showplace, *Jean Georges [→123] astonishes palates with new French flavour combinations and has managed to silence UWS restaurant sceptics. The tasteful, subdued dining-room has an air of privilege, with sky-high prices to match. Nougatine, its adjacent café, is slightly more affordable. The time-honoured *Café des Artistes [→124] cleaves to classic French cuisine in a formal, old-world setting – lush with flowers and paintings of frolicking nudes, it's a romantic sight to behold.

More modest budgets are accommodated at *Pampa [→127], a lively South American spot that satisfies from start to finish. Steaks, spit-roasted chicken and fish are all made (and consumed) with gusto. Rain is also a fun place for spicy and aromatic Thai-Vietnamese dishes. Golden hues, exposed brick and tropical plants evoke a colonial feel.

Alternatively, pan-Latino flavours are featured at *Calle Ocho ✔ [→127], a magically-designed place, with warm colours, where chef Alex Garcia packs a punch with shrimp chowder and Cuban steak with yuca fries.

There are several pricey restaurants around the Lincoln Center, but walk a few blocks up to Sesso for a pre-concert deal. This cosy duplex serves hearty American and Italian specialties, with a very reasonable three-course set menu (5–7pm Sun–Thu). At any time of the day, Avenue, a French country charmer with brick walls and dark wooden tables, delivers quality food at moderate prices, including a cornucopia of delicious baked goods. Josie's, an attractive, 'earth-friendly' hangout, is the place to be after dusk. Do your body a favour and feast on the myriad of fresh juices, free-range meats and innovative vegan choices.

cafés

A beloved deli that's been around forever and feels straight out of Seinfeld, *Barney Greengrass is a veritable Jewish general store. Its few tables are completely packed for weekend brunches, so stop in during the week for bagels, pickled herring, and knishes (closes 6pm, & all day Mon). Meanwhile the pretty, European-style Café Lalo is an ideal date place which has a full coffee and liquor menu as well as light salads and sandwiches – make sure you save room for their luscious desserts. Café con Leche is a more casual hang, cramped and colourful, with great coffee, Cuban-style rice and beans, crispy chicken and roast pork. Their early-bird special (4–7pm Mon–Thu) offers a full dinner for around $8. Gabriela's, with Guadalajara-style home cooking, is highly popular for low-priced, massively portioned enchiladas, tamales and roast chicken. The atmosphere is old luncheonette crossed with a Mexican fiesta. More of a dive, the 24-hour *Big Nick's Burger serves gargantuan hamburgers.

bars

There's a reason Seinfeld always met his buddies at the local diner – he lived in the UWS which, unlike most of Manhattan, has limited nightlife options. Apart from junior yuppie watering holes and Ivy League meat markets, unlimited coffee refills are your main option.

Coffee and booze are both on the menu at ***Drip**, a quirky singles' bar. If you're up for it, fill out a questionnaire for the noticeboard and peruse fellow customers profiles to spot someone you'd like to be set up on a date with. Being picked

up is far easier at **Saints** (no paperwork, just eye-contact), a hetero-friendly gay bar frequented by Columbia University students and anyone wishing to cruise them. Columbia students can also be found slamming shots at **Smoke** and **Night Café**. The former, a smoky jazz dive, tends to attract a more mellow crowd, while the latter is a favourite of the edgier UWS set. Expect a competitive pool table, and a number of Nietzsche fans. Escape from Engels, Marx and talk of marginalized peoples at **Dive Bar**. Located a safe 20 blocks

south of Columbia, this is one of the few tolerable neighbourhood joints – if you don't mind the cigar smoke. New addition **Potion Lounge** is altogether swankier, a kind of downtown lounge transplanted across the street from the American Museum of Natural History. A heartier, happier haunt is the swell Irish **Malachy's Donegal Inn**. Loud, local sports fans gather round the big-screen TV for games, and their shouting is only rivalled by the jukebox. Perfect for a wolfing down a burger and swilling a beer or two.

🖈 directory

Allan & Suzi ⌀A6
416 Amsterdam Ave
724-7445

Avenue ⌀B6
520 Columbus Avenue
579-3194 $$

Barney Greengrass ⌀B5
541 Amsterdam Ave
724-4707 $–$$

Big Nick's Burger ⌀A7
2175 Broadway
362-9238 $

Café con Leche ⌀A6
424 Amsterdam Ave
595-7000 $

Café des Artistes ⌀C9
1 W 67th Street
877-3500 $$$

Café Lalo ⌀A6
201 W 83rd Street
496-6031 $

Calle Ocho ⌀B6
446 Columbus Avenue
873-5025 $$–$$$

Dive Bar ⌀B3
732 Amsterdam Ave
749-4358 ◖

Drip ⌀B6
489 Amsterdam Ave
875-1032 ◖

Face Stockholm ⌀B7
224 Columbus Avenue
769-1420

Fairways ⌀A7
2127 Broadway
595-1888

Gabriela's ⌀B4
685 Amsterdam Ave
961-0574 $–$$

Jean Georges ⌀C10
Trump International Hotel, 1 Central Park W
299-3900 $$$$

Josie's ⌀B8
300 Amsterdam Ave
769-1212 $$

Malachy's Donegal Inn ⌀B8
103 W 72nd Street
874-4268 ◖ $

Maxilla & Mandible ⌀B6
451 Columbus Avenue
724-6173

Naughty & Nice ⌀A7
212 W 80th Street
787-1212

Night Café ⌀B2
938 Amsterdam Ave
864-8889 ◖

Nougatine ⌀C10
Trump International Hotel, 1 Central Park W
299-3900 $$

Olive & Bette's ⌀B8
252 W 72nd Street
579-2178

Only Hearts ⌀B7
386 Columbus Avenue
724-5608

Pampa ⌀B3
768 Amsterdam Ave
865-2929 $–$$

Potion Lounge ⌀B7
370 Columbus Avenue
721-4386

Rain ⌀B6
100 W 82nd Street
501-0776 $$

Reebok Sports Club ⌀B9
160 Columbus Avenue
595-1480

Saints ⌀B1
992 Amsterdam Ave
222-2431

Sesso ⌀B8
285 Columbus Avenue
501-0607 $–$$

Smoke ⌀A2
2751 Broadway
316-3737

Zabar's ⌀A5
2245 Broadway
787-2000

take the a train

Harlem holds an essential place in African-American history: the great jazz musicians lived here in the 20's; in the 60's this was the centre for black activism; and in the 80's the first rappers honed their skills on its mean streets. Although still predominantly black in population, more and more young New Yorkers are fleeing Downtown's steep rents and making the move Uptown. While you still see the signs of urban decay which gave Harlem a bad rap, counteract that with rows of beautiful brownstones, cheap eateries and the colourful chaos of 125th Street. Just south, the neighbourhood of Morningside Heights is home to Columbia University, so the streets are flooded with students and lined with bookstores and cafés.

day

🏛 125th Street, Harlem's main drag, is lined with stores selling bargain sportswear, ethnic goods and eats at the local markets. Going to church on Sunday is an event in itself.

👁 Central Park [→90]; The Cloisters [→85]; Morris-Jumel Mansion Museum [→83]; St John the Divine [→75]; Schomburg Center for Research in Black Culture [→88]; Studio Museum of Harlem [→88].

night

🍴 Harlem's colourful eateries are big on African and soul food.

☆ Lots of venues for jazz and contemporary music, including the Apollo Theatre [→147] although you'll have to factor in the cost of a cab home again.

Ⓜ A to 125th or 145th St; B•C to Cathedral Pkwy, 116th, 125th, 135th or 145th Sts; 1•9 to Cathedral Pkwy, 116th St-Columbia University, 125th, 137th or 145th Sts; 2•3 to Central Pk N, 116th, 125th, or 135th Sts; 3 to 145th St or Harlem-148th St.

🚌 M1 15th Ave; M2 ←Central Pk N; M3 ←→ Central Pk N via St Nicholas Ave; M4 Central Pk N via Broadway; M7 ↕Lenox Ave; M10 ↕ Central Pk W; M11 ↕Amsterdam Ave; M60, M100 & M101 ←→125th St; M102 ↕Lenox Ave; M104 ↕Broadway; M116 ←→116th St.

harlem & the heights

shopping

fashion, accessories & interiors

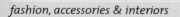

Although Harlem is changing, the neighbourhood stores are still very local. The heart of the district, 125th Street, offers everything from slick, Italian sportswear to all things Afrocentric, both inexpensive and pricey.

The younger generation of urban homeboys continues

its mad love affair with classic/preppy casual chic. **Scheme,** a major fashion outpost in the neighbourhood, carries lots of labels like Iceberg, Moschino, Nautica and Polo, plus a wide array of edgy trainers and must-have boots from Timberland and Vasque. There's also a fashion-forward selection of leather

jackets to pull the whole look together. If you're thinking local instead of global, then **The Harlem Collective** ▲ is the right place to be. It features clothes for men and women, accessories, jewellery, art, books and small pieces of furniture; many of the artisans and designers are neighbourhood residents,

→ more shops | restaurants & cafés | bars | directory & map

and much of the merch is ethnic. A showcase for all things African – garments, home furnishings, art, and tie-dye – **African Paradise** is just that. And if you're really into making a total statement, you'll need an 'ear spear' by designer Lavalais of **Bamboozle Studio**. These heavy but elegant carved earrings are made from bone, bamboo, turquoise and silver in both artistic and tribal styles.

At the centre of Harlem is the Studio Museum [→88],

devoted to modern African-American culture and African history. The **Studio Museum Gift Shop** stocks all manner of related goodies – books, posters, decorative objects, games and jewellery. If a visit here inspires you to create your own African-style outfit, then head over to **Kaarta Imports**, the place for all kinds of African fabrics – prints and solids, traditional mud cloth – and almost all of it 100% cotton.

markets

Across the street from the legendary Apollo Theatre [→147], sits the aptly-named **Mart 125**. All under one roof are many different outlets for African food, clothes, fabrics, music and more. Open daily, the market is very much the shopping hub of the neighbourhood. The outdoor version, with an even grander selection of merchandise, is the ***Malcom Shabazz Harlem Market**, in its new, $3.1 million headquarters.

eating & drinking

restaurants & cafés

For a fun night out in Harlem, head up to ***Copeland's** [→124] – especially on Saturdays when live jazz plays all night. Good Southern-style soul food and spicy Louisiana specialties are served in a faded, genteel dining room. Homey ***Sylvia's** (the 'queen of soul food') attracts bus loads of tourists so the food is not as carefully prepared. Still, the Sunday gospel brunch is enjoyable, and the ladies in fancy church hats a vision. **Africa** is very authentic, a mellow Senegalese restaurant adorned with African fabrics and chairs carved with animal figures. Look out for grilled fish, couscous and lamb stew with peanut butter. In Morningside Heights at the top of an elegant residential building is **The Terrace**, a pricey French restaurant which offers a breathtaking view of the city, even if its interior resembles that of a cruise ship.

*Tom's Restaurant [→126] is the diner immortalized by *Seinfeld* and, while you'd think it would be overrun

with tourists by now, it's still filled with neighbourhood sitcom types. It's great for cheap and reliable diner fare (24 hours Thu–Sat; 1.30am Sun–Wed). Across the street from the Cathedral of St John the Divine [→75], the **Hungarian Pastry Shop** is an old, softly-lit café with pastries, croissants, strudel and great coffee. You can sit here long enough to write a book without anyone bothering you. Further north is **Obaa Koryoe**, a friendly, relaxed nook attached to a shop stocked with unique *tchotchkes*. Specializing in exotic West African cuisine, people flood in on Sundays for the great value all-you-can-eat buffet brunch served until 11pm. **Slice of Harlem** ⚓ is a more boisterous scene, with one wall splashed by a huge mural of black history and pop culture – just the ticket for cheesy pizza by the slice, garlic knots and sausage rolls. And for dessert, you must try one of **Krispy Kreme's** light glazed donuts from its outpost near the Apollo Theatre – one taste and you'll be hooked.

bars

The city-wide drop in crime, combined with increasingly high Downtown rents, has spurred a nightlife renaissance in the upper reaches of Harlem and neighbouring Washington Heights.

True to the neighbourhood's history, jazz bars continue to be favourite haunts in Harlem, and shoebox-sized **St Nick's Pub** is one of the oldest. Jazz musicians perform here all week, and Monday nights feature saxophonist Patience Higgins jamming with the Sugar Hill Jazz Quartet. **Lenox Lounge**, another Harlem institution, is beginning to attract a younger crowd thanks to aggressive party promoters, DJs and superb live jazz. While St Nick's and Lenox Lounge start filling up at 11pm, **Café Largo**, a much newer bar and restaurant, caters to an early-evening crowd, with live jazz performances starting at 8pm, and lazy jazz brunches served on Sundays.

Head to Washington Heights and Sugar Hill, farther north, where Latin bars are still key to the neighbourhood's night-life. One of the most popular is **Zapatas Manoletas**, a fantastic bar filled with bull-fighting posters and glittery tropical murals. Patrons are partial to salsa and the crowd tends to be older. A younger Latin scene can be found at **Audubon Bar & Grill**, which hosts late-night dance parties, as well as comedy nights.

Poets and rappers take the stage at **Sugar Shack**, a homey soul-food restaurant with open-mic nights, while karaoke fans flock to *Coogan's, a spacious Irish sports bar. Large-screen TVs make it a local favourite during any play-offs, and karaoke nights have been known to get raucous.

directory

Africa ♫ B9
247 W 116th Street
666-9400 $

African Paradise ♫ C8
27 W 125th Street

Audubon Bar & Grill ♫ A2
3956 Broadway
928-5200 ◐ $–$$

Bamboozle Studio ♫ B9
171 E 118th Street
360-6848

Café Largo ♫ A6
3387 Broadway
862-8142 ◐ $–$$

Coogan's ♫ A1
4015 Broadway
928-1234 ◐

Copeland's ♫ A5
547 W 145th Street
234-2357 $–$$$

The Harlem Collective ♫ B8
2533 Eighth Avenue
368-0520

Hungarian Pastry Shop ♫ A10
1030 Amsterdam Ave
866-4230 $

Kaarta Imports ♫ C8
121 W 125th Street
866-4062

Krispy Kreme's ♫ B8
280 W 125th Street
531-0111 $

Lenox Lounge ♫ C8
288 Lenox Avenue
427-0253 ◐

Malcolm Shabazz Harlem Market ♫ C9
Lenox Avenue
987-8131

Mart 125 ♫ B8
260 W 125th Street
316-3340

Obaa Koryoe ♫ A8
3143 Broadway
316-2950 $

St Nick's Pub ♫ A4
73 St Nicolas Avenue
283-9728 ◐

Scheme ♫ B8
201–303 W 125th Street
678-2146

Slice of Harlem ♫ B6
2527 Eighth Avenue
862-4089 $

Studio Museum Gift Shop ♫ B8
144 W 125th Street
864-0014

Sugar Shack ♫ B6
2611 Eighth Avenue
491-4422 ◐ $–$$

Sylvia's ♫ C8
328 Lenox Avenue
996-0660 $–$$

Tom's Restaurant ♫ A10
2880 Broadway
864-6137 $

The Terrace ♫ A9
400 W 119th Street
666-9490 $$$

Zapatas Manoletas ♫ A1
1218 St Nicholas Ave
923-9769 ◐

over the east river

brooklyn

As Manhattan rents continue to skyrocket, Brooklyn, the biggest of NY's five boroughs, is becoming an increasingly appealing alternative for those who want to live with light and space without paying a fortune. Generations of immigrants have settled here over the last 150 years, and many long-term residents still mourn the defection of legendary local baseball team, The Dodgers, in 57.

Thanks to the huge diversity of Brooklynites, the neighbourhoods vary wildly, from up-and-coming Fort Greene, artsy Williamsburg, and quietly elegant Brooklyn Heights, to the irresistibly tacky Coney Island and the atmospheric Russian enclave of Brighton Beach. Recently gentrified neighbourhoods may provide the requisite cool cafés, boutiques and restaurants to meet the needs of new residents, but the borough remains forever Brooklyn. Those black-clad figures are just as likely to be Hassidim as fashionable bohos.

day

Williamsburg: shops and cafés get going around noon. The local gallery scene is ad-hoc, so pick up the *Waterfront Week* to check what's on, especially at the Williamsburg Art & Historical Center (also has shows, events, movies and concerts ☎ 1-718-486-7372).
Fort Greene: pretty laid back by day, except at weekends. UrbanGlass opens its glass-blowing studios to the public one Sunday each month ☎ 1-718-625-3685.
Cobble Hill & Carroll Gardens: great to wander around in the day, though the new boutiques only open around noon.
Coney Island & Brighton Beach: in summer crowds throng the seaside attractions, including the world-famous funfair [→96]. Off season, the area's much quieter, but not without a certain charm.

👁 Brooklyn Botanical Gardens [→91]; Brooklyn Museum of Art [→86]; Prospect Park [→91].

night

Williamsburg: buzzy bars and eateries. Galapagos hosts events and screens art-house movies on Sundays ☎ 1-718-388-8713. **Fort Greene**: the Brooklyn Academy of Music (BAM) [→143] has a great concert, dance and movie programme, and nearby restaurants stay open late. **Carroll Gardens**: the serious restaurants are open, but not much else. **Brighton Beach**: wild partying in the Russian nightclubs and restaurants; at Coney Island little stirs.

❶ Wherever you are, it's best to avoid deserted-looking blocks at night.

Ⓜ Williamsburg: L to Bedford Ave; J•M•Z to Marcy Ave. Fort Greene: D•Q•N•R•M to Dekalb Ave; D•G•2•3•4•5 to Atlantic Ave; A•C to Lafayette Ave. Carroll Gardens: F•G to Carroll St. Coney Island/Brighton Beach: B•D•F to Stillwell Ave; D•Q to Brighton Beach.

williamsburg

Along Williamsburg's gritty streets, traditionally home to Hispanics and Hassidic jews, groovy boites sit next to die-hard bodegas and Polish bakeries. The cool zone is small: along Bedford Avenue and the parallel Berry Street between N 5th to N 12th Streets.

shopping

Right on Bedford, you can't miss **Ugly Luggage**, which is crammed with trading cards, ashtrays, lunch-boxes and assorted memorabilia. **Max & Roebling** sells arty, interesting clothes from local designers, as well as leather bags and beaded dresses from India, while **Ear Wax** has an eclectic, unusual mix of CDs and some LPs. A few blocks over on Wythe Avenue there's a row of great bric-a-brac and furniture stores: R is a good, if pricey source of covetable post-World War II furniture

(in good condition), and at **Junk**, you'll find that Depression-era glass candy dish, or light-up beer sign you've been searching for. Up and down Bedford there are used-clothing places, but it's worth going a little further afield to the legendary **Domsey's Warehouse Outlet** a megastore for the thrifty, with racks and racks of used clothing and housewares, for literally next-to-nothing.

restaurants, cafés & bars

The neighbourhood's most relaxed places for casual food are the **L Café**, (good sandwiches and salads, mismatched tables and chairs) and **Kasia's**, (tasty Polish and diner grub in a log-cabinesque setting). For more attitude, try **Oznot's Dish** ✔, where quirky decor meets Middle Eastern cuisine (and there's a garden), **Plan Eat Thailand** (excellent Thai food), and **Diner**, which serves vogueish, vaguely French cuisine in an actual chrome-and-tile diner. The closest place to a club – tiny, peppy **Vera Cruz** – dishes up Mexican food, margaritas and, on Monday nights, mambo dancing. **Teddy's** ▲ is the mellowest local hangout –

a perennial favourite with its majestic wooden bar and big windows that are opened out in good weather. The **Brooklyn Ale House** has a parade of serious beer including some made at the **Brooklyn Brewery** (free tours Saturday afternoons – with samples! – also open Friday nights for happy hour).

Brooklyn Ale House
103 Berry Street (at N 8th St)
☎ 1-718-302-9811 ◖

Brooklyn Brewery
79 N 11th Street (at Wythe Ave)
☎ 1-718-486-7422

Diner
85 Broadway (at Berry St)
☎ 1-718-486-3077 $–$$

Domsey's Warehouse Outlet
431 Kent Avenue
(bet. S 9th & S 10th Sts)
☎ 1-718-384-6000

Ear Wax
204 Bedford Avenue
(bet. N 5th & N 6th Sts)
☎ 1-718-218-9608

Junk
320 Wythe Avenue
(bet. Grand & S 1st Sts)
☎ 1-718-782-7780

Kasia's
146 Bedford Avenue
(at N 9th St)
☎ 1-718-387-8780 $

L Café
189 Bedford Avenue
(bet. N 6th & N 7th Sts)
☎ 1-718-388-6792 $–$$

Max & Roebling
189 Bedford Avenue
(bet. N 6th & N 7th Sts)
☎ 1-718-387-0045

Oznot's Dish
79 Berry Street (at N 9th St)
☎ 1-718-599-6596 $$

Plan Eat Thailand
184 Bedford Avenue
(bet. N 6th & N 7th Sts)
☎ 1-718-599-5758 $

R
326 Wythe Avenue
(bet. Grand & S 1st Sts)
☎ 1-718-599-4385

Teddy's
96 Berry Street (at N 8th St)
☎ 1-718-384-9787 ◖

Ugly Luggage
214 Bedford Avenue
(bet. N 5th & N 6th Sts)
☎ 1-718-384-0724

Vera Cruz
195 Bedford Avenue
(bet. N 6th & N 7th Sts)
☎ 1-718-599-7914 $–$$

fort greene

Tranquil Fort Greene is booming: apartments in beautiful brownstones are being snapped up and the area's become the focus of an African-American artistic renaissance that's brought artists, writers and interesting stores to its gracious, tree-lined streets.

shopping

While you'll find antique shops for browsing on Fulton Street, the real retail thrill here is clothes, for both men and women. At **Moshood**, they're bold and simple, urban and African (and on weekends you'll see live mannequins modelling them in the window). **4W Circle of Art** features more traditional African wear (lots of kente cloth), created by neighbour-

hood designers, as well as jewellery, candles and cards. The collection at **Courtney Washington** is simply exquisite: flowing, clean-lined clothes in crunchy natural fabrics dubbed 'ethnic-European' and made on the premises, while **Exodus Industrial Sport** is a small place that carries more somber, yet chic clothes for day and night.

eating & drinking

Across the street from BAM, the stylish **New City Café** offers French-American bistro food in a cool, airy setting. Also with an American menu, this time with African accents, is **Lucien Blue**, a spacious bar-restaurant that wouldn't look out of place in Soho. Nearby, **Brooklyn Mod** also caters to a young,

fashionable crowd, serving American and international classics while DJs spin tunes (the upstairs bar is ideal for lounging). At the less sleek but no less charming **SEA Cambodian** (NY's only Cambodian restaurant), the fragrant, spicy food is great value, while **Miss Ann's**, a true hole-in-the-wall, serves sublime Southern dishes – but to only 12 people at a time. Or, at the popular **Keur 'n' Dye**, you'll get Senegalese cooking in a pleasant, calming environment. There's a livelier scene at the intimate **Brooklyn Moon Café**, where the chatty crowd gets big at the Friday night open-mic sessions [→146]. **Tillie's of Brooklyn** is an arty coffee bar, with jazz on the weekends (and occasional sightings of Rosie Perez who lives locally). [directory→70]

Brooklyn Mod
271 Adelphi Street
(at Dekalb Ave)
☎ 1-718-522-1669 $–$$

Brooklyn Moon Café
745 Fulton Street (bet. S
Portland Sts & S Elliot Sts)
☎ 1-718-243-0424 $–$$

S.E.A Cambodian
87 S Elliott Place (bet. Hanson
Pl & Lafayette Ave)
☎ 1-718-858-3262 $–$$

Courtney Washington
674 Fulton Street (bet. S
Portland and S Elliott Sts)
☎ 1-718-852-1464

Exodus Industrial Sport
771 Fulton Street (bet. S
Oxford & S Portland Sts)
☎ 1-718-246-0321

4W Circle of Art
704 Fulton Street (bet. S
Portland and S Oxford Sts)
☎ 1-718-875-6500

Keur 'n' Dye
737 Fulton Street (bet. S Elliott
& S Portland Sts)
☎ 1-718-875-4937 $–$$

Lucien Blue
63 Lafayette Avenue
(at Fulton St)
☎ 1-718-422-0093 $$

Miss Ann's
86 S Portland Street (bet.
Hanson Pl & Lafayette Ave)
☎ 1-718-858-6997 $

Moshood
698 Fulton Street (bet. S
Portland & S Oxford Sts)
☎ 1-718-243-9433

New City Café
25 Lafayette Avenue (bet.
Flatbush Ave and Ashland Pl)
☎ 1-718-622-5607 $–$$

Tillie's of Brooklyn
248 DeKalb Avenue
(at Vanderbilt Ave)
☎ 1-718-783-6140 $

carroll gardens

This quiet old Italian neighbourhood, with its tree-lined streets and predominance of young families, has chic little stores in among its delis, old-time bakeries and front-yard shrines.

shopping

Smith Street is where the action is. **Refinery** has discreetly stylish, one-off bags made of vintage and recycled materials. **Frida's Closet** (inspired by Frida Kahlo) is a pristine space with racks of classic handmade women's clothes and jewellery, and at **Stacia New York**, the adorably feminine clothes are made (on the premises) by the owner, who used to work for Cynthia Rowley. Satisfy your schlock-horror movie-poster needs at **Main Street Ephemera/Paper Collectibles**, while 3D home wares (cocktail shakers, clunky lamps and spindly dinette sets) can be found at the all-retro **Astroturf**.

eating & drinking

The most atmospheric local saloon is **PJ Hanley's** – a dark, comfy 100-year-old place with an ornate bar, frequented by plumbers and bond-traders alike. Brooklyn's true bohemians are more likely to be in the **Fall Café** – a haven of big

sofas, little tables, cool music, art on the walls and artistic types dawdling over chilli, sandwiches and coffee.

Respectable bagels (12 kinds), plus knishes and burritos, are available at the low-key **Bagels by the Park**, but lunch at **Vinny's of Carroll Gardens** if you want to soak up the sound of some authentic 'Brooklynese'. Whether you choose the clam spaghetti or the tortellini *en brodo*, portions are huge. **Helen's Place** is another old-fashioned Italian joint, with white tablecloths, wood-panelled walls, a linoleum floor, and atmosphere courtesy of the radio and memory. Top off any lunch with Italian pastries or ices from long-standing **Monteleone's**, (the delicate lemon ice is a winner) , or exquisite soufflé cakes, madeleines, and fruit tarts from the more recently arrived **Sweet Melissa** ➚

In the evenings, **Patois**, a French-American bistro, is frequently jammed; fortunately, its waiting area (through the kitchen and out back, under casbah-like draperies) is beguiling. The pace at pretty **Rosina's** is less frenetic, and the Mediterranean food, like *caldo gallego* and Moroccan spiced shrimp, is thoughtfully prepared. For organic steaks and Argentinian specialties, try rowdy, friendly **Sur**.

Astroturf
290 Smith Street
(bet. Union & Sackett Sts)
☎ 1-718-522-6182

Bagels by the Park
323 Smith St (at President St)
☎ 1-718-246-1321 $

Fall Café
301 Smith Street
(bet. President & Union Sts)
☎ 1-718-403-0230 $

Frida's Closet
296 Smith Street
(bet. Union & Sackett Sts)
☎ 1-718-855-0311

Helen's Place
396 Court Street
(bet. 1st Pl & Carroll Street)
☎ 1-718-855-9128 $–$$

**Main Street Ephemera/
Paper Collectibles**
172 Smith Street
(bet. Sackett & DeGraw Sts)
☎ 1-718-858-6541

Monteleone
355 Court Street
(bet. President & Union Sts)
☎ 1-718-624-9253 $

Patois
255 Smith Street
(bet. DeGraw & Douglass Sts)
☎ 1-718-855-1535 $$

PJ Hanley's
449 Court Street (at 4th Pl)
☎ 1-718-834-8223

Refinery
254 Smith Street
(bet. DeGraw & Douglass Sts)
☎ 1-718-643-7861

Rosina's
288 Smith Street (at Sackett St)
☎ 1-718-855-0681 $–$$

Stacia New York
267 Smith St (at DeGraw St)
☎ 1-718-237-0078

Sur
232 Smith Street
(bet. Douglass & Butler Sts)
☎ 1-718-875-1716 $–$$

Sweet Melissa
276 Court Street
(bet. Douglass & Butler Sts)
☎ 1-718-855-3410 $

Vinny's of Carroll Gardens
295 Smith Street
(bet. Union & Sackett Sts)
☎ 1-718-875-5600 $–$$

coney Island & brighton beach

Even during the rather desolate winter months, Coney Island – tattered and faded – has a unique mix of people, a swathe of boardwalk, an atmospheric funfair (closed in winter), an expanse of beach, and a lingering feeling of good times gone by. In neighbouring Brighton Beach, the Russian language prevails, giving rise to its nickname 'Little Odessa by the Sea'.

shopping

People don't come to this part of the world to shop, but it's hard to avoid the temptation of **Philip's Candy Store** right in the Coney Island subway station. Philip's has been selling made-on-the-premises candies for over 40 years. Off Surf Avenue, underneath the elevated subway tracks, is an eccentric, if rather sad, flea market: more of a curiosity than a place for real bargains.

Brighton Beach, just a short stroll away along the Boardwalk, has America's largest concentration of Russian emigrés. And they love food, from serious smoked fish to great gooey cakes, all abundantly – and we mean abundantly – displayed in the numerous delis and shops. Good bargains (such as salmon caviar for around $16 per pound) can be easily found. The chaotic **M&I** is *the* serious gourmet store, but you'll have to be persistent to get anyone to wait on you. For an easier shopping experience, try the **Sea Lane Bakery** or the elegant **Odessa**, which offers fancy prepared foods like duck legs with apples and coubiliac of salmon. Far less showy is the great (if basic) **Mrs Stahl's Knishery**, making cheap, rib-sticking snacks to go, in flavours like mushroom and potato or blueberry. **Isay's Leather** – crammed with interesting items from the former USSR: amber jewellery, nesting dolls, hand-painted boxes and leather goods – is the neighbourhood's only non-food shop worth mentioning.

restaurants, cafés & clubs

Forget healthy, be gone wholesome! The essential Coney Island dining experience is **Nathan's Famous Restaurant**, serving the best hot dog in the universe (as well as sublime fries and sauerkraut) in pretty basic surroundings – best get some to go. Up on the boardwalk, **Ruby's Old Thyme Bar** (open summer only) is a reliquary with a liquor licence. Cluttered with memorabilia, everything in it – including much of the clientele – harks back to Coney's glory days.

If your tastes run to cigarette smoke and vodka, the Russian cafés off Brighton Beach will delight. Whatever the weather, whatever the time of day, you'll find hardy fur-clad locals sitting outside among the seagulls at the **Tatiana Café** (elegant) or the **Café Restaurant Volna** (more basic), slugging down the Stoli and inhaling deeply. You could substitute sushi or blintzes.

Brighton Beach's nightclubs are legendary and keep going into the small hours every night, with a truly OTT party atmosphere at weekends. From the outside, the clubs look like funeral parlours or KGB headquarters. Inside, they're huge, glitzy places where you eat a heavy, multi-course meal (the appetizers are the best part), surrounded by Russians in sequins and shantung, hell-bent on partying. These places are said to be associated with the Russian mob, so be nice. Knock back the vodka, experience Vegas-type acts and flail around on the dance floor under a mirrored ball. The veteran **Primorski** has the best food and the smallest dance floor; **Rasputin** is the most glamorous (book way in advance), while the **Winter Garden**

offers a winning combination of location (on the Boardwalk), excellent food (cherry dumplings, breast of duck), and a 'groovy' floorshow (perfumed smoke, glamour and 70's sounds). Call to book, wear all your jewellery, go in a rowdy group (if you can), and call a car to get home.

Café Restaurant Volna,
3145 B 4th St (bet. Brighton Beach Ave & Boardwalk)
☎ 1-718-332-0341 $

Isay's Leather
292 Brighton Beach Avenue (at 3rd St)
☎ 1-718-769-8775

M&I
249 Brighton Beach Avenue (bet. 2nd & 3rd St)
☎ 1-718-615-1011

Mrs Stahl's Knishery
1001 Brighton Beach Avenue (at Coney Island Ave)
☎ 1-718-648-0210 $

Nathan's Famous Restaurant
1310 Surf Avenue (at Stillwell Ave)
☎ 1-718-946-2202 $

Odessa
1113 Brighton Beach Avenue (bet. B 13th & B 14th Sts)
☎ 1-718-332-3223

Philip's Candy Store
1237 Surf Avenue (in the Stillwell Avenue-Coney Island subway station)
☎ 1-718-372-8783

Primorski
282B Brighton Beach Avenue (at B 3rd St)
☎ 1-718-891-3111 $

Rasputin
2670 Coney Island Avenue (at Avenue X)
☎ 1-718-332-9187 $

Ruby's Old Thyme Bar
1213 Boardwalk (at W 12th St)
☎ no phone

Sea Lane Bakery
615 Brighton Beach Avenue (bet. 6th & 7th Sts)
☎ 1-718-934-8877

Tatiana Café
3145 B 4th Street (bet. Brighton Beach Ave & the Boardwalk)
☎ 1-718-646-7630 $–$$

Winter Garden
3152 B 6th Street (bet. Brighton Beach Ave & the Boardwalk)
☎ 1-718-934-6666 $–$$

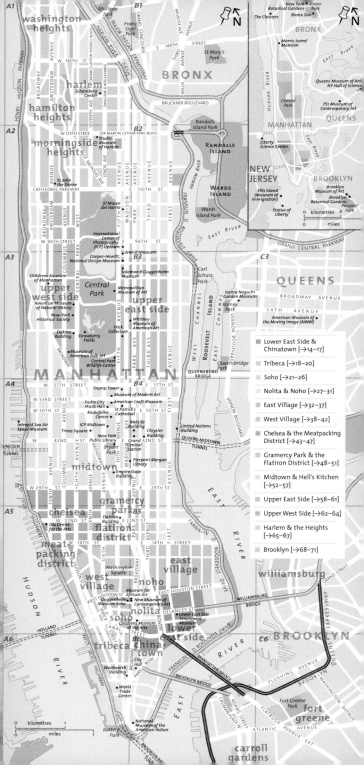

new york's top sights, museums & galleries

directory

American Craft Museum *♭A4* [→85]

American Museum of the Moving Image *♭C3* [→81]

American Museum of Natural History *♭A3* [→79]

Battery Park *♭A6–B6* [→91]

Bronx Zoo *♭see locator* [→92]

Brooklyn Botanical Garden *♭see locator* [→91]

Brooklyn Bridge *♭B6* [→74]

Brooklyn Museum of Art *♭see locator* [→86]

Bryant Park *♭A4* [→91]

Central Park *♭A2–A3* [→90]

Central Park Wildlife Center *♭A3* [→92]

Children's Museum of the Arts *♭B5* [→92]

Children's Museum of Manhattan *♭A3* [→92]

Chrysler Building *♭B4* [→74]

City Hall *♭B6* [→74]

The Cloisters *♭see locator* [→85]

Cooper-Hewitt, National Design Museum *♭B3* [→82]

Dakota Building *♭A3* [→75]

Dia Center for the Arts *♭A5* [→86]

Ellis Island (Museum of Immigration) *♭see locator* [→77]

El Museo del Barrio *♭B2* [→84]

Empire State Building *♭A4* [→78]

Flatiron Building *♭B5* [→74]

Frick Collection *♭B3* [→82]

Grand Central Station *♭B4* [→78]

Guggenheim Museum Soho *♭B5* [→80]

International Center of Photography (ICP) Midtown *♭A4* [→87]

International Center of Photography (ICP) Uptown *♭B2* [→87]

Intrepid Sea Air Space Museum *♭A4* [→93]

Isamu Noguchi Garden Museum *♭B3* [→87]

Jewish Museum *♭B3* [→83]

Liberty Science Center *♭see locator* [→93]

Lower East Side Tenement Museum *♭B5* [→82]

MetLife Building *♭B4* [→75]

Metropolitan Museum of Art *♭A3* [→79]

Morris-Jumel Mansion Museum *♭see locator* [→83]

Museum of American Folk Art *♭A3* [→85]

Museum of Modern Art *♭A4* [→80]

Museum for African Art *♭B5* [→84]

National Museum of the American Indian *♭B6* [→84]

New Museum of Contemporary Art *♭B5* [→87]

New York Botanical Gardens *♭see locator* [→81]

New-York Historical Society *♭A3* [→86]

New York Public Library *♭A4* [→77]

NY Hall of Science *♭see locator* [→81]

Pierpont Morgan Library *♭B4* [→83]

Prospect Park *♭see locator* [→91]

PS1 Museum of Contemporary Art *♭C4* [→88]

Queens Museum of Art *♭see locator* [→91]

Radio City Music Hall *♭A4* [→75]

Rockefeller Center *♭A4* [→75]

St John the Divine *♭A2* [→75]

St Patrick's Cathedral *♭B4* [→75]

Schomberg Center for Research in Black Culture *♭A1* [→88]

Solomon R Guggenheim Museum *♭B3* [→80]

Statue of Liberty *♭see locator* [→77]

Strawberry Fields *♭A3* [→75]

Studio Museum of Harlem *♭A2* [→88]

Times Square *♭A4* [→76]

Trump Tower *♭B4* [→76]

UN Building *♭B4* [→76]

Whitney Museum of American Art *♭B3* [→81]

Woolworth Building *♭B6* [→76]

World Trade Center *♭A6* [→76]

getting your bearings

---

tours

boat tours

Circle Line
☎ 563-3200
Ⓜ A·C·E to 42nd St ⌖ $18–$22
◑ Apr–Nov: 3-hr trip; Jun–Aug: 2-hr evening cruise. Other tours also available.

bus tours

Gray Line
☎ 397-2600
w www.graylinenewyork.com
⌖ $17–$49 ◑ 7.45am–8pm daily. Choose from more than 20 different tours.

New York Double-Decker Tours
☎ 967-6008 ⌖ $15–$25 (hop on-hop off; ticket valid for 10 days. ◑ 9am–5pm daily, every 30 min–1 hr.

Harlem Spirituals
☎ 391-0900
w www.harlemspirituals.com
⌖ $33–$75 ◑ vary. Tours of the Bronx, Manhattan, Brooklyn, and Harlem, including gospel tours. Also walking tours.

Hassidic New York
4-hr tour of Williamsburg & Crown Heights, Brooklyn. Bus meets by the lion sculptures in front of the New York Public Library [→77] ☎ 1-718-953-5244 to book **w** www.jewishtours.com
⌖ $36 ◑ 9.30am Sun.

Helicopter tours

Liberty Helicopters
Midtown Heliport (at Twelfth Ave & 30th St) ☎ 967-4550 Downtown Heliport (at Wall Street/Pier 6) ☎ 487-4777
⌖ Mon–Thu $46 for 4 min, $79 for 10 min and $149 for 15 min; Fri–Sun $50 for 4 min, $99 for 10 min and $159 for 15 min.
◑ 8.45am–8.45pm daily; every 10 min. Private tours available.

walking tours

Big Apple Greeter
☎ 669-3685
w www.bigapplegreeter. org
⌖ free ◑ 9.30am–5pm Mon–Fri. A volunteer friend shows you around your choice of neighbourhood. Book 3–4 days ahead.

Big Onion Walking Tours
☎ 439-1090 **w** www.bigonion. com ⌖ $10 ◑ vary. Specializes in ethnic and historic neighbourhood tours.

Street Smarts
☎ 969-8262 ⌖ $10 ◑ 2-hr tours Sat–Sun. Specializes in walks around the oldest parts of town.

CulturePass

This ensures unlimited free admissions (valid for periods of up to 3 days to one year) to many of NY's finest museums. There are also CulturePass special events, such as private museum tours, and discount offers on tickets for jazz clubs and Broadway shows. Available from the New York Convention and Visitors' Bureau (810 Seventh Ave, bet. 52nd & 53rd Sts) ☎ 484-1200 and at selected American Express travel service offices in Manhattan, or call toll-free ☎ 1-877-278-7277. An adult pass costs $25 for 3 days; an annual family pass is $99.95.
w www.culturepass.com

Citypass

Save 50% on admission costs, and avoid queues with this pass (valid for nine days), that covers the Metropolitan Museum of Art, Empire State Building, Museum of Modern Art, American Museum of Natural History, Intrepid Sea Air Space Museum and the World Trade Center. The cost for adults is $26.75, and the pass is available at any of the above attractions.

big apple highlights

Immigrants from all over the world have contributed to the palimpsest that is New York: a heritage exemplified by the city's mosaic of museums and cultural institutions.

↓ manhattan landmarks

Brooklyn Bridge
When this 1596-ft bridge (the first to employ steel-wire suspension) was unveiled in 1883, it was the world's longest. The Williamsburg Bridge beat it by 4 ft 20 years later, but the walkway of one of New York's most visible landmarks still commands unrivaled views. Catch the Brooklyn Bridge live camera at www.romdog.com/bridge/brooklyn.html.

Chrysler Building | Lexington Ave | Midtown
Unmistakable in the midtown skyline, the 77-storey art deco skyscraper was built as a celebration of the motor car's rise to success in the 1930's. Exterior details are based on car motifs like the gargoyles modelled on hood ornaments; inside, Edward Trumball's ceiling mural glows above the red marble lobby.

City Hall | City Hall Park | Lower Manhattan
A prime example of Federal architecture, this has been home to the mayor and seat of NYC government since 1812. It's also the traditional finishing point of tickertape parades along Broadway. The apple trees in the park opposite were used as gallows by the British before Independence.

Empire State Building | Fifth Avenue | Midtown
Recognisable from its role in the film classic *King Kong*, the 1,250-ft high building is visible from almost anywhere in NY. The coloured lights illuminating the top floors mark special occasions: pink for Gay Pride Day, orange for Halloween, red for Memorial Day.....

Flatiron Building | Broadway | Flatiron District
NYC's first skyscraper, this building got its shape and name from its plot at the intersection of Broadway, Fifth Avenue and 23rd Street. The site was a favourite with turn-of-the-century voyeurs as swirling drafts raised women's skirts: policemen who chased them away gave rise to the expression '23 skidoo'.

Grand Central Station | 42nd Street | Midtown
Opened in 1913, this beaux arts belle was officially recognized as a landmark sight in 1978. It's most impressive for its cathedral-like concourse and ingenious design which separates train, car and pedestrian traffic; outside, statues of Mercury, Hercules and Minerva hover around its famous clock [→78].

The MetLife Building | Park Avenue | Midtown

Built for Pan Am in 1963 by a team of architects which included Bauhaus founder Walter Gropius, and now owned by Metropolitan Life Insurance Company, this may well be most hated building in the city. Not only does it block the Fifth Avenue view, but it glowers over Grand Central Station.

Radio City Music Hall | Sixth Ave | Midtown

Part of the Rockefeller Center, and resplendent in its art deco finery, cascading chandeliers (the world's largest) and sweeping staircases, Radio City defines the opulence of 1930's New York. As well as the resident Rockettes, acts as varied as Barry Manilow and Riverdance have shared the stage in its vast auditorium.

Rockefeller Center | Sixth Avenue | Midtown

JD Rockefeller Jr, the benevolent billionaire, created many jobs during the Depression with the construction of this monument to business – a gift to his city. Mitsubishi is now the major shareholder of the complex, which boasts 19 buildings, 40 restaurants, and one of NYC's best seasonal ice rinks.

St John the Divine | Amsterdam Ave | Harlem

Begun in 1892 – and still unfinished. If it is ever completed, this cathedral church will be the largest in the world (work in progress can be seen in the stoneyard). The annual 'animal blessing' sees a parade of New Yorkers and their pets, in line for benediction.

St Patrick's Cathedral | Fifth Avenue | Midtown

Once set in rolling hills, the largest Roman Catholic church in the USA, and the seat of the archdiocese of New York, now resides in the shadows of Midtown's skyscrapers. The relief-figure on the central doors is Anne Seton – the first American-born saint.

Statue of Liberty | Liberty Island

Representations of Lady Liberty – modelled on the sculptor Bartholdi's mother, and the quintessential symbol of freedom – abound. The real McCoy stands proud guarding the tip of lower Manhattan [→77].

Strawberry Fields & the Dakota Building
Central Park West | Upper West Side

Tucked in Central Park, a leafy shrine commemorates the life of John Lennon who was killed outside his home in the Dakota building opposite. NYC's first luxury apartments (built in 1884) were so far from the city that 'society' named them Dakota after Indian territory in the Wild West.

sights, museums & galleries

more landmarks | views

Times Square

Once the heart of NY's Theatre District, after the Depression this area declined and became the epitome of sleaze. Beneath the trademark neon signs of this now spruced-up part of town, gawping out-of-towners shuffle by the fast-disappearing strip clubs. *The* place to be on New Year's Eve in the Big Apple.

Trump Tower | Fifth Avenue | Midtown

Often called gauche, tacky and over-the-top, Donald Trump's erection stands tall; a tribute to the days when *Dallas* was considered chic. Above the atrium's shiny brass and pink marble five-storey waterfall are 20 floors of offices and ritzy apartments – most worth well over one million dollars.

UN Building | First Avenue | Midtown

Overlooking the East River, the three buildings (greatly influenced by Le Corbusier's design philosophy) that make up the UN's head-quarters are flanked by the flags of its 180-member nations. The site is actually an inter-national zone and not part of US territory.

Woolworth Building | Broadway | Lower Manhattan

Until the sad demise of 'Woolies' in 1997, the 60-storey 'cathedral of commerce' was the headquarters of the five-and-dime store empire. A comical sculpture inside the building shows founder, Frank Woolworth counting the coins that made his fortune.

World Trade Center | West St | Lower Manhattan

Some 50,000 workers occupy 12 million sq ft of office space in the five buildings of the WTC. Its two stainless steel and glass towers, a quarter of a mile high, have transformed the Manhattan skyline. In 1993, six people died in a terrorist bombing that shook more than just the foundations of the building.

At street level the city seems a crazy maze of concrete and steel, but you can rise above it all...

↓ uplift yourself

Brooklyn Heights Promenade
Ⓜ 2·3 to Clark St; N·R to Court St

Empire State Building
350 Fifth Ave (at W 34th St) 💳 $6 ◐ *9.30am–midnight daily.* ☎ 736-3100 Ⓜ B·D·F·N·Q·R to 34th St-Herald Sq

Riverside Church Observatory
490 Riverside Dr (at W 120th St) ☎ 870-6700 💳 $2 ◐ *11am–4pm Tue–Sat; 12.30–4pm Sun.* Ⓜ 1·9 to 116th St-Columbia Uni

Rooftop Sculpture Garden
Metropolitan Museum of Art, 1000 Fifth Ave (at E 82nd St) ☎ 535-7710 💳 suggested $8 ◐ *May–Nov: 10am– 5.15pm*

Tue–Sun (8.30pm Fri & Sat) Ⓜ 4·5·6 86th St

Roosevelt Island Tramway
Second Ave & E 60th St ☎ 832-4543 💳 $1.50 ◐ *6–2am daily (3.30am Fri–Sat).* Ⓜ 4·5·6 to 59th St

Staten Island Ferry
Battery Park ☎ 1-800-573-7469 💳 free ◐ *24 hrs daily.* Ⓜ 1·9 to Whitehall St

Subway
B·D·Q across the East River

World Trade Center Observation Deck
2 World Trade Center, West St ☎ 323-2340 💳 $8 ◐ *9.30am–9.30pm daily (11.30pm Jul–Aug).* Ⓜ C·E to World Trade Center; 1·9 to Cortlandt St See also the Greatest Bar on Earth [→136]

↓ consume with a view

The Rainbow Room
30 Rockefeller Plaza, W 50th Sts (bet. 5th & 6th Aves) ☎ 632-5000 Ⓜ B·D·F·Q to 47th-50th Sts-Rockefeller Center

The Top of the Tower
Beekman Tower, 3 Mitchell Pl (bet. Beekman Pl & First Ave), ☎ 355-7300 Ⓜ 6 to 51st St [→136]

The View Lounge
Marriot Marquis, 1700 Broad-way (at W 44th St) ☎ 398-1900 Ⓜ N·R·S· 1·2·3· 7·9· to Times Sq-42nd St

↓ one-offs

Ellis Island
(Museum of Immigration)

Ellis Island stands as a testament to the millions of European immigrants who dared to venture into the 'new world', forced from their homes because of famine and political unrest. By 1892, the number of immigrants had reached such a phenomenal level – one million a day at its peak – that a huge complex was built on Ellis Island, comprising dormitories, a baggage room, a registration room and a hospital. Over the next 60 years, the station processed 17 million successful immigrants, mainly from Ireland, Germany, southern Italy and the old Russian empire.

Some people say that recent renovations have resulted in an overly sanitized atmosphere. But seeing the personal testimonies, belongings and photographs, and hearing voice-recordings of some immigrants, you can go some way to imagining their anguish and hope. It is even more poignant if you remember that just under half of all US citizens have ancestors who were registered at Ellis Island. The highlight is the beautiful Registry Hall, where each new arrival waited anxiously for medical and legal processing. If you can bear the rather corny tone of the 30-min documentary film *Island of Hope, Island of Tears* (shown continuously in two theatres), you can glean some fascinating insights.

❶ Bring provisions. Queues get incredibly long in summer when it can be so crowded that it's hard to appreciate the atmosphere; going early in the day helps.

☎ 363-3200; 269-5755 (ferry information)
🚇 4•5 to Bowling Green; 1•9 to South Ferry
💲 $7 return ferry ticket – from Castle Clinton, Battery Park – includes entrance to Ellis Island Museum and Liberty Island.
🚢 none ❶ 9.30am–3.15pm, every 30 min, daily (may change in winter). ♿🎧

New York Public Library

The lions 'Patience' and 'Fortitude' sit majestically either side of the white marble-columned entrance to this stunning beaux-arts building, and the steps outside are a popular meeting place and impromptu picnic spot for both visitors and locals. Its cool rooms and ice-cold marble floors are reason enough to visit in summer, and the hushed tones throughout the building are incredibly soothing. The public reading room is a must-see, its beautiful ceiling restored to reveal a vibrantly painted blue sky with scudding clouds; the bronze reading lamps and rows of polished tables are in immaculate condition. Around twelve million manuscripts, three million pictures and six million books, as well as some real literary treasures are housed here. Among them are original manuscripts of TS Eliot's *The Wasteland*, the diaries of Virginia Woolf, Charlotte Brontë's writing desk and even the original stuffed animals on which AA Milne based his *Winnie the Pooh* stories. There are frequent free exhibitions in the library's long corri dors – always excellently researched if a little understated. Imaginative and varied exhibitions are held in the Gottesman Hall.

❶ Free internet access on 24 computer terminals in the Bill Blass Public Catalog Room.

Fifth Avenue (at 42nd St)
☎ 930-0800 📠 869-8089
🚇 B•D•F•Q to 42nd St
💲 free ❶ 11am–7.30pm Tue–Wed; 10am–6pm Thu–Sat. ♿
[→Midtown 52–57]

Statue of Liberty

So thoroughly has Lady Liberty come to symbolize America and the values upheld by the American Constitution that it is easy to forget her European origins. A gift from the French people in 1886, the 151-ft-high statue was designed by sculptor Frédéric Auguste Bartholdi, together with Gustave Eiffel. The latter was the brain behind designing Liberty's flexible 'skeleton', which allows the statue some give during high winds. The separately designed pedestal – a formidable structure in its own right at 89 ft – now houses the museum and elevator (taking visitors as high as Liberty's feet). The climb to the top of the crown (the narrow, steep route up

sights, museums & galleries

more sights | museums

the torch is now prohibited for safety reasons) is the equivalent of a 22-storey trek, and is not for those who are claustrophobic or prone to vertigo. In her right hand Liberty carries a burning torch, metaphorically lighting the way for millions of immigrants whose first sight of America was her awesome silhouette. The tablet in her left hand is inscribed with the date of Independence Day, 4 July 1776, and the broken shackles at her feet represent the end of slavery and escape from tyranny. To modern visitors, her comparatively diminutive size (now that she is dominated by the skyscrapers of Manhattan) may well be a little disappointing.

❶ In the summer months waiting times to climb to the crown can exceed 3 hours, and access to the crown is limited. Come early. There is still an excellent view from the top of the pedestal which you can reach by elevator. If you're going on to Ellis Island, don't delay – visiting both sites can easily take all day.

☎ 363-3200; 269-5755 (ferry information) Ⓜ 4·5 to Bowling Green; 1·9 to South Ferry ⊞ $7 return ferry ticket – from Castle Clinton, Battery Park – includes entrance to Liberty Island and Ellis Island Museum. 🚇 none ❶ 9.30am–3.15pm, every 30 min, daily (may change in winter). Informative tours are given by the National Park Service Rangers; call in advance for group bookings ☎ 363-7620 ♿

Empire State Building

Probably the best-known stack of bricks, cement and glass in New York. Aside from being the city's second highest building at 1450 ft, the Empire State Building holds a special place in the heart of New York: it was the secret meeting spot for a highly romantic rendezvous in *An Affair to Remember*, Spiderman used to climb it at the beginning of every episode, and King Kong hung from the point at the top. Spectacular panoramic views – as far as 80 miles on a clear day – can be seen from two observatories: an outdoor one on the 86th floor and an enclosed glass one on the 102nd floor. There are no extra gimmicks, frills or thrills, though if that's what you crave, the Skyride on the 2nd floor simulates a flight over the city.

❶ 102nd floor observatory is closed at weekends. 350 Fifth Avenue ☎ 736-3100 Ⓜ B·D·F·N·Q·R to 34th St-Herald Sq; 6 to 33rd St ⊞ $6 ❶ 9.30am–midnight, daily. 🚇 none ♿ (Skyride: ☎ 279-9777 ⊞ $11.50 ❶ 9am–10pm daily) [→Midtown 52–57]

Grand Central Station ▼

Even New Yorkers are blown away by the transformation of Grand Central Station (officially Grand Central Terminal) following its recent facelift. The marble interior is now so clean it's almost translucent. Huge, sparkling chandeliers and 2500 lights – representing the constellations of a winter sky and set in the vaulted ceiling – light the main concourse. The vast wall of windows, recognizable from so many of Hollywood's best black-and-whites, lets the sun stream into the main hall in dusty shafts of light, illuminating the clock in the centre of the hall – *the* place to meet. Original brass fixtures and wrought-iron ticket-booth window grates have been put back in place with the same attention to detail that has evidently gone into the whole restoration process. The downside with the renovation is that parts of the station have been transformed into a shopping mall.

Two new restaurants overlook the main concourse, but they are tastefully kitted out and don't detract from the grandeur of the space. For the authentic Grand Central encounter, however, descend through the confusing maze of tunnels to the lower concourse. Down here, directly outside the Oyster Bar [→125], the 'Whispering Gallery' phenomenon takes effect – acoustics are so fine-tuned that murmured secrets don't stay secret for long.

E 42nd Street (at Park Ave) ☎ 340-2583 Ⓜ 4·5·6·7 to Grand Central-42nd St ⊞ free ❶ 5.30–1.30am daily. ☞ The Municipal Arts Society's free tours take you through the common areas, lower level passageways & behind the wall of windows (12pm Wed) ♿ [→Midtown 52–57]

American Museum of Natural History ►

Visitors here are greeted by a soaring skeletal tableau of a three-storey-high *Barosaurus* protecting its frightened young from the attack of a ferocious *Allosaurus*. If any of this makes sense to you, then you will probably want to head up to the top floor for more prehistoric skeletons, from mammoth and sabre-toothed tiger to the Mike Tyson of the dinosaur world, the flesh-devouring *Tyrannosaurus Rex*. This is undeniably one of the top museums in the world; the American Museum of Natural History (abbreviated to the barely pronounceable AMNH) has been working on its presentation since 1869, and it's time that has been well spent.

With a mission to study all of mankind, civilizations around the globe and the complete history of the earth – oh, and the celestial universe as well – it will come as no surprise that the museum's five sprawling floors are crammed with one fantastic, in-your-face display after another. That said, it does have its more serene corners, such as the dark but quietly dazzling Hall of Minerals, which glitters with polished rocks and crystals. A super-big-screen IMAX theatre is on the first floor, with hourly screenings of nature films all day, and 3D laser shows accompanied by rock music on Friday and Saturday nights. Even the Ocean Life Café in the basement is set amidst stuffed walruses and seals, with a 100-ft model of a blue whale suspended overhead.

▶ The Hayden Planetarium is due to open early in the year 2000 when it will be housed in a new 'floating' sphere.
◉ The Star of India, the world's biggest blue sapphire (ground flr); the 16-ft cross-section of a Giant Sequoia trunk (1st flr).
❶ Visit 5–8.45pm on a Friday or Saturday when crowds are minimal. If you only want a quick look, the museum offers free admission for the last hour of opening each day.

Central Park W (at 79th St)
☎ 769-5000
📠 769-5100
w www.amnh.org
Ⓜ B·C to 81st St-Museum of Natural History

79

💲 \$8 suggested donation AE/MC/V
🕐 10am–5.45pm daily (10am–8.45pm Fri–Sat).
📱 ♿ 🎧 🎭 ⏱ 🛍
[→Upper West Side 62–64]

sights, museums & galleries

Metropolitan Museum of Art ▼

The Met is New York's cultural behemoth. Its list of galleries and departments reads like the artistic equivalent of a Roman banquet: Assyrian sculpture, the classical art of the Greek empire, galleries packed with African, Asian and Islamic treasures, Roman sculpture, a pre-Columbian gold treasury, early Flemish and Netherlandish paintings, a succession of 19th- and 20th-century galleries and much, much more besides. Museums simply don't get any better than this, and each of the 22 curatorial departments has its own stunning highlight, whether it be the polished steel of arms and armour or the dandyish delights of Tiffany and La Farge (the latter displayed in a lovely garden setting). The Temple of Dendur stands in timeless repose on its own plinth in the Egyptian wing and, in the summertime, the huge rooftop garden provides its own attraction as a place to

more museums

drink coffee, view a changing selection of sculpture and breathe in the spectacular treetop views over Central Park.

👁 The Temple of Dendur, Roof Garden.
❶ Evenings, especially Fridays and Saturdays are quieter times to visit popular exhibitions. No pushchairs allowed on Sundays.

1000 Fifth Avenue (at 82nd St)
☎ 570-3951
📠 535-7710
w www.metmuseum.org
🚇 4•5•6 to 86th St
💲 $8 suggested donation 🚌 none ⏰ 9.30am–5.30pm Tue–Sun (9pm Fri–Sat). ❏ ♿ ☞ 🎧 ♨ ✆ 🛗
[→Upper East Side 58–61]

Museum of Modern Art (MoMA)

The pre-eminent modern art museum in the US, if not the world, MoMA has more than 100,000 art works in its permanent collection, with only about 12% on view at any one time. This is the holy writ of modernism told the American way. Through its holdings, MoMA presents a resolutely triumphalist view of the progress of modern art, beginning in France with the Impressionists and Post-Impressionists, and opening a new chapter with Picasso, before making the giant leap across the Atlantic to Pollock, Rothko, Newman and Reinhardt.

Special exhibitions of painting, sculpture, prints, drawings, photography and architecture regularly rewrite art history – or at least scribble a few important notes in the margin. High up in the fourth floor's atrium a dangling helicopter lets you know you've hit the design department. The bright enclave of the sculpture garden exemplifies the aesthetic links between the pleasures of classicism and modernism, whilst also providing a fine location for refreshments in the summertime. In the basement the museum has a movie theatre with an extensive alternative film programme, which is great if you want a rest.

👁 Rousseau's The Dream, Gauguin's The Moon and the Earth, Picasso's Les Demoiselles d'Avignon, Monet's Waterlilies and Van Gogh's Starry Night.
❶ Admission is by donation 4.30–8.30pm Fri – pay as much as you wish. Lunchtime lectures are usually on Tuesdays and Thursdays, while there's live jazz in the garden on Friday nights (in the café in winter).

11 W 53rd Street (bet. Fifth & Sixth Aves)
☎ 708-9400
w www.moma.org
🚇 E•F to Fifth Ave
💲 $9.50 🚌 none ⏰ 10.30am–5.45pm Thu–Tue (Fri 8.15pm). ❏ ♿ ☞ 🎧 ♨ ✆ 🛗
[→Midtown 52–57]

Solomon R Guggenheim Museum ►

Though never quite as sharp or pristine as it appears in photographs, the spiralling rotunda of Frank Lloyd Wright's final work, the Guggenheim Museum, is one of the great architectural achievements of the 20th century; fortunately, the collection of modern and contemporary art housed here is equal to its home. Works from the permanent collection (Chagall, Picasso, Brancusi, Kandinsky and Gauguin are all represented), are mostly hung in the tower, which was added to the back of the building in the 1990's. There's a small selection of impressionist, post-impressionist and early modernist works in the small rotunda. The rotunda is the counterbalance to the main spiral, which is the focus for all temporary exhibitions. There are two ways to view the temporary shows – by a spiralling ascent on foot or heading straight to the elevator and making your way down this cultural helter-skelter (less tiring!); whichever you choose, you are bound to spend as much time looking at the building as the art. The museum shop is packed with books and Gugg memorabilia, including ceramic mugs inspired by the building's distinctive shape.

👁 Picasso's voluptuous sleeping Woman with Yellow Hair and Kandinsky's vibrant Dominant Curve.
❶ Admission is by donation 6–8pm Fri.

575 Broadway (bet. Prince & Houston)
☎ 423-3500
w www.guggenheim.org
🚇 4•5•6 to 86th St
💲 $12 🚌 AE/MC/V ⏰ 10am–6pm Fri–Wed (8pm Fri–Sat). ❏ ♿ ☞ 🎧 ♨ ✆ 🛗
[→Upper East Side 58–61]

Guggenheim Museum Soho

Far from Fifth Avenue's museum mile is the downtown Guggenheim – established in 1992 on the first two floors of a cavernous brick loft building on Broadway. The museum makes good use of the extensive Guggenheim

Bauhaus-designed building, this is *the* leading collection of American art in the world. A selection from its permanent collection (including works by Edward Hopper, Jasper Johns, Georgia O'Keeffe and Andy Warhol) is usually on show alongside temporary exhibitions, or its famed biennials of contemporary American art – US national pride writ large in paint on canvas. Anachronism or barometer? You decide.

Until recently, it seemed that the Whitney loved to make trouble. The 1993 biennial, for instance, had a 40-ft-long replica of a toy firetruck parked out front, two artists dressed like natives in a cage in the basement, and the world's largest puddle of plastic vomit on the floor upstairs. Bad press and low attendance curtailed such amusing artistic tantrums, and the museum is now better-mannered, garnering praise for its retrospectives (recently of restrained abstract painters such as Mark Rothko, Richard Diebenkorn and the like) and other grand-scale exhibits.

collection: the temporary exhibitions tend to flit between the historical and the contemporary, and it may be that this lack of a clear agenda has contributed to the gallery's rumoured financial problems. This aside, the curators always have some interesting, and occasionally irreverent ideas up their sleeves, and the separate museum store is one of the coolest in town. Who could resist a Guggenheim snow-shaker?

❶ Admission is by donation 6–8pm Sat.

575 Broadway (at Prince St)
☎ 423-3500
w www.guggenheim.org
Ⓜ N·R to Prince St; B·D·F·Q to Broadway-Layfayette St 🎫 $8 🚇 AE/MC/V ❶ 11am–6pm Wed–Sun (8pm Sat). ❑ ♿ ⬩ ☞ ♫ ⓭ ⬚ ⬚
[→Soho 21–26]

Whitney Museum of American Art

Founded in 1930 in the studio of Gertrude Vanderbilt Whitney, and now occupying a wonderful

▶ Until the end of Jan 2000, the entire exhibition space is given over to the American Century: Art and Culture exhibition, a wide-ranging overview of America's identity through the eyes of its artists.
❶ Admission is by donation 6–8pm on the first Thu of each month – pay as much as you wish.

945 Madison Avenue (at 75th St)
☎ 570-3676
w www.whitney.org
Ⓜ 6 to 77th St
🎫 $12.50 🚇 AE/MC/V ❶ 11am–6pm Tue–Wed & Fri–Sun; 1–8pm Thu.
❑ ♿ ☞ book in advance ♫ ⬚ ⬩ ⬚
[→Upper East Side 58–61]

sights, museums & galleries

↓ off manhattan

American Museum of the Moving Image (AMMI)
American Spielbergs can experiment with sound effects and editing techniques.

35th Ave (bet. 36th & 37th Sts), Astoria, Queens
☎ 1-718-784-0077
Ⓜ R to Steinway St
❶ make your own video flip book
🎫 $8.50 ❶ 12–5pm Tue–Fri; 11am–6pm Sat–Sun.
♿ ☞ 3pm Mon–Fri ⬩ ⬚

NY Botanical Gardens
A blooming 250-acre urban oasis (based on London's Kew Gardens), spectacular at any time of the year.

❶ free 10am–6pm Wed & 10am–12pm Sat

Southern Boulevard (at 200th St), Bronx
☎ 1-718-817-8705
Ⓜ C·D·4 to Bedford Park, then Bx26 bus
🎫 $3 ❶ Apr–Oct: 10am–6pm Tue–Sun. ⬩ ⬚

NY Hall of Science
Science is made fun with lots of exciting, hands-on exhibits.

4701 11th St (at 48th Ave), Flushing Meadows, Corona Park, Queens
☎ 1-718-699-0005
Ⓜ 7 to 111th St
🎫 $6 ❶ Sep–Jun: 9.30am–2pm daily (5pm Thu–Sun); Jul–Aug: 9.30am–5pm daily (2pm Mon).

Queens Museum of Art
Best known for its amazing Panorama – an incredibly detailed scale model of NYC.

New York City Building, Flushing Meadows, Corona Park, Queens
☎ 1-718-592-9700 x223
Ⓜ 7 to 111th St
🎫 $4 (suggested voluntary donation)
❶ 10am–5pm Wed–Fri; 12–5pm Sat–Sun.
♿ ☞ ♫ ⬚

more museums

↓ historic houses

Cooper-Hewitt, National Design Museum

This museum – the only one in the US devoted entirely to design – is housed within the dark, wood-panelled walls, of a mansion that was built for the super-rich and highly philanthropic steel magnate Andrew Carnegie.

The opulent atmosphere provides a strange background to some of the more adventurous short-term exhibitions, such as the one of Latino culture in Los Angeles, but such juxtapositions are all part of this museum's attraction. The focus of other temporary exhibitions have ranged from Huguenot silverware to the classically modern furniture of Charles and Ray Eames. Every three years, the Cooper-Hewitt hosts the National Design Triennial, which lasts for four months and offers an overview of the issues and ideas animating design in the States. The museum's collection of over 250,000 items – including one-off and mass-produced prints, textiles and furniture – is available for personal study, but only by prior appointment.

▣ The next opportunity to see the National Design Triennial is in Spring 2000.
❶ Admission is free 5–9pm Tue. School groups tend to visit in the mornings.

2 E 91st Street (at Fifth Ave)
☎ 849-8400
w www.si.edu/ndm
Ⓜ 4•5•6 to 86th St
Ⓔ $5 ⊟ none ❶ 10am–5pm Tue–Sat (9pm Tue); 12–5pm Sun. ▢ ♿☞🛈🛅
[→Upper East Side 58–61]

Frick Collection

If the Cooper-Hewitt has whet your appetite for leisurely strolls through echoing halls and sumptuous rooms, then head for the Frick Collection on Fifth Avenue. This mansion was the home of a steel industrialist of a more acquisitive kind, Henry Clay Frick. In the few years

he spent here before his death in 1919, he covered the walls with European art, carpeted the floors in oriental rugs, and adorned the 18th-century French furniture with porcelain and other fanciful *objets d'art* to indulge his decorative whims.

Today, the Frick is perhaps the most elegant small museum in the country. It features some 20 rooms filled with about 175 paintings by masters ranging from Gainsborough to Vermeer and El Greco, plus a music room for concerts and a new basement gallery for temporary exhibitions. The acutely observant may notice traces of similarity between this mansion and the NY Public Library, for the two buildings share a common architect – Thomas Hastings. His design for the indoor courtyard provides a light and serene haven in the midst of the city.

◉ Bellini's *St Francis in the Desert*, Rembrandt's monumental, great last *Self Portrait*, Goya's dark and muscular *The Forge*, Vermeer's light-strewn *Officer and A Laughing Girl* and two rooms of lovely rococo romance – Fragonard's six-painting cycle *The Progress of Love* and Boucher's eight-painting decorative scheme *The Arts and Sciences*.
❶ No children under 10.

1 E 70th Street (at Fifth Ave)
☎ 288-0700
e info@frick.org
w www.frick.org
Ⓜ 4•5•6 to 68th St-Hunter College
Ⓔ $7 ⊟ none ❶ 10am–6pm Tue–Sat; 1–6pm Sun. ▢ ♿🛈🛅
[→Upper East Side 58–61]

Lower East Side Tenement Museum ◄

Tenement blocks are integral to the character and history of New York. These were the buildings that were thrown up all across town in the 19th century to house the swelling tides of immigrants landing upon the eastern shore of America. Often built without plumbing or running water, such expeditious and economical construction was necessary to meet the demands of this expanding city-port.

The tenement at No. 97 Orchard Street was built in 1864, and its useful life was just 70 years – the building being sealed due to its unsafe condition in 1935. During its short lifespan, however, it was home to an estimated 10,000 people from 20 countries. The building stood idle for 52 years until 1987, when, with the process of gentrification transforming many of the former poor, run down and slum neighbourhoods, this tenement was selected to become a testament to the urban poor who built the multi-ethnic, tough-talking character of New York that the city still trades on today.

The Tenement Museum preserves three apartments as they once were – homes to German, Italian and Lithuanian families – complete with furnishings and personal effects. The museum can be visited only by joining a guided tour. There is also a more lighthearted tour (designed for kids) where the guide plays the part of an Italian matron of 1916, welcoming relatives to the new country, while dispensing advice and admonitions in equal measure to her young charges.

◉ The scale model of the building on the ground floor for a bird's eye view.
❶ Tours around the tenement are limited to 15 people – call ahead to book tickets. If you do have to queue, there's a video to watch.

90 Orchard Street (at
Broome St)
☎ 431-0233
w www.wnet.org/tenement
Ⓜ F·J·M·Z to Delancey St-
Essex St; B·D·Q to Grand St.
⊞ $8 ⊟ AE/MC/V ◑ *12–5pm
Tue–Sun* (11am Sat–Sun).
▢ ☞ compulsory ☡ 🏛
[→Lower East Side 14–17]

Morris-Jumel Mansion Museum

Said to be the oldest exist-
ing house in New York, this
classical mansion's white
façade now looks a little
frayed, though still remains
an amazing landmark. This
lavishly-proportioned summer villa, built in 1765 for
one Lt. Col Roger Morris,
stands on the island's
northeast corner in a
neighbourhood that has
clearly seen better days.
George Washington lived
here during the Revo-
lutionary War while he
drew up battle plans, but
the house's most infamous
resident was Madame Eliza
Jumel, a scandalous and
wealthy widow who
resided here in the 1830's
(a former prostitute,
apparently she allowed her
rich husband to bleed to
death so she could inherit
his fortune). The mansion
opened as a museum in
1907, and to this day you
can admire the interior
decor which includes
period wallpaper, stained-
glass roundels and many
items from the time of
Eliza's occupation including her mesmerizing obitu-
ary which details
her raucous life.

👁 Eliza's bed (said to have
once belonged to Napoleon),
the octagonal sitting room,
George Washington's study.
❶ If there are no groups on
Mondays & Tuesdays, the
museum opens to individuals
– phone ahead to check.

65 Jumel Terrace (bet. 160th
& 162nd Sts)
☎ 923-8008
Ⓜ C to 163rd St-Amsterdam Ave
⊞ $3 ⊟ MC/V ◑ *10am–4pm
Wed–Sun.* ▢ 🅰 limited ☞ pre-
book a month in advance ☡ 🏛
[→Harlem 65–67]

Pierpont Morgan Library ⚲

This gorgeous 1902 library
houses one of the finest
collections of manuscripts
in the world. It was built as
a library and study for the
financier and avid manu-
script collector, JP Morgan,
whose son (JP Morgan Jr)
bequeathed the building
and its collection to the
city in 1924. Temporary
exhibits change regularly:
you might get a glimpse at
such delights as Mozart's
multicoloured music script
for a horn concerto, John
Tenniel's illustrations for
Lewis Carroll's *Alice*, or
recent acquisitions from

20th century literature (in
December, an original of
Dicken's *Christmas Carrol* is
always on show). After
you've taken in the current
displays in the annexed
exhibition space, explore
the two sumptuous rooms
of the actual library and
study, lavishly decorated
with Italian motifs and
heavy with furniture and
paintings. But if the wealth
of edifying visual material
makes you a little weary,
there is a light and airy
courtyard café in which to
take a breather and boost
your reserves. The muse-
um's shop is has a particularly lovely selection of
books and gifts.

👁 Old Master drawings,
ancient Near Eastern cylinder
seals.

29 E 36th Street (bet.
Madison & Park Aves)
☎ 685-0610
Ⓜ 6 to 33rd St
⊞ $7 ⊟ none ◑ *10.30am–
5pm Tue–Sat (8pm Fri; 6pm
Sat); 12–6pm Sun.*
▢ 🅰 ☞ ☡ 👓 🏛
[→Midtown 52–57]

sights, museums & galleries

more museums

↓ melting pot

Jewish Museum

It seems only appropriate
that the biggest collection
of Jewish artifacts outside
Israel can be found in New
York. In spite of a wealth of
Jewish history to draw
upon – 4000 years to be
precise – the Jewish
Museum has always been
something of an avant-
garde pioneer, staging
exhibitions that explore
the twin strands of mini-
mal and conceptual art. Its
curators consistently haz-

ard shows on such contro-
versial subjects as the
Arab-Israeli conflict, as well
as mounting retrospec-
tives of crowd-pleasers
such as Mark Chagall,
Camille Pissarro and
Chaim Soutine on two of
the museum's four mag-
nificent floors. In the
remaining space is the
permanent collection,
where you can see
Canaanite cult idols from
800 BC (the kind of things
that got Moses' flock into
such trouble), slingshot

ammo (clay balls capable of
slaying a Goliath) and one
of the earliest surviving tax
records on a 4th-century
Babylonian cuneiform
tablet – as now, so then,
death and taxes are life's
only certainties.

❶ admission free 5–8pm Tue.

1105 Fifth Avenue (at 92nd St)
☎ 423-3230 **w** www.
thejewishmuseum.org
Ⓜ 4·5·6 to 96th St
⊞ $8 ⊟ none ◑ *11am–
5.45pm Sun–Thu (8pm Tue).*
▢ 🅰 ☞ 🎧 ☡ 👓 🏛

sights, museums & galleries

El Museo del Barrio

El Museo has become *the* place to see frequently vibrant and life-affirming exhibitions chronicling the art that stems, either geographically or socio-politically, from the Caribbean and Latin America. It was founded in 1969 by a Puerto Rican community group as a cultural focus for East Harlem's Spanish-speaking 'el barrio', a low-rent neighbourhood that is still home to immigrants and the descendants of immigrants from Latin America and the Caribbean (particularly Puerto Rico). Some of the exhibitions explore and document the folklore and history of the Latin American peoples, but much is contemporary and tackles varied and universal issues. The museum's temporary shows are always worth a look, and recently gallery space has been given over to investigations of Afro-Caribbean Sacred Spaces and the perennial Search for Miracles. The small gift shop specializes in unusual examples of folk art, supplied locally or imported from Mexico and South America.

1230 Fifth Avenue (at 104th St)
☎ 831-7272
e elmuseo@aol.com
w www.elmuseo.org
Ⓜ 6 to 103rd St
$4 (suggested donation)
◑ 11am–5pm Wed–Sun
(Jun–Sep: 8pm Thu).
⌨ ♿ ☞ 🖥 🛈

Museum for African Art

This relatively young museum, founded in an Upper East Side townhouse in 1984 and moved to Soho in 1992, occupies two cosy floors of galleries designed by Maya Lin, whose previous work includes the National Vietnam Veterans Memorial in Washington, DC. Until recently the museum has specialized in exhibitions of classical African art, whether focusing on surveys of artefacts made by individual peoples, or the broader-based holdings of collectors. However, under new director Elsie Crum McCabe, the Museum for African Art is widening its remit into contemporary African social and political issues. This is borne out in recent and up-and-coming shows, which cover broad-ranging subjects such as political machinations of the Congo in the post-colonial era, the art emerging from South Africa since the end of apartheid and a serious look at style through the Language of Hair in African Art and Culture. A regular series of gallery talks and discussions contributes to the sense of analysis and debate. As well as a fair selection of books on African art, the museum shop, which occupies the lobby area, also sells jewellery, textiles, crafts and even furniture.

❶ Free admission on Sundays in February.

593 Broadway (bet. Houston & Prince Sts)
☎ 966-4444
🖷 966-1313
e museum@africanart.org
w www.africanart.org
Ⓜ N•R to Prince St; B•D•F•Q to Broadway-Lafayette St
$5 🖷 AE/MC/V
◑ 10.30am–5.30pm Tue–Fri; 12–6pm Sat–Sun.
⌨ ♿ ☞ 🖥 🛈
[→Soho 21–26]

National Museum of the American Indian ✓

At the southern end of Manhattan Island, between the green tip of Battery Park and a bronze statue of a charging bull, is the Alexander Hamilton US Customs House. Built in 1890 on the site of the colonial-era Fort Amsterdam, the Customs House is a marvel of limestone and multicoloured marble, its façade ornamented with a dozen faux Corinthian columns and four massive allegorical figure groups representing the continents. This astonishing beaux-arts structure is home to one of New York's newest museums (opened in 1994), the George Gustav Heye Center of the National Museum of the American Indian (to give it its full, illustrious title).

The museum presents its wares within a rigorously educational context, com-

plete with high-tech touch-screen video stations, dioramas and installations. Though such window-dressing is often unnecessary (and even tacky) the incredible beauty of the artefacts shines through regardless. Huron moccasins decorated with moose hair and porcupine quills, a 19th-century ledger with drawings of Lakota chiefs on horseback by Red Dog, an Algonquin duck decoy made of woven reeds – all such items can be found in the museum's two permanent installations; All Roads Are Good: Native Voices on Life, and Culture and Creation's Journey: Masterworks of Native American Identity and Belief. Temporary exhibitions frequently showcase contemporary art by Native Americans living in the US as well as the traditional art and artefacts of indians from around the world. The museum shop has a wealth of books, jewellery, textiles and crafts for sale, while a second floor is devoted to things for kids. Among its offerings is a 'talking feather', which is held by the speaker at a powwow while everyone else must remain silent (at $3.50 this could be an inexpensive way to settle traditional family hostilities).

George Gustave Heye Center, US Custom House,
1 Bowling Green (bet. State & Whitehall Sts)
☎ 668-6624
Ⓜ 1•9 to South Ferry; N•R to Whitehall St
free ◑ 10am–5pm daily.
⌨ ♿ ☞ 🛈

↓ in the mix

American Craft Museum

The applied arts at their most exotic and imaginative are found in the American Craft Museum. The museum has done pioneering work as a centre and clearing-house for information on traditional crafts, and gone further to explore that strange twilight world between craft and art. There are ceramics of every shape and size, blown and cast glass, contemporary fibre art and quirky quilts, bizarre furniture, stained glass, a glittering array of jewellery and much more besides. Located across the street from the Museum of Modern Art in ground-level galleries in Deutsche Bank's high-rise headquarters, the museum has something of a showroom ambience, filled as it is with fancy home furnishings. But the exhibitions are consistently entrancing: In addition to theme exhibitions, which often cover historical material (art nouveau porcelain, for instance), the museum also mounts retrospective surveys of work by the leading lights of contemporary crafts. Like so many American museums in this era of dwindling government support, the museum shop fills the lobby and offers sleek high-end wares from artisans.

❶ Admission is by donation 6–8pm Thu – pay as much as you wish.

20 W 53rd Street
(bet. Fifth & Sixth Aves)
☎ 514-3700
📠 956-4707
🚇 E•F to 5th Ave
💲 $5 🏧 AE/MC/V ◑ 10am–6pm Tue–Sun (8pm Thu).
❑ ♿ ☞ 🍴
[→Midtown 52–57]

The Cloisters ✔

If you make only one trip to a museum beyond Museum Mile make this the one. Located at the northern tip of Manhattan in Fort Tryon Park, The Cloisters is the branch of the Metropolitan Museum devoted to the art and architecture of medieval Europe. Not only is the museum itself an absolute treasure-trove of delights, but the location – within a wild and rocky 56-acre preserve – will show you an entirely different side to New York from the adrenalin-fired life of Downtown.

The Cloisters is a 20th-century recreation of a medieval monastic complex that incorporates genuine architectural features pillaged from Europe, such as the secluded central cloister with its 12th-century Romanesque arcade. In fact, the whole building is a wonderful hodge-podge of sections taken from five Romanesque and Gothic cloisters that originated in France. This fabulous place was the brainchild of John D Rockefeller, who not only donated much of the money to buy the buildings in 1925, but provided the land, an endowment and the bulk of the collection, which numbers about 4000 items.

There are incredible examples of polychrome sculpture, stained glass, Spanish lustreware and carved oak furniture, as well as a handful of pieces that deserve special mention: the *Belles Heures de Jean, Duc de Berry* (a staggeringly intricate and beautiful illuminated manuscript); Robert Campin's small but perfectly formed Merode Altarpiece (*Triptych of the Annunciation*); and the freshly conserved and presented Unicorn Tapestries from Brussels, made in around 1500 AD.

The Bonnefont and Trie cloisters enclose gardens containing hundreds of plants and herbs used in the Middle Ages, either medicinally or for culinary purposes. The shop offers up a pretty good selection of reproduction jewellery and other medieval-style keepsakes, as well as tapes and CDs of monks humming their ecclesiastical medleys – very relaxing.

👁 Unicorn Tapestries, Fuentidueña chapel with its fresco of the Virgin and Child ❶ Ticket also valid for Metropolitan Museum.

Fort Tryon Park
☎ 923-3700
w www.metmuseum.org
🚇 A to 190th St, then M4 bus
💲 $8 (suggested donation)
🚭 none ◑ Mar–Oct: 9.30am–5.30pm Tue–Sun; Nov–Feb: 9.30am–4.45pm Tue–Sun.
❑ ♿ limited ☞ 🍴 🏛

Museum of American Folk Art

'We all have little obsessive concerns,' wrote Robert Penn Warren in an essay about folk art, the umbrella term for the imaginative and heartfelt artefacts and crafts produced by untutored, often rural people as a part of their everyday lives. Recently, folk art has come to overlap with 'outsider art', which tends to describe art made by untrained artists and those in institutions. The permanent collection includes duck decoys, religious art, woven coverlets and quilts, painted trays and boxes, weathervanes, dolls and devotional figures, carvings and paintings – a small, jewel-like selection is always on show in a special gallery. Though the facility has something of the feel of a commercial mall, its three galleries devoted to two temporary exhibitions do justice to the fascinating works of art.

2 Lincoln Square, Columbus Avenue (bet. 65th & 66th Sts)
☎ 595-9533
w www.folkartmuse.org
Ⓜ 1·9 to 66th St-Lincoln Center
💲 $3 (suggested donation)
🕐 11.30am–7.30pm Tue–Sun.
◻ & ☞ 🅰 🏧
[→Upper East Side 58–64]

New-York Historical Society

Where else but in the strange world of the New-York Historical Society could you find three centuries of New York restaurant menus, a sample of George Washington's hair, and more Tiffany lamps than you could shake a stick at. Founded in 1804, the society – complete with the archaic hyphen in New-York – is often referred to as the city's attic, a description that suggests a musty storehouse filled with junk that no one in the family really wants. To be fair, although the Historical Society was hit by scandalous revelations in the early 1990's over mismanagement and neglect, its multifarious acquisitions could never be described as junk. Now brought back from the brink of fiscal disaster, the museum has become widely recognized as a source of artefacts in which resides the physical presence of New York (and US) history. Not only does it hold the nation's largest collection of Tiffany lamps (113 in all) and the 431 original watercolours for Audubon's *Birds of America*, but it is also home to the five-part series *The Course of Empire* painted by Thomas Cole, founder of the Hudson River School, and has more than 500,000 19th- and 20th-century American photographs. The society stages temporary exhibitions as well as its permanent collection on subjects such as how Manhattan was purchased from the indigenous population for a mere $24 and a handful of beads.

2 W 77th Street (at Central Park W)
☎ 873-3400
w www.nyhistory.org
Ⓜ B·C to 81st St
💲 $5 🍽 none 🕐 11am–5pm Tue–Sun. ◻ & ☞ 1pm & 3pm daily 🅰 🏧
[→Upper West Side 62–64]

↓ in the picture

Brooklyn Museum of Art ▶

This is a browser's pleasure palace – the delightful epitome of a provincial museum, that brings together a miscellany of exhibits from Rodin sculptures to full-scale Dutch farmhouses of the 18th century. It was founded approximately 175 years ago as the Brooklyn Museum, and only recently added the 'of Art' to its name. Apparently, visitors didn't realize quite what it was about and kept asking to see the dinosaurs!

The museum's encyclopedic collection, spread through a spacious five-storey building, includes assemblages of both African and Egyptian art that have few matches in the US. The first floor has a gallery dedicated to temporary shows, and a small space for contemporary art, often devoted to showing work by members of Brooklyn's burgeoning artist population. Asian art is on two – look for an elegant Chinese wine jar with a cobalt blue design of fish and waterplants on white ceramic from the Yuan dynasty – while Egyptology takes up a fair slice of the third floor. The Dutch farmhouses are on the fourth floor, which gives some indication of the size of the museum, nestled alongside 28 period rooms – Brooklyn was the first museum to present this kind of exhibit. Among the American and European paintings on the fifth floor is a selection of 58 works by Rodin. Brooklynites (and others, of course) flock to the 'happenings' the museum organizes on the first Saturday of each month, a series of events, which is topped by a live dance band in the main lobby.

👁 The Egyptian exhibits include a brilliantly painted mummy cartonnage (a type of elaborately decorated coffin) of Nespenetjerenpare, as well as the gilded coffin for an ibis. On the first floor, be sure to check out the Haida totem poles and the 2000-year-old, richly embroidered Paracas Textile from Peru.
❶ On the first Saturday of each month there's a special free programme (including a band and Latin dancing) 5pm–11pm. Don't forget the adjacent Brooklyn Botanical Garden [→91].

200 Eastern Parkway, Brooklyn
☎ 1-718-638-5000
w www.brooklynart.org
Ⓜ 2·3 to Eastern Parkway-

Brooklyn Museum
💲 free 🕐 10am–5pm Wed–Fri; 11am–6pm Sat–Sun.
◻ & ☞ 🎧 🅰 ♻ 🏧

Dia Center for the Arts

Located since 1987 in a 40,000-sq-ft warehouse in Chelsea, Dia specializes in lavish, long-term exhibitions of works by contemporary artists from around the world, ranging from Francesco Clemente and Alighiero e Boetti to Jenny Holzer, Andy Warhol and Richard Serra. Launched in the 1970's, Dia was part of a visionary scheme to provide long-term or permanent installations of major works by a select handful of primarily Minimalist and Conceptual artists.

One work by Dan Graham and two by Walter de Maria are still maintained in New York. One of Graham's trademark glass pavilions is permanently sited on the roof and is a good spot to watch the sun set over the Hudson. The Walter de Maria pieces are over in the Soho district and are worth a special visit: the New York Earth Room takes up a floor of a loft at 141 Wooster, where soil 2 ft deep has been spread throughout the gallery; viewers stand at the door, behind a perspex sheet which holds back the earth, taking in the dank smell and pointing out the occasional sprouting of grass. The second work, the Broken Kilometer at 393 West Broadway, is composed of 1066 yards of solid brass rod, divided into 500 upended lengths arranged in a formation that subtly plays with your sense of perspective.

❶ Don't forget to visit the space across the street from the main gallery. Check Dia's calendar for poetry readings, lectures and performances.

548 W 22nd Street (bet. Tenth & Eleventh Aves)
☎ 989-5566
w www.diacenter.org
Ⓜ C•E to 23rd St
💲 $6 🚇 AE/MC/V ❶ 16 Sep–12 Jun: 12–6pm Wed–Sun.
❑ ♿ ✆ 🛍
[→Chelsea 43–47]

International Center of Photography

New York's only museum dedicated solely to photography was established in 1974 by photojournalist Cornell Capa, brother of the late war photographer Robert. Due to its distinctive heritage, the ICP regularly shows work with a journalistic slant, as opposed to oeuvres of artist-photographers. The museum's headquarters are located Uptown on Museum Mile, where there are two floors of intimate gallery space within an imposing early 20th-century brick building that previously housed the National Audubon Society. A second two-storey facility, grey-carpeted in corporate style, is located a block away from Times Square. Regular and multiple exhibitions draw on the ICP's extensive archive and include a recent Robert Capa retrospective as well

as other displays of the masters of this fascinating art form. The shop is a great resource for photo books.

❶ Admission is by donation 6–8pm Fri – pay as much as you wish.

1130 Fifth Ave (at 94th St)
☎ 860-1777
e info@icp.org
w www.icp.org
Ⓜ 6 to 96th St-Lexington Ave
💲 $6 🚇 none ❶ 10am–5pm Tue–Sun (8pm Fri; 6pm Sat–Sun).
❑ ♿ 🛍
[→Upper East Side 58–61]

1133 Sixth Ave (at 43rd St)
☎ 768-4682
e info@icp.org
w www.icp.org
Ⓜ B•D•F•Q to 42nd St
💲 $6 🚇 none ❶ 10am–5pm Tue–Sun (8pm Fri; 6pm Sat–Sun).
❑ ♿ 🛍
[→Midtown 52–57]

Isamu Noguchi Garden Museum ⓘ

The minimalism of high modernism meets the traditions of Zen Buddhism in this stylishly asymmetrical, one-storey museum, designed by the Japanese–American sculptor Isamu Noguchi (1904–1988) and dedicated in 1985. This is one of the most serene spaces in all of the city, and it houses more than 250 of his works, spread throughout 13 galleries.

Noguchi made a virtue of creating simple abstract forms that became part of the everyday environment – sculptures in stone and metal, models for public art projects, playground sculptures and dance sets (including 20 sets for Martha Graham). The museum includes one of the artist's small, meditative gardens (closed during winter months), with weeping cherry trees, bam-

boo, juniper and ivy, as well as major granite and basalt sculptures. One of the large cubes also functions as a tranquil fountain that gently bubbles its water supply. The museum shop offers a complete line of Noguchi's Akari lamps – light-sculptures inspired by classical Japanese lanterns of bamboo and pleated paper. A programme of films on Noguchi's life and work runs continuously.

👁 The artist's unusual musical weathervane, as well as his biomorphic glass-topped coffee table, a design which has been sold by Herman Miller since 1949.
❶ $5 round trip by shuttle-bus, hourly at weekends from the Asia Society, E 70th Street (at Park Ave). Check out the Socrates Sculpture Park in nearby Rainey Park.

32–37 Vernon Boulevard, Long Island City, Queens
☎ 1-718-721-1932
e museum@noguchi.org
w www.noguchi.org
Ⓜ N to Broadway (Queens)
💲 $4 (suggested donation only) 🚇 AE/MC/V ❶ 10am–5pm Wed–Fri; 11am–6pm Sat–Sun. ❑ ♿ limited ✆ 🛍

New Museum of Contemporary Art

With its recently renovated, three-storey facility and new director – former Whitney curator Lisa Phillips – the New Museum is poised to take on the art of the new millennium. The museum doesn't have a permanent collection, but can be counted on each year for a dozen or so challenging temporary exhibitions of new art from around the globe. Much of it is likely to be political, community-based and funky, as it endeavours to catch the best artists of our times on the way up. Previous exhibitions

sights, museums & galleries

more museums | galleries

have showcased Jeff Koons and Christian Boltanski.

▶ The 1999–2000 season will include a retrospective of British artist Keith Piper and the first museum show dedicated to hypermuscular women, Picturing the Modern Amazon.
❶ Admission is free
6–8pm Thu.

583 Broadway (bet. Houston & Prince Sts)
☎ 219-1222
e newmu@newmuseum.org
w www.newmuseum.org
Ⓜ 6 to Spring St or Bleecker St; N·R to Prince St; B·D·F·Q to Broadway-Lafayette St
💲 $5 🚇 AE/MC/V ◑ 12pm–6pm Wed–Sun (8pm Thu–Sat).
❑ ♿ ☞ 🎫

PS1 Museum of Contemporary Art

Out amid the industrial units of Queens is a unique New York art institution that captures the lively spirit of contemporary art – PS1. A ramshackle, four-storey, red-brick school that was converted into an art centre over 20 years ago, PS1 combines exhibition galleries with artists' studios. In 1998, with the help of an $8 million grant from the city, the museum got a new brutalist courtyard designed by architect Frederick Fischer, and spruced up its galleries considerably, though it still has a refreshing informality.

What makes the place seem particularly energetic are the long-term special projects by artists all around the building, from the Robert Ryman painting bolted to the wall next to the furnace in the basement, to the picnic table on the roof decorated by Julian Schnabel (where you can also take in a dramatic view of the Manhattan skyline and the Queensboro Bridge). There's a tiny, sexy video by Pipilotti Rist embedded in the hallway floor and a perplexing neon sculpture installed by Keith Sonnier in the airshaft above the foyer. All this is in addition to the major temporary exhibitions (check the listings magazines for current shows) and the artists-in-residence programme that opens up the studios for public inspections once in a while.

❶ Be sure to wait till dusk and see *Meeting* by James Turrell, the leading US master of inflecting space with colour. It's in Room 306 in the south wing, a carpeted space ringed with wooden seating, artfully lit and open to the sky – the effect of light and hue is phenomenal.

22–25 Jackson Avenue, Long Island City, Queens
☎ 1-718-784-2084
w www.ps1.org
Ⓜ E·F 23rd St (Ely Ave)
💲 $5 suggested donation
◑ 12–6pm Wed–Sun.
❑ ♿ ☞ 🎫 🐾

Schomburg Center for Research in Black Culture

This lodestone of African American learning is the biggest resource of its kind in America. Home to a massive collection of books, artworks, artifacts and documents (5 million at the last count), the Schomburg is actually a branch of the New York Public Library [→77] and as such it continues to elucidate and inform. The centre was named after the Puerto Rican-born black scholar and bibliophile, Arturo Alfonso Schomburg, who was once told there was no such thing as black history and decided to prove otherwise. He added his personal collection to the library's Division of Negro Literature, History and Prints in 1926 and served as the collection's curator from 1932 until his death in 1938, and in 1940 it was renamed in Schomburg's honour. The collection includes publications in over 200 indigenous African and Creole languages and dialects, and more than 300,000 photographs and prints, ranging from 18th-century graphics to contemporary works, all serving to document the history and culture of peoples of African descent worldwide. Schomburg's red-brick, modernist facility, located in the heart of Harlem, is also home to a lively community centre with two exhibition spaces and a theatre – there's always something going on, whether it be concerts, jazz performances or readings. There are several New York-

oriented exhibition mounted in the library each year.

❶ Saturdays after 3pm are a quiet time to visit. Phone for details of concerts and special programmes. An appointment is required to view the library's extensive holdings of art objects, rare books and manuscripts.

515 Lenox Ave (at 135th St)
☎ 491-2200
w www.nypl.org
Ⓜ 2·3 to 135th St
💲 free ◑ 12–8pm Mon–Wed; 10am–6pm Thu–Sat; 1–5pm Sun.
❑ ♿ ☞ by appointment 🎫
[→Harlem 65–67]

Studio Museum of Harlem

Founded in 1967 by a group that included abstract painter William T Williams, and some staffers from the Museum of Modern Art, the Studio Museum in Harlem grew out of the Black Art movement of the 1960's and is now the linchpin of the Upper Manhattan art scene. Its special quality comes from the constant involvement of artists – indeed, of its four or five exhibitions each year, one is always dedicated to work by the three yearly participants in the museum's artists-in-residence programme. To commemorate the museum's 30th anniversary, construction has started on new (in fact, the first ever) galleries for the permanent collection, which include works by Romare Bearden, Elizabeth Catlett, Robert Colescott and Jacob Lawrence. Among the offerings in the museum shop are exhibition catalogues for 30 years of exhibitions at the museum, plus African jewellery, textiles and woven containers.

❶ Free admission on the first Saturday of the month.

144 W 125th Street (bet Seventh St & Lenox Ave)
☎ 864-4500
📠 864-4500 X230
w www.studiomuseumin harlem.org
Ⓜ 2·3 to 125th Street
💲 $5 🚇 none ◑ 10am–5pm Wed–Fri; 1–6pm Sat–Sun.
❑ ♿ ☞ 🍴 🎫
[→Harlem 65–67]

Whether you're itching for action on the hardwood or want to take in some hot dogs and sun at the ballpark, NY's got all the bases covered

↓ a piece of the action

American football

This is a game of testosterone and touchdowns. NY has two teams, the Jets and the Giants, both based at Meadowlands Sports Complex, and each with its own rabid fan base. Tickets are hard to come by for either team. Season: Sep–Dec with the Superbowl played on the 3rd Sun in Jan.

Baseball

Touted as the most American of sports, baseball maintains a strong tradition. New York has two teams, the Yankees and the Mets. The Yankees are the most recognized franchise name in baseball and the Mets (based at the Shea Stadium) are the often the most maligned. Tickets are easy to get and nothing beats the combination of summer sun, beer and baseball. Season: Apr–Oct.

Basketball

Fast and furious, basketball is exciting to watch even if you're not so hot on all the rules. The two men's professional teams in the New York area are the NY Knickerbockers (Knicks), who play at Madison Square Garden and the New Jersey Nets (based at the Meadowlands Sports Complex). Tickets are expensive and difficult to get hold of. Season: Nov–Jun. Alternatively, go to a women's basketball league game. Tickets for NY Liberty (who play at Madison Square Garden) are reasonably priced, easily available (though book ahead for good seats) and fun. Season: Jun–Sep.

Boxing

A few of the mega-money, bloody bouts take place at Madison Square Garden each year. The Golden Gloves, a NY tradition and amateur boxing's biggest event, takes place every April. Call for ticket prices of individual fights.

Ice hockey

'Went to the fight and a hockey game broke out' is a common description of a night at the rink. Despite the frequent pummellings, hockey is an incredibly swift and often graceful game to watch – if you can keep up with the puck. The three area teams are the New York Rangers (Madison Square Garden), New York Islanders (Nassau Coliseum) and the New Jersey Devils (Meadowlands Sports Complex). It's a popular game and tickets may not be easily available if the team has done well in past seasons. Plan ahead. Season: Oct–Apr.

Tennis

The US Open is the USA's top tennis event and held at the Arthur Ashe Stadium at the end of August or early September. Tickets go on sale from May 31, but are incredibly difficult to get for the big matches. Chance a scalper or try your luck at the Will Call window for corporate tickets that are returned. Madison Square Garden also boasts elite women's international tennis matches (the Chase Championships) held in November. Tickets on sale in April.

directory

Arthur Ashe Stadium
USTA Tennis Center,
Flushing, Queens
☎ 1-718-760-6200
🚇 7 to Willets Point-Shea
Stadium ⌚ $30–$65 ♿

Meadowlands Sports Complex
50 Route 120 N, East Rutherford, New Jersey
☎ 1-201-935-3900
🚌 from Port Authority Bus Terminal 42nd St & 8th Ave

American Football: Jets & Giants ⌚ $20–$65 ♿
Basketball: Nets ⌚ $10–$500 ♿
Ice Hockey: Devils
⌚ $20–$65 ♿

Madison Square Garden
W 33rd St & Seventh Ave
☎ 465-6741
🚇 A·C·E·1·2·3·9 to 34th St-Penn Station

Basketball: Knicks ⌚ $22–$220 ♿; Liberty ⌚ $8–$55 ♿
Boxing: ⌚ $15– $35 for Golden Gloves ♿
Tennis: ⌚ $15–$45 ♿
Ice Hockey: Rangers
⌚ $22–$65 ♿

Nassau Coliseum
Hempstead Turnpike, Uniondale
☎ 1-516-794-9300
🚆 LIRR from Penn Station to Hempstead, then bus N70, N71 or N72 from Hempstead bus terminal (one block away)
Ice Hockey: Islanders
⌚ $19–$60 ♿

Shea Stadium
126th St (at Roosevelt Ave), Queens
☎ 1-718-507-8499
🚇 7 to Willets Point-Shea Stadium ⌚ $9–$24 ♿

Yankee Stadium
161st St & River Ave, Bronx
☎ 1-718-293-6000
🚇 C·D·4 to 161st St-Yankee Stadium ⌚ $12–$23 ♿

Websites
(all preceded by www.)
baseball
sports.excite.com/mlb/
basketball nba.com (men's) & wnba.com (women's)
boxing and all other Madison Square Garden events
thegarden.com
football nfl.com
horse racing
sports.excite.com/rah/
ice hockey nhl.com
soccer sports.excite.com/mls/
tennis sports.excite.com/ten/

booking tickets & what's on

Sports are very popular with the locals so it's best to get tickets as early as possible. Most events can be booked ahead in person, by phone or online with a credit card and collected at the gate. First try the stadium's box office, then call **Ticketmaster** ☎ 307-7171. When all else fails, you can call a ticketing agency such as **Ticket Window** ☎ 1-800-765-3688. Scalping (buying a ticket from an individual, usually on the day of the event outside the arena at an inflated price) is illegal, risky and subject to police crackdowns of late. If you come up empty handed, simply catch the action on TV or if you'd like some company try one of the sports bars [→136].

The *Daily News*, *NY Post* and *NY Times* all give in-depth coverage and listings of sports as do the local TV newscasts. WFAN radio at 660 AM broadcasts sports talk and play around the clock. For schedule, ticket and seating info look in the front of the *Manhattan Yellow Pages* or go to any team's website through the listed league sites.

spectator sports

parks & beaches

↓ turf 'n' surf

When the 24-hour pace gets tough, take a hike into the great urban outdoors: whether it's the planned expanse of Central Park or the ad-hoc gardens of Alphabet City, New Yorkers have an unexpected sense of pastoral pride.

Central Park

Completely man-made, Central Park (lush in summer, bleak in winter) is the quintessential city park. Designed in 1858, with a view to preserve a green space in the heart of Manhattan, it stretches for about 50 blocks, and contains woodland, lawns, bridle trails, plants and ponds – all kept in impressive shape by the ever present City Parks folk. Cars are allowed on the East and West Drives (just inside the park's periphery): but not between 10am–3pm and 7–10pm Mon–Fri; 7pm Fri–6am Mon, or from 7pm the night before until 6am the day after a public holiday. Distinctive areas, from Strawberry Fields to The Mall, as well as popular landmarks such as the Hans Christian Andersen and Alice in Wonderland statues, are part of the park's unique appeal. Vast and fascinating to explore, it's easy to lose your bearings and so worth remembering the old New Yorker navigation-trick: look at the numbers on the lampposts – they indicate the equivalent street outside the park. (Addresses within the park are given as street coordinates.)

① Belvedere Lake and Castle
A mock medieval creation at the park's highest point – home of the Park Rangers' HQ and the Meteorological Observatory's weather centre.

② The Ramble
Scary after dark, but romantic by day. Officially the paths and groves are good for bird watching; but they're also the place for a gay pick up.

③ Strawberry Fields
Yoko Ono's tribute to her late husband who was murdered nearby [→75].

④ The Mall
Ever since amplified sound was welcomed at this spot, it has been a performance mayhem of drummers, mime artists and trick-skaters.

⑤ Sheep Meadow
In summer, hacky-sack, frisbee and general posing are the order of the day – some even sunbathe topless (now legal in NY State).

⑥ Rumsey Playfield
Music, spoken word and dance acts take place throughout humid summer months [→140].

Roller Disco between The Mall & Sheep Meadow.
The Carousel 64th St at mid park
☎ 879-0244 ⊠ 90¢ ◐ 10.30am–5pm Mon–Fri; 10.30am– 6pm Sat–Sun.
Wollman Rink [→97].
Loeb boathouse: Fifth Ave & E 74th St ☎ 517-4723 Bike rentals ⊠ from $8 per hr. Rowboat & gondola ⊠ $10 per hr (plus $30 deposit). ◐ 10am–5pm daily (summer only).
Claremont Riding Academy: 175 W 89th St ☎ 724-5100 ◐ 6.30am–10pm Mon–Fri; 6am–5pm Sat–Sun ⊠ $35 per hr (exp. riders only).
Park View at the Boathouse [→130];
Leaping Frog Café.

☎ **Useful Numbers**
Central Park Information: ☎ 360-3444
Central Park Police Precinct: ☎ 570-4820
Visitor centres:
The Dairy ☎ 794-6564; **Belvedere Castle** ☎ 772-0210 and **The Charles A Dana Discovery Center** ☎ 860-1370
The Urban Park Rangers offer walking tours, general and emergency assistance in all major Manhattan parks ☎ 628-2345.

parks & beaches

Battery Park

Battery Park proper occupies the southern tip of Manhattan, and contains the Civil War-era Castle Clinton (now essentially the ticket office for ferries to Liberty and Ellis Islands). Adjoining it, and flanking the Hudson River, is Battery Park City, a former wasteland, now revamped and teeming with life. It encompasses lush grassy areas, an esplanade that is popular for post-brunch strolls, the Museum of Jewish Heritage and for gawpers – a dock housing millionaires' yachts, on-board helicopters and all.
♫ Gorgeous sunsets; outdoor jazz and blues in the summer.

Battery Place & State St
☎ 797-3143/3133
Ⓜ 4·5 to Bowling Green; 1·9 to South Ferry
Ⓢ basketball; cycling; fishing; soccer; softball; rollerblading; etc

Brooklyn Botanical Gardens

Set back from the sprawling Prospect Park, the Botanical Gardens is a place out of time. In spring the Cherry Orchard, with a variety of cherry trees unmatched outside of Japan, and the Herb Garden with its 300 kinds of fragrant plants, perfume the air. In the winter months the conservatory is a treat; the Tropical Pavilion includes plants from the Amazon basin and the Bonsai Museum has trees over a century in the growing.
♫ The Osbourne Garden's kaleidoscope of colour; the Shakespeare Garden with over 80 species mentioned by the great bard.

900 Washington Ave at E Parkway, Brooklyn
☎ 1-718-623-7200
Ⓜ D·Q to Prospect Park; 2·3 to Eastern Parkway-Brooklyn Museum ⬧ $3 adults
❶ free all day Tue & 10am–12pm Sat
◑ Apr–Sep: 8am–6pm Tue–Sun (10am Sat–Sun); Oct–Mar: 8am–4.30pm Tue–Sun (10am Sat–Sun)
☞ 1pm Sat–Sun ⬧
[→Brooklyn 68–71]

Bryant Park

Being the only open space in this section of Midtown, Bryant Park is very popular with the lunchtime crowd – 'brown-bagging it' as a workers' picnic is known. Its large lawn is enclosed by overflowing flowerbeds and trees; green garden chairs are scattered throughout, and two small concession stands sell over-priced beverages when the weather is good. In the summer the park takes on a life of its own with a boisterous, boozy singles scene at the Bryant Park Grill & Café [→54], and the occasional classical or rock concert. Sitting in the park, surrounded on all sides by skyscrapers, it's amazing to think that less than 180 years ago the site was just a potter's field.
♫ Free movies every Monday night in summer.

Sixth Avenue (at 42nd St)
☎ 983-4142
Ⓜ N·R·1·2·3·7·9 to 42nd St-Times Sq ◑ 24 hours daily ⬧
[→Midtown 52–57]

Lower East Side Gardens

Birdsong, frog-burps and butterflies – common sights and sounds on a summer's day in the Big Apple? The gardens of Alphabet City defy the cliché of what used to be one of the dodgiest areas in Manhattan. Proudly maintained by the local community groups, there's a garden on almost every block: ponds, stone chess tables and weeping willows offer shady relief from the blaring salsa of the Puerto Rican neighbourhood and heat of the summer.

Ⓜ F to 2nd Ave; L·N·R·4·5·6 to 14th St-Union Sq
◑ 8am–sundown Sat–Sun.
☞ Big Onion Walking Tours ☎439-1090
[→East Village 32–37]

Prospect Park

Landscaped by the architects who designed Central Park, Brooklyn's Prospect Park has some of the same features – a boating lake, an ice-rink, woodland areas and miles of pedestrian footpaths – but it also has attributes all of its own. The less manicured fields give it a much more rural feel; there's a stream that runs through a small valley; and areas that can make you feel like an explorer stumbling on uncharted territory. In summer the local neighbourhood residents pour into the park in droves – the BBQ areas are teeming with families of all ethnic diversities and kiteflying, games of soccer and volleyball are open to anyone.
♫ A summer music programme – for details see listings mags.

Flatbush Ave (at Grand Army Plaza), Brooklyn
☎ 1-718-965-8999 (events hotline) Ⓜ 2·3 to Grand Army Plaza ⬧ free ◑ dawn–dusk.
Ⓢ soccer, volleyball, etc
[→Brooklyn 68–71]

beaches

Brighton Beach & Coney Island Beach [→96]

Packed during the summer, but worth it for a juicy slice of Brooklyn life.

Ⓜ B·D·F to Brighton Beach or Stillwell Ave-Coney Island ◑ year round

Jones Beach

When buying your train ticket, ask for the 'special', which includes the bus ride (approx 15 min) to the beach. The beach bus makes three stops; the first is best for families, the second a little more youth-oriented, and the third is less crowded and leads to the gay beach farther down.

Ⓜ LIRR from Penn Station to Freeport, then bus.
◑ Memorial Day–Labor Day

Robert Moses State Park

The extra 30 min or so on the journey is well worth it to experience the white sands and untouched dunes of Fire Island. It's always pretty mellow, even in the height of summer – and the water is cleaner too.

Ⓜ LIRR from Penn Station to Babylon, then bus to the beach (again, ask for the special).
◑ Memorial Day–Labor Day

Rockaway Beach

This seven-mile stretch of beach is not necessarily the most beautiful you'll ever see, but it's close to the city and is used mainly by locals.

Ⓜ A·S to any stop along the beach, from Rockaway Park Beach 116th St to Beach 25th St ◑ year round

Always intense and exciting – from the roar of an urban zoo to the intrigue of a futuristic science center – NYC is cool for kids. Go have some fun.

↓ kids' corner

kids' eats

Ellen's Stardust Diner

Owned by Ellen Hart, Miss Subway 1959, this vintage subway car-shaped diner with a dinnertime show was made for kids. The food is standard American with cleverly named kids' dishes, inspired by hugely popular kids' TV channel Nickelodeon.

1650 Broadway (at 51st Street)
☎ 956-5151
Ⓜ 1/9 to 50th St
🕐 7.30am–midnight Sun–Thu;
7.30am–1am Fri–Sat.
🍴 all ages
[→Midtown 52–57]

Two Boots

This is a very family-friendly, funky, eclectic pizzeria with a strong Cajun influence. All kids get colouring books and, depending on age, some can even drink from boot-shaped mugs. Specialties include kid-size personalized pizzas, little-tot-size ravioli and the ubiquitous chicken fingers.

37 Avenue A (at 2nd Street)
☎ 505-2276
Ⓜ F to 2nd Ave
🕐 12pm–midnight daily.
🍴 all ages
[→East Village 32–37]

Cowgirl Hall of Fame

Round up those kiddies and bring them to this Western wonderland of cowhide, lassos and steer horns. Full kids' menu with a Tex-Mex, Southern feel. There's a great room in the back for romping around with other kids, which is stocked with toys and games. Crayons and colouring materials are also available.

519 Hudson St (at 10th St)
☎ 633-1133
Ⓜ A/C/E to 14th St; 1/9 to Christopher St
🕐 12–11pm Sun–Thu;
12pm–midnight Fri–Sat.
🍴 all ages
[→West Village 38–42]

Serendipity 3

Kids are wild about their dreamy 'frozen hot chocolate', fountain sodas and ice-cream sundaes. The whimsical nostalgic setting also houses a general toy store out front. They serve standard American lunch and dinner, but leave plenty of room for their famously outrageous desserts.

225 E 60th Street (bet. Second & Third Avenues)
☎ 838-3531
Ⓜ 4/5/6 to 59th St
🕐 11.30am–midnight daily.
🍴 all ages
[→Upper East Side 58–61]

animal adventures

Bronx Zoo

This is the largest urban zoo in America with a special children's zoo where kids can try out the exhilarating 'spider web' rope climb and see life underground in the 'prairie dog burrow'. The World of Darkness, full of bats, should also prove a big hit. There are camel rides; and trams, buses, and a monorail offering a narrated journey through Wild Asia make it easy to get around, but it's a big place and may become too much for kids under four.

Bronx River Parkway
Fordham Road, Bronx
☎ 1-718-367 1010
w www.wcs.org
Ⓜ 2 to East Tremont
🎟 $6 adults, $3 2–12 yrs, Wed free; monorail $2
🕐 10am–4.30pm daily.
🍴 all ages

Central Park Wildlife Center

Children can get up close and personal with the wild things at the Petting Zoo in this, the biggest of Manhattan's parks [→90]. They can also look at, but not touch, penguins, puffins, sea lions and monkeys through eye-level Plexiglas. Divided into three zones: the Polar Circle, Temperate Territory and Tropical Zone, the centre's intimate atmosphere and convenient locale make it a great choice for some outdoor fun.

Entrance at Fifth Ave & 64th St
☎ 861-6030
w www.centralpark.org
Ⓜ N/R to 5th Ave or 6 to 68th St
🎟 $3.50 adults, 50¢ 3–12 yrs
🕐 10am–4.30pm daily.
🍴 all ages

New York Aquarium

Kids get the feel of smaller sea-life in the touch pool or marvel at sea-mammal shows held several times daily at the open-air amphitheatre. There are over 10,000 specimens, including such favourites as Beluga whales and dolphins, and interactive displays aimed at kids. The aquarium is situated near the famous Coney Island boardwalk and amusement park – a fascinating slice of Americana – which is an ideal distraction for older children and teens.

W 8th St (at Surf Ave), Coney Island ☎ 1-718-265-3474
w www.wcs.org/zoos/aquarium/index.html
Ⓜ B/D/F/N to Stillwell Ave, Coney Island
🎟 $7.75 adults, $3.50 2–12 yrs
🕐 10am–6pm daily.
🍴 2 & up
[→Brooklyn 68–71]

kid culture

Children's Museum of the Arts

A true celebration of the art of play, this museum allows kids to get to grips with painting, sculpture, theatre, music and even graphic design. Sessions are tailored to match attention-spans and allow children to roam from one interest to the next. There's also an additional infant playroom.

182 Lafayette St (bet. Broome & Grand Sts)
☎ 941-9198
Ⓜ 6 to Spring St
🎟 $5 (under 12 months free)
🕐 12–5pm Thu–Sun; 12–7pm Wed. 🍴 10 & under
[→Nolita & Noho 27–31]

Children's Museum of Manhattan ↓

Another interactive museum where children run free and explore myriad make-believe worlds. They can cook green eggs and ham in the area dedicated to Dr Seuss, shoot down an artery in the Body Odyssey or produce their own TV show in the Media Center. With the Winnie the Pooh playland, added attractions for the under fours, storytelling, face painting and theatre, it all makes for an enjoyable full schedule.

212 W 83rd St (bet. Broadway & Amsterdam Ave)
☎ 721-1234
w www.cmoc.org
🚇 1/9 to 86th St 💳 $5 (under 12 months free) ◑ 10am–5pm Wed–Sun. 🅑 all ages 🏛
[→Upper West Side 62–64]

Intrepid Sea Air Space Museum

A 900-ft former aircraft carrier, the *Intrepid* is the centrepiece of this engrossing interactive museum, which also features a submarine, helicopters, lunar-landing modules, and simulators. It's packed with displays and models, and anecdotes from retired sea-dogs spice up your visit even more.

Pier 86, W 46th St and 12th Ave.
☎ 245-2533
🚇 A/C/E to 42nd St. Then M42 bus. 💳 $10 adults, $7.50 12–17 yrs, $5 6–11 yrs, $1 2–5 yrs. ◑ Apr–Sep 10am–5pm Mon–Fri (6pm Sat–Sun); Oct–Mar 10am–5pm Wed–Sun 🅑 all ages 🐾 🏛

gifts & goodies

Enchanted Forest

Toys Я Art rather than Toys Я Us. Handmade stuffed animals, puppets, masks and instruments are discreetly displayed in the branches of this shop's mock forest. Highly recommended for beautiful, top-quality, one-of-a-kind toys.

85 Mercer St (bet. Spring & Broome Sts) ☎ 925-6677
🚇 6 to Spring St ◑ 11am–7pm Mon–Sat, 12–6 Sun.
[→Soho 21–26]

Tootsie's Children's Books

A recently renovated and expanded three-storey townhouse full of books for all ages – from highbrow to high adventure. Children can also enjoy the extensive playspace, art classes and story hours. Call for details.

555 Hudson St (at Perry St)
☎ 242-0182
🚇 1·9 to Christopher St
◑ 11am–6pm daily.
[→West Village 38–42]

show time

Central Park [→90] is packed with free performances during the summer. You can count on both the Crowtations puppet show at Bethesda Fountain, and storytelling at the Hans Christian Andersen statue. For details of all park events call 794-6564 or 360-3444. The Swedish Marionette Theater has year-round indoor shows. If you are looking for big-screen entertainment, Manhattan has two IMAX cinemas. Other notable venues include the New Victory Theater, with everything from opera for kids to circus; the Grove Street Playhouse, which does great adaptations of children's classics; and Theatreworks/USA for wild and witty musicals. For a wide variety of shows from The Wiz to Shakespeare, check out the New York Youth Theater and Here. Call for showtimes, age recommendations and prices.

FAO Schwarz

The larger-than-life stuffed animals, huge music box-cum-clock and extensive train set will have you and the kids marvelling at this, the grand-daddy of all toy stores. Highly commercial, it has everything a child could want.

767 Fifth Ave (at 58th St)
☎ 644 9400
🚇 E/F/N/R to 5th Ave
◑ 10am–6pm Mon–Sat (11 am Sun).
[→Midtown 52–57]

Penny Whistle Toys

An uptown treasure-trove of time-tested toys for newborns through to teens. Parents will love their high-quality, educational aspects, while the bubble-blowing bears outside and the satisfying toys inside keep the children happy.

448 Columbus Ave (at 81st St)
☎ 873–9090
🚇 B/C to 81st St; 1/9 to 79th St ◑ 10am–7pm Mon–Fri (6pm Sat); 11am–5pm Sun.
[→Upper West Side 62–64]

new frontiers

Liberty Science Center

Here, more than 250 scientific exhibits offer kids a chance to touch and test the physical world. Large-scale displays include a geodesic dome, a lighthouse, a solar telescope and a fully-equipped ambulance. Informative staff encourage participation. The museum also houses the largest domed IMAX cinema in the USA. The center's observation deck offers a pleasant café and great views of Lady Liberty and the city skyline.

251 Philip Street, Jersey City
☎ 1–201–200–1000
w www.lsc.org
🚢 NY Waterway ferry (1-800-533-3779) from World Financial Center to Colgate Piers, then free shuttle bus 💳 $9.50 adults, $6.50 2–12 yrs, (OMNI) IMAX cinema $2

◑ 9.30am–5.30pm daily (3 Sep–30 Mar closed Mon).
🅑 2 & up 🐾 🏛

Sony Wonder Technology Lab ▲

Four floors of hi-tech tinkering, with numerous interactive gadgets from robots to ultra-sound scanners. Everyone gets a card-key imprinted with their image, name and voice, which personalizes each of the exhibits when used. Print-outs of the experience provide a permanent memento.

550 Madison Ave (at 56th St)
☎ 833-8100
w www.wondertechlab.sony.com
🚇 E/F to 5th Ave
💳 free ◑ 10am–6pm Tue–Sat (8pm Thu); 12–6pm Sun.
🅑 8 and up 🐾 🏛
[→Midtown 52–57]

ⓘ Midtown is littered with theme stores and restaurants (Disney, Warner, Niketown, Planet Hollywood et al). Big on razzle dazzle and long lines, they are real black holes of merchandising, but if you can say 'no', the interactive exhibits can be great fun.

showtime venues & cinemas

Grove Street Playhouse
39 Grove Street
(bet. Seventh Ave & Bleecker St)
☎ 741-6436
Here
145 Sixth Avenue (at Spring St)
☎ 647-0202
IMAX
Sony Theater
Broadway (at 68th St)
☎ 336-5000
Naturemax (IMAX)
American Museum of Natural History, Central Park West (at 79th St) ☎ 769-5100
New Victory Theater
209 W 42nd St (bet. Broadway & Eighth Avenue) ☎ 382-4000
New York Youth Theater
Central Presbyterian Church, 593 Park Avenue (at 64th St)
☎ 888-0696
Swedish Marionette Theater
Central Park
(at 81st St on westside)
☎ 988-9093
Theatreworks/USA
Promenade Theater
2162 Broadway (at 76th St)
☎ 647-1100

NYC is famous for a lot of things and being peaceful just ain't one of 'em. If you find yourself in need of some pampering, tranquillity, or a place to let it all sweat out, these are some of the best Gotham City has to offer.

↓ feelgood factor

top spas

The Avon Center

Given that Avon is a rather old-fashioned name, this place is surprisingly chic – with make-up lessons ($85), applications ($50), and a hair salon. You can get made up for free if you buy a product or have a facial. The whole range of treatments is covered, from half leg wax ($35) to paraffin body wrap ($150).

725 Fifth Avenue (bet. 56th & 57th Sts) ☎ 755-2866 Ⓜ N·R to Lexington Ave; 4·5·6 to 59th St ◑ 9am–6pm Mon–Sat (8pm Thu). ⊟ AE/MC/V ⓑ

Bliss ✔

When Uma Thurman, Winona Ryder and Gwyneth Paltrow crave R&R, they hit Bliss, the city's most talked-about and hottest day-spa for men and women. From the buffet of champagne and chocolates, and the lavish boutique of beauty products, to the menu of ultra-luxurious treatments ($50–$225), such as a facial exfoliation with micro-crystals, a 2-hour rub down with crushed ginger and oils, a hot almond-milk pedicure and a mint body mask, the Bliss mantra is simple: indulge! Book anything from 2 weeks to 2 months ahead.

568 Broadway (bet. W Houston & Prince Sts) ☎ 219-8970 Ⓜ N·R to Prince St ◑ 9.30am–8.30pm Mon–Fri; 9.30am–6.30pm Sat. ⊟ AE/MC/V ⓑ

Carapan

This is an intimate, sage-scented haven, decked out with rustic furnishings, which aims to heal the body (men's and women's) inside and out. Their specialties are massage, aromatherapy, reflexology and cranio-sacral work ($95 per session).

5 W 16th Street (bet. Fifth & Sixth Aves) ☎ 633-6220 Ⓜ L·N·R·4·5·6 to 14th St-Union Sq ◑ 10am–10pm daily. ⊟ AE/MC/V

Origins Feel Good Day Spa

All the usual massages (from $40 for 25 min) and facials ($70) using their world-famous, all-natural products; but Origins also offers a 'light tank' – a capsule where you can lie and absorb rays of light which help you relax, pep up or even cure jet-lag ($25 for 30 min).

Pier 60, The Sports Center, Chelsea Piers ☎ 336-6780 Ⓜ C·E to 23rd St ◑ 9am–9pm Mon–Sat (8pm Sat); 11am–7pm Sun. ⊟ AE/MC/V ⓑ

Soho Sanctuary

This women-only day-spa is so tranquil, you'll feel transported. They offer massages and facials (both $85 for 1 hour), body treatments, yoga and meditation ($20 per class), and perhaps the best steam-room in town (mosaic tiles and delicious herbal scents).

119 Mercer Street (bet. Prince & Spring Sts) ☎ 334-5550 Ⓜ N·R to Prince St; 6 to Spring St ◑ 10am–9pm Tue & Thu; 9am–9pm Wed & Fri; 10am–6pm Sat; 12–6pm Sun. ⊟ AE/MC/V ⓑ

fitness & dance

Crunch

These gyms are known for their 'no judgements' policy, so leave your self-consciousness behind. At the Lafayette Street locale, which is by far the biggest, there are 2 floors of cardio equipment, a boxing ring, tanning facilities and fun classes like firefighter training (a real firefighter has you lugging hoses and dragging bodies). It's $22 per day whatever you choose to do, but don't sweat at the price, they have state-of-the-art machinery to make the most of your work-out.

404 Lafayette Street (bet. E 4th St & Astor Pl) ☎ 614-0120 Ⓜ 6 to Astor Pl ◑ 24 hours Mon–Fri; closes 9pm Sat; 8am–9pm Sun. ⊟ all ⓑ

162 W 83rd Street (bet. Amsterdam & Columbus Aves) ☎ 875-1902 Ⓜ 1·9 to 86th St ◑ 6am–11pm Mon–Thu (10pm Fri); 8am–9pm Sat–Sun. ⊟ all ⓑ

Fred Astaire Dance Studio

To pick up some smooth moves – swing, ballroom, Latin, waltz, tango, foxtrot, rumba or cha-cha-cha – you'll need to take a few lessons ($25 each). Call ahead to fit into a programme of classes or, for more instant success, a private session ($88). Don't expect a grand setting – facilities are basic.

666 Broadway (bet. Bond & Bleecker Sts) ☎ 475-7776 Ⓜ 6 to Bleecker St ◑ 1.30–10.30pm Mon–Fri; 12.30–6pm Sat. ⊟ AE/MC/V

697 E 43rd Street (at Second Ave) ☎ 697-6535 Ⓜ 4·5·6·7 to Grand Central-42nd St ◑ 1.30–10.30pm Mon–Fri; 11am–5pm Sat. ⊟ AE/MC/V

Power Pilates

The business of stretching the body and releasing toxins and fluids is so hot, and Pilates is one of the latest ways for the supermodels and celebs to get fit. The rigorous mat-based classes last 1 hour ($15) or you can have a semi-private (3 people) machine session for $40, or a one-to-one for $65–$100.

138 Fifth Avenue (bet. 18th & 19th Sts) ☎ 337-9952 Ⓜ N·R·6 to 23rd St ◑ 7am–9pm Mon–Wed & Fri (8pm Thu); 9am–3pm Sat; 10am–4pm Sun. ⊟ MC/V ⓑ

Revolution

Sans frills and fancy stuff, Revolution is exactly what a gym is supposed to be – a place to sweat. Classes range from spinning (static cycling), boxing and body-conditioning to the more eclectic holistic self-defence, Thai kick-boxing, and strength and alignment sessions. Just pay by the class ($12). And if you're looking for some personal attention, they have some of the most educated and bodily aware trainers in the business. ❶ BYOT (towel)!

104 W 14th Street (bet. Sixth & Seventh Aves) ☎ 206-8785 Ⓜ L·N·R·4·5·6 to 14th St-Union Sq ◑ 6am–10pm Mon–Fri; 8am–4pm Sat–Sun. ⊟ all ⓑ

alternative therapies

Genesis Center ▼

Tune into your 'bodymind's orchestra' with Genesis's bio-entrainment treatment. You lie down on a suspended bed and let the music penetrate every pore of your body ($80). Speakers and sensors modify your vital signs and the vibe, volume and beat of the music changes depending on how you feel. You get to choose your music too.

Soho Health & Wellness Center, 177 Prince Street (bet. Sullivan & Thompson Sts), Suite 4B
☎ 777-4890
Ⓜ N·R to Prince St; 6 to Spring St
◑ by appointment only.
🚻 AE/MC/V & limited

Jivamukti

Anyone hooked on yoga will dig this huge centre ($15 for any class, including astanga, and their unique jivamukti yoga). The peaceful setting is complete with a waterfall, pastel-painted rooms, each with an incense-laden altar, and a boutique dedicated to satisfying your spiritual needs – incense, books, clothes, music etc. Keep your eyes peeled – you might be contorting next to Sting.

404 Lafayette Street, 3rd floor (at E 4th St)
☎ 353-0214
Ⓜ B·D·F·Q to Broadway-Lafayette St; 6 to Astor Pl
◑ 6.45am–10pm daily. 🚻 all &

Open Center

This is a serene oasis in which to learn the arts of belly-dancing, yoga, tai chi, martial arts, astrology and more, at the centre's lectures, seminars and cool classes. There's also a free meditation room (donations welcome).

83 Spring Street (bet. Crosby St & Broadway)
☎ 219-2527
Ⓜ N·R to Prince St; 6 to Spring St ◑ 10am–10pm daily (6pm Sun). 🚻 AE/MC/V &

Osaka Health Center

One of the best remedies for an achy body is a shiatsu massage. The approach of this parlour is pretty intense – there are ropes above the

tables for therapists to hold on to while they walk on your back and dig their toes into your pressure points – but it's worth it ($50–$100, including hot and cold tub, and sauna).

50 W 56th Street (bet. Fifth & Sixth Aves)
☎ 682-1778
Ⓜ N·R to 57th St
◑ 10am–midnight daily.
🚻 AE/MC/V &

beauty treatments

J Sisters

Famous for their pedicures (for $55 they'll even dig and get rid of in-grown toe-nails), and bikini wax service ($45), this glam venue has professionals who'll go places your partner wouldn't!

35 W 57th Street (bet. Fifth & Sixth Aves)
☎ 750-2485
Ⓜ B·N·Q·R to 57th St
◑ 9am–5.30pm Tue–Sat (7.30pm Wed–Thu). 🚻 MC/V

Ling

The shape of your brows can make or break your face. Ling's got the best eyebrow 'designers' in town. They do all the models and actors and know how to sculpt the perfect arch ($22).

10 E 16th Street (bet. Fifth & Sixth Aves)
☎ 989-8833
Ⓜ N·R·L·4·5·6 to 14th St-Union Sq; F to 14th St; L to 6th Ave ◑ 10am–7pm Mon–Fri; 9.30am–5pm Sat.
🚻 all &

The Service Station

Even the man in the street is taking better care of himself these days, and the Service Station is here to make sure it's a pleasurable experience. Kitted out like an old gas station, this is the original pampering place for men (although some women come too). They do tanning, massage ($60 per hour), manicures ($10), pedicures ($20) and hair ($35 for men; $45 for women).

137 Eighth Avenue (at 16th Street)
☎ 243-7770 Ⓜ A·C·E to 14th St; L to 8th Ave ◑ 10am–10pm Mon–Sat; 12–8pm Sun.
🚻 AE/MC/V &

hair care

Devachan

Having a haircut at Devachan – an airy Soho loft – is a spiritual experience...it all starts when they get you to lie down on a massage table, while they shampoo and give you a 10-min head massage

($60–$125 for cut; $65 and up for colour).
❶ If you have curly hair, try to see the owner Lorraine – she'll teach you how to 'cultivate your curls'.

558 Broadway (bet. Prince & Spring Sts)
☎ 274-8686
Ⓜ N·R to Prince St; 6 to Spring St
◑ 11am–7.30pm Tue–Fri; 10am–5pm Sat. 🚻 AE/MC/V

Jerry's Men's Hair Styling Salon

An old-school barbers, Jerry's gives shaves (with a steam towel), shoe shines, hair cuts ($20) and manicures. Walk in scruffy and leave like a gentleman.

635 Fifth Avenue (in the Rockefeller Center)
☎ 246-3151
Ⓜ B·D·F·Q to 47–50th Sts-Rockefeller Ctr; 6 to 51st St
◑ 8am–6pm Mon–Fri. 🚻 AE &

Mark Garrison Salon

This is as far away as you can get from the trad East Village hole-in-the-wall salon, where the specialty is usually crazy colour and funky cuts. One of the most chichi spots in town, this salon is beautiful, posh and a real indulgence. They'll give you that perfect cut (approx $100) and change your hair forever. For a true splurge, see Mark for $200.

820 Madison Ave (at 67th St)
☎ 570-2455
Ⓜ 6 to 68th St-Hunter College
◑ 9am–6pm Mon–Sat (8pm Tue & Thu). 🚻 MC/V

body art

Body Adorned

Looking to decorate your skin with some piercings or tattoos? Then head for the East Village. This neighbourhood is loaded with little haunts, but the ultra-hygienic Body Adorned is an especially friendly set-up. They have design books you can sift through for tattoo inspiration, and the professional artists (some of the most talented in town) will give you their advice before inflicting pain. Aside from tattoos (prices start at $75), they also have mendhei painters ($20 for a hand print), and a piercing service.

47 Second Avenue (bet. 2nd & 3rd Sts)
☎ 473-0007
Ⓜ F to 2nd Ave
◑ 12–8pm Sun–Thu (10pm Fri–Sat). 🚻 all &

u might have been there or done that, but to get the feel of the
...y, open wide and really get your teeth into the Big Apple by
joining the locals (plus those who long to be) at play...

↓ have a blast

Bowling

You can bowl your heart out all day long in the Big Apple, but for a different spin, why not 'rock 'n' bowl' at **Bowlmor Lanes** (Mon 10pm–4am) with Night Strike, NY's premier 'lights out' neon bowling party for the over-18's. Or, at **AMS Chelsea Bowl**, try 'extreme bowling' when the lights go out, pins and balls go day-glo and you're surrounded by a laser light show. There's also a huge video games room.

Bowlmor Lanes
110 University Pl (at E 13th St)
☎ 255-8188
Ⓜ L•N•R•4•5•6 to 14th St-Union Sq. 💲 $4.95 per game Mon–Fri (10pm–4am Mon $12 unlimited games), $5.95 Sat–Sun. Shoe rental $3. ⏱ 10–1am daily (4am Mon & Fri–Sat; 2am Thu). ♿☕

AMS Chelsea Bowl
Pier 60 (bet. 20th St & Twelfth Ave) ☎ 835-2695
Ⓜ C•E to 23rd St 💲 $6.25 per game. Shoe rental $4 ⏱ 9am–midnight (4am Fri–Sat). ♿☕

Chess

For activity of a more cerebral kind, bring or pair up with a chess partner at **Chess Forum**. You can even brush up on your moves beforehand with a private lesson or two. However, the quintessential NY chess experience is to challenge one of the local chess masters/hustlers who hang out in **Washington Square Park**. But, should they suggest a wager, and you win the first game, it might be best to quit while you're ahead; there are a lot of scam artists out there...

Chess Forum
219 Thompson Street (bet. W 3rd & Bleecker Sts)
☎ 475-2369
Ⓜ A•B•C•D•E•F•Q to W 4th St-Washington Sq 💲 $1; private lessons $25 per hour ⏱ 11–3.30am daily. ♿☕

Washington Square Park
Ⓜ A•B•C•D•E•F•Q to W 4th St-Washington Sq

Coney Island [→71]

The masses started coming to Coney Island in the early 1900's, and this Brooklyn outpost is still a great bet for an afternoon of amusement and some summer fun. Visit the 150 ft-high Wonder Wheel (built in 1920) or the world-famous **Astroland**, home of the Cyclone (built in 1927), a 100-second, nine-hill roller-coaster ride that does its best to make you lose your cool – and your lunch. **Sideshows by the Seashore** is the last remaining 10-in-1 (10 acts, one admission price) sideshow in the US; expect bearded ladies, sword-swallowers and escape artists.

Astroland Amusement Park
1000 Surf Ave (at W 10th St)
☎ 1-718-372-0275
Ⓜ B•D•N•F to Stillwell Ave-Coney Island 💲$12.99 for unlimited major rides; single rides $1-75–$4
⏱ Memorial Day–Labor Day: 12pm–midnight daily. ♿

Sideshows by the Seashore
1208 Surf Ave (at W 12th St)
☎ 1-718-372-5159 Ⓜ B•D•F•N to Stillwell Ave-Coney Island 💲$3 ⏱ May 1–Memorial Day: 1pm–midnight, Sat–Sun; Memorial Day–Labor Day: 2–10pm Fri; 1pm–midnight, Sat–Sun; 2–8pm public holidays. ♿

Dance

For a full evening's entertainment, take advantage of the fact that swing is the hottest thing to hit the dance scene since Saturday Night Fever. At the **Supper Club**, zoot suits are prevalent and big bands blast until the small hours. Before or after an optional dinner, you can practise your footwork in the lavish ballroom setting. Beginners, relax – you can pick up lessons. On your own-eo? No sweat, there's a hopping singles scene. And if you can't wait for the weekend, try the **Swing 46 Jazz & Supper Club**, where there are more live big band sounds to help you 'get hip, get hep, get right in step'.

Supper Club
240 W 47th Street (bet. Broadway & Eighth Ave)
☎ 921-1940
Ⓜ 1•9 to 50th St 💲 $25 before 8pm, $20 thereafter.
⏱ 5.30pm–4am Fri–Sat. ☐☕

Swing 46 Jazz & Supper Club
349 W 46th Street (bet. Eighth & Ninth Aves) ☎ 262-9554
ⓦ www.swing46.com
Ⓜ 1•9 to 50th St 💲 $7 Sun–Wed, $12 Thu–Sat. Price includes free class at 11pm.
⏱ 12pm–4am daily. ☐☕

Games & Sports

NY is a great place to find your inner child. At **Hackers, Hitters & Hoops**, you can go mini-golfing, run an obstacle course, toss a football, strike out in a batting cage, slam dunk a basketball, spike a volleyball, kick a soccer ball, pick up a game of air hockey or pump quarters into video games for hours.

A less frenetic game of pool or ping-pong might be more up your street. If so, **Fat Cat Billiards** is the real deal – a dingy hole-in-the-wall where you can kick back, shoot pool, slap a ping-pong ball around (with a net surround for minimum effort) and nurse a beer for hours. Or, for a more up-to-date take on games, **XS New York** is cyber heaven for those who dig state-of-the-art virtual reality games and simulated sports. You might not want to eat lunch before you climb into the simulated airplane/spaceship 'M4' or 'Indy 500 racecar' with surround sound and slam-bam realistic movement. Lazer Tag beckons in the basement.

Hackers, Hitters, & Hoops
123 W 18th Street (bet Sixth & Seventh Aves) ☎ 929-7482
Ⓜ 1•9 to 18th St 💲 $3 entrance, game prices vary eg Lazer Tag $5 ⏱ 11am–7pm daily (midnight Tue–Thu; 2am Fri–Sat). ♿

games & activities

Fat Cat Billiards

75 Christopher Street (at Seventh Ave) ☎ 675-6056
Ⓜ 1·9 to Christopher St
Ⓢ $3.75 per hour per player.
❶ 2pm–2am daily. 🅿 ♿

XS New York

1450 Broadway (bet. 41st & 42nd Sts)
☎ 398-5467 Ⓜ N·R·1·2·3·7·9 to 42nd St-Times Sq
Ⓢ video and virtual reality games $1.50–$5. Internet access $4.20 for 20 min.
❶ 12–10pm daily (2am Fri–Sat) (over 18's only after 8pm). ♿ ♿

Showtime

For a Chinese meal that's a little out of the ordinary, try Lucky Chengs, where their specialty is service with a song. There are three cabaret shows a night (7.30, 8.30 and 10pm). If you're (un)lucky, your waitress may put whipped cream all over you and then lick it off, dance on your table and generally slither sexily around the room! If that's not your bag, there's Kabuki Karaoke downstairs. The service is fun, but the food... well, you don't come for the food.

Lips will also give you a good lip sync show and better than average American cuisine. The ambience is laid-back downtown – banquettes, sofas and sexy red lights. Don't get too ga ga over your outrageously leggy waitress at either place, she's really a man in drag.

Lucky Chengs

24 First Ave (bet 1st & 2nd Sts) ☎ 473-0516
Ⓜ F to 2nd Ave Ⓢ appetizers $5–$11, entrées $12–$23
❶ 6pm–midnight for dinner (2am for drinks) daily. ♿

Lips

4 Bank Street (bet. Greenwich Ave & Waverly Pl) ☎ 675-7710
Ⓜ 1·2·3·9 to 14th St-Union Sq
Ⓢ average meal: $30 (with appetizer and drink)
❶ 5.30pm–midnight Mon–Thu (1am Fri–Sat); 11.30am–4.30pm Sun brunch. ♿

Skate City

Ice-skating is big in NYC, and the city has several rinks. In the mid of Central Park [→90] is the secluded Wollman Rink, offering the great outdoors, music and, if you're looking and lucky, a little romance. It's especially busy at Christmas season weekends. The park is also prime rollerblading territory (especially in summer), but if you feel like taking to the streets with a crowd, join the huge number of bladers who gather on Wednesday evenings (summer months only) in Union Square for the weekly ritual.

Turn back the clock and head to the Roxy, a dance club where they turn the floor into a roller-rink on Wednesday nights. The DJ spins 70's and 80's disco tunes while some of the best skaters around trip the light fantastic. Even if you're not so hot on wheels, you'll appreciate others' talents – and it's a crazy flashback to headbands, glitter and bad hair. For 21's and over.

Union Square Mass Blade: meet by the parking lot on the east side of the square
Ⓜ L·N·R·4·5·6 to Union Sq-14th St ❶ 8pm Wed.

The Roxy

515 W 18th Street (bet. Tenth & Eleventh Ave) ☎ 645-5156
Ⓜ A·C·E to 14th St Ⓢ $15 admission, $5 for skate hire, $10 for blade hire.
❶ 8pm–2am daily. 🅿

Wollman Rink

Park entrance at 59th St and Sixth Ave ☎ 396-1010

Ⓜ N·R to 5th Ave
Ⓢ $7 (6–9.30pm Wed $3.50). $3.50 skate hire. ❶ Nov–Mar only: 10am–3pm daily (9.30pm Wed; 5pm Thu; 11pm Fri–Sat; 9pm Sun).

❶ swing night (7–9pm Thu) with 30-min lesson. Adults only Ⓢ $15

Travel in Style

Who wouldn't willingly part with a few extra dollars to live the life of a celebrity For a few hours you can, by cruising Manhattan in the ultimate luxury, the stretch limo. Dress up, bring your friends – and pretend.

❶ bring your own booze.

Dav-El Limousine Service

☎ 247-0711 Ⓢ $85 per hour (minimum 2 hours after 6pm)

Delancey Car Service

☎ 228-3301 Ⓢ $50 per hour (minimum 2 hours)

Tiara Luxury Transportation

☎ 398-5466 Ⓢ $75 per hour (minimum 3 hours)

TV Heaven

Find yourself lamenting those missed episodes of Baywatch or wishing to revisit your childhood and a favourite Lost in Space show? Run, don't walk, to the world's most comprehensive collection of TV shows and radio clips at the Museum of Television and Radio. Around 100,000 programmes are available for private viewing or listening on individual consoles, and you can see everything from a classic I Love Lucy to a wrap up of this year's Super Bowl commercials. There are also daily screenings and seminars in the museum's two screening rooms.

Museum of Television and Radio

25 W 52nd Street (bet. Fifth & Sixth Aves) ☎ 621-6800
Ⓜ E·F to 53rd St; N·R to 49th St; 1·9 50th St; B·D·F·Q to 47th-50th Sts at Rockefeller Center Ⓢ $6 ❶ 12–6pm Tue–Sun (8pm Thu; 9pm Fri for screenings only). ♿ 🅸

---

lottery

The New York State Lottery offers 10 different games to gamble with and you can grab a ticket in over 6500 locations citywide – look for the yellow and blue Lottery sign. Some games are more popular than others: if you need instant gratification, try the $1 and $2 scratch cards – the overall chances are 1 in 6, and you can win anything from $2 to $1 million. On Mon, Tue, Thu and Fri, a $1 TAKE 5 offers you a 1 in 9 chance of winning prizes worth up to $300,000. Choose five numbers and watch

ABC TV (Channel 7) at 11.21pm to see if your numbers come up. If you want the big bucks, play $1 LOTTO on Wed and Sat where the jackpot prize starts at $3 million. If no one wins, the winnings go up to $8, $12 and then $25 million. So what if the odds of winning the jackpot are only 1 in 12,913583! You must be 18 or older to participate.

☎ 383-1300 for information on claiming prizes and checking numbers.

new york's top shopping zones

directory (downtown–uptown)

getting your bearings

West Broadway (*bet. Varick & Reade Sts*) ♿B6: Cutting-edge home furnishings and interesting up-and-coming designers.

Franklin Street (*bet. Broadway & Church St*) ♿B6: More cutting-edge home furnishings and interesting up-and-coming designers.

Canal Street (*bet. Bowery & West Broadway*) ♿B6–C6: Street vendors selling all manner of fruit and veg, knock-off designer watches and bags, cheap and gold jewellery, electronics, and the Pearl River Mart [→111].

Broadway (*bet. Canal & Houston Sts*) ♿B6: Below Houston are superstores like Banana Republic and Sephora, plus lots of sportswear stores selling cut-price sneakers and trainers.

Houston to Grand Street (*bet. Broadway & Bowery*) ♿B6–C6: The moment's hottest one-off boutiques, young designers, and precious accessories stores, and some very cool home furnishings.

Houston to Canal Street (*bet. Broadway & Sullivan St*) ♿B6: Peppered with major inter-national designers from Anna Sui [→101] to Yohji Yamamoto [→101], upscale home furnishing stores, unique boutiques and commercial art galleries.

Ludlow and Orchard Streets (*bet. Delancey & Houston Sts*) ♿C6: One-off boutiques selling cool clothing as well as vintage stores and record shops, plus traditional bargain vendors selling cut-price leather goods,

bags and sportswear. There's a Sunday market for bags, toys, general accessories like T-shirts and socks on Orchard Street.

Lafayette Street (*bet. Spring & Houston Sts*) ♿C6: Cool clothing boutiques which cater to a young, downtown crowd. Vintage home furnishing stores selling Americana.

Broadway (*bet. Houston & 12th Sts*) ♿B5: More sportswear and clothing boutiques, Tower Records and good bookstores like Shakespeare and Co, and Strand.

Christopher Street (*bet. Sixth Ave & Bleecker St*) ♿B5: Erotic boutiques, gift stores and interesting one-offs.

Bleecker Street (*bet. Hudson St & Sixth Ave*) ♿B5: Interesting one-off gift boutiques, some record stores, food shops.

Sixth Avenue (*bet. 12th & W 4th Sts*) ♿B5: Historic stores like Balducci's [→114] and Bigelow's [→109], and chains like Urban Outfitters and Foot Locker.

E 7th Street (*bet. Ave A & Second Ave*) ♿C5: Interesting one-offs, vintage furnishings, funky gift boutiques, cool clothing stores with a boho edge.

8th Street (*bet. Broadway & Sixth Ave*) ♿B5: Shoes of all descriptions.

St Mark's Place (*bet. Second & Third Aves*) ♿C5: Record stores, vendors selling cheap jewellery and sunglasses.

Chelsea (*bet. 22nd & 24th Sts*) ♿A4: A burgeoning commercial gallery scene, plus radical chic from the Commes des Garçons boutique [→101] and Jeffrey's department store [→101].

E 9th Street (*bet. Ave A & Second Ave*) ♿C5: More interesting one-offs, vintage furnishings, funky gift boutiques, and cool clothing stores with a boho edge.

Avenue A (*bet. E 2nd & E 9th Sts*) ♿C5: One-off kooky gift boutiques and home accessories stores.

Broadway (*bet. 12th & 14th Sts*) ♿B5: A cluster of antique stores.

Fifth Avenue (*bet. 14th & 30th Sts*) ♿B4–B5: Interesting lesser known designer stores like Paul Smith [→103] and Intermix, big name chains such as Zara and Banana Republic, designer emporiums like Armani.

Broadway (*bet. Union Sq & 23rd St*) ♿C4: One of a kind superstores like Paragon sports [→108] and ABC Carpet and Home [→110], with the emphasis firmly on home furnishings.

Sixth Avenue (*bet. 17th & 26th Sts*) ♿B4: Megastores like Bed Bath Beyond [→110], discount stores like Daffy's [→107].

W 18th and W 19th Streets (*bet. Fifth & Sixth Aves*) ♿B4: Bookstores for new and used books, including Barnes & Noble [→112].

W 25th and W 26th Streets (*around Sixth Ave*) ♿B4: Antique showrooms and the Annex Flea Market [→115].

W 28th Street (*bet. Broadway & Seventh Ave*) ♿B4: Flower shops.

Sixth Avenue (*bet. 30th & 36th Sts*) ♿B3 and **34th Street** (*bet. Madison & Sixth Aves*) ♿B3: Around Herald Square are Macy's department store [→100], the Manhattan Mall, HMV, and sportswear chain stores like Footlocker and Modell's.

W 47th Street (*bet. Fifth & Sixth Aves*) ♿B2: The jewellery stores of the Diamond District and the Gotham Book Mart.

Fifth Avenue (*bet. 48th & 59th Sts*) ♿B2: Department stores like Saks Fifth Avenue [→100] and Bergdorf Goodman [→100], designer flagships like Gucci, Prada and Versace, the Gap flagship, historic one-of-a-kind stores like Tiffany's, and theme stores like the Disney Store [→108].

57th Street (*bet. Madison & Seventh Aves*) ♿B2: Theme stores like Niketown [→108] and Warner Bros Studio Store [→108], commercial galleries, and Rizzoli book store.

Lexington Avenue (*bet. 57th & 64th Sts*) ♿C1–C2: Bloomingdales [→100], the Diesel and Zara flagships, chain stores like Banana Republic, Express and 9 West shoes.

Madison Avenue (*bet. 57th & 74th Sts*) ♿C1–C2: Every name designer in the known universe from Prada and Versace to Chlöe and Calvin Klein. Major designer 'event' flagships like the Ralph Lauren mansion [→102], cool department stores like Barneys New York [→100].

Columbus Avenue (*bet. Broadway & 81st St*) ♿A1: Chains like Barnes & Noble and Gap. Interesting boutiques selling kids clothes and home furnishings.

125th Street (*bet. Fifth & Eighth Aves*) ♿off map: Bargain stores, sportswear chains, ethnic stores, and the Studio Museum store.

■ Lower East Side & Chinatown [→14–17]

■ Tribeca [→18–20]

■ Soho [→21–26]

■ Nolita & Noho [→27–31]

■ East Village [→32–37]

■ West Village [→38–42]

■ Chelsea & the Meatpacking District [→43–47]

■ Gramercy Park & the Flatiron District [→48–51]

■ Midtown & Hell's Kitchen [→52–57]

■ Upper East Side [→58–61]

■ Upper West Side [→62–64]

■ Harlem & the Heights [→65–67]

■ Brooklyn [→68–71]

The epicentre of the shopping universe, New York has everything from big buck couture to bargain sneakers. If you can't find it here, you won't find it anywhere...

retail therapy

↓ department stores

shops

Barneys New York

Since the demise of its Downtown location, Barneys brilliant buyers continue to seek out the very best in modern design for the remaining Uptown outpost. Fashion-forward clothing by such luminaries as McQueen and Margiela line the racks upstairs. On the ground floor the collection of accessories is breathtaking, and the two shoe departments hold some of the most interesting footwear around. The annual warehouse sale is as anticipated by New Yorkers as fireworks on the Fourth of July. $$$

660 Madison Ave (at 61st St) ☎ 826-8900 Ⓜ E·F·N·R to 5th Ave ◐ 10am–8pm Mon–Sat (7pm Sat); 12–6pm Sun. 🖃 AE/MC/V

Bergdorf Goodman

For pure elegance, the one and only Bergdorf's is hard to top. Exclusives by designers such as Philip Treacy and Jo Malone attract fashionistas here likes bees to a honey pot. But don't be intimidated by the big names, there are inspiring lines of casualwear and accessories too. The men's version is across the street. $$$

754 Fifth Ave (at 58th St) ☎ 753-7300 Ⓜ N·R to 5th Ave ◐ 10am–6pm Mon–Sat (8pm Thu; 7pm Sat). 🖃 AE/MC/V

Bloomingdales

Bloomingdales (aka Bloomie's) has seen better days, but it's making an effort to catch up fashion-wise by including some high-end urbanwear by the likes of Sean John (that's Puff Daddy to you and me). It is still a key destination for New Yorkers looking for home furnishings. Make sure you check out the Barbie Boutique on the fifth floor, and the in-store chocolate factory on the sixth. $$–$$$

1000 Third Ave (at 59th St) ☎ 355-5900 Ⓜ N·R to Lexington Ave; 4·5·6 to 59th St ◐ 10am–8.30pm Mon–Sat (7pm Sat); 11am–7pm Sun. 🖃 AE/MC/V

Jeffrey

Jeffrey Kalinsky, the ex shoe-buyer at Barneys, has built up a huge following. With this 18,000 sq-ft repository of designer clothes, shoes, accessories and home products, Jeffrey has emerged to fill the void the now defunct Downtown Barneys left behind. Jil Sander, Helmut

Lang and Alexander McQueen are all on board. The store also carries its very own private unisex label: KR. The prices may be high, but can you put a cost on style? $$–$$$

449 W 14th Street (at Ninth Ave) Ⓜ A·C·E·L to 14th St 🖃 AE/MC/V

Macy's

Famous for its sponsorship of the annual Thanksgiving Day parade [→154], Macy's also claims to be the world's largest department store. There's virtually nothing you can't buy here. With brand names ranging from Armani to Zenith, as well as cheaper, casual lines, Macy's covers all the bases. The Cellar, in the basement of course, carries home furnishings and there's also Eatzi's, an excellent deli. Don't miss Macy's notorious one-day sales. $$–$$$

151 W 34th St (bet. Seventh Ave & Broadway) ☎ 695-4400 Ⓜ B·D·F·N·Q·R to 34th St-Herald Sq ◐ 10am–8.30pm Mon–Sat; 11am–7pm Sun. 🖃 AE/MC/V

Saks Fifth Avenue

Historic Saks should be visited as much for its famed setting on Fifth Avenue as anything else. Best for top-of-the-line custom menswear and the exhaustive (and exhausting) bridal section, but the shoe and lingerie departments are loaded with treasures too. Also worth discovering is the surprisingly cutting-edge women's fashion on the fifth floor. Don't miss Café SFA, perhaps the best in-store restaurant in NYC. $$–$$$

611 Fifth Ave (bet. 49th & 50th Sts) ☎ 753-4000 ◐ 10am–7pm Mon–Sat (8pm Thu; 6pm Sat); 12–6pm Sun. Ⓜ B·D·F·Q to 47–50th Sts-Rockefeller Center; E·F to 53rd St 🖃 all

Takashimaya

A very elegant Japanese department store, where every object has been carefully chosen. Whether you are looking for the perfect tea service, elegant home furnishings or an opulent piece of clothing, this is your store. The jungle-like garden shop on the ground floor is filled with fresh flowers by Christian Tortu, and the tea room in the basement is appropriately serene. $$–$$$

693 Fifth Ave (bet. 54th & 55th Sts) ☎ 350-0100 Ⓜ F to 53rd St ◐ 10am–7pm Mon–Sat. 🖃 all

New York, fashion capital of the USA, offers up a myriad of stylish options. Check out the glittering flagships of the major designers, or experiment with the city's edgy local names at funky one-off boutiques. You can spend a lot, or just a little, and still go home happy.

↓ fashion

for men & women

→ more shops

Anna Sui

Always young, fresh, fun and more than a little bit rock 'n' roll, Anna Sui's purple boutique in Soho is filled with clothes for the sartorially courageous, including a small men's collection popular with rock stars and male models. All of this NY designer's leather coats are perfection, her shoes are the funkiest, and the accessories legendary. Recently, Sui's own make-up line (including lots of sparkly nailpolish) has been added to the mix. $$

113 Greene St (bet. Prince & Spring Sts)
☎ 941-8406 🅼 N•R to Prince St ◑ *12–7pm daily (6pm Sun).* 🚍 AE/MC/V

APC

The high-style basics from this French design company keep all those fashion-insider types well-dressed. Classically-cut clothes are made in interesting, contemporary fabrics. Even the T-shirts and underwear are luxe. $$

131 Mercer St (bet. Prince & Spring Sts)
☎ 966-0069 🅼 N•R to Prince St ◑ *11am–7pm Mon–Sat; 12–6pm Sun.* 🚍 AE/MC/V

Calvin Klein ▲

In Klein's spartan house of minimalist chic, designed by trendy Brit architect John Pawson, you'll find the full complement of the designer's unfussy, clean-lined clothing for men and women. Also here is the cheaper CK line, a wide range of accessories (including a new handbag collection), plus the latest bed and bath range from one of America's favourite designers. $$–$$$

654 Madison Ave (at E 60th St) ☎ 292-9000
🅼 4•5•6 to 59th St ◑ *10am–6pm Mon–Sat (8pm Thu); 12–6pm Sun.* 🚍 AE

Commes des Garçons

The far west Chelsea shop of fashion pioneers Commes des Garçons is as happening as many of the area's trendy art galleries. The clothes are always experimental and beautifully-made and while all this fabulousness doesn't come cheap, Rei Kawakubo's brilliance makes every piece highly-collectible. $$$

520 W 22nd St (bet. Tenth & Eleventh Aves)
☎ 604-9200 🅼 C•E to 23rd St ◑ *11am–7pm Tue–Sat; 12–6pm Sun.* 🚍 all

Costume National

In a store that looks like the inside of a very dark, monochrome space ship, Ennio Capasso's clothes are streamlined, sexy and artistic. While the fashion is pure genius, everybody really wants the shoes. Terminally trendy, the men's styles, especially, are unique and very flattering. $–$$$

108 Wooster St (bet. Prince & Spring Sts)
☎ 431-1530 🅼 N•R to Prince St; C•E to Spring St ◑ *11am–7pm Mon–Sat; 12–6pm Sun.* 🚍 all

Diesel

The riotous Diesel flagship can sometimes seem as surreal as those ubiquitous adverts. Amidst the loud music and the 'art exhibits', you'll find urban, street-wise clothes that are casual with a cutting-edge twist. Even the underwear is trendy. Take a break from it all at the in-store café. $$

770 Lexington Ave (at 60th St) ☎ 308-0055
🅼 N•R to Lexington Ave-59th St ◑ *10am–8pm Mon–Sat; 12–6pm Sun.* 🚍 all

D/L Cerney

Based mostly on vintage wear from the 40's, 50's and 60's, the collection here features casual, inexpensive, and well-cut clothing in good fabrics. Strong on hand-tailored shirts, an essential basic, as well as blazers, fitted pants, and lots of feminine shift dresses. $–$$

222 West Broadway (bet. Prince & Spring Sts)
☎ 941-0530 🅼 N•R to Prince St ◑ *12–7pm Mon–Sat (11am Sat).* 🚍 AE/MC/V

Dolce & Gabbanna

The Italian design duo's fabulously sexy clothing will bring out the Sophia Loren (or Marcello Mastroanni) in you. Choose between the glamorous, high-end label, or the 'cheaper' D & G line which repeats themes from the Uptown collection like lavish embroidery and flashy metallics: Each collection has its own store. $$–$$$

825 Madison Ave (bet. 68th & 69th Sts)
☎ 249-4100 🚇 6 to 68th St-Hunter College
🕐 *10am–6pm Mon–Sat (7pm Thu).*
💳 AE/MC/V

434 W Broadway (bet. Prince & Spring Sts)
☎ 966-2868 🚇 B•D•F•Q to Boadway-Lafayette
🕐 *11am–7pm Mon–Sat; 12–6pm Sun.*
💳 AE/MC/V

DKNY

Donna Karan's new flagship is just across the street from her all-American rival Calvin Klein. This is where she keeps her younger, DKNY line – the shapes borrow from classic sportwear silhouettes and the T-shirts make a great New York souvenir. $$

655 Madison Avenue, opening in Aug
☎ 768-5800
🚇 4•5•6 to 59th St

Emporio Armani

Armani is synonymous with Italian high-style. Minimalist chic from the master means simple shapes, decorated with lots of glitter and shine, and classic men's suits in rich fabrics. Downtown at the Armani Exchange, Italian ingenuity is applied to more sporty designs. $–$$$

760 Madison Ave (bet. 65th & 66th Sts)
☎ 988-9191 🚇 6 to 68th St-Hunter College
🕐 *10am–6pm Mon–Sat (7pm Thu).* 💳 AE/MC/V
110 Fifth Ave (at 16th St) ☎ 727-3240
🚇 L•N•R•4•5•6 to 14th St-Union Sq 🕐 *11am–8pm Mon–Sat (7pm Sat); 12–6pm Sun.* 💳 all

Gucci ✎

Tom Ford, who has radically changed the Gucci look, never fails to impress with his sensual, of-the-moment clothes for both sexes. The severely stylish also hanker after the amazing shoes and unbelievably tasteful home furnishings. $$$

10 W 57th St (bet. Fifth & Sixth Aves) ☎ 826-2600 🚇 E•F to 5th Ave 🕐 *9.30am–6pm Mon–Sat (7.30pm Thu); 12–6pm Sun.* 💳 all

Helmut Lang

Lang (say it Long) is beloved of fashionable New Yorkers, who never say no to lots of expensive black designs in 'interesting' shapes. The spartan store houses his stark, poetic clothing including stunning men's suits and seemingly simple, yet high-constructed, frocks for women.$$$

80 Greene Street (bet. Broome & Spring Sts)
☎ 925-7214 🚇 6 to Spring St; N•R to Prince St
🕐 *11am–7pm Mon–Sat; 12–6pm Sun.*
💳 AE/MC/V

Hotel Venus

The Soho outlet for Downtown style maven Patricia Field, this is the place for outlandish, clubby wear with a dash of class. Hotel Venus carries labels like Courrèges and Stephen Sprouse, plenty of fetish-inspired outerwear, stilettos, adorable accessories from Japan, and rhinestones for every occasion. $–$$

382 W Broadway (bet. Broome & Spring Sts)
☎ 966-4066 🚇 A•C to Spring St 🕐 *12–8pm daily.* 💳 AE/MC/V

If Soho New York

With an intriguing mix of international fashion icons and brilliant newcomers, If Soho New York really gives any serious shopper a taste of the truly avant-garde. The entire Commes des Garçons collection is here, along with Martin Margiela and Dries Van Noten, plus edgy local stars Mark Kroeker and Susan Cianciolo. $$$

94 Grand St (bet. Greene & Mercer Sts)
☎ 334-4964 🚇 N•R to Prince St; C•E to Spring St 🕐 *11am–7pm daily (6.30 Sun).* 💳 AE/MC/V

Prada

No matter which lime green Prada store you happen into, plan on spending big bucks for some of the most modish clothes available anywhere. While her bags, shoes and shapes are endlessly imitated in the chain stores, Miuccia Prada's original and clean-lined designs for men and women are worth every penny. $$$

841 Madison Ave (at 70th St) ☎ 327-4200
🚇 6 to 68th St-Hunter College 🕐 *10am–6pm Mon–Sat (7pm Thu).* 💳 AE/MC/V Other branches, phone for details.

Prada Sport

For those who worship at the altar of Prada, this latest addition to Muiccia's empire is a must. Filled with highly-designed sport clothes, utility wear and shoes. $$

116 Wooster St (bet. Prince & Spring Sts) ☎ 925-2221 🚇 N•R to Prince St; C•E to Spring St 🕐 *11am–7pm Mon–Sat; 12–6pm Sun.* 💳 AE/MC/V

Ralph Lauren

This historic, Upper East Side mansion provides the perfect environment for Ralph Lauren's classic look for men and women. Just as the setting appropriates the trappings of an English country castle, the clothing encorporates old world elegance with new world ease. The Polo Sport store (with its sporty creations) is just across the avenue. $$–$$$

867 Madison Ave (at 72nd St)
☎ 606-2100 🚇 6 to 68th St-Hunter College
🕐 *10am–6pm Mon–Sat.* 💳 AE/MC/V

Shanghai Tang ⚑

Ultra-luxe clothes from China are the main attraction in this impressive, brightly-coloured art-deco store, which includes an in-store tailor who makes up garments in rich, expensive silks (3rd flr). There are lots of mandarin-style jackets and gorgeous cashmere sweaters and a few, select home furnishings too. $–$$

667 Madison Ave (bet. 61st & 62nd Sts)
☎ 888-0111 🚇 N•R to 5th Ave ◗ 10.15am–7pm Mon–Sat; 12–6pm Sun. 💳 AE/MC/V

Steven-Alan

The eponymous owner is famous for his ability to sniff out new, young design talent before anybody else. His main women's store regularly showcases young designers who combine casual chic with a Downtown aesthetic. $$

60 Wooster St (bet. Broome & Spring Sts)
☎ 334-6354 🚇 N•R to Prince St; C•E to Spring St ◗ 1–8pm daily. 💳 AE/MC/V
330 E 11th St (bet. 1st & 2nd Aves) ☎ 982-2881 🚇 N•R to 8th St; 6 to Astor Pl ◗ 1–8pm Tue–Sun. 💳 AE/MC/V Other branches (menswear and outlet stores), phone for details.

Untitled

Nestled among the inexpensive shoe shops on 8th Street, this two-storey abode carries a selection of clothes from hot, young designers from around the globe. Upstairs, the duds are mostly for dudes, and include desirable gear by Dirk Bikkemberg, Martin Margiela, John Richmond, Gaultier and more. Downstairs, the women's clothes are equally illustrious and the accessories are divine. $$

26 W 8th St (bet. Fifth & Sixth Aves) ☎ 505-9725 🚇 A•B•C•D•E•F•Q to W 4th St-Washington Sq ◗ 11.30am–9pm Mon–Sat; 12–9pm Sun. 💳 AE/MC/V

Versace

Beloved by exhibitionist types (including lots of celebs), the entire Versace collection shines in a multi-level shop that is as lavish and vivid as the clothes it contains. Even if the colossal price tags are out of your league, stop in just for the wild Versace experience. $$$

815 Madison Ave (at 68th St) ☎ 744-6868 🚇 6 to 68thSt-Hunter College ◗ 10am–6pm Mon–Sat (7pm Thu). 💳 AE/MC/V Flagship at 645 5th Ave (bet. 51st & 52nd Sts) ☎ 317-0224 for details.

Vivienne Westwood

British icon Vivienne Westwood has opened her first store stateside. The space (once a Soho art gallery) is filled with the entire range of Westwood's quirky English tailoring, including the hard-to-find Anglomania collection, and her newest Oceania sportswear. There are also loads of distinctive bags. $$$

71 Greene St (bet. Broome & Spring Sts)
☎ 334-1500 🚇 N•R to Prince St ◗ 11am–7pm Mon–Sat; 12–6pm Sun. 💳 AE/MC/V

Yohji Yamamoto

Yamamoto's all-white shrine of a store pushes forward the boundaries of fashion – so no wonder the sales help behave as if every item were a work of art. Consistently inventive and suprisingly wearable, Yamamoto's designs are like nothing else you'll see. $$$

103 Grand St (at Mercer St) ☎ 966-9066 🚇 J•M•N•R•Z•6 to Canal St ◗ 11am–7pm Mon–Sat; 12–6pm Sun. 💳 all

men's fashion

Nova USA

Nova offers occasionally severe, sporty clothes (like the perfect drawstring pants), meant for men, but worn by lots of women who appreciate the classic cut. $–$$

100 Stanton St (at Ludlow St) ☎ 228-6844 🚇 F to 2nd Ave ◗ 11am–8pm Mon–Sat; 12–7pm Sun. 💳 AE/MC/V

Paul Smith

Paul Smith's clothes are classically English but slightly wacky. His sweaters and shirts are highly-designed and made from luxe (ie expensive) materials, the ties often whimsical, and the suits amazing for both style and quality. There is a wonderful selection of toney accessories too. $$

108 Fifth Ave (bet. 15th & 16th Sts) ☎ 627-9770 🚇 L•N•R•4•5•6 to 14th St-Union Sq ◗ 11am–7pm Mon–Sat (8pm Thu); 12–6pm Sun. 💳 AE/MC/V

Sean

A recent addition to the menswear scene, Sean offers sporty clothes that are stylish without trying too hard. Ranging from corduroy shirts to tailored jackets, everything here is very wearable, with reasonable price tags. $$

132 Thompson St (bet. Houston & Prince Sts) ☎ 598-5980 🚇 Prince St ◗ 12–7pm daily (6pm Sun). 💳 all

➔ more shops

Yves Saint Laurent Rive Gauche

The elegant and spacious store is one of the few really stylish men-only outlets in Soho. With a new designer (Hedi Slimane) at the wheel, YSL Men is recycling the classics, but there's also a modern (and very dapper) aesthetic for guys who aren't afraid to make a fashion statement. $$$

88 Wooster St (bet. Broome & Spring Sts)
☎ 274-0522 🚇 N•R to Prince St; C•E to Spring St ◑ 11am–7pm Mon–Sat; 12–6pm Sun. 🚪 AE/MC/V

women's fashion

Antique Boutique

This space-age store offers some of the best Downtown fashion around. There are lots of up-and-coming local designers represented, plus many burgeoning European stars too. Things are grouped according to colour rather than designer, and err towards the avant-garde. $$

712 Broadway (bet. Astor Pl & 4th St)
☎ 460-8830 🚇 N•R to 8th St; 6 to Astor Pl ◑ 11am–10pm Mon–Sat; 12–8pm Sun. 🚪 all

Betsey Johnson

Soho fashion pioneer (and survivor), Betsey Johnson, has decorated her flagship store in her signature and ultra-girly flower print, and it looks a bit like an upscale bordello. The clothes are directed at femmes of all shapes, sizes and ages: when you wear one of Betsey's frocks, you know you'll have lots of fun. $$

138 Wooster St (at Prince St) ☎ 995-5048
🚇 N•R to Prince St ◑ 11am–7pm Mon–Sat; 12–7pm Sun. 🚪 AE/MC/V Other branches, phone for details.

Calypso St Barths

This store is filled with a vibrant collection of truly pretty and feminine clothes from various designers. Along with the I-enjoy-being-a-girl outfits, there are brilliant little bags and accessories that can make getting dressed up a pleasure. Owner Christiane Celle's mini-empire also includes Jamin Puech [→108]. $$

280 Mott St (bet. Houston & Prince Sts)
☎ 274-0449 🚇 B•D•F•Q to Broadway-Lafayette St; 6 to Bleecker St ◑ 11am–7pm Mon–Sat; 12–6pm Sun. 🚪 all

Catherine

Well-known Parisian stylist, Catherine Maladrino has created a shop that looks like a very groovy, mid-60's living room. It's filled with colour-coordinated clothes that range from pretty beaded skirts to leathers, and lots of perfect tops to complete the outfit. Maladrino is also known for her high-style cowgirl hat in an array of pastel colours. $$

468 Broome St (bet. Greene & Mercer Sts)
☎ 927-6765 🚇 N•R to Prince St; C•E to Spring St ◑ 11am–7pm Mon–Sat; 12–6pm Sun. 🚪 AE/MC/V

Cynthia Rowley

Cute, sexy and all-girl is the theme at this wild and eclectic store. New York designer, Rowley does dresses the best: pretty fabrics, lots of beading and colour, plus cute accessories like charm bracelets and lipstick bags. Don't miss the fantastic collection of very femme shoes. $$

112 Wooster St (bet. Prince & Spring Sts),
☎ 334-1144 🚇 N•R to Prince St ◑ 11am–7pm Mon–Sat (8pm Thu–Fri); 12–6pm Sun. 🚪 all

Daryl K

Transplanted from Ireland, Daryl K has become an international style luminary with a huge, celebrity following (so much so her clothes are endlessley imitated by Seventh Avenue designers). In her futuristic cavern-of-a-store are sophisticated clothes under the Daryl K label, as well as funky and less-expensive pants and tops from her K-189 collection. $$

21 Bond St (at Lafayette St) ☎ 777-0713
🚇 6 to Astor Pl; N•R to Prince St ◑ 12–7pm daily. 🚪 AE/MC/V

Fendi

The fabulous Fendi sisters continue to create super-stylish, offbeat clothes, using lots of fake fur and funky leather. But what everyone craves, season after season, are the 'baguette' bags, designed by Karl Lagerfeld, decorated with big 'F' buckles and even bigger price tags. $$$

720 Fifth Ave (at 56th St) ☎ 767-0100
🚇 E•F to 5th Ave ◑ 10am–6pm Mon–Sat (7pm Thu). 🚪 all

Issey Miyake Pleats Please

The store itself is as entertaining as the merch within – check out the windows which change from clear to opaque as you walk by. The clothes, which come in neutrals and bright patterns, are all totally pleated, and slide on the body like a second skin. It's a distinctive look, if you're feeling especially experimental. $$

128 Wooster St (at Prince St) ☎ 226-3600
🚇 N•R to Prince St; C•E to Spring St ◑ 11am–7pm Mon–Sat (6pm Sun). 🚪 AE/MC/V

Marc Jacobs

Marc Jacobs has made a name for himself as the premier young American designer. Having been dubbed 'the new Calvin Klein', Jacobs lives up to the moniker with refined, minimalist designs that are continuously fun, fresh, and really expensive. His cashmere sweaters are so popular, there's rumoured to be a long waiting list to get one. $$$

163 Mercer St (bet. Houston & Prince Sts)
☎ 343-1490 🚇 N•R to Prince St ◑ 11am–7pm Mon–Sat; 12–6pm Sun. 🚪 all

Miu Miu

This is the younger, sexier, slightly less expensive line from Prada. There are lots of little skirts, tops, dresses and coats that are modern yet flirtatious, with unique bags to match. Check out the super-trendy shoes too. $$

100 Prince St (bet. Greene & Mercer Sts)
☎ 334-5156 Ⓜ N•R to Prince St ◑ 11am–7pm Mon–Sat, 12pm–6pm Sun. 🖃 all

Morgan Le Fay

The world of Morgan Le Fay is totally original: meant to be layered, one piece on top of the other, the clothes are gypsy-meets-fairytale princess. This look is meant for the supremely-confident artsy type who likes to be noticed. $$$

151 Spring St (at Broome St)
☎ 925-0144 Ⓜ N•R to Prince St; C•E to Spring St ◑ 11am–7pm daily. 🖃 AC/MC/V

Olive & Bette ◄

In this cute neighbourhood shop (there's a sister store on the UES), the focus is on happening young designers like Daryl K and Vivienne Tam, along with genius jeans from Earl, those must-have T-shirts from 3 Dot and the most recent thing from Fiorucci. $–$$

252 W 72nd St (at Columbus Avenue)
☎ 579-2178 Ⓜ B•C to 72nd St
◑ 11am–7pm Mon–Sun. 🖃 AE/MC/V

Scoop

One of Downtown's favourite fashion outposts. Owner Stephanie Grenfield's taste in clothing runs from girly frocks to bold separates: young designers from New York and Europe are the lure, with lots of cute accessories to finish the look. Don't miss colourful T-shirts by Juicy USA – the best bargains in the store. $$

532 Broadway (bet. Prince & Spring Sts),
☎ 925-2886 Ⓜ C•E to Spring St ◑ 11am–8pm daily (7pm Sun). 🖃 all
Branch in UES, phone for details.

TG-170

Owner Terri Gillis was one of the original pioneers in the now happening LES fashion scene. This is one of the most distinctive and edgy collections in any store in New York, and many a designer has been launched here. The prices are impressively low for all this daring style. $–$$

170 Ludlow St (bet. Houston & Stanton Sts)
☎ 995-8660 Ⓜ F to 2nd Ave ◑ 1–8pm daily.
🖃 AE/MC/V

Tracey Feith

The interior here is all elegant dark wood and white walls – the perfect place to display Feith's colourful and seductive dresses, many of them inspired by vintage silhouettes and fabrics. There are darling shoes and bags, and plenty of room for Raj, the designer's less-expensive, hippie-gypsy clothes, that all Downtown girls love. $$

209 Mulberry St (bet. Broome & Spring Sts)
☎ 334-3097 Ⓜ C•E to Spring St
◑ 11am–7pm daily. 🖃 AE/MC/V

→ more shops

chain stores

Once a suburban phenomenon, chain stores have become the first port of call for affordable copycat fashion. Indeed, it's not unusual to see catwalk trends translated to the chains before they reach the actual designer stores. The best places to look for the big names are Broadway (bet. 8th & Canal Sts), Herald Square, Fifth and Sixth Avenues, Lexington Avenue (bet. 57th & 61st Sts) Soho, South Street Seaport and the World Trade Center. Most carry both men's and women's apparel as well as footwear and accessories.

*All-American department store, **Kmart**, is one of the best-priced with rock bottom bargains for the entire family. Also for all ages, the ubiquitous, unisex **Gap** features reasonably-priced understated basics like chinos and white T-shirts. The prime store is on Herald Square. **Old Navy** is in the same vein with even cheaper prices. **J Crew** and **Banana Republic** are good bets for time-*

*less casualwear. But the more upbeat **XOXO** carries sexy clothing for female style vixens, while **Guess?** features the same sexy look at a higher price point. Other mid-priced stores include: **Express**, mainstream fashion for women, and its male counterpart, **Structure**. For streetwear, **Urban Outfitters** lives up to its name, offering the latest youth-oriented fashions. **Zara** injects a bit of European flair with its sleek separates, casualwear and shoes. **Club Monaco** and **French Connection** fit into the slightly more upscale and interesting, but still reasonably-priced, category. For something more rugged **Eddie Bauer** handles outdoorwear for men and women, while the more buttoned-down will appreciate the conservative **Brooks Bros** tailored suits. Its Wall Street style goes a long way with men, and the line of preppy womenswear is building momentum.*

↓ shoes

Europeans may be surprised to find the selection of footwear on offer in New York is not as great as the choice at home, but, hey, the sneakers are cheap (for good deals, trek up Broadway between Canal Street as far as 8th Street). If your credit is limitless, however, and you aren't afraid of vertigo, **Manolo Blahnik's** heels are the kind no *Vogue* editor leaves the house without. In the same ultra-luxury category, Brit **Jimmy Choo** has just opened a snazzy, new boutique to house his collection of pretty heels and mules. Fellow European **Stephane Kélian's** more outlandish creations are in the same, high-end price bracket. Along the block on Madison is the recently opened **Tod's** store. The brand's beloved (and expensive) leather 'driving loafer' is the kind worn by slumming movie stars.

Less pricey and infinitely more inventive are the 60's-style, mod designs on offer at **Sigerson Morrison**, one of the best little shoe stores in town. **Jutta Neuman's** handmade sandals are also a bit of a bargain, considering the work that's gone into them. Career shoe shoppers, however, depend on the **Tootsi Plohound** mini-chain for the best selection of high-fashion shoes by various big names such as Freelance. You can actually find the entire **Freelance** range of imaginative footwear at their Soho store. For bargains, you'll

have to head for 8th Street between Sixth Avenue and Broadway, where upwards of 20 one-off stores line the blocks (try **Le Petit Peton** for starters). And if your feet are worn out after looking for something to slip them into, you can get complimentary reflexology at the new **Rockport** 'concept' store in Soho where, thankfully, comfy footwear is the lure.

Freelance
155 Spring St (bet. W Broadway & Wooster St) ☎ 965-9231 ⓜ C·E to Spring St ◐ 11.30am–7.30pm Mon–Fri; 11am–8pm Sat; 12–7pm Sun. ⊟ all $–$$

Jimmy Choo
645 Fifth Ave (at 51st St) ☎ 593-0800 ⓜ E·F to 5th Ave ◐ 10am–6pm Mon–Sat. ⊟ all $$$

Jutta Neumann
317 E 9th St (bet. 1st & 2nd Aves) ☎ 982-7048 ⓜ 6 to Astor Pl ◐ 12–8pm Tue–Sat. ⊟ all $–$$

Le Petit Peton
27 W 8th St (bet. 5th & 6th Aves) ☎ 677-3730 ⓜ A·B·C·D·E·F·Q to W 4th St–Washington Sq ◐ 11am–9pm Mon–Sat; 12–8.30pm Sun. ⊟ AE/MC/V $

Manolo Blahnik
31 W 54th St (bet. Fifth & Sixth Aves) ☎ 582-3007 ⓜ E·F to 5th Ave ◐ 10.30am–6pm Mon–Fri (5pm Sat). ⊟ AE/MC/V $$$

Rockport
465 W Broadway (bet. Prince & W Houston Sts) ☎ 529-0209 ⓜ N·R to Prince St ◐ 11am–7pm Mon– Sat; 12–6pm Sun. ⊟ AE/MC/V $–$$

Stephane Kélian
717 Madison Ave (bet. 63rd & 64th Sts) ☎ 980-1919 ⓜ N·R to 5th Ave ◐ 10am–6pm Mon–Sat. ⊟ all $$$

Sigerson Morrison
242 Mott Street (bet. Houston & Prince Sts) ☎ 219-3893 ⓜ B·D·F·Q to Broadway-Lafayette ◐ 11am–7pm Mon–Fri; 12–6pm Sun. ⊟ all $–$$

Tod's
650 Madison Ave (bet. 59th & 60th Sts) ☎ 644-5945 ⓜ N·R to 5th Ave ◐ 10am–6pm Mon–Sat (7pm Thu); 12–5pm Sun. ⊟ all $$$

Tootsi Plohound
413 W Broadway (bet. Prince & Spring Sts) ☎ 925-8931 ⓜ N·R to Prince St; 6 to Spring St ◐ 10.45am–8.30pm Mon–Sat; 11.30am–7.30pm Sun. ⊟ all $$–$$$ Other branches, phone for details

shoe chains

The ubiquitous **Nine West** always has plenty of well-priced styles which 'pay hommage' to the likes of Prada and Gucci. **9 & Co** is just as fashion-friendly, and in an even cheaper price bracket. **Kenneth Cole** is a favourite with smart, young New Yorkers of both sexes who appreciate his cool, wearable styles and general affordability (his bags and sharp separates are here too). Far more ostentacious are the platforms and fun sneakers on offer at **Steve Madden**, whose shoes are beloved of the dazed and confused set. **Sacco** is an excellent outpost for women's shoes and boots – although prices are a little higher than some of the other chains, sophistication is the payoff. For a more conservative look, **Joan & David** has a reliable selection with price tags to match. **Juno's** carries more edgy footwear, as well as a competitive selection of men's shoes. But for the ultimate bargain, **Payless** has footwear for men women for as little as $10. Just don't expect these shoes to outlive the month.

↓ vintage & secondhand

It's tough finding deals on vintage and antique clothing in New York where savvy store owners tend to know the value of a decent pair of used Levis. Although you might find some 'deadstock' (never-before worn vintage clothing), most stuff is pre-owned, so inspect all clothes well

before purchasing as most places have a final sale only policy. The flea markets are a good place to start; after that, head to the East Village and the Lower East Side where you'll find the biggest concentration of stores. **Resurrection** is crammed with museum-quality antique and vin-

tage pieces, which acts as a magnet to shoppers and stylists. At **Timtoum**, the eclectic mix is more laid back and less expensive. Along the block, **Cherry** is a store devoted to collectible clothing and accessories (sometimes complete with original tags) from post-World War II forward.

shops

Elsewhere, **Stella Dallas,** in the West Village, has a girly collection of dresses, slips and nighties from the 30's and 40's at reasonable prices. **Darrow 7's** ↖ immaculate womenswear from the 40's to the 70's, including a great selection of shoes and hats, is a little more expensive, but of very high quality. In Noho, **Screaming Mimi's** and the **Center for the Dull** are both purveyors of groovy yet chic threads, shoes, sunglasses and bags from the 60's, 70's and 80's. Hit the lower level of **Canal Jeans** on Broadway to find racks of vintage Levis, polyester shirts, jackets and accessories at OK prices.

Consignment shops can also yield good buys. **Tokio 7** offers a broad spectrum of carefully-worn designer clothes with an avant-garde edge. But for the finest selection of preowned designer duds, go to **Ina,** which has stores for both men (Nolita) and women (Soho).

True bargains are to be found at **Housing Works Thrift Shop** and **Out of the Closet,** where the clothing (especially men's suits), books, furniture and trinkets are exceptionally low in price. Both stores benefit AIDS charities.

Canal
504 Broadway (bet. Spring & Broome Sts) ☎ 226-1130 Ⓜ 6 to Spring St; N·R to Prince St ◑ 9.30am–8pm Mon–Sat (9pm Fri–Sat); 10am–8pm Sun. ⊟ all $

Center for the Dull
216 Lafayette St (bet. Spring & Broome Sts) ☎ 925-9699 Ⓜ 6 to Spring St ◑ 12–7pm daily. ⊟ all $–$$

Cherry
185 Orchard St (bet. Houston & Stanton Aves) ☎ 358-7131 Ⓜ F to 2nd Ave ◑ mid Apr–Nov: 12–9pm Sun–Wed; 12–midnight Thu–Sat (call for winter hours). ⊟ AE/V/MC $–$$

Darrow 7
W 19th St (bet. 5th & 6th Aves) ☎ 255-1550 Ⓜ F·N·R to 23rd St ◑ 11am–7pm Mon–Sat (by appointment only Sun). ⊟ AE/MC/V $–$$

Housing Works Thrift Shop
143 W 17th St (bet. 6th & 7th Aves) ☎ 366-0820 Ⓜ 1·9 to 18th St ◑ 10am–6pm Mon–Sat; 12–5pm Sun. ⊟ AE/MC/V $

Ina
101 Thompson St (bet. Spring & Prince Sts) ☎ 941-4757 Ⓜ A·C·E to Spring St; N·R to Prince St ◑ 12–7pm daily ⊟ AE/MC/V $$
Also branch in Nolita, phone for details.

Out of the Closet
220 E 81st St (bet. 2nd & 3rd Aves) ☎ 472-3573 Ⓜ 4·5·6 to 86th St ◑ 10am–5pm Tue–Sat. ⊟ none $–$$

Resurrection
123 E 7th St (bet. 1st Ave & Ave A) ☎ 228-0063 Ⓜ F to 2nd Ave; L to 1st Ave; 6 to Astor Pl ◑ 1am–9pm daily (8pm Sun). ⊟ AE/MC/V $$
Also branch in Nolita, phone for details.

Screaming Mimi's
382 Lafayette St (at E 4th St) ☎ 677-6464 Ⓜ N·R to 8th St; 6 to Astor Pl ◑ 12–8pm daily (6pm Sun). ⊟ all $–$$

Stella Dallas
218 Thompson St (bet. Bleecker & W 3rd Sts) ☎ 674-0447 Ⓜ A·B·C·D·E·F·Q to W 4th St–Washington Sq ◑ 12–7pm daily. ⊟ AE/MC/V $–$$

Timtom
167 Orchard St (bet. E Houston & Stanton Sts) ☎ 780-0456 Ⓜ F to 2nd Ave ◑ 1–8pm daily. ⊟ MC/V $–$$

Tokio 7
64 E 7th St (bet. 1st & 2nd Aves) ☎ 353-8443 Ⓜ 6 to Astor Pl ◑ 12–8.30pm daily. ⊟ AE/MC/V $$

shops

---

discount stores

Century 21
Even Uptown fashionistas aren't beneath shopping at this infamous clearing house. The store features 16 departments with most designer names at 25–75% off, but it's a real endurance test to pluck the diamonds from the trash.

22 Cortlandt St (bet. Broadway & Church St) ☎ 227-9092 Ⓜ N·R·1·9 to Cortlandt St ◑ 7.45am–7.30 Mon–Fri (8.30pm Thu, 8pm Fri); 10am–7.30pm Sat. ⊟ all $–$$ Also branch in Brooklyn, phone for details.

Daffy's
The masters of the outfit for under $100. Fight your way through the overcrowded racks for eveningwear, lingerie, and men's and women's clothes and shoes.

131 Broadway (at 34th St) ☎ 736-4477 Ⓜ B·D·F·N·Q·R to 34th St–Herald Sq ◑ 10am–9pm Mon–Sat (8pm Sat); 11am–7pm Sun. ⊟ all $–$$ Other branches, phone for details.

Loehmann's
Known for carrying tremendous high-end designer merchandise from DKNY, Versace, Dries van Noten and many more – all at eye-popping prices.

101 Seventh Ave (bet 16th & 17th Sts) ☎ 353-0856 Ⓜ 1·9 to 18th St ◑ 9am–9pm Mon–Sat; 11am–7pm Sun. ⊟ all $–$$
Other branches, phone for details.

SSS Nice Price
Each week several designers offer up delicious samples, old and new, at below bargain prices. Marc Jacobs, Donna Karen, Urban Outfitters, and Kenar have all tested their wares here.

134 W 37th St (bet. Broadway & Seventh Ave) ☎ 947-8748 Ⓜ 1·2·3·9 to 34th St–Penn Stn ◑ times vary, phone ahead ⊟ AE/MC/V $–$$

➔ more shops

↓ accessories

bags

Jamin Puech

Entirely precious bags by this Parisian designer in jewel-like colours are housed in a gorgeous, teeny boutique. $$$

252 Mott St (bet. Houston & Prince Sts) ☎ 334-9730 Ⓜ B•D•F•Q to Broadway-Lafayette St ◑ 11am–7pm Mon–Sat; 12–7pm Sun. ✉ all

Kate Spade

Kate Spade's adorable bags are a New York status symbol, and range from everyday to evening glam. $$

454 Broome St (at Mercer St) ☎ 274-1991 Ⓜ N•R to Prince St; C•E to Spring St ◑ 11am–7pm Mon–Sat; 12–6pm Sun. ✉ all

Manhattan Portage

The bag brand that's been so popular in Europe is finally making an impact at home. Stop by to find backpacks and DJ bags in the strongest canvas and lots of colours. $

333 E 9th St (bet. 1st & 2nd Aves) ☎ 594-7068 Ⓜ 6 to Astor Place ◑ 11am–7pm daily. ✉ all

eyewear

Robert Marc

A New York staple for excellent eyewear, this tiny chain has a good selection including hard-to-find makes like Prosh and Beausoliel. $$–$$$

1300 Madison Ave (at 92nd St) ☎ 722-1600 Ⓜ 6 to 96th St ◑ 9.30am–6pm Mon–Sat; 12–5.30 Sun. ✉ all Other branches, call for details

Selima Optique

Selima's sexy, sleek line of eyewear is known for its cult-like following of everyone from the Dior-clad lady to edgy hipsters. There are loads of other designer frames too. $–$$

59 Wooster St (at Broome St) ☎ 343-9490 Ⓜ C•E to Spring St ◑ 11am–7pm Mon–Sat (8pm Thu); 12–7pm Sun. ✉ all Other branches, phone for details

hats

Amy Downs

Her hats are outrageous and take a degree of courage to wear; some make you think the Cat in the Hat went couture. $–$$

103 Stanton St (at Ludlow St) ☎ 598-4189 Ⓜ F to 2nd Ave ◑ 1–6pm Wed–Sun. ✉ all

Kelly Christie

Beautifully crafted, handmade hats, there's something for everyone. $–$$

235 Elizabeth St (bet. Houston & Prince Sts) ☎ 965-0686 Ⓜ N•R to Prince St ◑ 12–7pm daily (to 6pm Sun). ✉ all

jewellery

Bond 07

Another store by the owner of Selima Optique. This one is filled with divine accessories (hats, glasses, shoes and trinkets), including lots of unique and beautiful jewellery. All irresistible. $$

7 Bond St (bet. Broadway & Lafayette St) ☎ 677-8487 Ⓜ 6 to Bleecker St; B•D•F•Q to Broadway-Lafayette St

◑ 11am–7pm Mon–Fri; 12–7pm Sun. ✉ all

Fragments

Owner's Goldman and Moore keep this pretty Soho store filled with the inventive creations of 30 or so designers. Expect anything from Indian beadwork to rhinestone-studded bracelets, and even the occasional diamond. $$

107 Greene St (bet. Prince & Spring Sts) ☎ 334-9588 Ⓜ 6 to Spring St; N•R to Prince St ◑ 11am–7pm Mon–Sat; 12–6 Sun. ✉ all

sports gear

Foot Locker

901 Sixth Ave (at 33rd St) ☎ 268-7146 Ⓜ B•D•F•N•Q•R to 34th St-Herald Sq ◑ 10am–8pm Mon–Sat; 11am–6pm Sun. ✉ all Other branches, phone for details $

Modell's

901 Sixth Ave (at 33rd St) ☎ 594-1830 Ⓜ B•D•F•N•Q•R to 34th St-Herald Sq ◑ 10am–8pm Mon–Sat; 11am–6pm Sun. ✉ all Other branches, phone for details $

Paragon

876 Broadway (at 18th St) ☎ 255-8036 Ⓜ L•N•R•4•5•6 to 14th St-Union Sq ◑ 10am–8pm Mon–Sat; 11am–6.30pm Sun. ✉ all $–$$

Reebok Concept Store

160 Columbus Ave (bet. 67th & 68th Sts) ☎ 595-1480 Ⓜ 1•9 to 66th St ◑ 10am–8pm Mon–Sat; 12–6pm Sun. ✉ all $–$$$

---

theme stores

Disney Store

Strictly for kids and their adult companions, Disney is Mickey and more in an OTT setting. $–$$

210 W 42nd St (bet. 7th & 8th Aves) ☎ 221-0430 Ⓜ A•C•E•N•R•1•2•3•7•9 to 42nd St ◑ 10am–9pm Mon–Sat (midnight Wed–Sat); 12–10pm Sun. ✉ all Other branches, phone for details

Niketown

At this temple to the 'swoosh', the experience of visiting is invigorating, even if the service is slow. $–$$

6 E 57th St (bet. 5th & Madison Aves) ☎ 891-6453

Ⓜ E•F•N•R to 5th Ave ◑ 10am–8pm Mon–Sat; 11am–6pm Sun. ✉ AE/MC/V

Original Levi's Store

Four floors of this all-American brand, including non-denim clothing and accessories. Can't find a pair that fits? The store will custom-make some for you. $–$$

3 E 57th St (bet. 5th & Madison Aves) ☎ 838-2188 Ⓜ E•F•N•R to 5th Ave; B•Q to 57th St ◑ 10am–8pm Mon–Sat; 12–6pm Sun. ✉ all

Sony Style

Shop for gadgets or simply test drive the Playstations

in this technophile's paradise. $–$$$

550 Madison Ave (bet. 55th & 56th Sts) ☎ 833-8800 Ⓜ 4•5•6 to 51st St; E•F to 5th Ave ◑ 10am–6pm Tue–Sat (9pm Thu); 12–6pm Sun. ✉ all

Warner Bros Studio Store

Products galore from the WB's cartoons, movies and TV shows plus interactive games on the top floor.

1 E 57th St (at 5th Ave) ☎ 754-0305 Ⓜ E•F•N•R to 5th Ave; B•Q to 57th St; 4•5•6 to 59th St ◑ 10am–8pm Mon–Sat; 12–8pm Sun. ✉ all $–$$

↓ beauty

Aveda

This elegant space is easily the best smelling store in the world. If you're not going for Aveda's amazing hair care, aromabath and body collection, pop in for, at the very least, the soothing environment. The hair salon is upstairs, the spa is nearby on Spring Street. $$

456 W Broadway (bet. Houston & Prince Sts) ☎ 473-0280 🚇 C·E to Spring St; N·R to Prince St; 1·9 to Houston St ◑ 10am–9pm Sun–Thu (7pm Sun); 9am–8pm Fri–Sat. 💳 AE/MC/V Also a branch in Midtown, phone for details

Bigelow Pharmacy

Founded in 1838, Bigelow's boasts a thoroughly modern variety of beauty products (hair accessories, essential oils, homeopathic remedies, and lots of good make-up). Spot the celebs at this quintessential West Village pharmacy. $$

414 Sixth Ave (bet. 8th & 9th Sts) ☎ 533-2700 🚇 A·B·C·D·E·F·Q to W 4th St-Washington Sq ◑ 7.30am–9pm Mon–Fri; 8.30am–7pm Sat; 8.30am–5.30pm Sun. 💳 AE/MC/V

Bliss Spa

While the who's who is making a bee-line to Bliss for spa treatments, the real treat at this chichi oasis is the boutique. All of the products are hand-picked by the spa's owner, skin-guru Marcia Kilgore. In addition to lines like Decleor and Yonka, Bliss sells everything you ever wanted beauty-wise, like upscale tooth-whitening paste and an at-home paraffin manicure kit. $$$

2nd flr, 568 Broadway (bet. Houston & Prince Sts) ☎ 219-8970 🚇 N·R to Prince St; B·D·F·Q to Broadway-Lafayette St; 6 to Spring St ◑ 9.30am–8.30pm Mon–Sat (6.30pm Sat). 💳 AE/MC/V

Face Stockholm

Face products have become a favourite amongst top make-up artists and the glitterati. You can choose from a bevy of all-natural beauty supplies – from make-up and utensils to bath gels and lotions. Check out the lip gloss – it's the best. $$

224 Columbus Ave (bet. 70th & 71st Sts) ☎ 769-1420 🚇 1·9 to 72nd St ◑ 11am–7pm daily. 💳 AE/MC/V Also branches in Soho & Midtown, phone for details

Kiehl's

Kiehl's is more than a beauty supply store – it's an American institution. This pharmacy-turned-beauty-brand's natural approach to products, and friendly, informative staff, make it a pleasure for you to financially submit (cost accumulates quite easily). They're best known for their lip balm and unisex appeal. $$

109 Third Ave (bet. 13th & 14th Sts) ☎ 677-3171 🚇 N·R·4·5·6 to 14th St-Union Sq; L to 3rd Ave. ◑ 10am–6.30pm Mon–Fri (7.30pm Thu); 10am–6pm Sat. 💳 AE/MC/V

M.A.C.

If you want the trendiest new colour for your lips, eyes, nails, or cheeks, then M.A.C. is the place to be. This make-up collection, which was created by a professional make-up artist, is known for its cutting-edge palette and sleek packaging. $$

113 Spring St (bet. Greene & Mercer Sts) ☎ 334-4641 🚇 N·R to Prince St ◑ 11am–7pm Mon–Sat; 12–6pm Sun. 💳 AE/MC/V Also a branch in West Village, phone for details

Ricky's

This store is a magnet for girlies who like their beauty products cheap and cheerful. The Soho branch has everything from fun-coloured wigs and nail polish to typical drugstore necessities. They also sell high-end products by the likes of Aveda, Phyto and Nexus at discounted prices. $

590 Broadway (bet. Prince & W Houston Sts) ☎ 226-5552 🚇 N·R to Prince St; 6 to Spring St ◑ 8am–9pm Mon–Fri; 9am–9pm Sat–Sun. 💳 AE/ MC/V Other branches, phone for details

Sephora

Product princesses will feel as if they've died and gone to heaven here. It's like a major department store, but just for cosmetics. Bath goods, make-up, perfume, skincare, and everything in between from big-name brands (Chanel, Lancôme, Dior) to more eclectic labels. $–$$$

555 Broadway (at Spring St) ☎ 625-1309 🚇 6 to Spring St ◑ 10am–8pm Mon–Sat (9pm Thu–Fri); 12–7pm Sun. 💳 AE/MC/V Also a branch in Midtown, phone for details

Shu Uemura ▼

The Armani of make-up, but from Japan. The store – and merchandise – has a Zen-like appeal in that less is more. Shu Uemura is not all about the moment's most fashionable colours, but minimalist beauty and quality. $$

121 Greene St (bet. Prince & W Houston Sts) ☎ 979-5500 🚇 N·R to Prince St; 6 to Spring St ◑ 11am–7pm Mon–Sat; 12–6pm Sun. 💳 AE/MC/V

shops

→ **more shops**

↓ interiors

ABC Carpet & Home

One of the most popular and unique stores in NYC, it's got six floors crammed with the most luxurious items for bed, bath, table and kitchen – plus fine fabrics and trim, antiques and, of course, carpets. On the ground floor there's a great café and an exotic food shop. $–$$$

888 Broadway (at 19th St) ☎ 473-3000
Ⓜ L•N•R•4•5•6 to 14th St-Union Sq
◑ 10am–8pm Mon–Sat (7pm Sat); 11am–6.30pm Sun. ☷ AE/MC/V

Ad-Hoc Software

Ad-Hoc Software's creative items always manage to fit the bill. Along with covetable bed and bath accessories (including some of the finest sheets and towels anywhere), there are lots of luxuries like French scented candles, gorgeous table linens, edgy dishware and cutlery, and even the latest in watch design. $–$$

410 W Broadway (at Spring St) ☎ 925-2652
Ⓜ C•E to Spring St ◑ 11am–7pm Sat; 11.30am–6pm Sun. ☷ AE/MC/V

Bed Bath Beyond

This gigantic superstore is the first place to check out when you're furnishing a new apartment. It carries a vast range of things for the home – some of it high-end and expensive, some of it a real bargain. For people used to shopping in crowded spaces with limited options, this place is a real treat, and the quality of the merchandise is pretty good. $–$$

620 Sixth Ave (at 19th St) ☎ 255-3550
Ⓜ 1•9 to 18th St; F to 23rd St ◑ 9.15am–9pm daily. ☷ AE/MC/V

Fishs Eddy

Dishes are the name of the game at Fishs Eddy. The owners of this clever shop buy up sets of decorated dishes from country clubs, schools, hotels and other unlikely institutions, and sell them here. They also do their own retro designs – the one with the New York skyline is fab. $

889 Broadway (at 19th St) ☎ 420-9020
Ⓜ L•N•R•4•5•6 to 14th St-Union Sq; N•R to 23rd St ◑ 10am–9pm Mon–Sat; 11am–8pm Sun. ☷ AE/MC/V

Gracious Home

Taking up almost both sides of one block, Gracious Home has all you need to line your nest. Everything here, from hardware to cleaning products, imported linens and towels, is sleek and highly-designed. $$

1217 & 1220 Third Ave (bet. 70th & 71st Sts)
☎ 517-6300 Ⓜ 6 to 68th St-Hunter College
◑ 8am–7pm Mon–Sat (9am Sat); 10am– 6pm Sun. ☷ AE/MC/V

Jonathan Adler

Designer of the moment, Adler is known for his whimsical home accessories blessed with bold, graphic designs. He has assembled a charming and aesthetically-pleasing selection of vases and tableware, along with other desirable objects culled from trips to flea markets – clearly his obsession. $$

465 Broome St (bet. Greene & Mercer Sts)
☎ 941-8950 Ⓜ N•R to Prince St ◑ 11am–7pm Mon–Sat; 12–6pm Sun. ☷ AE/MC/V

Las Venus

A staple for fashionable Downtowners, Las Venus is all about 20th-century pop culture. It carries lots of graphic furniture and other colourful home furnishings (some of them quite kitsch) that any trendster would crave. $–$$

163 Ludlow St (bet. Stanton & E Houston Sts)
☎ 982-0608 Ⓜ F to 2nd Ave ◑ 12–9pm Mon–Thu (11pm Thu); 12pm–midnight Fri–Sat; 12–8pm Sun. ☷ AE/MC/V

Moss

A showcase of the best designs past and present: if you like things for your home that are both functional and slick, Moss is nirvana. There are silver pieces from Alessi, fanciful glassware, jewel-toned Swedish crystal, and vases made from resin. The shop sometimes serves as a gallery for up-and-coming designers. $$

146 Greene St (bet. Houston & Prince Sts)
☎ 226-2190 Ⓜ N•R to Prince St ◑ 11am–7pm Tue–Fri; 12–7pm Sat; 12–6pm Sun. ☷ AE/MC/V

Pottery Barn

As quintessentially American as Gap, Pottery Barn is a mass-market outlet for well-designed, countrified home furnishings at reasonable prices; it's hard to find anyone in New York who doesn't shop here. $–$$

2109 Broadway (at 73rd St) ☎ 633-8405
Ⓜ 1•2•3•9 to 72nd St ◑ 10am–9pm Mon–Sat; 11am–7pm Sun. ☷ AE/MC/V Other branches, phone for details

Shabby Chic

No false advertising here: the owners of this influential design store have made quite an impact with their laid-back take on contemporary elegance (think cosy, over-stuffed sofas and piles of downy pillows). The sheets made from T-shirt material have been much imitated. $$

93 Greene Street (bet. Spring & Prince Sts)
☎ 274-9842 Ⓜ C•E•6 to Spring St; N•R to Prince St ◑ 10am–7pm Mon–Sat; 12–7pm Sun. ☷ AE/MC/V

TOTEM

One of the most modern home furnishing stores in the city, everything here is beautifully-designed; colourful, slick and functional. They carry loads of stylish plastic accessories, along with clean-lined furniture and distinctive rugs. $–$$

71 Franklin St (bet. Church St & Broadway) ☎ 925-5506 🚇 1•9 to Franklin St ◐ 11am–7pm Mon–Sat; 12–5pm Sun. 🖃 AE/MC/V

Williams-Sonoma

A big chain store from California, everything here is top-of-the-line: there are dishes from Italy, Calphon pans, plenty of glassware, food and gadgets that you can't do without. The real bargains here are the linens and napkins that look expensive but aren't. $–$$

110 Seventh Ave (bet. 16th & 17th Sts) ☎ 633-2203 🚇 1•9 to 18th St; 1•2•3•9 to 14th St ◐ 10am–8pm Mon–Sat (7pm Sat); 12–6pm Sun. 🖃 AE/MC/V

Wyeth

A pristine selection of 20th-century collectibles are harmoniously displayed in this loft-like store: furniture, many different styles of lighting, decorative objects, and that hot home furnishing of the moment – the vintage metal cabinet. $–$$$

151 Franklin St (bet. Varick & Hudson Sts) ☎ 925-5278 🚇 1•9 to Franklin St; A•C•E to Canal St ◐ 11am–6pm Mon–Sat. 🖃 AE/MC/V

Zona

Zona brings a bit of country life to the urban jungle. Filled with furniture and other items from around the world; the stock here is eclectic, deluxe and colourful. There are lots of little doodads that will brighten your pad, and don't cost much. The cult item here is the store's own hand-rolled candles that come in a rainbow of colours. $–$$

97 Greene St (bet. Prince & Spring Sts) ☎ 925-6750 🚇 C•E•6 to Spring St ◐ 11am–7pm Mon–Sat; 12–6pm Sun. 🖃 AE/MC/V

shops

↓ gift & museum stores

Cooper-Hewitt, National Museum of Design Store

The former music room of the Carnegie Mansion offers unexpected and unusual items that often tie in with the exhibitions: unique building toys, kitchen gadgets, stationery, and artsy books. Leave yourself a lot of time to browse. $$

2 E 91st Street (bet. Fifth & Madison Aves) ☎ 849-8355 🚇 4•5•6 to 86th St ◐ 10am–5pm Tue–Sat (9pm Tue); 12–5pm Sun. 🖃 all

Felissimo

New York's most unusual department store appeals to the rich hippy set. Brimful of amazing gift ideas, from wooden carvings to coloured candles, and beautifully stationery to indoor fountains, the products here are gathered from all over the world. Home furnishings, books and divine accessories are upstairs, as well as an elegant tearoom. $$

10 W 56th St (bet. Fifth & Sixth Aves) ☎ 247-5656 🚇 B•Q to 57th St ◐ 10am–6pm Mon–Sat (8pm Thu). 🖃 all

Guggenheim Museum Store

Pricey merchandise for the art lover (and materialist) in you: Chinese paint and ink sets, geometric-shaped Japanese mobiles, decorated chopsticks as well as museum store staples like posters, prints, scarves, T-shirts and shoulder bags. $$

1071 Fifth Avenue (bet. 88th & 89th Sts) ☎ 423-3615 🚇 4•5•6 to 86th St ◐ 10am–4pm daily (6pm Sun–Wed; 8pm Fri–Sat). 🖃 AE/MC/V

Metropolitan Museum of Art Store

The mother of all museum shops, the Met's three spacious, colourful floors are an ode to art and commerce, and the book department can equal any art bookstore in the city. $$

Fifth Avenue (bet. 80th & 84th Sts) ☎ 650-2850 🚇 4•5•6 to 86th St ◐ 9.30am–5.15pm Tue–Sun (9pm Fri–Sat). 🖃 all

Museum of Modern Art Store

Most of the goods in the MoMA shop relate directly to the museum's permanent exhibits: its calendars, posters, monographs and books all make great gifts. Don't miss the MoMA design store across the street, which features rugs and kitchen accessories as well as contemporary remakes of furniture by designers like Charles Rennie Mackintosh. $$

11 W 53rd Street (bet. Fifth & Sixth Aves) ☎ 708-9700/767-1050 🚇 E•F to 5th Ave ◐ 10am–7pm daily (9pm Fri). 🖃 AE/MC/V

Pearl River Mart

This Chinese emporium is packed with goodies: Chinese pyjamas and dresses, plain white T-shirts, great slippers, sandals, and loads and loads of oriental *tchotchkes*. Load up your baskets. $

277 Canal St (at Broadway) ☎ 431-4770 🚇 B•Q to Grand St; N•R to Canal St ◐ 10am–7.30pm daily. 🖃 all

more shops →

Troy

Troy's superb collection of strong design pieces by various New York and European names is offset by a sleek, all-white space. Hunt for the best in 90's design: unique lamps, small furniture and cool accessories like clocks and candles. Everything has a strong graphic edge. $$

138 Greene St (bet. Houston & Prince Sts) ☎ 941-4777 🚇 N·R to Prince St; C·E to Spring St; 6 to Bleecker St ◷ 11am–7pm Tue–Sat (6pm Sat); 12–6pm Sun. 🖃 AE/MC/V

Shi

Spare, sleek and modern is the style of this store, and everything in it from tiny lights on strings to perfectly-shaped ash trays. Very Zen. $$

233 Elizabeth St (bet. Houston & Prince Sts) ☎ 334-4330 🚇 6 to Bleecker St ◷ 12–7pm Tue–Sat; 12–6pm Sun. 🖃 AE/MC/V

↓ books

In New York's ultra-competitive publishing world **Barnes & Noble** reigns supreme. With convenient locations in every pocket of New York (including Brooklyn), it carries selected hardcover new releases at 30% off. Author readings occur nightly and their cafés have a reputation as the pick-up bars of the 90's. In a similar vein, but with fewer locations, **Borders** has a wide range of titles at reasonable prices. Of the smaller chains, the excellent **Rizzoli**'s is best for art and design books and **Shakespeare & Co** is strong on fiction, drama, film titles and British imports.

Other specialty bookstores fill the niches the chains haven't covered. **Tower Books** focuses on music titles, whereas the atmospheric **A Photographer's Place** offers secondhand photo books to stack up on the coffee table. East Village subversives adore their local **St Mark's Bookshop**, which puts the emphasis on politics, theory and the cutting-edge. The West Village literary set prefer New York's prettiest bookstore, **Three Lives and Company**, with its large fiction section. Judging by the number of mystery bookstores in town, New Yorkers have a voracious appetite for intrigue. **Murder Ink** is among the best of the bunch. Sci-fi, comic and graphic novel fans, meanwhile, will appreciate the massive range at **Forbidden Planet**. But if your idea of adventure is the rise and fall of a soufflé, then **Kitchen Arts & Letters** is home sweet home. **A Different Light ►** is the largest gay and lesbian bookshop in NY. It's a genuinely fun place to hang out with a buzzing café where events are held regularly.

With a purported 8 miles of used books to choose from, **The Strand** has enough dusty tomes to keep the most avid bibliophile busy for days. Look out for new hardcovers at significant discounts too. For used books in a less intimidating environment, visit 80-year-old **Gotham Book Mart**, a NY literary landmark. Replete with used books on all subjects, its walls are lined with photos of folk who have read and met here over the years.

A Different Light
151 W 19th St (bet. 6th & 7th Aves) ☎ 989-4850 🚇 F·1·2·3·9 to 14th St; L to 6th Ave ◷ 10am–midnight daily. 🖃 all $–$$

A Photographer's Place
133 Mercer St (bet. Prince & Spring Sts) ☎ 966-2356 🚇 C·E·6 to Spring St; N·R to Prince St ◷ 11am–8pm Mon–Sat; 12–6pm Sun. 🖃 all $–$$

Barnes & Noble
105 Fifth Ave (at 18th St) ☎ 807-0099 🚇 L·N·R·4·5·6 to 14th St-Union Sq ◷ 9.30am–7.45pm Mon–Sat (6.15pm Sat); 11am–5.45pm Sun. 🖃 all $ Other branches, phone for details

Borders
5 World Trade Center (bet. Church & Vesey Sts) ☎ 839-8049 🚇 C·E to World Trade Center ◷ 7am–8.30pm Mon–Sat (10am Sat); 11am–8.30pm Sun. 🖃 all $–$$ Other branches, phone for details.

Forbidden Planet
840 Broadway (at 12th St) ☎ 473-1576 🚇 all 4·5·6 to 14th St-Union Sq ◷ 10am–8.30pm daily. 🖃 all $–$$

Gotham Book Mart
41 W 47th St (bet. 5th & 6th Aves) ☎ 719-4448 🚇 B·D·F·Q to 47th–50th Sts-Rockefeller Ctr ◷ 9.30am–6.30pm Mon–Sat (6pm Sat). 🖃 AE/MC/V $

Kitchen Arts & Letters
1435 Lexington Ave (bet. 93rd & 94th Sts) ☎ 876-5550 🚇 6 to 96th St ◷ 1–6pm Mon; 10am–6.30pm Tue–Fri; 11am–6pm Sat (closed Sat & Sun Jul–Aug). 🖃 MC/V $–$$

Murder Ink
2486 Broadway (bet. 92nd & 93rd Sts) ☎ 362-8905 🚇 1·2·3·9 to 96th St ◷ 10am–7.30pm Mon–Sat; 11am–6pm Sun. 🖃 AE/MC/V $–$$

Rizzoli
31 W 57th St (bet. 6th & 7th Aves) ☎ 759-2424 🚇 B·N·Q·R to 57th St ◷ 10.30am–9pm Mon–Sat; 12–7pm Sun. 🖃 all $–$$ Other branches, phone for details.

St Mark's Bookshop
31 Third Ave (bet. 8th & 9th Sts) ☎ 260-7853 🚇 6 to Astor Pl ◷ 10am–midnight daily (11am Sun). 🖃 all $–$$

Shakespeare & Co
716 Broadway (at Washington Pl) ☎ 529-1330 🚇 6 to Astor Pl ◷ 10am–11pm daily (midnight Fri–Sat). 🖃 all $–$$ Other branches, phone for details.

The Strand
828 Broadway (at 12th St) ☎ 473-1452 🚇 L·N·R·4·5·6 to 14th St-Union Sq ◷ 9.30am–9.30pm daily (11am Sun). 🖃 all $–$$

Three Lives & Company
154 W 10th St (at Waverly Pl) ☎ 741-2069 🚇 A·B·C·D·E·F·Q to W 4th St-Washington Sq ◷ 1pm–8pm daily (11am Thu–Sat; 7pm Sun). 🖃 AE/MC/V $–$$

Tower Books
383 Lafayette St (at E 4th St) ☎ 258-5100 🚇 6 to Astor Pl; B·D·F·Q to Broadway-Lafayette St ◷ 9am–midnight daily. 🖃 all $–$$

↓ electronics

For camera and electrical items go to any one of the numerous stores between 30th and 50th Streets, from Fifth to Park Avenues. They appreciate a good haggle but beware of inferior goods and fakes (which are plentiful). Comparative shopping is always your best bet, though some sales people are willing to lower on their prices to close the deal – especially if you're paying cash. **Nobody Beats the Wiz** and **Radio Shack** are the main chains. The Wiz specializes in television and sound equipment, and their bargains make up for the slow service. For years, consumers have thought of Radio Shack as a cheap imitation of the electronic big boys. But recently, their products have taken a giant step

forward in quality, and the slightly higher costs reflect it. A good one-off, **J & R Music & Computer World** has all the top-name computer and stereo equipment you could ever hope to use. There's also **B & H Photo-Video**, the home from home for many photographers looking for the best deal on professional quality lenses and bodies. For gadget freaks, the **Sharper Image** is your destination.

B & H Photo-Video
420 Ninth Ave (bet. 33rd & 34th Sts) ☎ 239-7500 Ⓜ A•C•E to 34th St-Penn Stn ◑ 9am–7pm Mon–Thu; 9am–1pm Fri; 10am–5pm Sun. ▤ all $-$$

J & R Music & Computer World
23 Park Row (bet. Beekman & Ann Sts) ☎ 238-9100 Ⓜ J•M•Z•2•3•4•5 to Fulton St-Broadway Nassau; N•R•4•5•6 to City Hall ◑ 9am–7pm

Mon–Sat (7.30pm Thu); 10.30am–6.30pm Sun. ▤ all $-$$

Nobody Beats the Wiz
555 Fifth Ave (at 46th St) ☎ 557-7770 Ⓜ B•D•F•Q to 47–50th Sts-Rockefeller Center; E•F to 5th Ave ◑ 9am–8.30pm Mon–Sat; 11am–7pm Sun. ▤ all $-$$ Other branches, phone for details

Radio Shack
626 Broadway (bet. Houston & Bleecker Sts) ☎ 677-7069 Ⓜ B•D•F•Q to Broadway-Lafayette St ◑ 10am–8pm Mon–Sat; 11am–6pm Sun. ▤ all $$ Other branches, phone for details

Sharper Image
4 W 57th St (bet. 5th & 6th Aves) ☎ 265-2550 Ⓜ B•D•F•Q to 47–50th Sts-Rockefeller Center; E•F to 5th Ave ◑ 10am–7pm Mon–Sat (6pm Sat); 12–5pm Sun. ▤ all $$

shops

↓ cds, records & tapes

NYC has every kind of record store from big-name chains to kooky specialty stores. **Tower Records** is a virtual music supermarket, its three floors of merchandise making a good starting point for any mainstream release. **HMV** is another giant with thousands of titles to browse as an in-store DJ entertains you. And the **Virgin Megastore** has the most comprehensive selection, which compensates for the slightly higher prices.

There's a string of music stores along St Mark's Place, which are good for price and selection. The best of these is **Kim's Video & Music**, with a great range and helpful staff. It's also a good spot for used CDs. **J & R Music & Computer World** is the best for bargains and carries all new releases at discount. There are separate departments for jazz and classical CDs.

DJs make their way to **Dancetracks** where all the latest dance music is car-

ried on vinyl. **8 Ball Records**, the record label's own store, is also excellent for house and other dance music. But for the newest in hip-hop, push your way past the DJs into **Fat Beats**, although DJs looking for bargains tend to frequent **Record Explosion**. For used CDs that also include fairly new pop hits, **Disco Rama** is hard to surpass.

If you want to go back in time, **Bleecker Bob's Golden Oldies** has vintage and collectible vinyl and the tour T-shirts to match. To pick up tour posters and recordings of your favourite live show, **Generation Records** is a gold mine. Jazz aficionados regularly make pilgrimages to the **Jazz Record Center** to get their fix, while those who love musicals head to **Footlight Records**. On Broadway, **Colony Records** also has an extensive collection of show tunes with the sheet music too. On a more classical note, **Academy Books & Records** is especially good for used classical CDs. Hard-to-find titles are

tracked down by **Other Music**. The knowledge of their staff alone might make it the best record store in the city.

Academy Books & Records
10 w 18th St (bet. 5th & 6th Aves) ☎ 242-4848 Ⓜ L•N•R•4•5•6 to Union Sq ◑ 11am–7pm daily. ▤ AE/MC/V $

Bleecker Bob's Golden Oldies
118 W 3rd St (at MacDougal St) ☎ 475-9677 Ⓜ A•B•C•D•E•F•Q to W 4th St-Washinshgton Sq ◑ 12pm–1am daily (3am Fri–Sat). ▤ all $-$$

Colony Records
1619 Broadway (at 49th St) ☎ 265-2050 Ⓜ N•R to 49th St; 1•9 to 50th St ◑ 9.30am–midnight daily. ▤ all $-$$

Dancetracks
91 E 3rd St (at 1st Ave) ☎ 260-8729 Ⓜ F to 2nd Ave ◑ 12–9pm Mon–Sun (10pm Fri). ▤ AE/MC/V $

Disco Rama
186 W 4th St (bet. 6th & 7th Aves) ☎ 206-8417 Ⓜ A•B•C•D•E•F•Q to W 4th St-Washinshgton Sq ◑ 10.30am–10.30pm Mon–Sat (11.30pm Fri; 12.30am Sat); 11.30am–8pm Sun. ▤ all $

8 Ball Records
105 E 9th St (bet. 3rd & 4th Aves) ☎ 473-6343 Ⓜ 6 to Astor Pl; N•R to 8th St ◑ 12–9pm Mon–Sat; 1–7pm Sun. ▤ AE/MC/V $

[more directory →114]

→ more shops

Fat Beats

406 Sixth Ave (bet. 8th & 9th Sts) ☎ 673-3883 ▥ A·B·C·D· E·F·Q to W 4th St-Washinshgton Sq ◑ 12–9pm daily (10pm Fri–Sat; 6 pm Sun). ▣ MC/V $–$$

Footlight Records

113 E 12th St (bet. 3rd & 4th Aves) ☎ 533-1572 ▥ L·N·R·4· 5·6 to 14th St-Union Sq ◑ 11am–7pm Mon–Fri; 10am–8pm Sat; 11am–5pm Sun. ▣ AE/MC/V $–$$

Generation Records

210 Thompson St (bet. Bleecker & W 3rd Sts) ☎ 254-1100 ▥ A·B·C·D·E·F·Q to W 4th St-Washington Sq ◑ 11am–10pm Mon– Fri; 11–11am Sq; 12–10pm Sun. ▣ AE/MC/V $–$$

HMV

57 W 34th St (at 6th Ave) ☎ 629-0900 ▥ B·D·F·N·R·Q to 34th St-Herald Sq ◑ 9am–

10pm Mon–Sat; 11am–9pm Sun. ▣ AE/MC/V $–$$ Also branch in Midtown, phone for details.

Jazz Record Center

8th flr, 236 W 26th St (bet. 7th & 8th Aves) ☎ 675-4480 ▥ C·E·1·9 to 23rd St ◑ 10am–6pm Tue–Sat. ▣ AE/MC/V $

J & R Music & Computer World

23 Park Row (bet. Beekman & Ann Sts) ☎ 238-9000 ▥ J·M·Z 2·3·4·5 to Fulton St-Broadway Nassau; N·R·4·5·6 to City Hall ◑ 9am–7pm Mon–Sat (7:30pm Thu); 10.30am-6.30pm Sun. ▣ all $–$$

Kim's Video & Music

6 St Mark's Place (bet. 2nd & 3rd Aves) ☎ 598-9985 ▥ 6 to Astor Pl ◑ 9am–midnight daily. ▣ AE/MC/V $

Other Music

15 E 4th St (bet. Broadway &

Lafayette St) ☎ 477-8150 ▥ 6 to Bleecker St; B·D·F·Q to Broadway-Lafayette St ◑ 12–9pm daily (10pm Fri; 7pm Sun). ▣ AE/MC/V $–$$

Record Explosion

142 W 34th St (bet. 6th & 7th Aves) ☎ 714-0450 ▥ B·D·F·N·Q·R to 34th St-Herald Sq ◑ 9am–8.30pm Mon–Sat (9pm Sat); 10am–8pm Sun. ▣ all $

Tower Records

692 Broadway (at E 4th St) ☎ 505-1500 ▥ 6 to Bleecker St ◑ 11am–11pm daily. ▣ all $–$$

Virgin Megastore

1540 Broadway (bet. 45th & 46th Sts) ☎ 921-1020 ▥ A·C·E·N·R·1·2·3·7·9 42nd St-Times Sq ◑ 9–1am daily (2am Fri–Sat). ▣ all $$

↓ food stores

lower east side

Russ & Daughters

This cherished, spic-and-span Jewish deli has survived since World War I due to personalized service, and top quality smoked salmon (eight varieties), chopped liver, whitefish salad, sophisticated cheeses and dried fruits. So proud of their stock, they urge tastings on you (Eat!). $–$$

179 E Houston St (bet. Allen & Orchard Sts) ☎ 475-4880 ▥ F to 2nd Ave ◑ 9am–7pm Mon–Sat; 8am–5.30pm Sun. ▣ MC/V

soho

Dean & Deluca

A huge white gallery with hundreds of mustards, vinegars, olive oils and herbs, plus gourmet cheeses, gorgeous breads, exotic flowers, professional kitchenware and cookbooks. Up front is a popular espresso bar. $$–$$$

560 Broadway (at Prince St) ☎ 226-6800 ▥ N·R to Prince St ◑ 10am–8pm daily (7pm Sun). ▣ MC/V Other branches, phone for details.

Gourmet Garage

Groovy, food-conscious Downtown types are always roaming the aisles here, filling their baskets with organic produce, European cheeses, house olive oil, salsa, tortilla chips and ice cream. Also a funky stop for bagels, sandwiches and soups to go. $–$$

453 Broome St (at Mercer St) ☎ 941-5850 ▥ N·R to Prince St

◑ 7am–9pm daily. ▣ AE/MC/V Other branches, phone for details

east village

Astor Wines & Spirits

Manhattan's biggest liquor store, with row upon row of bottles from around the world, including a trustworthy wine selection from New York State. The staff know their stuff and you can't beat the prices (check out the house brand liquors). Free wine tastings 3–6pm every Sat, and often 5–8pm Thu–Fri. $

12 Astor Pl (at Lafayette St) ☎ 674-7500 ▥ 6 to Astor Pl ◑ 9am–9pm Mon–Sat. ▣ AE/MC/V

west village

Balducci's

Open since 46, this virtual horn of plenty will astound you with its exquisite fruits and vegetables as well as lovely cheeses, pastries, chocolates, charcuterie and prepared foods. Most of it's costly, so sometimes it's just fun to look. $$–$$$

424 Sixth Ave (at 9th St) ☎ 673-2600 ▥ A·B·C·D·E·F·Q to W 4th St-Washington Sq ◑ 7am–8.30pm Mon–Sun. ▣ MC/V

Murray's Cheese Shop

Manhattan's oldest cheese purveyor (opened 36 years ago) is beloved by foodies and locals alike – an old-world cornucopia of well-chosen international dairy produce, sold by a knowledgeable staff

who have the gift of the gab. A fun Village stop for antipasti and sandwiches as well. $–$$

257 Bleecker St (bet. 6th & 7th Aves) ☎ 243-3289 ▥ 1·9 to Christopher St ◑ 8am–8pm Mon–Sat; 9am–6pm Sun. ▣ AE/MC/V

chelsea

Garden of Eden

Both the Chelsea and East Village (314 Third Ave) locations display exotic, fascinating fruits you've never heard of: 'ugly fruit' from Jamaica, gold tamarilo from New Zealand, kiwana-horned melons, sweet feijoa, etc. This is a global, decently-priced farmers' market with dozens of types of marinated olives, fantastic prepared foods and cured meats. $–$$

162 W 23rd St (bet. 6th & 7th Aves) ☎ 675-6300 ▥ 1·9 to 23rd St ◑ 7am–10pm daily (9.30pm Sun). ▣ AE/MC/V

upper east side

Best Cellars

Instead of classifying wines by grape or origin, here sections are labelled 'luscious', 'juicy', 'smooth', 'big', etc, so you can match them with mood or food. Better yet, every bottle is under $10 and has an evocative description to go with it. Free tastings daily from 5–8pm. $

1291 Lexington Ave (bet. 86th & 87th Sts) ☎ 426-4200 ▥ 4·5·6 to 86th St ◑ 10am–9pm Mon–Sun (10pm Fri–Sat). ▣ AE/MC/V

Eli's Bread at The Vinegar Factory

Eli's is famous citywide for its cavernous warehouse of grocery items (the space formerly housed a vinegar factory). A salad bar holds dozens of choices and 10 fresh soups; the seafood counter, homemade potato chips and fresh squeezed juices also make it worth the trek. Upstairs is a café and exclusive housewares department. $$

431 E 91st St (bet. 1st & York Aves) ☎ 987-0885 Ⓜ 4•5•6 to 86th St ◑ *7am–9pm daily.* 💳 AE/MC/V

upper west side

Zabar's ►

Beloved by New Yorkers and tourists alike, this landmark, labyrinthine store has a dizzying array of cheeses, coffee beans, bargain caviar, imported candies, baked goods and smoked salmon. Upstairs are housewares at the cheapest prices in town. Nutty on the weekends. $

2245 Broadway (at 80th St) ☎ 787-2000 Ⓜ 1•9 to 79th St ◑ *8am–7.30pm Mon–Sat (8pm Sat); 9am–6pm Sun.* 💳 AE/MC/V

↓ markets

Shopping al fresco is an alternative New York experience. Spring officially begins in the city when weekend street vendors put up their stands on streets like Astor Place, Columbus Avenue or along the sidewalks in the West Village to sell cheap clothes, handmade jewellery, and corndogs. A stall's merchandise tends to reflect the taste of the neighbourhood's residents. So it's Downtown for hand-painted hash pipes, nose rings and kaftans and Uptown for silk scarves, crystal necklaces and polished antiques.

Apart from street stalls, there are, luckily, several fixed markets which operate year round. On Sundays, **Orchard Street** is closed to traffic so local vendors can sell underwear, leather goods, and toys to the masses. Also on the weekend, the **Tower Market** is a small but crowded lot filled with knitted caps, T-shirts, and tapes. The **Spring Street Market** offers more of the same, with a particularly good selection of affordable knock-offs. Southeast of Central Park South's strip of hotels is **Columbus Circle Market** peddling art and antiques; it's a known hot spot for tourists, so prices tend to be higher. Uptown, the indoor and outdoor stalls at **PS 44** and **PS 183** sell upscale antiques, needlework, and various other arts and crafts. And way up in Harlem, the **Malcolm Shabazz Harlem Market** ↗ is *the* place for colourful African imports.

Or have a rummage in one of the city's plentiful flea markets. The biggest and the best is Chelsea's **Annex Flea Market** which sells anything and everything. The next best place to check out is the **Soho Antique Fair Collectibles Market** on Broadway, which sells vintage clothing, old cameras, and crafts. **Columbus Flea** is, like Soho, on a much smaller scale than the Annex.

Farmers' markets sell fresh produce from New Jersey and Upstate New York. The open air one in **Union Square**, which sells fruit and vegetables, maple syrup, jams, flowers, and plants, is open year round. The indoor **Chelsea Market** houses about two dozen shops, specializing in delicious baked goods, seasonal produce, meat and fish.

Annex Flea Market
Sixth Ave (bet. 24th & 26th Sts) Ⓜ F to 23rd St ◑ *9am–5pm Sat–Sun.*

Chelsea Market
75 Ninth Ave (bet. 15th & 16th Sts) ☎ 243-5678 Ⓜ A•C•E to 14th St; L to 8th Ave ◑ *7am–7pm Mon–Sat; 10am–6pm Sun.*

Columbus Circle Market
58th St & Eighth Ave Ⓜ A•B•C•D•1•9 to 59th St-Columbus Circle ◑ *11am–7pm daily.*

Columbus Flea
77th St & Columbus Ave Ⓜ B•C to 81st St-Museum of Natural History ◑ *10am–5.30pm Sun.*

Malcolm Shabazz Harlem Market
118 Lenox Ave (bet. 116th & 117th Sts) ☎987-8131 Ⓜ 2•3 to 116th St ◑ *8am–9pm daily.*

Orchard Street
Orchard St (bet. Delancey & Houston Sts) Ⓜ F to Delancey St-Essex St ◑ *Sun.*

PS 183
419 E 67th St (bet. 1st & York Aves) Ⓜ 6 to 68th St ◑ *10am–6pm Sat.*

PS 44
Columbus Ave (bet. 76th & 77th Sts) Ⓜ 1•9 to 79th St; B•C to 81st St ◑ *10am–5.30pm Sun.*

Soho Antique Fair Collectibles Market
Broadway & Grand St (nw corner) Ⓜ J•M•N•R•Z•6 to Canal St ◑ *9am–5pm Sat–Sun.*

Spring Street Market
Spring & Wooster Sts Ⓜ C•E to Spring St ◑ *10am–7pm daily.*

Tower Flea Market
Broadway (bet. W 4th & 3rd Sts) Ⓜ B•D•F•Q to Broadway-Lafayette St ◑ *10am–7pm Sat–Sun.*

Union Square
(bet. 17th St & Broadway) Ⓜ L•N•R•4•5•6 to 14th St-Union Sq ◑ *8am–5pm Mon, Wed, & Fri–Sat.*

new york's night-time hot spots

directory

Brighton Beach *♪off map*

Infamous Russian owned nightclubs and restaurants, popular with hen and stag nights, are sure to deliver too much vodka and kitsch floor shows

Chelsea *♪A5*

Lots of bustling restaurants and gay-slanted bars on Seventh and Eighth Avenues, plus some Off-Off Broadway theatres. Megaclubs Twilo [→151] and Tunnel [→150] are located on the far west side.

Chinatown *♪B6*

Not great for bars or clubs, rather the streets here are thronged with those in search of excellent quality and reasonably-priced oriental food. The quintessential Chinatown.

East Village *♪B5*

One of New York's most active night-time hotspots, with abundant and varied restaurants, cool bars, live music venues, clubs and alternative theatre spaces.

Fort Greene *♪C6*

Nightlife tends to be dominated by the Brooklyn Academy of Music (BAM) [→145], which also has its own cinema. Nearby restaurants and cafés keep going into the early hours. Spoken word aficionados should investigate.

Harlem *♪A1–A2*

Once strictly no-go by day, let alone by night, Harlem is now quite a night-time destination, but it's still not advisable to loiter on quieter streets. Down by Columbia University, the scene is dominated by students.

Lower East Side *♪B5*

Ludlow and Orchard Streets are the focus for a happening bar and club scene; a mix of well-established and brand new – with something for everyone. There are also some interesting alternative performance spaces and lots of small live music venues.

Meatpacking District *♪A5*

A real happening hotspot. Several excellent nightclubs like Mother [→150] and the Cooler [→146] are situated here, plus a smattering of restaurants and bars.

Midtown *♪A4*

Away from the Theater District [→Theater District], there are lots of cinemas, and a good choice of restaurants and swank hotel bars.

Noho *♪B5*

Exceedingly hip restaurants, bars, and lounges are crammed into this tiny area. Also the location of the well-respected Joseph Papp Public Theater [→140].

Nolita *♪B5*

Neighbouring Nolita has an even greater concentration of bars and eateries including some of the moment's most fashionable destinations in NYC.

Soho *♪A5–A5*

Super-stylish restaurants and bars, loungey bar-clubs with velvet ropes and strict door policies. Club music venue Shine [→150] is located here, plus New York's leading arthouse cinema The Angelika [→142]. Very *Sex in the City*.

Theater District *♪A4*

The jewel in Midtown's crown. The location of around 30 Broadway theatres, plus lots of Off-Broadway ones too – as well as restaurants catering to the early evening theatre crowd. Times Square might be a shadow of its former seedy self, but the bright neon lights still cannot fail to impress. There are a few old-time dive bars around Hell's Kitchen, and lots of restaurants, especially those along Ninth Avenue.

Tribeca *♪A6*

Quite a well-behaved and local nightlife scene, centered around lots of restaurants and a few bars and lounges. Great music venues such as the Knitting Factory [→146], as well as the movie house, the Screening Room [→142].

Upper West Side *♪A3*

The Lincoln Center is the hub of nightlife in the lower reaches of the UWS, with its various concert and performance halls, great for opera, dance, classical and the occasional world music and jazz. Also many restaurants and bars in the 70's along Columbus Avenue.

Washington Heights *♪A1*

To the north of Harlem is Washington Heights with a happening bar scene, including lots of live music, especially jazz and Latin. Again, not an area to stroll around after dark.

West Village *♪A5*

Cosy Off-Off Broadway theatres, lots of smoky jazz clubs and laid back music cafes. A great number of excellent restaurants of all shapes and sizes, plus diverse lounges and bars, many for gay men and women, and their friends.

restaurants & bars
what's where

↓ brooklyn heights

Grimaldi's | $$ [→126] ☏

↓ chelsea/meatpacking district

Cafeteria | $$ [→121 & 133] ☏
Ciel Rouge [→135] ▯
Empire Diner | $–$$ [→126] ☏
Florent | $–$$ [→124] ▯ ☏
Hell [→134] ▯
Hudson Bar & Books [→135] ▯
Mustang Sally's Saloon [→136] ▯
O Padeiro | $–$$ [→132] ☏ ▯

↓ east village

Angelica Kitchen | $–$$ [→131] ☏
Angel's Share [→137] ▯ ☏
Baraza [→134] ▯
Barmacy [→137] ▯
The Cock [→138] ▯
Decibel [→137] ▯ ☏
Dick's [→138] ▯
First | $–$$$ [→132] ☏ ▯
Il Bagatto | $ [→121] ☏ ▯
KGB [→138] ▯
Lakeside Lounge [→135] ▯
Lei Bar [→138] ▯
Nevada Smith's [→136] ▯
Old Devil Moon | $–$$ [→126] ☏ ▯
Pisces | $–$$ [→133] ☏ ▯
Second Avenue Deli | $–$$ [→123] ☏
7A | $ [→131] ☏
Takahachi | $$–$$$ [→128] ☏
2A [→137] ▯
Wonder Bar [→138] ▯
Yaffa Café | $ [→133] ☏

↓ gramercy park/flatiron district/
union square/madison square

Eleven Madison Park | $$–$$$ [→121] ☏ ▯
Gramercy Tavern | $$–$$$ [→125] ☏ ▯
Mesa Grill | $$–$$$ [→128 & 131] ☏ ▯
Park Avenue Country Club [→136] ▯
Patria | $$$ [→128] ☏ ▯
Tabla | $$$ [→128] ☏ ▯
Union Pacific | $$$ [→131] ☏
Union Square Café | $$$ [→125] ☏ ▯

Verbena | $$$ [→131] ☏ ▯
Veritas | $$$ [→133] ☏ ▯
Zen Palate | $–$$ [→131] ☏

↓ harlem/morningside heights/
washington heights

Coogan's [→136] ▯
Copeland's | $–$$$ [→124] ☏ ▯
Sylvia's | $–$$ [→131] ☏
Tom's Restaurant | $ [→126] ☏

↓ lower east side/chinatown

Baby Jupiter [→134] ▯ ☏
Bereket | $ [→133] ☏
Joe's Shanghai | $–$$$ [→128] ☏
Katz's Deli | $ [→123] ☏
Kush [→138] ▯
Lansky Lounge [→134] ▯ ☏
Max Fish [→137] ▯
Meow Mix [→135] ▯
Orchard Bar [→134] ▯
Tonic [→135] ▯ ☏
Winnie's [→135] ▯ ☏

↓ midtown/hell's kitchen

Aquavit | $$$ [→122] ☏ ▯
Blue Bar [→137] ▯
Cho Dang Gol | $–$$ [→127] ☏
Ess-a-Bagel | $ [→123] ☏
Island Burgers & Shakes | $ [→129] ☏
King Cole Bar [→135] ▯
La Bonne Soupe | $–$$ [→129] ☏ ▯
Le Bernardin | $$$ [→123] ☏ ▯
Lespinasse | $$$ [→123] ☏ ▯
Oyster Bar | $–$$$ [→125] ☏ ▯
Regents [→138] ▯ ☏
The Russian Samovar [→138] ▯ ☏
Siberia [→137] ▯
Swine on Nine [→138] ▯ ☏
Top of the Tower [→136] ▯ ☏
Trattoria dell'Arte | $$–$$$ [→125] ☏ ▯
'21' Club | $$$ [→125] ☏ ▯

↓ nolita/noho

Acquario | $–$$ [→132] 🍽️
Balthazar | $$–$$$ [→120] 🍽️ 🍺
B-Bar | [→120 & 134] 🍺 🍽️
Bond St | $$–$$$ [→120] 🍽️ 🍺
Botanica | [→134] 🍺
Il Buco | $–$$$ [→121] 🍽️ 🍺
Joe's Pub | [→135] 🍺 🍽️
Le Jardin Bistrot | $$–$$$ [→130] 🍽️
Lombardi's | $$ [→126] 🍽️
Mare Chiaro | [→137] 🍺
Rialto | $$ [→129] 🍽️
Sweet & Vicious | [→134] 🍺

↓ soho

Alison on Dominick Street | $$$ [→129] 🍽️ 🍺
Bar 89 | [→135] 🍺 🍽️
Blue Ribbon | $–$$$ [→132] 🍽️ 🍺
Circa Tabac | [→135] 🍺
Grand Bar | [→136] 🍺 🍽️
Jerry's | $$ [→124] 🍽️ 🍺
Mercer Kitchen | $–$$$ [→121] 🍽️ 🍺
Pepe Rosso | $ [→127] 🍽️ 🍺
Quilty's | $$$ [→130] 🍽️ 🍺
Raoul's | [→136] 🍺 🍽️
357 | [→136] 🍺 🍽️
Void | [→138] 🍺

↓ tribeca/lower manhattan

American Park | $$–$$$ [→129] 🍽️
Bayard's | $$$ [→122] 🍽️ 🍺
Bouley Bakery | $$$ [→122] 🍽️
Bubble Lounge | [→136] 🍺 🍽️
Capsouto Frères | $$–$$$ [→129] 🍽️ 🍺
The Greatest Bar on Earth | [→136] 🍺 🍽️
Nancy Whiskey Pub | [→137] 🍺 🍽️
Nobu | $$$ [→124] 🍽️ 🍺
Odeon | $$–$$$ [→125 & 131] 🍽️ 🍺
Rosemarie's | $$–$$$ [→130] 🍽️ 🍺
Screening Room | $$–$$$ [→130] 🍽️ 🍺
Spartina | $$–$$$ [→130] 🍽️ 🍺

↓ upper east side/central park

Café Boulud | $$$ [→122] 🍽️ 🍺
Café Carlyle | [→135] 🍺 🍽️
Club Macanudo | [→135] 🍺
Comfort Diner | $–$$ [→126] 🍽️
Daniel | $$$ [→122] 🍽️ 🍺
Elaine's | [→136] 🍺 🍽️
Harry Cipriani | $$$$ [→136] 🍺 🍽️
Jackson Hole | $ [→129] 🍽️
Park View at the Boathouse | $$–$$$ [→130] 🍽️ 🍺
Payard Patisserie & Bistro | $$–$$$ [→133] 🍽️ 🍺

↓ upper west side

Barney Greengrass | $–$$ [→123] 🍽️
Big Nick's Burger | $ [→129] 🍽️
Café des Artistes | $$$ [→124] 🍽️ 🍺
Calle Ocho | $$–$$$ [→127] 🍽️ 🍺
Drip | [→138] 🍺 🍽️
Jean Georges | $$$ [→123] 🍽️ 🍺
Pampa | $–$$ [→127] 🍽️

↓ west village

Babbo | $$–$$$ [→120] 🍽️ 🍺
Bar d'O | [→135] 🍺
Bar Pitti | $–$$ [→132] 🍽️ 🍺
Chumley's | [→136] 🍺 🍽️
Corner Bistro | $ [→129] 🍽️ 🍺
French Roast | $–$$ [→133] 🍽️
Gotham Bar and Grill | $$$ [→123] 🍽️ 🍺
Grange Hall | $$–$$$ [→132] 🍽️ 🍺
'Ino | $ [→126] 🍽️ 🍺
Japonica | $$–$$$ [→127] 🍽️
Joe Jr's | $ [→126] 🍽️
Moomba | [→134] 🍺 🍽️
Pó | $$ [→133] 🍽️ 🍺
Surya | $–$$$ [→128] 🍽️ 🍺
Tea & Sympathy | $–$$ [→127] 🍽️
Waterloo | $$$ [→121] 🍽️ 🍺

Key

$	main courses up to $10
$$	main courses up to $20
$$$	main courses above $20
🍽️	restaurant/café
🍺	bar/pub

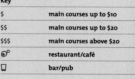

restaurants & bars chart

➜ more restaurants | cafés | bars

eat up

New York has always been a major chowtown but never so much as today – even the most dedicated foodie has trouble keeping up. You'd need a King Kong appetite and a Rockefeller-sized fortune to try it all, so sample what you can of the amazing variety of eateries – high-priced and low – in neighbourhoods all over the city.

↓ talk of the town

Babbo 110 Waverly Pl (bet. MacDougal St & Sixth Ave) | West Village

Everything good you hear about Mario Batali's gorgeous place in the old Coach House is true. Two spacious lemon-yellow rooms (upstairs is fancier), and meticulous service are merely the backdrop to the most original Italian food around. Read and salivate: goat's cheese tortellini with dried orange and wild fennel pollen; chestnut gnocchi with wild boar – and that's just the primi. Entrées are equally imaginative and desserts such as poached kumquats with gorgonzola are delectable.

$$–$$$ ($17–$29)

🚇 A·B·C·D·E·F·Q to W 4th St-Washington Sq

☎ 777-0303

◑ 5.30–11.30pm Mon–Sat; 5–11pm Sun.

🍴100 ☒ all Ⓢ tasting menus $49–$59
♿ limited ▯ ▤

B-Bar 40 E 4th St (bet. Bowery & 4th St) | Noho

Here, in the sexy, aviary-themed dining room, in the huge bar and out on the enclosed patio, interesting faces and fashions are sure to be seen. Even though it's been around a few years, B-Bar (formerly the Bowery Bar) still hosts tons of private music biz parties, and there's always a line of stretch limos purring outside. American favourites, like crab cakes and roast chicken with mash, are dead certs.

$–$$$ ($9–$21)

🚇 6 to Astor Pl

☎ 475-2220

◑ 11.30am–1am Mon–Sat (midnight Mon; 10.30am Sat); 10.30–midnight Sun.

🍴180 ☒ all ♿ ▯ ⊿
▤ ▨ Ⓥ

Balthazar 80 Spring St (bet. Broadway & Crosby St) | Nolita

When this spot-on facsimile of the perfect Parisian bistro opened in 87, it was a too-hot-to-handle celebrity-model night-mare, but now it's assumed its rightful place as the young sibling of New York's most lovable restaurant, Odeon [→125]. Order very good renditions of French faves – plateau de fruits de mer; the Balthazar salad of greens, green beans, sheep's cheese and truffle oil; steak-frites; rabbit pappardelle – all accompanied by fine sour-dough bread baked at the next-door boulangerie. This is a guaranteed fun meal out.

$$–$$$ ($12–$29)

🚇 N·R to Prince St; 6 to Spring St

☎ 965-1414

◑ 7.30–2am Sat–Thu (3am Sat–Sun).

🍴150 ☒ all ♿ ▯
⊿ bar only ▤

Bond St 6 Bond St (bet. Broadway & Lafayette Sts) | Noho

This is the three-storey Japanese restaurant that out-Nobus Nobu. The lower ground floor is a loud bar where you pick your sake by personality, eg 'cool, subtle and refined' or 'warm, rich and complex'; above, there are two floors of packed, dimly-lit, minimalist dining rooms. Drop your entire budget on *osetra* caviar sushi, select spotted sardine, needle fish and basil-smoked salmon *nigiri*, or get fab, fun rolls like sesame-crusted shrimp with orange curry dressing. Absolutley not your everyday sushi joint.

$$–$$$ ($18–$26)

🚇 B·D·F·Q to Broadway-Lafayette St; 6 to Bleecker St

☎ 777-2500

◑ 6pm–midnight Mon–Sun (11pm Sun).

🍴135 ☒ all Ⓢ tasting menu from $60 ▯
⊿ bar only ▤

Prices quoted correspond to the cost of a main course

Cafeteria 119 Seventh Ave (at 17th St) | Chelsea

Don't be fooled by the name – this is the furthest thing from a typical cafeteria. In fact, it's one of the city's sleeker hot spots, so try not to gawp when Kate Moss, Calvin Klein or Evan Dando sit at the cushy booth right next to you and order from a menu packed with cholesterol-rich comfort food like old-fashioned macaroni cheese, fries, milk shakes, and jaw-breakingly huge sandwiches. Downstairs, there's a funky lounge where late-night crawling lizards may languish.

$$ ($10.95–$17.95)
L·1·2·3·9 to 14th St
☎ 414-1717
24 hours daily.
♠80 ⊟ all ♿ limited

Eleven Madison Park 11 Madison Park (at 14th St) | Gramercy Park

Danny Meyer, restaurateur supreme (Union Square Café, Gramercy Tavern, Tabla) scores another success with this swanky eaterie located in a former bank. It's most corporate place, from the lobby-like soaring marble-floored room to the Yankee-French food and the suits at the tables. Menus read like a butcher's display: foie gras several ways (with pomegranate essence, toasted walnuts and sage), braised pork shoulder, dry-aged sirloin strip, loin of lamb, saddle of venison, roast chicken (with potato speck tart); accompaniments are invariably hearty. Not for vegetarians, anorexics or dates.

$$–$$$ ($19–$34)
N·R to 23 St
☎ 889-0905
5.30–10.30pm Mon–Sat (11pm Sat & 9.30pm Sun).
♠168 ⊟ all ♿ ▢ ▤

Il Bagatto 192 E 2nd St (bet. Aves A & B) | East Village

If you never had the stereotypical Italian mamma (you know... killer cook, killer instinct) but always felt the need, head to this charming restaurant, where there are two rules: no cheese on seafood pasta, and be on time. While the service is often offhand and the seating cramped, the homemade gnocchi and lasagne will leave you begging for more. Everything is stuffed full of the best, hand-picked ingredients and made with love, so it's no wonder that the jewel box of a space is always packed with a hip crowd of downtown gurus, models and celebs. Warning: smoking's allowed here, and everyone does – with gusto.

$ ($7–$10)
F to Second Ave
☎ 228-0977
6.30–11.30pm Mon–Sat (midnight Sat); 6–10.30pm Sun.
♠34 ⊟ none ▢ ♿ ⊿

Il Buco 47 Bond St (bet. Bowery & Lafayette St) | Noho

On any night of the week, well-coiffed young debs and their Newport-type dates mob this dark, romantic restaurant filled with vintage toys and bookshelves of wine bottles. Long-haired, carefully dishevelled downtown artists also gather around the big wooden tables. A rustic Spanish/Italian theme is carried through from the country decor to such luscious tapas plates as polenta with goose ragu and duck prosciutto with port wine. Pasta specials are heavenly, like penne with artichoke, pancetta and cream. The wine list is wide-ranging and discriminating.

$–$$$ ($6–$25)
6 to Bleecker St
☎ 533-1932
6pm–midnight Mon–Sat; 5–11pm Sun.
♠80 ⊟ AE ♿ ▢ ⊿ ▤

Mercer Kitchen 147 Mercer St (at Prince St) | Soho

Raw tuna pizza, black sea bass carpaccio, slow-cooked rabbit, garlic-spiked duck – you can't go wrong with anything you order in this ultra-cool, roomy subterranean restaurant in the fashionable Mercer Hotel [→ 144]. The food (prepared by one of New York's most acclaimed chefs, Jean Georges Vongerichten) is superb, though the crowd, decked out in the latest creations by Gucci, Prada and Helmut do their best to outshine the menu. Whether you're a fashionista or Madonna, so long as you look the part, the staff will treat you like a star. Book way ahead.

$–$$$ ($12–$35)
N·R to Prince St
☎ 966-5454
8–10.45am, 12–2.45pm & 6pm–midnight daily.
♠150 ⊟ all ♿ ▢
⊿ bar only

more restaurants & cafés ➔

Waterloo 145 Charles St (at Washington St) | West Village

If you aren't in a good mood when you arrive here, you will be when you leave – the party-on atmosphere is up there with the best. The industrial, flatteringly-lit dining room is filled with arty types, and the tight seating promotes merrymaking. Sharing a black kettle of mussels and frites over a delicious Belgian beer is a bonding experience, and you'll also want to dig into each other's full-flavoured Belgian-accented chocolatey-rich desserts. One of the best of a new crop of Belgian eateries.

$$$ ($22–$26)
1·9 to Christopher St
☎ 352-1119
6pm–1am Mon–Sun (2am Fri–Sat).
♠75 ⊟ AE/MC/V ♿ ▢
⊿ bar only ▤

big bucks

Aquavit 13 W 54th St (bet. Fifth & Sixth Aves) | Midtown

$$$ ($22–$25)

M E•F to 5th Ave

☎ 307-7311

◑ 12–2.15pm Mon–Fri; 5.30–10.30pm Mon–Sat; 12–4pm Sun.

♦75 ▭ all Ⓢ 3-course, pre-theatre menu $39, 7-course tasting menu $75; 7-course vegetarian menu $58 ▯ ◡ 🗐 Ⓥ

Named after an icy eau de vie, Aquavit aptly offers a broad selection of fluid flavours infused with lemon, dill or anise. They go best with herring (four types of saltwater fillets are available), and other unusual Swedish specialties, like crispy smoked salmon with fingerling dumplings and dill-sevruga broth. Chef Marcus Samuelsson experiments with global influences, both in the intimate (and less expensive) upstairs café and in the formal downstairs atrium, which dramatically shoots up six storeys towards the skylights. A sculpted waterfall whispers in the background.

Bayard's India House | 1 Hanover Sq | Lower Manhattan

$$$ ($22–$35)

M 2•3 to Wall St

☎ 514-9454

◑ 3.30–10pm Mon–Fri; 5.30–11pm Sat. Closed Sun.

♦85 ▭ all ▯ ◡ 🗐

Maritime history and gentlemen's club elegance evoke an aura of privilege. Even though you might think Bayard's is just for Wall Street tycoons, you're wrong. Everyone who walks through the hallowed India House doors is treated like royalty by one of the best-trained, most personable staffs in the city. Sensational contemporary French cuisine is by chef Luc Dendievel; sautéed Hudson Valley foie gras, poached Maine lobster, and loin of venison in red wine are all divine, as is the wine list.

Bouley Bakery 120 W Broadway (at Duane St) | Tribeca

$$$ ($28–$34)

M 1•9 to Chambers St

☎ 964-2525

◑ 11.30am–3pm & 5.30–11.30pm daily.

♦80 ▭ AE/MC/V Ⓢ $35 lunch for 3 courses ♿

Some describe the space at Bouley as 'intimate' – others go for 'cramped'. But regardless, everyone agrees on the food: it's succulent and flavourful, an unadulterated party for your tastebuds. Chef David Bouley has long been revered for his creations, and despite the name 'Bakery' this is a fully-fledged NY culinary hotspot. Think filo-crusted shrimp with Maine crab meat and baby squid, Maple Leaf Farm duck with glazed turnips. While the service is often quite surly, tables are booked way ahead, and even though the prices get steep, no one seems to mind or complain. It's delish!

Café Boulud 20 E 76th St (bet. Fifth & Madison Aves) | UES

$$$ ($24–$30)

M 6 to 77th St

☎ 772-2600

◑ 12–2.30pm & 5.45–11pm Tue–Sat; 5.45–11pm Sun–Mon.

♦90 ▭ all ♿ ▯ 🗐 🌸 Ⓥ

Since chef/owner Daniel Boulud is busy over at his four-star restaurant Daniel, he has appointed rising star Andrew Carmellini to man the stove at the smaller, more relaxed Café Boulud. His take on traditional French (chicken fricassee), seasonal specialties (smoked salmon latkes with caviar), vegetarian creations (cassoulet of root vegetables with garlic crust), and featured world cuisines (anything from Basque to Louisiana cooking) is subtle and deeply resonant. The warm, cosmopolitan room is plushly upholstered and usually filled with powerbrokers (but ties aren't required).

Daniel 60 E 65th St (bet. Madison & Park Aves) | UES

$$$ ($68)

M 6 to 68th St

☎ 288-0033

◑ 12–2pm & 5.45–11pm Mon–Sat.

♦130 ▭ all Ⓢ tasting menus $68–$99 ▯ ◡ bar only 🗐

Daniel Boulud is a god-like chef, and this pink parlour vindicates his reputation. He does serious, sit-up-straight French cuisine: incredible dishes include a chestnut-celery root soup with a braised apple slice and a tranche of foie gras immersed within; a *boeuf aux carottes* – perfect, peasanty braised beef and carrots; or roasted Arctic char with béarnaise and baby vegetables. Desserts are equally sublime – an espresso cup of foamy chocolate with a thick chocolaty bottom; a fruit soup with apple beignets... To die for.

↓ eat-in delis

Barney Greengrass 541 Amsterdam Ave (bet. 86th & 87th Sts) | UWS
Topnotch Jewish specialties, velvety lox and knishes big as baseballs.
☎ 724-4707 **$–$$**

Ess-a-Bagel 831 Third Ave (bet. 50th & 51st Sts)| Midtown
Charmless atmosphere but bagels like no other, plus everything else under the sun.
☎ 980-1010 **$**

Katz's Deli 205 E Houston St (at Ludlow St)| LES
A funky cafeteria with incredible pastrami and chopped liver, around forever for good reason.
☎ 254-2246 **$**

Second Avenue Deli 156 Second Ave (at 10th St) | East Village
Always a line but worth it for huge portions of quality meats and homemade pickles.
☎ 677-0606 **$–$$**

restaurants & cafés

Gotham Bar and Grill 12 E 12th St (bet. Fifth Ave & University Pl) | West Village

Alfred Portale's edible sculptures have been amazing New Yorkers since 85. His kitchen has been a training ground for several of the city's top chefs, educated in his visionary architecture of flavours and beauty.The soaring room is lit by billowy parachutes, a great environment to carefully savour sweetwater shrimp salad with papaya and curry vinaigrette, and seared yellowfin tuna with pappardelle and caponata. The polished, friendly service also sets the standard, and the crowd is sophisticated too.

$$$ ($26.50–$35)
Ⓜ L•N•R•4•5•6 to 14th St-Union Sq
☎ 620-4020
◗ 12–2.15pm Mon–Fri; 5.30–10pm daily (11pm Fri–Sat & 9.45pm Sun).
♟153 ▭ all Ⓢ ▯ ▤

Jean Georges Trump International Hotel | 1 Central Park W (bet. 60th & 61st Sts) | UWS

Eating at this four-star mega blockbuster is not going to be easy. Tables are booked 30 days in advance with every foodie in town eager to explore Jean-Georges Vongerichten's eclectic palette, which might include black sea bass with Sicilian pistachio crust, and loin of lamb dusted with black trumpet mushrooms and leek purée. The dining room's floor-to-ceiling windows and neutral canvas of colours is a soothing backdrop for the smart, refined clientele, who discuss their dishes in low, thrilled tones. The kitchen also turns out grilled meats, salads and cold soups for the Mistral Terrace (summer only) which overlooks Central Park.

$$$ ($85)
Ⓜ A•B•C•D•1•9 to 59th St-Columbus Circle
☎ 299-3900
◗ 12–2.30pm & 5.30–11pm Mon–Fri; 5.30–11pm Sat. Closed Sun.
♟70 ▭ all Ⓢ $85 for 3 courses, $115 for 7 course tasting menu ♿ ▯ ▤ ▤

Le Bernardin 155 W 51st St (bet. Sixth & Seventh Aves) | Midtown

Chef Eric Ripert is so skilled he might spoil you for seafood pre-pared by anyone else. Based in corporate, moneyed Midtown, Le Bernardin has started to attract a cool, younger clientele flush with newfound-but-not-obnoxious wealth. The quiet, wood-lined dining room is Frank Lloyd Wright-inspired, embel-lished with gorgeous floral arrangements. It's flying first class all the way. Sit in the kitchen (six available seats) to observe the French master more closely, but only the very brave would try to duplicate dishes like roasted lobster tail with finely diced foie gras or skate in goosefat with caramelized confit of arti-chokes and fennel.

$$$ ($72)
Ⓜ N•R to 49th St; 1•9 to 50th St
☎ 489-1515
◗ 12–2.30pm Mon–Fri; 5.30–10.30pm Mon–Sat (6pm Mon; 11pm Fri–Sat). Closed Sun.
♟120 ▭ AE/MC/V Ⓢ $72 for 3 courses, $120 tasting menu for 5 courses ♿ ▯ �__ ▤

Lespinasse St Regis Hotel | 2 E 55th St (bet. Fifth & Madison Aves) | Midtown

The grandest of Gotham City's French restaurants is named for Mademoiselle Lespinasse who, during Louis XV's reign, enter-tained philosophers, nobles and diplomats in her Paris salon. The restaurant's exquisite atmosphere may evoke a past era, but you'll hear big money deals discussed more than ideas. Chef Christian Delouvrier is highly trained in classic French tech-niques, using only the best ingredients in dishes like hare stew in red wine, and confit of baby pig in rich cassoulet. Before or after dinner, take time to luxuriate in the glowing King Cole Bar.

$$$ ($37–$44)
☎ 339-6719
◗ 7–10.30am, 12–2pm & 5.30–10pm Tue–Sat. Closed Sun & Mon.
♟88 ▭ AE/MC/V ♿ ▯ ▤

more restaurants & cafés

Nobu 105 Hudson St (at Franklin St) | Tribeca

Nobu's nouvelle-Japanese morsels are remarkable in flavour, freshness and sheer artistry. With no holds barred, dinner for two in this dramatic blond-wood setting easily costs $200 with items like abalone and sea urchins on the menu, but eating here for half that amount is possible if you stick to regular sushi items with salmon, squid, mackerel or white fish. (The more intriguing-sounding sakes and seafood specialties can really add up.) Film and music big-shots, and a galaxy of pretty faces fill the soaring, dramatic stage where the sushi bar stools look like oversized chopsticks, wall sconces resemble crossed samurai swords, and lights are embedded within towering birch tree sculptures.

$$$ ($22–$27)

Ⓜ 1·9 to Franklin St

☎ 219-0500

Ⓛ 11.45am–2.15pm & 5.45–10.15pm Mon–Fri; 5.45–10.15pm Sat–Sun.

♠140 ▭ all ♿ 🖵 🔲

↓ timeless classics

Café des Artistes 1 W 67th St (bet. Columbus & Central Park W) | UWS

Intimate and extravagantly filled with flowers and sensual murals, Café des Artistes is not for the claustrophobic. Patrons are well-heeled and it's perfect for cosy dates and smart family dinners. The French fare is consistent and classic, with salmon served four ways (smoked, poached, dill-marinated and tartare) a highlight. Hungarian owner George Lang has also sneaked in some of his native dishes (like chicken paprika, and goulash soup). Service is cutely formal, and it's tough getting a reservation. The polished bar is romantic for drinks.

$$$ ($22–$40)

Ⓜ B·C to 72nd St; 1·9 to 66th St

☎ 877-3500

Ⓛ 12–2.30pm (11am Sat, 10am Sun) & 5.30pm– midnight daily.

♠110 ▭ all ♿ 🖵 ⬛ 🔲

Copeland's 547 W 145th St (bet. Amsterdam Ave & Broadway) | Harlem

If you're curious about Harlem, Copeland's is an excellent introduction, easy to reach by subway. There's a veneer of formality and decor that recalls a 70's-style country club. The wine list is economical and the homey Southern cooking accomplished: fried chicken, collard greens, spicy Louisiana gumbo, and delectable candied yams. Sunday brunch features gospel, and every night it's live, glorious jazz (no cover charge).

$–$$$ ($8.95–$25)

Ⓜ 1·9 to 145th St

☎ 234-2357

Ⓛ 4.30–11pm Tue–Sat (midnight Fri–Sat); 12–11pm Sun

♠85 ▭ AE/MC/V Ⓢ 14.95 buffet Tue–Thu ♿ 🖵 ⬛ 🔲 ✎ Tue–Sun

Florent 69 Gansevoort St (bet. Greenwich & Washington Sts) | Meatpacking District

Fêted institutions should often be avoided, but this drag queens' French diner on a cobblestone street is so much fun. You'll go away hoarse and deaf (especially late on weekends) and will eat amply, if not memorably. Best bets are roast chicken with mustard sauce and mash, boudin noir and fries, mussels, smoked trout, French toast, or steak frites. It's an ideal pit-stop on your way home after an exhausting evening. Best to be decisive about what you want because some of the waiters are verging on cruel.

$–$$ ($7–$17)

Ⓜ A·C·E·L to 14th St

☎ 989-5779

Ⓛ 9–5am Mon–Thu; open 24 hrs Fri–Sun.

♠70 ▭ none ♿ 🖵 ⬛ bar only 🔲 Ⓥ

Jerry's 101 Prince St (bet. Greene & Mercer Sts) | Soho

Nearly the only soulful restaurant in the Soho 'mall', Jerry's red booths, mosaic-tiled floor, zinc bar and zebra-striped walls have held up well over time, as has much of the American comfort food with slight pretensions – well, mostly. Portions – of roast chicken; seasonal vegetable plate; cajun shrimp salad; devilishly good chocolate brick cake – aren't exactly diner-sized, but the French toast, made with baguette, is the best in town. Watch out for the brunch crush, and occasionally deranged service.

$$ ($11–$22)

Ⓜ N·R to Prince St

☎ 966-9464

Ⓛ 9am–11pm Mon–Sat (11.30pm Fri–Sat); 10.30am–5pm Sun.

♠70 ▭ all ♿ 🖵 ⬛ Ⓥ

Gramercy Tavern 42 E 20th St (bet. Broadway & Park Ave A) | Gramercy

If your pocket's not up to it, you can sidestep the gastronomic prix fixe dinner at this extremely popular and lively temple to new American cuisine by sauntering into the tavern area (no reservations needed) where lower-priced à la carte items are featured. The wine selection is excellent, and they'll open just about anything for you to try by the glass. Everything – either in the tavern or in the dining room – is well prepared, such as fondue of sea urchin and crabmeat with curry essence, and roasted monkfish with pancetta and truffle vinaigrette. Lunch is happening, too, with a more reasonable set menu.

$$–$$$ ($62 dining room; $12–$18 tavern)

Ⓜ N·R to 23rd St

☎ 477-0777

❶ Dining room: 12–2pm Mon–Fri; 5.30–11pm Sat–Sun (11pm Fri–Sat). Tavern: 12–11pm Sun–Thu; 12pm–midnight Fri–Sat.

♠ 140 (dining room); 52 (tavern) 🍴 all
Ⓢ gastronomic $62; lunch $32 ♿ 🖥 ⌄ 🖩

Odeon 147 W Broadway (bet. Duane & Thomas Sts) | Tribeca

If Downtown had to eliminate all but one restaurant, the vote would definitely be to keep Odeon, the ideal place for all occasions (date, birthday, hunger), all hours (still busy at midnight Mondays), all moods (it can cure misery), and all types (though predominantly arty and cool). In the early 80's art boom, it was the place to be seen (Warhol et al), then it died a little, now it's here to stay. Food is American bistro (burgers, seared tuna, beet and fennel salad, steak frites); service is brisk. Enjoy.

$$–$$$ ($14–$24)

Ⓜ A·1·2·3·9 to Chambers St

☎ 233-0507

❶ 11.45–1am Mon–Wed; 11.30–3am Thu–Sat; 11.30–1am Sun.

♠120 🍴 all ♿ limited 🖥 ⌄ bar only 🖩 🚭 Ⓥ

Oyster Bar Lower Level | Grand Central Station | Midtown

Somehow, visiting the Oyster Bar is a little like going to Coney Island: corny yet peculiarly charming. Essentially, it's expensive, ultra-fresh fish and seafood in an old-fashioned setting with gruff yet winsome servers who've been at it for decades. The vaulted space is vast and sitting at the counter for chowder, fresh oysters (tons of different types) and a glass of beer is an after-work treat. House specials include bouillabaisse, Maryland crab cakes and Arctic char. The big, dark bar at the back feels like a wood-lined steamship cabin.

$–$$$ ($9.95–$27.95)

Ⓜ 4·5·6·7 to Grand Central-42nd St

☎ 490-6650

❶ 11.30am–9.30pm Mon–Fri; 5.30–9.30pm Sat.

♠480 🍴 all ♿ 🖥 ⌄ 🖩

Trattoria dell'Arte 900 Seventh Ave (at 57th St) | Midtown

The price of the cracker-thin, fresh clam pizza makes you wonder if the little molluscs were flown in first class from the ocean, but you know what? It's worth it. So is the creative antipasti, and there is a special fish dish every day. An illustrious set regularly gathers at this attractive, bustling Italian establishment, with Tina Brown, Steve Martin and actor William Baldwin being spotted in a single lunch sitting. If no stars are around, feast your eyes on the strange art bedecking the walls.

$$–$$$ ($17–$37.50)

Ⓜ N·R to 57th St

☎ 245-9800

❶ 11.30am–2.45pm & 5–11.45pm Mon–Sun (to 10.45pm Sun).

♠300 🍴 all ♿ 🖥 ⌄ 🖩

'21' Club 21 W 52nd St (bet. Fifth & Sixth Aves) | Midtown

What?! You might harrumph at paying $27 for a hamburger (potatoes and green beans included!), or $33 for chicken hash (Joe DiMaggio's favourite). But this Prohibition-era speakeasy is such a charming landmark it's hard to be curmudgeonly. Newish chef Erik Blauberg, a culinary historian, has taken standards to a new level of excellence. Flaming baked Alaska and caramelized banana flan lit with Malibu rum produce exciting pyrotechnics. Hang out at the bar and feel the tippling spirits of old regulars Ernest Hemingway and Humphrey Bogart.

$$$ ($27–$42)

Ⓜ E·F to 5th Ave

☎ 582-7200

❶ 12–2.30pm Mon–Fri & 5.30–10.15pm Mon–Sat (11pm Fri–Sat). Closed Sun.

♠140 🍴 all ♿ 🖥 ⌄

Union Square Café 21 E 16th St (bet. Fifth Ave & Union Sq W) | Union Square

You can see clear to America's heartland through chef Michael Romano's vibrant cooking, matched by a brilliant wine list. The ambience is streamlined and comfortable. Serving such innovative delights as risotto with foie gras, savoy cabbage and sage, and lobster 'shepherd's pie', it is not surprising that this is many New Yorkers' favourite restaurant. If you can't get a table, swing by and request a seat at the bar, order some wine, a hamburger and hot garlic chips, and you'll feel like the smartest cookie in town.

$$$ ($22.50–$28)

Ⓜ L·N·R·4·5·6 to 14th St-Union Sq

☎ 243-4020

❶ 12–2.30pm & 6–10.30pm Mon–Sat (11.30pm Fri–Sat); 5.30–10pm Sun.

♠125 🍴 all ♿ 🖥 🖩

more restaurants & cafés

diners

Empire Diner 210 10th Avenue (at 22nd St) | Chelsea
Comfort food sassily served 24 hours a day, often accompanied by live piano music.
☎ 243-2736 $-$$

Joe Jr's 482 Sixth Avenue (at 12th St) | Chelsea
Cinematic diner dollhouse with lots of heart but no vitamin content.
☎ 924-5220 $

Tom's Restaurant 2880 Broadway (at 112th St) | Harlem
Immortalized by Seinfeld, with satisfying greasy-spoon specialties for student budgets.
☎ 864-6137 $

↓ bargain gourmet

Comfort Diner 142 E 86th St (at Lexington Ave) | UES

New York is filled with greasy spoon diners with acceptable grub, but at the Comfort Diner (two locations), it's butter, not bacon grease, that will shoot up your cholesterol level. Owned by a nostalgic soul named Ira Freehof, the place is polished to a sheen. The idea is kitschy, but also authentic, with crunchy grilled cheese sandwiches, macaroni and cheese, and thick chocolate malteds. Soups and lighter sandwiches cater to healthier tastes.

$-$$ ($5.95–$12.95)
Ⓜ 4·5·6 to 86th St
☎ 369-8628
◑ 7.30am–11pm daily (9am Sat–Sun).
♣140 🍴 all ♿ 🈳 no alcohol served

Grimaldi's 19 Old Fulton St (bet. Front & Water Sts) | Brooklyn Heights

Beneath the Brooklyn Bridge lies a paean to pizza lovers and Frank Sinatra (walls are littered with autographed photos of him as well as other bygone celebrities). Even the 'small' pizza is obscenely huge, the crust slightly charred, the fresh mozzarella bubbling from the brick oven. Conventional toppings are generous, the only gourmet touches being fresh basil leaves and a twist of fresh ground pepper. It may look tacky, and crass pop plays more than Ol' Blue Eyes, but it's hard to find a better pie.

$$ ($12–$16)
Ⓜ A·C to High St; 2·3 to Clark St
☎ 1-718-858-4300
◑ 11.30am–10.45pm Mon & Wed–Fri (midnight Fri); 2pm–midnight Sat; 2–11pm Sun. Closed Tue.
♣ 70 🍴 none ♿ 🈳 Ⓥ

`Ino 21 Bedford St (bet. Sixth Ave & Downing St) | West Village

Tucked down a little West Village side street, this is exactly the kind of cheery nook you'd love to find on a roadside in Italy. The staff are warm and don't rush you, allowing time to sit and read, think, or chatter all afternoon and night. What's more, the light snacking food is delicious: marinated olives, bruschetta with a number of toppings and flavourful panini with quality ingredients. Smooth music and interesting wines served by the glass, half carafe and bottle help wash cares away.

$ ($2–$10)
Ⓜ A·B·C·D·E·F·Q to W 4th St–Washington Sq
☎ 989-5769
◑ 8am–2am Mon–Fri, 11am–2am Sat–Sun.
♣21 🍴 none ♿ 🈳 ⌖ Ⓥ

Lombardi's 32 Spring St (bet. Mott & Mulberry Sts) | Nolita

This little place is satisfyingly cinematic, with its brick walls and chequered cloths, but the point is the 1905 coal oven and the pizza that emerges from it, which is – honest – the best in Manhattan. The crust is the crispest, the mozzarella the freshest, the toppings (pancetta, sweet Italian sausage, anchovies, roasted peppers, fresh basil, etc) the finest. They also do a fresh clam pie without tomato or cheese, and a white pizza (no tomato), with mozzarella, romano, ricotta and garlic, with a salad on the side. That's all you need.

$$ ($10.50–$20)
Ⓜ 6 to Spring St
☎ 941-7994
◑ 11.30am–11pm daily (midnight Fri–Sat).
♣60 🍴 none ♿ ⌖ 🈳 Ⓥ

Old Devil Moon 511 E 12th St (bet. Aves A & B) | East Village

This is where your 'white trash diner' meets the edgy East Village. In a funky-looking flea market of mismatched chairs, booths, kitsch and fairy lights, gigantic portions of meatloaf with mash, stews, salads and – the best dish – country ham are served by unbelievably sweet waitpersons. The pies (peanut butter cream and the like) are so loved, that you can place orders for whole pies, to go.

$-$$ ($9–$18)
Ⓜ F to 2nd Ave
☎475-4357
◑ 5–11pm Mon–Fri; 10am–midnight Sat–Sun.
♣60 🍴 all ♿ 🈳 ⌖ 🈳 ✍ Ⓥ

Prices quoted correspond to the cost of a main course

Pampa 768 Amsterdam Ave (bet. 97th & 98th Sts) | UWS

If you're looking for a festive place to meet friends, you can't beat Pampa, even though they don't take reservations. It's a cool, lively spot and cheap enough for everyone. Argentine steaks, fries coated in garlic and parsley, juicy roasted chicken, flaky empanadas, and South American wines that start at $15 – all justifying the trip Uptown. Waiters are so cute and sweet you'll want to take them home.

$–$$ ($6.50–$13.95)

ⓜ 1•2•3•9 to 96th St

☎ 865-2929

◑ 4–11pm Mon; 4pm–midnight Tue–Thu; 12pm–midnight Fri–Sun (11pm Sun).

♨85 ▱ none ♿ ⌣ ⌀ ▤

Pepe Rosso 110 St Mark's Pl (bet. Ave A & First Ave) | Soho

Stop by Pepe Rosso's tiny Sullivan Street shop in Soho for a delicious hunk of focaccia to snack on while strolling around. With just a few cramped tables, it's not very comfortable to linger. However, their larger outpost in the East Village is a destination on its own. Dirt cheap pastas (spaghetti with pesto for $5.95!), salads and grilled vegetables are robustly flavoured. The dark, funky setting is utterly without pretension and wine is poured in fat, stemless glasses. Service is haphazard but when the food's this cheap and good, who cares?

$ ($4.95–$7.95)

ⓜ N•R to 8th St; 6 to Astor Pl

☎ 677-6563

◑ 12pm–midnight daily.

♨55 ▱ none ♿ ⌣ bar only ▯ ▤ ▢

Tea & Sympathy 108 Greenwich Ave (bet. 12th & 13th Sts) | West Village

Anglos and Anglophiles alike can't get enough of Tea & Sympathy which is why it's often packed tight. Authentic English breakfasts, typical pub items (shepherd's pie, bangers and mash) and tea from mismatched pots are low-priced and satisfying. It looks like your favourite auntie's living room, the one who still cries over Diana (Royals' memorabilia is everywhere).

$–$$ ($8.50–$11.95)

ⓜ A•C•E• 1•2•3•9 to 14th St

☎ 807-8329

◑ 11.15am–10.30pm Mon–Fri; 10.30am–10.30pm Sat–Sun (10pm Sun).

♨23 ▱ none ⌣ ▤ ▢

↓ ethnic spice

Calle Ocho 446 Columbus Ave (bet. 81st & 82nd Sts) | UWS

Past a warren of secret loungey nooks is a cavernous, dazzling dining room lit by huge burlap lampshades that resemble hoop skirts. One wall is dominated by a dramatic, faux-aged Cuban mural, and more Cuban imagery is evoked when wonderful rolls and muffins arrive in a lined cigar box. Alex Garcia's stimulating Pan-Latino cooking radiates fragrance and spice (octopus and calamari with palm hearts, chick peas and olives, or side dishes like malanga mash and green plantains), while fun rum drinks like *mojitos* and *caipirinhas* prime the palate.

$$–$$$ ($16–$21)

ⓜ 1•9 to 79th St

☎ 873-5025

◑ 6–11pm Mon–Fri (midnight Fri); 5pm–midnight Sat–Sun (10pm Sun).

♨180 ▱ all ♿ ▯ ⌣ bar only ▤

Cho Dang Gol 55 W 35th St (bet. Fifth & Sixth Aves) | Midtown

This may be the only Korean restaurant that makes its own tofu, which sounds a missable experience, until, that is, you try the Doo-Boo-Doo-Roo-Chi-Gi (kimchi fermented cabbage with tofu and pork) or the Mo-Doo-Boo Nak-Ji-Bok-Um (octopus with tofu, vegetables and noodles), after your Pa-Jun – a delicious, thin, chewy pancake – and the Panjan of assorted fiery vegetable and fish side dishes. No place in Koreatown is friendlier. The lovely people seem to like helping neophytes with the mysteries of the menu.

$–$$ ($7.95–$15.95)

ⓜ B•D•F•N•Q•R to 34th St-Herald Sq

☎ 695-8222

◑ 11.40am–10.30pm daily.

♨90 ▱ all ♿ ▤ ▢

Japonica 100 University Place (at 12th St) | West Village

There has been a long-time debate in NY sushi-eating circles over which place serves the best. Now it's official – well at least among the sushi-eating set. Whether you're a die-hard Yama-ite, a Tomoe-addict or a dedicated Iso fan, Japonica has the best. The beautifully-presented sashimi and sushi is swimmingly fresh (albeit pricey), their cooked delights are delicious, and there's always a colourful selection of specials. It's short on atmosphere and long on queues (so book ahead), but it's about a taste of Japan, not the trend factor.

$$–$$$ ($16–$30)

ⓜ L•N•R•4•5•6•to 14th St-Union Sq

☎ 243-7752

◑ 12–10.30pm Mon–Fri (11pm Fri); 1–11pm Sat–Sun (10.30pm Sun).

♨90 ▱ AE/DC ♿

restaurants & cafés

more restaurants & cafés

Joe's Shanghai 9 Pell St (bet. Bowery & Mott St) | LES

The best joint in Chinatown. Sure, insane queues, borderline rude service and communal tables may be frustrating, but there is nothing like their soup dumplings (scoop 'em up in a spoon, bite the top off, drink the soup inside, and then eat the crab meat and pork filling) and fried ricecakes. Get the real Shanghai experience, over-order, over-eat and share with friends...

$–$$$ ($6.95–$25)

N·R·6 to Canal St; B·D·Q to Grand St

☎ 233-8888

🕙 11am–11pm daily.

♦110 none ♿ ▾

Mesa Grill 102 Fifth Ave (bet. 15th & 16th Sts) | Gramercy Park

Everything is oversized in the design of this airy, two-level space, from the huge pillars to the blown-up pop art, to fans as big as propellers on a B-52. The Southwestern flavours are tremendous, too. There's nothing cowardly about sweet potato and Scotch bonnet pepper ravioli, Yucatan-spiced venison or red snapper with roasted *poblano* sauce. Brunch is a standout, with Bloody Marys to knock your socks off. Cut down on the cost by visiting the long bar and sampling potent margaritas and spicy appetizers.

$$–$$$ ($18–$29)

L·N·R·4·5·6 to 14th St-Union Sq

☎ 807-7400

🕙 12–2.30pm & 5.30–10.30pm Mon–Fri; 11.30–3pm Sat–Sun

♦130 all ♿ ☐ ↵ bar only ▤ ▾

Patria 250 Park Ave S (at 20th St) | Gramercy Park

Patria is the patriarch of the Nuevo Latino trend, and electrifying for lunch or dinner. Even though many other restaurants have copied its use of South American and Latin American ingredients, nobody can match chef Andrew Dicataldo's exceptional brilliance. The spacious, creatively-designed dining room sports mosaic touches reminiscent of Gaudi. The three-course set menu features dishes like incredible crispy oysters, 'fire and ice' tuna ceviche, and plantain-coated *mahi mahi*.

$$$ ($54)

6 to 23rd St

☎ 777-6211

🕙 12–2.30pm & 6–11pm Mon–Fri; 5.30pm– midnight Fri–Sun (10.30pm Sun).

♦120 all ⑤ $54 for 3 courses ♿ ☐ ▤

Surya 302 Bleecker St (bet. Grove St & Seventh Ave S) | West Village

A former beauty queen from India is the hostess, setting the tone for a stylish room full of beautiful people. Exotic spices from Southern India blaze in dishes like *dosai* crêpes filled with sea bass, and grilled halibut with ginger and coconut cream. Unique vegetarian choices abound, making use of lentils in cakes, pancakes and soups; and spice-lifted aubergines, okra and potatoes in dishes served with mint rice or *paratha*. It's as modern as Indian restaurants get, also featuring spectacular, photogenic cocktails. The main dining room can be deafening, so when weather cooperates, opt for the serene courtyard.

$–$$$ ($9–$22)

1·9 to Christopher St-Sheridan Sq

☎ 807-7770

🕙 11am–3pm Sat–Sun; 6.30–11.30pm Sun–Thu; 6pm–midnight Fri–Sat.

♦63 all ♿ ☐ ↵ lounge & bar only ▤ ✍ ▾

Tabla 11 Madison Ave (at 25th St) | Gramercy Park

Want a typical Indian dinner? This is not the place. Chef Floyd Cardoz may be a Bombay native but he's more influenced by his training in haute cuisine at Lespinasse. Tabla's food is actually American with a profusion of Indian spices, the flavours intense and controversial, provoking feelings of love and hatred. See which way you turn with dishes like tandoori rabbit, or lobster with pink lentils and five-spice sauce. The fricassee of shellfish comes with turmeric mash and curry leaves. The beautiful, two-level space has dynamic views of Madison Square Park; downstairs is the more casual Bread Bar (lentil soup and lamb tandoori are delicious); upstairs there's a $48 set menu.

$$$ ($52 set menu)

N·R·6 to 23rd St

☎ 889-0667

🕙 12–2.30pm & 5.30–10.30pm Mon–Thu (11pm Fri); 5.30–1pm Sat. Closed Sun.

♦75 Bread Bar; 116 main dining room all ⑤ $52 ♿ ☐ ▤

Takahachi 85 Ave A (bet 5th & 6th Sts) | East Village

Unless you come before 7pm, you'll have to join the long line of East Village locals who know that the sushi here is worth the wait. Takahachi scores on its perfect, delicate *shumai* (steamed dumplings), its insistence on fresh crab instead of the stringy reconstituted stuff, and, in fact, the consistent super-freshness of everything. As an extra plus, it's also not too expensive and the portions are generous. The space is ugly standard-issue – pine tables and bright white light, but it's the food that people come back for.

$$–$$$ ($12–$40)

F to 2nd Ave

☎ 505-6524

🕙 5am–midnight daily.

♦79 all ▤ ▾

↓ romantic rendezvous

Alison on Dominick Street (No. 38 bet. Hudson & Varick Sts) | Soho

Eerily out of the way, once you find this honeymoon spot you'll never forget it. The small, low-ceilinged dining room is dimly lit, with plush navy velour banquettes and Billie Holiday softly playing in the background. Chef Dan Silverman won't blow you away with his creativity; rather, he prepares French and new American dishes simply and perfectly, especially the roasted duck breast and braised lamb shank. The extensive, international wine list heightens the experience, as does scrumptious bread pudding with apples.

$$$ ($27–$34)

Ⓜ C·E to Spring St; 1·9 to Houston St

☎ 727-1188

◑ 5.15–10.15pm daily (11pm Fri–Sat; 9.30pm Sun).

♫60 ▱ all ♿ ▯ ⊿ ▤

American Park Battery Park (opp 175 State St) | Lower Manhattan

Smack dab on the harbour and near the Staten Island ferry, American Park's towering windows afford an incomparable view of passing boats and the Statue of Liberty. But this is no tourist trap. The seafood tastes of the sea it just came from, and is swimming with global influences. How about grilled *mahi mahi* with Vietnamese rice noodles, Japanese eggplant and shiitake mushrooms in spicy lemongrass coconut broth. It works. A table on the outdoor patio at sunset is a lovely experience and service is friendly and proficient.

$$–$$$ ($18–$28)

Ⓜ 1·9 to South Ferry; 4·5 to Bowling Green

☎ 809-5508

◑ 12–3pm & 5–10pm Mon–Fri; 5–10pm Sat. Closed Sun. Outdoor Café: 12–10pm daily.

♫130 ▱ AE/MC/V ♿ ▯ ⊿ bar & patio only ▤

Capsouto Frères 451 Washington St (at Watts St) | Tribeca

The out-of-the-way address may exasperate your cab driver, but it really does exist, and it's well worth seeking out. Three brothers with lots of savvy opened this gracious Tribeca loftspace nearly 20 years ago, and new chef Eric Heinrich has recently reinvigorated the French cuisine. The temple to magnificent soufflés, saucisson chaud and fork-tender duckling now boasts creative specials like *tian* of venison with parsnip purée. Brunch is fab, the crowd distinguished but dressed down. And, oh, the wine list!

$$–$$$ ($15–$26)

Ⓜ 1·9 to Canal St

☎ 966-4900

◑ 6–10pm Mon; 12–3.30pm & 6–10pm Tue–Sun (11pm Fri–Sat).

♫90 ▱ all ♿ ▯ ⊿ bar only ▤

La Bonne Soupe 48 W 55th St (bet. Fifth & Sixth Aves) | Midtown

Utterly retro from the red-and-white check cloths to the fondues, this adorable bistro anachronism makes a fantastic Midtown bolt-hole. Ignore the terrifying menu prose ('this omelette masterpiece, almost austere in its simplicity', 'transformed by the art of France into a sophisticated delight'), because the food is just fine. Onion soup; Emmenthal fondue; great brandade and quiche; and little tables in two straight lines are the essence of cosy.

$–$$ ($8–$18)

Ⓜ E·F to 5th Ave

☎ 586-7650

◑ 11.30am–11pm daily.

♫70 ▱ AE
Ⓢ $12.95–$19.95 ♿ limited ▯ ⊿ bar only ▤

burgers

Big Nick's Burger 2175 Broadway (at 77th St) | UWS
24-hour Upper West Side dump that inspires affection; loosen your belt buckle.
☎ 362-9238 $

Corner Bistro 331 W 4th Street (at Jane St) | West Village
Cheap, juicy burgers in a dark saloon that do the trick after a night of drinking.
☎ 242-9502 $

Island Burgers & Shakes 766 Ninth Avenue (bet. 51st & 52nd Sts) | Midtown
Move over McDonald's. You can have it any way you like it here. But no fries.
☎ 307-7934 $

Jackson Hole 1270 Madison Avenue (at 91st St) | UES
Get lots of napkins for these messy burgers, especially good for kids.
☎ 427-2820 $

Rialto 265 Elizabeth Street (bet. Houston & Prince Sts) | Nolita
Groovy bistro with lots of inventive choices but nothing beats their thick, quality burgers and crispy fries.
☎ 334-7900 $$

more restaurants & cafés

Le Jardin Bistrot 25 Cleveland Pl (bet. Spring & Lafayette) | Nolita

One hesitates to recommend this perfect bistrot for fear of its being overwhelmed by success, but Breton chef-patron, Gérard Maurice, can surely handle it. The bucolic garden is full of grape vines, herb and tomato plants and Gérard's extensive collection of frog *tchotchkes*. Satisfy your yearnings for bouillabaisse, cassoulet, steak (or tuna) tartare, hangar steak, moules-frites and coq au vin; there is not a bad dish on the menu, though desserts (tarte tatin, chocolate marquise, creme caramel) tend not to be as successful.

$$–$$$ ($12–$29)
🚇 6 to Spring St
☎ 343-9599
🕐 12–3pm & 6–11.30pm Mon–Sat; 6–11pm Sun.
🍴80 🍽 AE/MC/V ♿ 📋 🖊

Park View at the Boathouse Central Park (bet. East Park Drive & 74th St)

A shuttle bus leaves from Fifth Avenue and 72nd Street every ten minutes to ferry customers to this rustic chalet in the middle of Central Park. Open all year round, the cosy interior glows from the slate fireplace in winter and there's a bar where you can warm up on hot toddies. In good weather the outdoor tables are romantically lakeside. The American menu with global touches is strong on seafood, such as Indian-spiced salmon tartare with mango, and spinach and potato crusted monkfish with Barolo sauce.

$$–$$$ ($18–$34)
🚇 6 to 68th St-Hunter College
☎ 517-2233
🕐 11.30am–4pm & 5pm–midnight Mon–Sat (1am Fri–Sat); 11am–4pm Sun.
🍴200 🍽 all ♿ 📋 ☕ 📋 🖊

Quilty's 177 Prince St (bet. Sullivan & Thompson Sts) | Soho

Chef Katy Sparks knows how to wow and woo diners with her spectacularly innovative cuisine. It is American food taken to a higher form of evolution, with Asian and French influences that accent each other in an eloquent way. For instance, you've never tasted anything quite like her tuna medallions with sesame-wilted Savoy cabbage, papaya coulis and macadamia couscous. The far-reaching wine list is nearly as amazing. Moneyed corporate types impress clients here with the cool Soho vibe, so go later for more quiet romance.

$$$ ($19–$28)
🚇 N·R to Prince St
☎ 254-1260
🕐 6–11pm Mon; 12–3pm (11.30am Sat–Sun) & 6–11pm Tue–Sun.
🍴60 🍽 all ♿ 📋 ☕ 📋 🖊

Rosemarie's 145 Duane St (bet. Church St & W Broadway) | Tribeca

Considering this excellent northern Italian in Tribeca doesn't put a foot wrong, it's remarkably underpopulated. The room is calm and grown up, the service is caring, and the small menu is good-to-spectacular. Go for wild mushrooms with polenta, pancetta and sage, or white bean crostini; a half order of pasta (*orecchiette* with Manila clams or rigatoni with lamb bolognese); then seared skate with brown butter over red cabbage, or a veal chop with porcini sauce – and your stomach will be happy. Buzz factor is low.

$$–$$$ ($16–$29)
🚇 1·9 to Franklin St
☎ 285-2610
🕐 12–2.30pm Mon–Fri; 5.30–9.30pm Mon–Sat.
🍴84 🍽 AE/MC/V ⑤ $22 for 3 courses ♿ 📋 ☕ bar only 📋

Screening Room 54 Varick St (bet. Canal & Laight Sts) | Tribeca

All under one roof, at The Screening Room you can enjoy cinematic cocktails at the bar (the 'Clockwork Orange', the 'Lolita'), tuck into rapturous dishes like pan-fried artichokes and cedar-planked salmon, and then move into the 40's-style theatre showing independent and foreign films. The attractive dining room is downtown casual, and the best deal is the $30 prix fixe, which includes three courses plus the screening. Brunch is also fun when they regularly show old cult favourites like *Breakfast at Tiffany's* and *Valley of the Dolls*.

$$–$$$ ($19–$24)
🚇 A·C·E·1·9 to Canal St
☎ 334-2100
🕐 12–3pm Mon–Thu; 5.30–11pm Thu–Sat (midnight Fri–Sat); 11.30am–3.30pm Sun.
🍴150 🍽 all ♿ 📋 ☕ 📋 🖊

Spartina 355 Greenwich St (at Harrison St) | Tribeca

Tribeca residents probably wish they could keep Spartina to themselves, but that's too bad. The warmth of the stylish room enfolds you, and the Mediterranean dishes further seduce. The place specializes in fish and seafood, such as roasted trout stuffed with brandade and wrapped in smoked bacon, but chef-co-owner Stephen Kalt also excels at slow-cooked short ribs and mash. Then there are the divine, crispy grilled pizzas, and over 80 types of wine. What more could you need?

$$–$$$ ($16–$25)
🚇 1·9 to Franklin St
☎ 274-9310
🕐 11.20am–3pm Mon–Fri; 5.30–11pm daily (midnight Thu–Sat).
🍴100 🍽 all ♿ 📋 ☕ bar only 📋 🖊

Prices quoted correspond to the cost of a main course

↓ brunch

Mesa Grill 102 Fifth Avenue (bet. 15th & 16th Sts) | Gramercy Park
Creative twists on Southwestern brunch, blazing with flavour – along with sensational drinks.
☎ 807-7400 $$–$$$

Odeon 145 W Broadway (bet. Duane & Thomas Sts) | Tribeca
Forever cool in every way, a delectable bread basket and big tables for brunching parties.
☎ 233-0507 $$–$$$

7A 109 Avenue A (at 7th St) | East Village
Cheap, hangover heaven. Bring sunglasses for sidewalk tables and reading material for the wait.
☎ 673-6583 $

Sylvia's 328 Lenox Avenue (bet. 126th & 127th Sts) | Harlem
Skip church and get your gospel here, along with church lady fashions.
☎ 996-0660 $–$$

restaurants & cafés

Union Pacific 111 E 22nd St (bet. Lexington & Park Ave S) | Gramercy Park

At this smart restaurant, expect some of the most succulent and creatively prepared seafood your tongue could hope to tangle with. Sashimi-quality Taylor Bay scallops with sea urchin; wild sturgeon with morels; and for the non-fish-eaters, there's always steak and chicken, prepared with the chef's innovative touch. And the richly-decorated space is just as smart as the menu – a plush lounge filled with chic velvet sofas and over-stuffed chairs in the basement level – it's the perfect place to impress.

$$$ ($65)
Ⓜ 6 to 23rd St
☎ 995-8500
◖ 12–2pm Mon–Fri; 5.30–10.30pm Mon–Sat (11pm Sat). Closed Sun.
♦109 ⊟ AE/MC/V
Ⓢ $35 for 3 courses (lunch); $65 for 3 courses (dinner) ♿ limited

Verbena 53 Irving Place (bet. 17th & 18th Sts) | Gramercy Park

If Edith Wharton were alive today, she would probably dine at Verbena; she lived near here and the place manages to be civilized and daring at the same time. The townhouse setting is lovely and spare, with two fireplaces, and botanical touches throughout. The courtyard garden is bordered by herbs and vegetables, which chef-owner Diane Forley employs in American dishes like butternut squash ravioli with roasted oranges and sage, and red snapper with braised cabbage and salsify.

$$$ ($23–$28)
Ⓜ L•N•R•4•5•6 to 14th St-Union Sq
☎ 260-5757
◖ 11.30am– 2.30pm Sun; 5.30–10.30pm daily (11pm Fri–Sat; 9.30pm Sun).
♦55 dining room; 75 garden ⊟ all ♿ 🚻 ▤ 🅿 Ⓥ

---

veg out

Angelica Kitchen 300 E 12th St (bet. 1st & 2nd Aves) | East Village

During the day Angelica Kitchen is a place to unwind over well-prepared dragon bowls of rice, beans, tofu and sea vegetables. Instead of salt and pepper on the tables, it's soy sauce and a shaker of sesame seeds. They also have good marinated tofu sandwiches and rich walnut-lentil paté. It's a homey, bright place with bronze Aztec-designed walls, an open kitchen and plain wood tabletops. At night it's more hectic so you won't absorb the same Zen-ness. Note: no alcohol served.

$–$$ ($5.50–$12.50)
Ⓜ L•N•R•4•5•6 to 14th St-Union Sq
☎ 228-2909
◖ 11.30am–10.30pm daily.
♦65 ⊟ none ♿ ▤ Ⓥ

Zen Palate 34 Union Square E (at 16th St) | Union Square

Luckily there is a Zen Palate Downtown, Midtown and Uptown so you never have to go too far to enjoy its meditative, unusual Asian compositions in a poetic atmosphere. The Union Square location is perhaps the most popular, with a busy downstairs area (and cheaper prices), and a tranquil, airy upstairs room (with fancier veggie offerings) affording views of the park. Patrons are chic but not horribly so. Real thought and creativity goes into dishes you feel you could eat into infinity. Note: no alcohol served.

$–$$ ($11–$17.50)
Ⓜ L•N•R•4•5•6 to 14th St-Union Sq
Ⓥ 614-9291
◖ 11am–11pm Mon–Sat; 12–10.30pm Sun.
♦200 ⊟ all ♿ ▤ Ⓥ

→ more restaurants & cafés

↓ neighbourhood standouts

Acquario 5 Bleecker St (at Bowery) | Noho

Apparently, everybody in this small, cosy brick-lined restaurant, sister to the popular Il Buco [→121] is from Europe, smokes and abuses cellphones, but don't let that discourage you. A Sicilian/Portuguese/Spanish menu offers no division between appetizers and mains, encouraging mix-and-match and sharing – *boquerones* with green pepper couscous and salsa verde; grilled octopus; baked Asiago cheese with prosciutto and fresh figs; clam linguine; grilled *gambas* with fennel and mache salad.

$–$$ ($9–$18)

Ⓜ B·D·F·Q to Broadway-Lafayette St; 6 Bleecker St

☎ 260-4666

◑ 12–3pm Mon & Wed–Sun; 6–11.30pm daily (midnight Sat–Sun).

♦40 ▭ none ☼ ⌣ ▤

Bar Pitti 268 Sixth Ave (bet. Bleeker & Houston Sts) | West Village

A simple Tuscan restaurant that's best in summer, when tables line up on the wide sidewalk, and the marble floors and white walls inside are super cool. The *fettunta* (bread salad) is the best dish on the menu, but the blackboard specials are all usually good, from spinach with garlic and lemon to marinated quail or homemade pasta. Bar Pitti feels genuinely European, as opposed to Eurotrashy (that's what Da Silvano, the expensive schmoozy joint next door, is for).

$–$$ ($7–$17)

Ⓜ A·B·C·D·E·F·Q to W 4th St-Washington Sq

☎ 982-3300

◑ 12pm–midnight daily.

♦77 ▭ none ☼ limited ▯ ▤ ✐ Ⓥ

Blue Ribbon 67 Sullivan St (bet. Prince & Spring Sts) | Soho

The waiting-in-line situation is absurd (even at 3am), but the people-watching (super-chic and supermodels) is almost an essential part of the experience. While it tends to get sceney, it's never obnoxious – because everyone is there for one thing ... fabulous, eclectic, innovative food, like the flavour-bursting fondue, roasted duck club sandwich and whole steamed flounder. Calorie counters, beware: it's impossible to stick to your diet here... and with a menu this diverse and tempting, you wouldn't want to.

$–$$$ ($9.50–$26.50)

Ⓜ C·E to Spring St

☎ 274-0404

◑ 4pm–4am Tue–Sun. Closed Mon.

♦55 ▭ AE/MC/V ▯

First 87 First Ave (bet. 5th & 6th Sts) | East Village

First has an undeniable groove, even though you'd never notice it passing by. The commodious booths are ideal for groups, and dim lighting enhances everybody's appearance. The new American cuisine is generously portioned, so beware the addictive warm bread with infused olive oil. Martinis are served in their own cute pitchers on ice, keeping them cold for refills. Pizza with condiments on the side (like fresh pesto) is wonderful, as is the vegetable extravaganza and grilled lamb steak.

$–$$$ ($9–$21)

☎ 674-3823

Ⓜ 6 to Astor Place; F to 2nd Ave

◑ 6pm–2am Mon–Sat (3am Fri–Sat); 11am–1am Sun.

♦90 ▭ AE/MC/V ☼ ▯ ▤ Ⓥ

Grange Hall 50 Commerce St (at Barrow St) | West Village

So homey, you'll feel like you're dining in your friend's ultra-cool art deco apartment. And the fact that it's nestled on one of NYC's most beautiful streets makes this restaurant even more of a draw. The service is sweet and the portions are waist-strainingly huge, so go hungry and prepare to scarf down some old-fashioned comfort food like creamy garlic mashed potatoes, herb-breaded organic chicken, and a big slab of aged shell-steak with pickles. It always brings in a crowd, especially for brunch (one of the most fattening weekend treats in town).

$$–$$$ ($12.50–$21.50)

Ⓜ 1·9 to Christopher St–Sheridan Sq

☎ 924-5246

◑ 12–3pm & 5.30–11pm Mon–Wed & Fri–Sun (11am Sat; 10.30am Sun; 11.30pm Tue–Wed; midnight Fri–Sat).

♦90 ▭ AE ▯

O Padeiro 641 Sixth Ave (bet. 19th & 20th Sts) | Chelsea

If you're in need of some hardcore carbohydrate action, then this adorable Portuguese bakery/tapas bar will be right up your alley. Their baked goods, and eclectic wine selections are outrageously good and their small-sized entrées (like salt cod layered with potato, chopped eggs and olives) demand indulgence. Every so often, a Portuguese singer adds a little more authentic flavour to the tile-embellished ambience.

$–$$ ($3–$3.75)

Ⓜ 1·9 to 23rd St

☎ 414-9661

◑ 7am–10pm Mon–Sat (11pm Fri–Sat); 10am–7pm Sun.

♦40 ▭ AE/MC/V ☼ ▯ ▤

Bereket 187 E Houston St (at Orchard St) | LES
A taxi driver's haven for speedy Turkish specialties sizzling on the grill.
☎ 475-7700 $

Cafeteria 119 Seventh Ave (at 17th St) | Chelsea
The cool kids' lunchroom any hour of the day.
☎ 414-1717 $–$$

French Roast 78 W 11th St (at Sixth Ave) | West Village
Dark, mellow hangout to unwind and refuel on a number of items.
☎ 533-2233 $–$$

Yaffa Café 97 St Mark's Pl (bet. Ave A & First Ave) | East Village
Eclectic spot, wide-ranging food, full of interesting, starving artist types.
☎ 674-9302 $

Payard Patisserie & Bistro 1032 Lexington Ave (bet. 73rd & 74th Sts) | UES

Children (and the child in you) will be filled with wonder at the tiers of tea cakes, tarts, éclairs, fancy pastries and handmade chocolates in the Parisian-style patisserie. A few small tables provide room for immediate gratification. Ladies who 'tea' will be entranced by the $14.50 afternoon delights of brioche, scones and madeleines. Those desirous of classic, but equally calorific, French fare can tuck into bouillabaisse and cassoulet in the bi-level bistro.

$$–$$$ ($19–$25)
Ⓜ 6 to 77th St
☎ 717-5252
Ⓞ Patisserie: 7am–11pm Mon–Sat. Bistro: 12–2.30pm (3pm Fri–Sat) & 6–10.30pm Mon–Sat (11pm Fri–Sat). Closed Sun.
♟100 ▱ all ♿ 🖵 🖩

Pisces 95 Ave A (at 6th St) | East Village

What's so great about Pisces is that you can get really fresh seafood prepared in eclectic ways and still walk out with money in your pocket. At weekends it's a challenge to snag a table even though they open the second deck upstairs for the overflow. In summer, the wraparound windows are flung open, making it feel like you're out at sea on Avenue A. Brunch is also a big attraction, with several egg dishes for under $8, which includes a Mimosa (champagne and OJ) and coffee.

$–$$ ($9.95–$19.95)
Ⓜ F to 2nd Ave; 6 to Astor Pl
☎ 260-6660
Ⓞ 5.30–11.30pm Sun–Thu; 5.30pm–1am Fri; 11.30–1am Sat–Sun (11.30pm Sun).
♟140 ▱ all ♿ 🖵 ⌕
🖩

Pó 31 Cornelia St (bet. Bleeker & W 4th Sts) | West Village

'Molto' Mario Batali is famous for his colourful TV cookery programme, popular cookbooks and two fine Italian restaurants, Pó and Babbo. Pó is the original, and still packed after a number of years. The small, unfussy space feels like a well-oiled machine, with every detail seen to in a professional, unpretentious manner. Garlicky white bean bruschetta comes gratis, and pastas are big in size and flavour. The six-course tasting menu is a real deal: an antipasto, two kinds of pasta, a main dish, cheese and dessert.

$$ ($12.50–$15)
Ⓜ 1·9 to Christopher St
☎ 645-2189
Ⓞ 5.30–11pm Tue; 11.30am–2.15pm & 5.30–11pm Wed–Sun (11.30pm Fri–Sat; 10pm Sun). Closed Mon.
♟34 ▱ AE Ⓢ $35 for 6-course tasting menu
♿ 🖵 🖩 Ⓥ

Veritas 43 E 20th St (bet. Broadway & Park Ave S) | Flatiron District

This muted, shimmering room gets rave reviews for one of the most astonishing wine lists in the city. What's more, bottles are not overpriced – certainly not for the quality and rare vintages. Owners Gino Diaferia and Scott Bryan are sharp guys, already having the extremely good Indigo and Siena restaurants under their belts. Veritas is their real showplace, with subtle yet exhilarating contemporary American inventions like warm truffled oysters with Riesling, roasted squab with foie gras emulsion, and pepper-crusted venison with sour cherry-Armagnac sauce.

$$$ ($22–$28)
Ⓜ N·R to 23rd St
☎ 353-3700
Ⓞ 12–2.30pm & 6–11pm Mon–Sat; 5–10pm Sun.
♟65 ▱ all ♿ 🖵 ⌕ 🖩

New York's bars are as varied as the city's denizens. Get louche in plush lounges, hang with the barflies at a local dive, or sip superb cocktails alongside the chic and sleek set. Everything's open until late, so you can take your time.

drink up

bars

club mode

Baby Jupiter

A bar, club, performance space and restaurant all squeezed into one, Baby Jupiter is always packed. Their popular club nights change frequently, so call ahead to confirm scheduling. Perfect for cheap dates and indecisive groups.

170 Orchard St (at Stanton St), LES ☎ 982-2229 🗒 F to 2nd Ave ◑ 11am–3 or 4am daily. 🖃 MC/V ⅄ ☜ ⬕ 🗐 ⬎ ⬤

Baraza ✔

Can't afford that tropical vacation? Take a trip to Baraza, an Alphabet City bar where DJs spin salsa and samba, bartenders serve *mojitos* and *caipirinhas* and the average duration of relationships formed on the premises is ten days.

133 Ave C (at 8th St), East Village ☎ 539-0811 🗒 L to 1st Ave ◑ 7.30pm–4am daily. 🖃 none ⅄ ⬎ 🗐 ☒ ⬤

B-Bar

Sink into a banquette and spy on starlets, fashionistas and celebrity slummers – B-Bar offers them all, as well as enough average Joes to keep things comfortable. In the summer, sip a few margaritas and stargaze in the garden.

4 E 4th St (at Bowery), Noho ☎ 475-2220 🗒 6 to Astor Pl ◑ 11.30am–2 to 4am daily. 🖃 all ⅄ ☜ ⬎ 🗐 ☒ ⬤ Mon–Sat

Botanica

Sick of the megaclubs? Come to Botanica for jungle, dub and drum 'n' bass spun by top DJs in a cosy basement lounge. Cheap drinks and a monthly surf music party too.

47 E Houston St (bet. Mott & Mulberry Sts), Noho ☎ 343-7251 🗒 B•D•F•Q to Broadway-Lafayette St ◑ 5pm–4am Mon–Fri; 6pm–4am Sat–Sun. 🖃 none ⅄ 🗐 ⬤ Mon–Fri & Sun

Hell

Hell is a gay bar that goes out of its way to welcome a mixed crowd. DJs spinning 70's and early 80's disco get the crowd moving on the dance floor, and Hell's potent house martinis (some more appealing than others) keep lazy loungers blissful.

55 Gansevoort St (bet. Greenwich & Washington Sts), Chelsea ☎ 727-1666 🗒 A•C•E to 14th St; L to 8th Ave ◑ 5pm–4am Fri; 7pm–4am Sat–Thu. 🖃 AE/MC/V ⅄ ⬎ 🗐 ⬤ Tue–Thu

Lansky Lounge

This bar may look like a Prohibition-era speakeasy, but don't let its tucked-away location fool you. Swing, Latin and lounge music nights draw capacity crowds, and fantastic flavoured martinis (try the mango) keep everyone lively.

104 Norfolk St (at Delancey St), LES ☎ 677-9489 🗒 F•J•M•Z to Delancey St-Essex St ◑ 8pm–3 or 4am Sat–Thu. 🖃 AE/MC/V ☜ ⬎ 🗐 ⬤ Thu & Sat

Moomba

Luckily, most of the hoopla that accompanied Moomba's opening in '98 has subsided, leaving in its wake a comfortably louche lounge, decent Asian fusion cuisine and a defanged wait staff. The velvet ropes are still in place, but don't let them fool you.

133 Seventh Ave S (at Charles St), West Village ☎ 989-1414 🗒 1•9 to Christopher St-Sheridan Sq ◑ 6pm–3am daily. 🖃 all ⅄ ground floor only ☜ ⬎ 🗐 ⬤

Orchard Bar

DJs spin all forms of electronica nightly in an atmosphere more reminiscent of a terrarium than a bar. From the foliage-filled glass tanks to the apples suspended in jars, an unnatural green glow pervades everything in the room – including visitors, who take excessive advantage of the bar's cheapish drinks.

200 Orchard St (bet. Houston & Stanton Sts), LES ☎ 673-5350 🗒 F to 2nd Ave ◑ 7pm–3am daily (4am Tue–Sat). 🖃 all ⅄ ⬎ 🗐 ⬤

Sweet & Vicious

The best time to enjoy this sleek, sexy lounge is on a Sunday night, when the weekend crowds have dissipated, DJs spin breakbeats and you can linger over your raki. Come summer, the garden is an urban oasis.

5 Spring St (at Elizabeth St), Noho ☎ 334-7915 🗒 6 to Spring St ◑ 5pm–3am daily. 🖃 none ⬎ 🗐 ☒ ⬤ Wed & Sun

live sounds

Bar d'O

New York's premiere venue for drag entertainment just keeps getting better. Intimate and glamorous, Bar d'O continues to attract a devoted following thanks to weekly performances by downtown legends Raven O and Joey Arias – a brilliant, Billie Holiday-esque chanteuse.

29 Bedford St (at Downing St), West Village ☎ 627-1580 🚇 1·9 to Houston St ● 7pm–3am daily. 🍴 none ⬗ 🍸 Sat, Sun & Tue ○ Mon & Wed–Sat

Café Carlyle

The reigning divas of cabaret often book a stint at Café Carlyle [→140]: intimate performances from the likes of Barbara Cook and the legendary Eartha Kitt – as well as a solid roster of classic cocktails – make this a New York favourite.

981 Madison Ave (bet. 76th & 77th Sts), UES ☎ 744-1600 🚇 6 to 77th St ● performances at 8.45pm & 10.45pm Mon–Sat (NB entrance fee for shows). 🍴 all ♿ ☮ 🍸 Mon–Sat

Ciel Rouge

More like Weimar Berlin than modern-day Chelsea, Ciel Rouge serves up sexy torch singers and exceptional cocktails in its plush, decadent lounge. When no one is performing, the CD player is partial to opera arias and Marlene Dietrich. Gorgeous garden, too.

176 Seventh Ave (at 20th St), Chelsea ☎ 929-5542 🚇 1·9 to 23rd St ● 7pm–2am daily (3.30am Fri–Sat). 🍴 none ♿ ⬗ 🍸 Tue, Wed & Thu

Joe's Pub

Built into the Public Theater and a recent addition to the Noho scene, Joe's Pub promises to remain one of New York's hottest nightspots long after the initial

buzz subsides. It is both an elegantly modern lounge and an intimate performance space [→141] with inebriated models performing unintentionally between sets.

425 Lafayette St (bet. Astor Pl & W 4th St), Noho ☎ 539-8770 🚇 6 to Astor Pl ● 5pm–4am daily (NB entrance fee for shows). 🍴 AE/MC/V ☮ ⬗ 🍸 vary ○ vary

Lakeside Lounge

Catch some of New York's best indie bands at Lakeside Lounge, before they hit the charts. A few big names play here as well, and, on nights when no one performs, you'll find plenty of out-of-work musicians slumped over their beers.

162–164 Ave B (at 10th St), East Village ☎ 529-8463 🚇 L to 1st Ave ● 4pm–4am daily. 🍴 MC/V ♿ ⬗ 🍸 vary

Meow Mix

Unlike its older, quieter counterparts in the West Village, Meow Mix – the only lesbian bar in the Lower East Side – offers live music seven nights a week and enough hard-rocking girls to keep the party going all night.

269 E Houston St (at Suffolk St), LES ☎ 254-0688 🚇 F to 2nd Ave ● 3pm–4am daily. 🍴 none ♿ ⬗ 🍸 ○ 🎤

Tonic

Ever had a drink in a giant wine barrel? This former Kosher wine shop now houses a performance space, an alternative press, and a basement bar featuring oversized casks that have been converted into miniature private rooms, complete with seating. Movies shown on Mondays.

107 Norfolk St (at Delancey St), LES ☎ 358-7504 🚇 F·J·M·Z to Delancey St-Essex St ● 11am–1am daily. 🍴 none ☮ ⬗ 🍸 Wed–Sun

Winnie's

Tucked away on a side street in Chinatown, Winnie's caters to both Asian and non-Asian karaoke fans. A makeshift stage inspires seasoned songsters to ham it up, while copious quantities of Tsing Tao beer encourage novices to screech at the bar. A fun, boisterous crowd.

104 Bayard St (bet. Mulberry & Baxter Sts), Chinatown ☎ 732-2384 🚇 J·M·N·R·Z·6 to Canal St ● 12pm–4am daily. 🍴 none ☮ ⬗ 🍸 karaoke nightly 🎤

cigar bars

Circa Tabac
32 Watts St (bet. Thompson St & Sixth Ave), Soho ☎ 941-1781 🚇 1·9 to Canal St ● 5pm–2am daily (4am Thu–Sat).

Club Macanudo
26 E 63rd St (bet. Park & Madison Aves), UES ☎ 752-8200 🚇 B·Q to Lexington Ave ● 4pm–12.30 Mon–Sat (1.30am Wed–Sat).

Hudson Bar & Books
636 Hudson St (bet. Horatio & Jane Sts), Chelsea ☎ 229-2642 🚇 A·C·E to 14th St ● 5.30pm–2am Mon–Fri (4am Fri); 6pm–4am Sat; 6pm–2am Sun.

King Cole Bar
St Regis Hotel, 5 E 55th St (bet. Fifth & Madison Aves), Midtown ☎ 339-6721 🚇 E·F to 5th Ave ● 11.30am–1am Mon–Sat (2am Fri & Sat); 12pm–midnight Sun.

live it up

Bar 89

Bar 89 was built for bull-market imbibing. If 40-ft ceilings and bottomless martinis aren't enough to make you feel like a master of the universe, steal one of the trophy girlfriends sitting at the banquettes.

89 Mercer St (at Spring St), Soho ☎ 274-0989 🚇 N·R to Prince St ● 1pm–2am daily. 🍴 AE/MC/V ♿ ☮ ⬗

bars

more bars

Bubble Lounge

Exceptional champagnes, tempting appetizers and enough platinum cards to buy a small Central American nation can all be found at the Bubble Lounge. Wear this season's Gucci to fit in.

228 W Broadway (at White St), Tribeca ☎ 431-3433 🚇 1•9 to Franklin St ⏰ 5pm–4am Mon–Sat. 🚫 AE/MC/V ♿ 🔊 🔉 ▤ 🔧 Mon &Tue

Grand Bar

Barely removed from the bustle of Soho, the Grand Bar is ideal for both stylish midday drinks and comfortable nightcaps à deux: just don't expect too much privacy at weekends when footsore shoppers and cultured-out gallery-goers take over the lounge.

Soho Grand Hotel, 310 W Broadway (at Canal St), Soho ☎ 965-3000 🚇 A•C•E to Canal St ⏰ 12pm–2am daily. 🚫 all ♿ 🔊 🔉 ▤

The Greatest Bar on Earth

The view from here is spectacular. Bring your friends, order a round of classic cocktails and stick someone else with the tab. After 10pm, the Wall Street crowd goes home and the kids come out for swing music and Sidecars. Be sure to visit on Wednesdays, when Lucien the Loungecore DJ spins kooky soundtracks and other lounge music staples.

107th Floor, 1 World Trade Center, Lower Manhattan ☎ 524-7011 🚇 N•R•1•9 to Cortlandt St; 2•3 to Park Pl; A•C•E to Chambers St ⏰ 12pm–midnight Mon–Sat (1am Wed–Sat); 11am–10pm Sun. 🚫 all ♿ 🔉 ▤ 🔧 Mon–Sat ● Mon–Sat

Harry Cipriani

Nostalgic for Italy? Visit Harry Cipriani, where bartenders pour the same Bellinis made famous at Harry's Bar in Venice. If power lunches frighten you, request your midday meal at the bar. (The downtown outpost of Harry's is worth a visit for its rooftop garden.)

781 Fifth Ave (at 59th St), UES ☎ 753-5566 🚇 N•R to 5th Ave ⏰ 12pm–10.30pm daily. 🚫 all 🔊 🔉 ▤ 🎵

357

A resolutely swanky champagne lounge serving both bubbly and booze by the bottle or glass. The crowd is equal parts downtown hipster and well-heeled Sohoite. Regular club nights – call ahead for DJ information.

357 W Broadway (at Broome St), Soho ☎ 965-1491 🚇 N•R to Prince St ⏰ 9pm–4am daily. 🚫 all ♿ 🔊 🔉 ▤ ● daily

Top of the Tower

Top of the Tower is the epitome of old New York elegance. The views from this art deco hotel bar – located on the 26th floor – are stunning. Ancient waiters (not aspiring actors) are on hand to serve

classic cocktails and a piano player performs nightly.

Beekman Tower Hotel, 3 Mitchell Place (bet. E 49th St & First Ave), Midtown ☎ 355-7300 🚇 E•6 to 51st St ⏰ 5pm–1am daily. 🚫 AE/MC/V ♿ 🔊 🔉 ▤ 🎵 🔧

the status quo

Chumley's

A former speakeasy with two secret entrances, Chumley's was once a literary hang-out for the likes of John Reed, Eugene O'Neill, John Dos Passos, TS Eliot and many others. Today, in this last remaining vestige of New York's prohibition era, there's a friendly neighbourhood crowd; a choice of over 25 beers on tap; and a varied steak and pasta menu.

86 Bedford St (bet. Bleecker St & Seventh Ave), West Village ☎ 675-4449 🚇 1•9 to Christopher St ⏰ 4pm–midnight daily (1am Sat–Sun). 🚫 all 🔊 🔉

Elaine's

This Upper East Side establishment has managed to maintain a loyal local clientele and attract enough swells to keep the gossip columnists busy. And yes, Billy Joel did write a song about it. Dress up for this chic Italian with fresco-like wall paintings and literary parties galore.

1703 Second Ave (at 88th St), UES ☎ 534-8103 🚇 4•5•6 to 86th St ⏰ 6pm–4am daily. 🚫 AE/MC/V 🔊 🔉 ▤

Raoul's

There may be no better end to the week than a glass of wine and Raoul's bar steak. Reservations are a must in the dining room, but you may prefer to eat at the pub-like bar, although this is crowded too.

180 Prince St (bet. Sullivan & Thompson Sts), Soho ☎ 966-3518 🚇 N•R to Prince St ⏰ 12pm–2am daily. 🚫 all 🔉 ▤

sports bars

Coogan's

4015 Broadway (bet. 168th & 169th Sts), Washington Heights ☎ 928-1234 🚇 A•B•C•1•9 to 168th St-Washington Heights ⏰ 11am–4am daily.

Mustang Sally's Saloon

324 Seventh Ave (bet. 28th & 29th Sts), Chelsea ☎ 695-3806 🚇 1•9 to 28th St ⏰ 10am–4am Mon–Sat; 12pm–2am Sun.

Nevada Smith's

74 Third Ave (bet. 11th & 12th Sts), East Village ☎ 982-2591 🚇 6 to Astor Pl ⏰ 12pm–3am daily.

Park Avenue Country Club

381 Park Ave (at 27th St), Gramercy Park ☎ 685-3636 🚇 6 to 28th St ⏰ 11.30am–2am Mon–Sat; 11.30am–10pm Sun.

2A

A pioneer of the Avenue A bar scene, 2A continues to thrive despite increasing competition from its neighbours. East Village rock kids and slumming college students pack the place to bursting each weekend. Heavy phone number trading begins at 11pm. Weekdays are similar, but not always as crowded.

25 Avenue A (at E 2nd St), East Village ☎ no phone ▥ F to 2nd Ave ◑ 7pm–4am daily. ▤ none ⌣ 🎵

great dives

Mare Chiaro

This is the quintessential Italian dive bar. Once a popular stop for visiting celebrities, and then a favourite haunt of downtown literati, Mare Chiaro is now seeing increased traffic from Nolita's fashionable new residents. Avoid weekends, when cigar-chomping bridge-and-tunnel types pour in from nearby restaurants.

176 Mulberry St (bet. Broome & Grand Sts), Nolita ☎ 226-9345 ▥ 6 to Spring St ◑ 12pm–1am daily (3am Fri–Sat). ▤ none ⌣ 🎵 ◐

Max Fish

The best dive bar in the Lower East Side is packed every evening with indie-rockers, students, artists and locals. Long since discovered by the outside world, Max Fish has managed to retain its edge without scaring off new visitors; the pool table, however, remains viciously competitive.

178 Ludlow St (bet. Houston & Stanton Sts), LES ☎ 253-1922 ▥ F to 2nd Ave ◑ 5.30pm–4am daily. ▤ none ♿ ⌣ 🎵

Nancy Whiskey Pub

A dive bar in Tribeca, Nancy Whiskey Pub is the real thing with a motley clientele, high-stakes shuffleboard tournaments, and a bartender who steals sips of your beer when you aren't looking.

1 Lispenard St (at 6th St), Tribeca ☎ 226-9943 ▥ A·C·E to Canal St ◑ 8.30am–3am daily. ▤ AE ♿ 🎵 🎵 🎵 ◐

Siberia ▲

Located in a subway station (and Russian only in decor) this joint is a welcome break from the overgrown theme palaces taking over Times Square above ground. The bar is tiny, the proprietor is gregarious and patrons are encouraged to cut loose, often with complimentary shots of chilled vodka. Not many dive bars can shut off your shy side like Siberia. Great jukebox, too.

1627 Broadway (at 50th St), Midtown ☎ 333-4141 ▥ 1·9 to 50th St ◑ 3pm–4am Mon–Sat; 8pm–4am Sun. ▤ none ⌣ 🎵 ◐

quiet retreats

Angel's Share

Don't come in a group: well-concealed Angel's Share enforces a strict four-person limit per group, making it most suitable for first-time dates and social recluses. The biggest draw here is the Japanese bartenders, known for mixing marvellous cocktails with expert precision.

8 Stuyvesant St (bet. Second & Third Aves), East Village ☎ 777-5415 ▥ 6 to Astor Pl ◑ 7pm–3am daily. ▤ AE/MC/V ♿ ⌣ 🎵

Blue Bar

The rarefied, literary atmosphere of the historic Algonquin Hotel [→156] provides the setting for this friendly, low-key midtown bar. Non-guests are warmly welcomed and the locquacious bartenders will brew you a warming Irish coffee on cold winter days.

59 W 44th St (bet. Fifth & Sixth Aves), Midtown ☎ 840-6800 ▥ B·D·F·Q to 42nd St (Bryant Park) ◑ 12pm–1am daily. ▤ all ♿

themes & schemes

Barmacy

A quirky downtown theme bar with all the trappings of a 50's pharmacy. East Village hipsters bond over cocktails and displays of vintage pharmaceuticals. DJs spin nightly.

538 E 14th St (at Ave A), East Village ☎ 228-2240 ◑ L to 1st Ave ◑ 5.30pm–4am Mon–Sat; 7.30pm–4am Sun. ▤ MC/V ♿ ⌣ 🎵 ◐

Decibel

Sample the sake at Decibel and you'll never settle for a flavourless flask of rice wine again. An impressive selection of premium sakes, mixed sake cocktails and Japanese munchies (hot peas, shrimp crackers) are offered at the bar, while full meals are served at the tables.

240 E 9th St (at 2nd St), East Village ☎ 979-2733 ▥ 6 to Astor Pl ◑ 8pm–3am Mon–Sat; 8pm–1am Sun. ▤ AE/MC/V ♿ ⌣ 🎵

→ more bars

Drip

Drip's kaleidoscopic decor is only rivalled by its house cocktails, an oddly colourful batch consisting of liqueurs you'd never dare order in a dive. An added attraction is the in-house dating system: visitors select someone from the profiles posted on the wall and Drip sets up the meeting.

489 Amsterdam Ave (at 83rd St), UWS ☎ 875-1032 🚇 1•9 to 86th St ◑ 8am–1am Mon–Sat (3am Fri–Sat); 8am–midnight Sun. 🚇 MC/V 👶 ☞ 🍴 📖 ◔

KGB

Don't be fooled by the commie-chic decor. Commercially successful authors read here regularly, as do a number of the literary world's brightest young stars. A haven for aspiring literati and anyone attracted to them.

85 E 4th St (bet. Bowery & Second Ave), East Village ☎ 505-3360 🚇 6 to Astor Pl ◑ 7.30pm–4am daily. 🚇 none 🍴 📖

Kush

Flop on a pillow-strewn couch, smoke a hookah and make believe you're in Marrakech. Kush brings the Middle East to the Lower East Side every Tuesday night with belly dancers, henna hand-painting and tarot card readings. Other nights feature live jazz or DJs but the vibe's still mellow.

183 Orchard St (bet. Houston & Stanton Sts), LES ☎ 677-7328 🚇 F to 2nd Ave ◑ 6pm–3am Mon–Sat; 7pm–3 or 4am Sun. 🚇 MC/V 👶 🍴 📖 ✎ Tue & Sun ◔ Mon–Sat

Lei Bar

Nestled in the basement of Niagara, this tiny East Village bar-within-a-bar boasts a DJ spinning surf-movie soundtracks and a bamboo-lined bar serving kitschy frozen drinks – all garnished with fruit kebabs and paper umbrellas.

112 Avenue A (at 7th St), East Village ☎ 420-9517 🚇 6 to Astor Pl ◑ 4pm–4am daily. 🚇 AE/MC/V 🍴 📖 ◔

The Russian Samovar

Idle Russian beauties line the bar; a piano tinkles in the background; dozens of infused vodkas beckon to be sampled: the Cold War may be over, but intrigue lingers on at this gaudy and elegant Theater District bar and restaurant. Bar snacks include herring and black bread.

56 W 52nd St (bet. Broadway & Eighth Ave), Midtown ☎ 757-0168 🚇 1•9 to 50th St ◑ 12pm–midnight daily (3am Thu–Sat). 🚇 all 👶 ☞ 🍴 📖 ✎ nightly

Swine on Nine

Swine on Nine may be the most garishly entertaining paean to pigs man has ever known. Pig murals, drawings and figurines line the walls, and a giant besuited boar greets visitors at the door. A dive at heart, Swine offers dirt-cheap drinks,

free chicken soup and a complimentary pink porcelain piggy bank for ladies.

693 Ninth Ave (bet. 47th & 48th Sts), Midtown ☎ 397-8356 🚇 C•E to 50th St ◑ 8am–4am Mon–Sat; 12pm–4am Sun. 🚇 none ☞ 🍴

Void

Dark, cavernous and striving for an air of deviance, Void has to be one of New York's best cyber bars, with film screenings (think *Blade Runner* and *Badlands*) every Wednesday, and DJs spinning electronica every Tuesday and Thursday, while punters surf the Web.

16 Mercer St (at Howard St), Soho ☎ 941-6492 🚇 N•R to Canal St ◑ 8pm–3am Tue–Sat. 🍴 📖 ◔ Tue & Thu.

gay thirst

The Cock

Drag thespians Sherry Vine and Jackie Beat are moonlighting as party hosts at the East Village's hottest gay bar. Homo heart-throb Mario Diaz and a gaggle of go-go dancers are on hand, while DJs spin classic rock 'n' roll, and more, nightly.

188 Ave A (bet. 11th & 12th Sts), East Village ☎ 777-6254 🚇 L to 1st Ave ◑ 10pm–4am daily. 🚇 none 👶 🍴 📖 ◔

Dick's

Famed for its cheap booze and superb jukebox, Dick's is one of Manhattan's best-loved gay dives. $2 shots and a few Morrissey singles should lower your inhibition. Cruising strongly encouraged.

192 Second Ave (at 12th St), East Village ☎ 475-2071 🚇 L to 1st Ave ◑ 2pm–4am daily. 🚇 none 👶 🍴 📖

Regents

A quiet focal point for the older gay male community, Regents is a swell midtown townhouse with a restaurant, lounge and piano bar. Casually but neatly dressed gentlemen gather round the piano to sing show tunes and standards, taking a break to stroll out onto the terrace or sit with friends. A heart-warming gem refreshingly free of young hustlers.

317 E 53rd St (at Second Ave), Midtown ☎ 593-3091 🚇 F to 53rd St ◑ 12pm–1am daily. 🚇 all ☞ 🍴 📖 ✎ ✎

Wonder Bar

One of the rare gay nightspots that welcomes straight friends without putting a damper on cruising. Excellent DJs keep the crowd happy, but some of the boys still pine for the old porn videos and curtained back room. Hey, it's Giuliani time.

505 E 6th St (at Ave A), East Village ☎ 777-9105 🚇 6 to Astor Pl ◑ 8pm–4am daily. 🚇 none 👶 🍴 📖 ◔

New York, the USA's undisputed cultural capital, throws up an infinite number of top-notch amusements on any given night. The only problem is how to choose between them...

that's entertainment

↓ get in on the act

Before there was Hollywood, there was Broadway, and the 'Great White Way' retains a unique spot in American popular consciousness. However, Broadway theatres aren't only on Broadway, but line the streets of the Theater District, which is approximately bounded by 41st and 53rd Streets, and Sixth and Eighth Avenues. More than 8 million visitors a year flock to its bright lights: this is where you'll find the power productions – the blockbuster musicals and dramas with star-studded casts.

After a loss of confidence on Broadway in the early 90's, the American musical is staging a comeback. Even Disney has got in on the act with a new stage version of its animated movie-musical *The Lion King* at the **New Amsterdam Theater**. Disney put the show in the hands of brilliant puppet-theatre director Julie Taymor and funky choreographer Garth Fagan – the result is a piece of theatrical excellence that remains one of the hottest tickets around. In addition to *The Lion King*, quality long-run musicals include the prizewinning production of *Rent* (**Nederlander Theatre**), the spectacular *Titanic* (**Lunt-Fontanne Theatre**), and revivals like *Cabaret* (**Studio 54**) and *Chicago* at the **Schubert**. This 70's musical didn't do so well with its first run on Broadway, but has triumphed this time round.

Now, serious plays (new and revivals) vie for attention with the big-time musicals on Broadway. Movie stars are being cast in major roles (yes, you can get to see the likes of Al

tickets & reviews

There are two central ticket agencies responsible for credit card phone orders for all the Broadway theaters: **Ticketmaster** ☎ 307-4100 and **Telecharge** ☎ 239-6200. Each makes a small surcharge for telephone reservations; tickets can then be picked up at the box office (show your credit card as proof of identity). Tickets can also be purchased directly over the internet from the Ticketmaster website www.ticketmaster.com. You can also buy tickets directly from the theatre box offices. There are often special discounts for those with disabilities: call Telecharge wheelchair hotline ☎ 899-8587.

On the day of the performance, you can get half-price tickets to both Broadway and Off-Broadway shows at the TKTS booths in Times Square (at 47th St) and at the World Trade Center (often less busy). Lines are long, but move quickly. Tickets for these booths cannot be purchased by phone or credit card (cash only).

☾ Broadway theatres are dark on Monday, and many shows are closed Sunday night as well. The main Broadway theatres usually have Wednesday, Saturday and Sunday matinees. Performances generally start at 8pm (matinees 2pm Wed & Sat; 3pm Sun).

♿ Phone the venues direct to get the low-down on seating. Many Broadway theatres now carry infra-red hearing enhancement (headsets available on request).

💲 Expect to pay $75 plus for the big Broadway shows; tickets for Off-Broadway shows are usually between $25 and $40, and Off-Off Broadway tickets are roughly $15 to $25.

❶ The *New York Times* prints theatre listings every day but the Friday and Sunday papers tend to have the most theatre coverage – critics on the *New York Times* and the *New Yorker* are especially well respected. There are also listings in the weekly magazines [→]148]. *New York City Onstage* ☎ 768-1818 gives recorded information on shows and *Playbill*'s website, www.playbill.com, has the low-down on what's on, plus seating plans for the main theatres.

Pacino close up), and box office takings are on the up. Revivals of modern classics, like Arthur Miller's *Death of a Salesman* at the **Eugene O'Neill Theatre**, are doing well, and a notable newcomer is Warren Leight's *Side Man* at the **Golden Theatre**. However some producers tend to run shy of home-grown drama, preferring to go with limited runs of London's West End smashhits like *Art* (**Royale Theatre**) or *Electra* with Zoe Wanamaker at the **Ethel Barrymore**.

Until the 60's, theatre in NY meant the blockbusters on Broadway, but today Off-Broadway is just as vital. These are the theatres that mounted the first productions of the works of playwrights like Tennessee Williams and David Mamet, and recently more than a few hits (like *Rent* for example) have originated here. Off-Broadway theatres tend to be more experimental and less commercial, and top writers and directors are lured here by the prospect of greater artistic freedom

→149 venue directory

than they get on Broadway. These theatres are technically venues with 100 to 499 seats but aren't necessarily outside the Theater District: Theater Row, the stretch of 42nd Street west of Ninth Avenue, sports a whole row of Off-Broadway (and even Off-Off Broadway theatres), including institutions such as **Playwright's Horizons,** which often presents earlier forms of plays that go on to play Broadway.

Granddaddy of the Off-Broadway, non-profit scene is the **Public Theater** in Noho, which legendary New York director Joseph Papp founded in 54. The Public presents productions in every stage of development, including a First Stages series which tests brand-new dramas and musicals in front of small audiences. The theatre has generated a legion of Broadway successes including the tap-dancing hit *Bring in Da Noise, Bring in Da Funk.*

Emulating the Public, the **Manhattan Theater Club** also presents readings of new work and fully-fledged stagings in its two small theatres at **City Center**, and has built up a healthy reputation of its own over the last 30 years. The **Atlantic Theater Company**, created out of workshops taught by William H Macy and David Mamet, also stages challenging scripts. And the **Mitzi E Newhouse Theater**'s polished productions of unknown plays almost come with a warranty.

As Off-Broadway became an increasingly established entity in its own right, the development of an even more alternative Off-Off-Broadway scene was inevitable. Anything goes on Off-Off Broadway, where even the definition of a 'theatre' is subject to interpretation. The theatres can be located anywhere from East Village to Brooklyn and they usually have less

than 100 seats. Off-Off Broadway shows tend to be hit or miss, but venues and companies that frequently show excellent productions are the **Jean Cocteau Repertory**, the **Adobe**, the **Irish Rep**, **PS 122**, the **Performing Garage** and **Second Stage**.

festivals

Shakespeare in the Park is the quintessential New York summertime theatre event [→153]. The **Lincoln Center Festival** (July) ☎ **875-5127** includes theatre in its broad and varied programme. During the regular season, the *Encores!* at **City Center** series presents three revivals of classic-but-forgotten American musicals, in concert version. Leading Broadway stars take time out from their regular shows to appear in the events, and the quality is consistently high. You have to be on the ball to get tickets.

↓ in the spotlight

When people hear the word 'cabaret' they often shudder and think 'showtunes'. True, you'll often find numbers from the best (and sometimes the worst) in American musical theatre in an evening of cabaret, but in New York – perhaps the world capital of cabaret – the scene is constantly reinventing itself and becoming a showcase for new, exciting music, in addition to the classic tunes of yesteryear.

For high glamour, try **Café Carlyle**. Cabaret legends Barbara Cook, Bobby Short and the outrageous Eartha Kitt frequently perform here. With a $50 cover charge, the night can get expensive, but you'll leave feeling it was worth every penny. **FireBird Café**, a tiny piano-bar, also boasts some top-notch talent. Catch the dapper Steve Ross channelling Cole Porter, and singer-pianist Daryl Sherman's after-hours' set of standards is one of the best-kept entertainment secrets in town. Nestled in

the Algonquin Hotel [→156] (yes, the Algonquin, of Dorothy Parker fame), **The Oak Room** is an intimate club where some of the biggest names in

cabaret play. Slip into a velvet banquette to hear timeless tunes interpreted by luminaries such as Andrea Marcovicci and Maureen McGovern.

tickets & reviews

There's no central booking agent, so contact venues directly to book tickets.

⏱ Most cabaret performances are Tuesday–Saturday, with a few smaller shows on Sundays and Mondays.

❶ Except for the big extravaganzas, almost all theatres are dark on Mondays, so you might find a singer from a Broadway musical doing a one-night-only event at a cabaret venue.

♪ Shows with very big names often sell out quickly, so reservations are highly recommended. Reservations are often not required for smaller shows, but it's a good idea to call ahead for seats.

💲 Most cabaret venues have a cover charge and a one- to two-drink minimum. Restaurants offering entertainment sometimes require guests to dine at earlier shows, so it's best to ask when making a reservation. Cover charges range from $10–$15 to $50 at more high-end spaces. Most smaller clubs take only cash, but the larger venues take credit cards.

❶ Cabaret listings change weekly, and the best resources are weekly publications like *Time Out New York*, *In Theater* and *Back Stage*. The *New York Times*, the *New York Daily News* and the *New York Post* often review performances, but you sometimes have to hunt to find cabaret coverage in between other entertainment news.

If you enjoy talent spotting, try **Don't Tell Mama**, where many a musical theatre career has been launched. You won't find any big names on the bill at this midtown bar, but there's always something for everyone. One of the friendliest spaces in town is the club **Eighty Eights** in West Village, which features an impressive range of more well-known cabaret singers. Names to watch include the coolly elegant Barbara Fasano and Joan Crowe. The venerable

Judy's lost its lease but has reappeared in a fabulous new space. **Judy's Chelsea** hosts a variety of new and traditional talent like award-winning singer-songwriter Bonnie Lee Sanders.

In the heart of Noho, **Joe's Pub** – a plush club in the Public Theater – manages to be hip and elegant at the same time [→30]. There's a great trend of recognizing new talent here: the incandescent Audra McDonald premiered her CD in this swanky space. Don't let the

cruisy atmosphere at **Wilson's** put you off: it's often home to Judy Barnett, whose velvety powerhouse of a voice and inventive jazz arrangements will have you cheering. **Torch**, an LES supper club [→16], is where you'll find Nicole Renaud, an enchanting Parisian songbird. Renaud's crystalline voice, clever play list (such as music from *The Umbrellas of Cherbourg*) and bizarrely beautiful costumes make for a decidedly different evening. Best of all, there's no cover charge.

↓ stand-up new york

If you're looking for comedy of the 'politically correct, fun-for-the-whole-family' variety in New York City, plop yourself in front of a TV set. But if it's irreverent, aggressive, take-no-prisoners entertainment that you're after, New York's top comedy clubs are sure to deliver. The majority of the acts you'll see in New York are stand-ups, but improv comedy is also starting to make big waves.

The city has a long tradition of nurturing breakaway talents like Jerry Seinfeld and Eddie Murphy. Recent, well-known comics who call the city home include Chris Rock (an edgy urban comedian), Janeane Garafolo (who you might recognize from the *Larry Sanders Show*), Colin Quinn (a down-to-earth Brooklynite) and Ray Romano (of *Everybody Loves Raymond* fame). Don't be surprised if any of these comedians makes an impromptu appearance, especially during the summer television-taping hiatus. Comedians like to frequent local clubs to test out new material before going on TV shows like *The Late Show with David Letterman*.

Starting Downtown, New York's alternative comedy scene centres round **Luna Lounge**, whose stark atmosphere epitomizes Lower East Side style. Some of the city's hippest comedians come here regularly to test

tickets & reviews

Make reservations by calling the club directly. Be sure to book a day or two in advance, especially for weekend shows or those with big-name headliners. All clubs mentioned take most major credit cards apart from Dangerfield's.

☉ As far as seasons go, comedy in New York never takes a vacation – clubs run shows year round. Typical weekday shows (Sun–Thu) run continuously from 9pm–midnight. Weekend shows (Fri & Sat) are more structured, with shows at 8pm, 10pm and 12.30am. The later the show, the racier the material gets.

♀ Reservations don't guarantee a seat: seating is first come, first served, so get there at least half an hour before show time otherwise you stand a good chance of paying $20 to watch the back of another punter's head.

💲 Cover charges range from $5– $25 and almost all clubs have a two-drink minimum, with prices ranging from $3 (non-alcoholic drinks) to $8 (mixed drinks).

❶ Check listings in the weekly mags [→148] but your best bet is to call the club direct: most venues have recorded listings detailing the week's lineups.

the water. Showcasing sassy comics who scoff at the notion of hitting the stage with polished material, the club typifies the belief that it is better to be daring than safely funny. The **Comedy Cellar**, in the heart of West Village, is home to many comedy legends like Robin Williams (who is known to drop by unannounced) and offers great comics in a cosy setting.

In Chelsea, the elegant **Gotham Comedy Club** has consistently strong lineups, and is one to check out if you're looking for comedy that pushes down barriers without pushing up your credit limit. Further Uptown you'll find New York's premier venue,

Caroline's on Broadway. This club will cost you, but its rich, 18-year tradition of hosting America's major comic talents (such as Jerry Seinfeld and Richard Belzer) will assure you of top acts. The Upper East Side is home to **Dangerfield's**, founded by comedy legend Rodney Dangerfield. The upscale club harks back to the days of the notorious Catskills comedy circuit, where Mel Brooks got started in the 50's. Lineups are a little uneven, but fairly strong. **Comic Strip Live** may not boast the best decor, but the lineups are good. Well-knowns like Chris Rock and Adam Sandler have been known to do sets on occasion.

↓ reel time

New York is, indisputably, the axis around which the international film world revolves, and on any given day the capital bursts with film-going options: if a recently released film isn't showing here, it very likely isn't worth the projector time.

New releases break in the Big Apple every week, usually before they open anywhere else. The city harbours approximately 185 screens, most of them occupied by the 60 or more films on current release. If big, Dolby-powered Hollywood blockbusters are up your street, there are enough screens in Manhattan, especially round the neon-lit Times Square, to meet your needs at practically any time of the day or night. In most listings magazines [→148] cinemas are conveniently listed by area so you can easily find a screen close by. The **Sony Lincoln Square** is New York's mega-cinema with 12 screens, and a 3D IMAX. But **Clearview's Ziegfeld** (once home to Ziegfeld Follies) is the ultimate movie-going experience, with its huge screen, great sound and ultra-comfy seats. It's the venue for many a glitzy pre-miere. For those on a budget, the **CO Encore World-wide** shows films which have recently completed their general release, at half the price.

Manhattan is awash with alternative movie venues. A good 40 screens, evenly distributed between Up- and Downtown, run imported, revived and avant-garde fare, sometimes with schedules that change every day. New York's indie showplace is the **Angelika Film Center**, which routinely screens the moment's finest low-budget films, and programmes the coolest midnight revivals. The beautifully restored **Paris Theatre** also shows regular revivals, especially of French films. The city's surviving repertory outlets are legendary – and deservedly so. **Film Forum**, on the edge of Soho, runs alternative film (documentaries, animations, underground and unorthodox indies) on one screen, and the city's most audience-friendly revival programming on another. **Quad** also includes documentaries in its programme as well as a healthy smattering of foreign films. And the **Anthology Film Archives**, another indie treasure, shows new experimental films and vintage art-film classics that no one else will touch; when Theo Angelopoulos's prize-winning *Ulysses' Gaze* came to town, this is where it was shown.

Even more off-beat movies are screened at the intimate **Cine-Noir Film Society** but only one night a week. For something more highbrow try the **Walter Reade Theater**, located in the Lincoln Center complex, with a comprehensive international series. More arcane, thanks to its curatorial agenda, is the **Museum of Modern Art**; it is always engaged in some series of rare screenings (such as a survey of Cuban films), which are free with museum admission. The **NYU Cantor Film Center** has an interesting programme of student cult revival movies and tickets won't break the bank.

Look out, as well, for foreign screenings at the **Asia Society**, the **Japan Society** (always good for some Kurosawa or Japanimation), **Goethe House** (for something German), the **French Institute** (for er...French films) and the **King Juan Carlos I Center** (for occasional screenings of Spanish movies).

During the summer, there are free *Cinema Paradiso*-esque outdoor screenings of golden oldies at **Bryant Park** [→81] every Monday ☎ 391-4248. **Two Boots**, a pizza parlour in the East Village, also has free screenings of classics movies in the downstairs basement, and the gay bookstore, **A Different Light**, shows a free gay-oriented film once a week.

For a night out with a difference, try **Void**, a cyber-age nightclub showing alternative classics, and the **Screening Room** for dinner and a movie; it mainly plays alternatives and classics, and is a great spot for late-night weekend screenings.

tickets & reviews

It's best to buy or book tickets in advance, and you can do this for most cinemas (but not some of the independents) via the credit-card reservation at ☎ 777-FILM (3456) – they charge a booking fee of $2 per ticket. The service is very easy to operate. It also gives preview information.

⟳ New films generally open on Fridays. Screening times vary, but usually start around 10am and finish up around midnight (there are many more midnight shows at the weekends). In general, movies have only a few trailers and maybe an ad preceding them, so don't assume there's masses of time to spare after the official programme start time.

♣ Automated booking services means the early bird gets the best seats.

▦ Ticket prices are currently about $9, and slightly less for the smaller, artier theatres.

❶ Film reviews and information about shows can be found in listings mags [→148]. Generally the quickest and hippest place to look for what's happening cinematically is the *Village Voice*, and *Time Out New York*. On the net, www.nytoday.com/movies will help you find a film nearby. The *New York Times* and *New York Observer* run regular film reviews.

festivals

The city hosts more than 30 film festivals during the year. The two biggest are the Lincoln Center's **New York Film Festival [→153]**; and MoMA's **New Directors/New Films Festival** (March) ☎ **708-9480**, which shows films from film-makers who are about to 'make it'. The **New York Underground Festival** is also in spring [→154]. This is followed by the **Women's Film Festival** in April ☎ **465-3435** at the NY Cantor Center and the **Gay and Lesbian Film Festival** in July ☎ **254-7228**.

movie landmarks

New York has constantly been featured on celluloid, and everywhere you go there are famous locations. The most obvious – and the most touted by the location itself – is Katz's diner (on Houston Street on the corner with Ludlow), the setting for the fake orgasm scene in **When Harry Met Sally.** *Also Downtown, the cab rank where Travis Bickle works in* **Taxi Driver** *is the real taxi hangout at the bottom of Sixth Avenue (just above Canal Street). And the scene where Madonna buys the sparkly boots in* **Desperately Seeking Susan** *was filmed in a store called Love Saves the Day on Second Avenue. Moving Uptown, the Daily Planet of* **Superman** *fame is based in the building inhabited by the Daily News (22 E 42nd Street). But the scariest movie ever made,* **Rosemary's Baby,** *took place in the Dakota Building [→67] – that creepy old apartment probably still echoes with Mia Farrow's screams.*

→ more classical music & opera | dance | poetry

cinema | classical music & opera

↓ new world symphonies

From grand opera at the Met to experimental performances at the avant-garde Kitchen, New York offers a breathtaking range of musical events. Lincoln Center alone boasts four major auditoria – the Metropolitan Opera House, the New York State Theater, Alice Tully Hall and Avery Fisher Hall – staging performances year round.

The **Metropolitan Opera House**, or Met (Oct–Apr), is arguably the best place in the world to see traditional productions of the standard repertory, but European-style stage direction, with its focus on reinterpreting opera for a contemporary audience, is still in its infancy. Met audiences dote on Franco Zeffirelli, who fills the stage with props, spectacle and casts of thousands in *Turandot* or *La Traviata*; but when Robert Wilson, whose distinctive, minimalist theatrical language is taken for granted in Europe, staged *Lohengrin* here, he was booed: the production was just too innovative for New York.

By contrast, **New York City Opera**, based next door in the **New York State Theater**, is more ambitious in the stage direction department. Here, singers who are younger and less well known than their Met counterparts, appear in innovative versions of both classics and recent American operas.

When there's no opera at the Met, there are other options. Year after year, the tiny **Amato Opera Theater** cranks out idiosyncratic productions on a shoestring, and the city's music schools, including **Mannes** (Sep–Jun) and the legendary **Juilliard**, stage full student performances. There's also the **Opera Orchestra of New York**, which gives three different operas a year in concert version at Carnegie Hall. Founder-conductor Eve Queler specializes in discovering new singers, and a lot of major stars have made their New York debut under her baton.

A symbol of New York's musical conservatism is the great **New York Philharmonic**. While former principal conductor Leonard Bernstein – one of America's best known artistes – is still lionized, the Philharmonic today has returned to the orchestral tradition's 19th-century European roots, offering the standard symphonic repertoire. The Philharmonic's home, **Avery Fisher Hall**, is one of Lincoln Center's ugliest buildings – the Beast, as it were, to the Beauty of **Carnegie Hall**, which has preserved its famous acoustic for more than a century. It also boasts a recital annexe, the **Weill Recital Hall**. Brooklyn's leading arts venue is the **Brooklyn Academy of Music** (BAM), the oldest academy in the US, where the wide and eclectic classical range extends from the **Brooklyn Philharmonic** to European opera productions.

For chamber music, the leader is, yet again, the Lincoln Center, where **Alice Tully** is the hall of preference. There's also **Merkin Concert Hall**, a couple of blocks north, another venue for chamber and lieder recitals. Across town, at the **92nd Street Y**, violinist Jaime Laredo runs the acclaimed chamber music series 'Chamber Music at the Y' and composer Ned Rorem has been presenting and performing here for the last 50 years.

Of course music isn't restricted to the concert hall stage. One insider tip is the acclaimed series of classical chamber concerts (sometimes with related lectures) at the **Metropolitan Museum of Art [→79]**. In

→149 venue directory

the same vein, the **Frick Collection [→82]** has presented recitals by such international soloists as James Levine. For cutting-edge performances and avant-garde music, the diminutive Downtown **Kitchen** is where it's at. And on a barge docked on the Brooklyn side of the East River, you can enjoy the Manhattan skyline while listening to chamber music presented by the popular series **BargeMusic**. For church concerts, check out **Trinity Church**, one of the oldest churches in New York, **St Ignatius Loyola** or, of course, the Cathedral of **St John the Divine** (see local listings for schedules).

festivals

Granddaddy of New York festivals is the **Mostly Mozart Festival** at Lincoln Center ☎ **546-2656** which has offered summertime classical concerts for over two decades. **The Lincoln Center Festival** ☎ **875-5127** in July brings in funky events from around the world, effectively serving as a summertime pendant to **BAM's Next Wave**

Festival every autumn ☎ **1-718-636-4111**. The epitome of summer in New York are the appearances of the Metropolitan Opera and New York Philharmonic in various city parks: picnickers enjoy performances like *Aida* under the stars ☎ **362-6000**.

tickets & reviews

Tickets for the Lincoln Center venues can only be booked through the agencies, with a surcharge of $4.80 to $5.50 per ticket. Call **Centercharge** ☎ **721-6500** for Alice Tully Hall and Avery Fisher Hall; **CarnegieCharge** ☎ **247-7800** for Carnegie Hall; and ☎ **362-6000** for the Metropolitan Opera. Tickets for other main venues, like the BAM, can be booked through **Ticketmaster** ☎ **307-4100** (surcharges vary by venue). Performances at smaller venues are less likely to be booked out; for tickets call the venues direct.

☞ Dress codes are a thing of the past: even at the Met, anything and everything goes, from jeans to tuxedos.

⏱ The Metropolitan Opera only plays from October–April. Evening performances generally begin at 8pm (occasionally, at 7 or 7.30pm). There are no Sunday performances at the Met. As a rule classical music performances generally begin at 8pm, but Sunday performances and recitals are sometimes earlier.

🕯 Binoculars are useful accessories in Lincoln Center's huge auditoria. Sitting at the top of the Met isn't necessarily a liability – the acoustics are great here.

💲 Tickets vary from $10 to $180 for events featuring the top performers. At the Met, standing-room tickets for the week go on sale the preceding Saturday morning; people line up before dawn to procure the $12 spots. At music schools, performances are often free.

❶ Listings of the week's cultural events appear in all the weekly mags [→148]. Classical music performances and opera are reviewed in most of the daily papers, usually two to three days after the event. The *New York Times* is the most respected but the critics on the *New York Post* and *Newsday* are usually spot on.

↓ perpetual motion

The New York dance scene is alive and kicking. At its heart is the **New York City Ballet**, created by the brilliant choreographer George Balanchine. Today, 16 years after his death, the choreographer's spare and elegant non-story ballets (Balanchine eschewed the word 'abstract') remain benchmarks of American dance. Current director, and former soloist, Peter Martins has kept up the company's Balanchine and Jerome Robbins (of *West Side Story* fame) classics, while adding his own new works. The **New York City Ballet** (NYCB) shares the **New York State Theater** with the New York City Opera; their seasons run from November to February, and April to June.

New York's other leading classical ballet company, the **American Ballet Theater** (ABT), based at the **Metropolitan Opera House** (April–June), presents a broad range of ballets, traditional and modern. Many are homegrown but big-name international companies like the Kirov and the Royal Ballet are also included in the programme. You are more than likely to see a star or two here.

What Balanchine was to ballet, **Martha Graham** was to modern dance; and her company continues to perform works from her repertoire. One Graham protégé was **Merce Cunningham**, a Graham soloist before founding his own avant-garde company, which he still heads today.

He has collaborated on productions with Andy Warhol and, more recently, Comme des Garçons. Another seminal, New York-based choreographer is the idiosyncratic and gifted **Twyla Tharp** (of *The Fugue* and *Push Comes to Shove* fame). She has her own touring outfit but tends to work with established companies like the NYCB. Another key figure is the inventive Paul Taylor who, in 57, established the renowned **Paul Taylor Dance Company**, which holds its New York season at City Center. Just as popular is the **Alvin Ailey American Dance Theater**, a troupe of mainly black dancers which, thanks to director Judith Jamison, maintains a strong international presence. Sadly, performances from the **Dance Theater of Harlem** are rare these days. It is now a New York institution but was started in a garage in 58 by NYCB dancer Arthur Mitchell, who wanted to give the kids of Harlem the opportunities he'd had.

These companies perform mainly at **City Center**, the **Brooklyn Academy of Music** (BAM), acknowledged as the New York centre of modern dance, and the smaller **Joyce Theater** in Chelsea. This former art deco-style cinema was converted into a dance venue by Cora Cahan and Eliot Feld, a fomer NYCB dancer. The Feld Ballet, recently re-incarnated as the more experimental **Ballet Tech**, is based here. The Joyce also presents the short seasons of a wide spectrum of companies both local and international, famous and less established.

Not far away, the **Dance Theater Workshop**, in the **Bessie Schonberg Theater**, provides young choreographers with a place to test their mettle. The other place to see truly cutting-edge choreographers is **PS 122** in the East Village. For all these venues, check the listings mags to find out what's on when [→148].

tickets & reviews

Some of the larger companies sell through ticket agencies such as Telecharge ☎ 307-7171. The TKTS booth (at Times Square and the World Trade Center) sometimes has dance tickets for City Center or Joyce performances. Tickets can only be purchased on the day, and they don't accept credit cards. Smaller venues have their own box office and booking system. Most companies' seasons last only a week or two. In smaller venues, there's often no assigned seating: first come, first served.

🕐 Most companies' seasons last only a week or two so you have to be on the ball to get tickets. Show times vary depending on the company and the length of the run. There are often weekend matinees.

🔭 It's advisable to bring binoculars for better viewing at the Met and the New York State Theater.

💺 Ticket prices vary from $10 for the smaller venues up to $200 for popular companies at the big venues.

❶ The listings mags [→148] are the best bet to find out what's going on. The main papers all review dance, but sporadically. *The Times* is the best bet but it's the luck of the draw as to which day reviews will run.

festivals

Known as a forum for many things new and interesting in the performing arts, the **BAM's Next Wave Festival** ☎ 636-4100 each autumn, always includes dance on its programme. At the Joyce, the **Altogether Different Dance Festival** (January) ☎ 242-0800, now in its 14th year, features choreographers working in novel directions. The **Lincoln Center Festival** ☎ 875-5127 (July) also features dance, and includes companies ranging from Merce Cunningham to the Stuttgart Ballet.

↓ urban verse

Poetry in NYC is becoming as omnipresent as yellow cabs; spoken word events and slams are taking place all over the city in all sorts of venues, from Barnes & Noble bookstores to Brooklyn cafés. Not since the 50's Beat generation has poetry been so big. The popularity of verse was confirmed by its appearance on the big screen in *Slam* (director Marc Levin's winner at the 98 Sundance Festival), which has inspired yet another generation to recycle their innermost thoughts in public.

When big names like Maya Angelou or John Ashbery want to reach the people live, they read in the stim-ulating, erudite atmosphere of the **92nd Street Y**, **Barnes & Noble** bookstores [→112] or the **New York Public Library**. On a cosier note, **Poets House** describes itself as a 'home to all the poetic traditions'. It boasts a 35,000 volume poetry library and literary centre. One of their signature series, *Passwords* presents poets reading and discussing the work of other poets.

Spoken word – poetry written for performance – is still riding high on the poetry and rap hybrid that originated in the city. It is a particularly New York phenomenon and the cross-fertilization was encouraged at clubs like **Fez**, where rap-pers read alongside scene stalwarts such as 99, poet-novelist Mike Tyler, Todd Colby, Edwin Torres and Tracie Morris. Morris, together with the legendary scene godmother, Jayne Cortez, comes from a long-standing tradition of combining poetry with politics and activism.

As ever, though, Downtown is where it's at, and superhip is the premier spoken word venue, the **Nuyorican Poets Café**. Founded by veterans Miguel Algarin, Bob Holman and Lois Elaine Griffith, it presents plays and verse, and it was within these bare brick walls that poetry slams (spoken word competitions),

→149 venue directory

poetry | music

triggered the appearance of spoken word on MTV. A bohemian, beatnik sanctuary of verse is the **Poetry Project at St Mark's**. This is where Allen Ginsberg performed, and Patti Smith has also read here recently. Its New Year's Eve marathon poetry all-nighters are a tradition. A few blocks further east, the ultra-fringe **A Gathering of Tribes** base their monthly rovings at the **Tribes Gallery** under the watchful eye of blind poetry guru Steve Cannon, who first encouraged Gil Scott-Heron and Ishmael Reed.

Way Uptown, every Friday night in Harlem, the **National Black Theatre** hosts the Hottest Poetry Slam, the live aspect of the Hottest Poets Radio Satellite Network (WEVD, 1050 AM). In the comparatively plush theatre setting, poets battle for a $500 prize. And Brooklyn boasts an ever-increasing number of cafés hosting poetry events, such as the **Brooklyn Moon Café** and the **Demu Café**, where hipsters can eat and enjoy music and open-mic sessions.

tickets & reviews

Tickets are usually available on the door but you'll need to book ahead for major performance poets or the big poetry slams.

○ Times of shows vary (check with venue) but they can start as early as 5pm and as late as 10.30/11pm.

⊠ Prices vary from free admission to $5–$10; special events are a bit more, but rarely over $15.

❶ The *Village Voice* features the Poetry Calendar of New York Council but other weekly mags have listings too [→148]; *Time Out New York* is probably the most comprehensive. The word often comes from the street: keep an eye out for flyers in cafés, bookshops or restaurants.

↓ the beat goes on

Even if Mayor Giuliani did bring the nightlife tempo down along with the murder rate, New York is still the city that never sleeps, with a wealth of musical performances happening every night. American and international music, from avant-garde to rock, jazz or blues, abounds in surroundings grand and down-home.

If it's international pop stars you're after, then the world-famous **Madison Square Garden** is a must, hosting big acts like the Rolling Stones. Stepping down in size, there are other seated venues like the beautiful **Beacon Theater**, which presents a mix of rock and reggae, ranging from Natalie Merchant to Bob Dylan. Be warned that many other venues are standing room only, like the enormous **Roseland**, a regular spot for big name acts, and the atmospheric **Irving Plaza**; despite its size, it still manages to be a cosy venue for rock, reggae and African artists. And there are always class acts at the **Hammerstein Ballroom,** the elegant **Webster Hall** and the **Bowery Ballroom**

where up-and-comers who are denting the charts hone their craft.

New York has a huge array of smaller, more cutting-edge venues too. In the mid-70's, the local rock scene that dared to call itself punk exploded out of **CBGB**. They launched Blondie and Talking Heads and have now given way to the likes of the Chainsaw Kittens. In the middle of St Mark's Place is **Coney Island High**, a popular rock venue for local bands and bigger names. On the traditional rock front, **The Bottom Line** is an institution dating back to the early 70's and is a regular record company showcase. But the LES and East Village is musically where it's at if you want to see the next generation of indie rock and folk stars in the making. Bars and clubs are teeming with aspiring artists and you can spend nights on end here hopping from gig to gig. Another music biz showcase is **Mercury Lounge,** the anchor of the buzzing Ludlow/Orchard Street scene. Really getting down and dirty, **Brownies** is a dark bar that showcases budding

rock stars for eager record company scouts. There's also ever-changing live action in small clubs like the lesbian bar **Meow Mix**, the **Luna Lounge**, **Max Fish**, **Tonic**, the **Living Room** and **Arlene Grocery**, a tiny but trendy club in a former grocery store, where all performances are free.

Musically speaking, the bastion of the avant-garde is the busy **Knitting Factory**. A small empire, it promotes art rock; John Cale, Yoko Ono and Lou Reed, among others, work out their new material here. In the heart of the Meatpacking District, the **Cooler** is named for its former purpose. It's a subterranean meat locker, called 'spooky-cool' by in-the-know locals. It isn't unusual to see experimental performances here by Thurston Moore and Beck.

New York is a dream made real for jazz fans – bands like the Vanguard Jazz Orchestra and Mingus Big Band all play here once a week. Big jazz names can be seen at deliciously close quarters in clubs like **Sweet Basil**, the **Village Vanguard**, **Smalls Underground** and

Fez. All of which vie for attention with the **Blue Note**, the renowned home of jazz. They've all gigged here, from Sonny Rollins to Dave Brubeck.

Self-appointed guardians of big-band jazz, **Jazz at Lincoln Center**, fronted by trumpeter Wynton Marsalis, has a programme of musical events aimed at keeping alive the work of artists like Duke Ellington. The premier jazz club **Birdland** is in itself a nod to jazz tradition, taking its name from Charlie 'Bird' Parker. Parker himself played here along with other big names in jazz. Across the road from Lincoln Center, the lurid, surreally decorated **Iridium** attracts vocalists of the calibre of Dee Dee Bridgewater. It's also worth taking the A train up to Harlem to explore the renaissance of jazz that's happening in intimate spots like **Nick's Pub** and **Perk's**. Meanwhile the **Supper Club**, a lovely ballroom in Midtown, holds big swing nights with the likes of the Charlie Watts Big Band providing the music. There are surprisingly few blues places in New York, but **Chicago BLUES** presents both local blues players and icons. For under $20, you can enjoy musicians such as Johnnie Johnson or Son Seals.

New York has a significant Latin and world music scene. The regular watering-hole of New York's Latin and world music aficionados is the venerable **SOB's** (Sounds of Brazil), with a stage that's usually overflowing with large Latin, African or Caribbean bands. The city's most elegant venue of world music is the **Town Hall**, a formal, classical space often booked out by the World Music Institute. For the pop-ier sides of world music, see what's happening at **Symphony Space**. If you're in search of salsa, dance your pants off at big halls like **Latin Quarter** and the **Copacabana**. Or way up in the Bronx is the lively pan-Latin hangout, **Jimmy's Bronx Café**, run by the redoubtable Jimmy himself, with live salsa and

merengue on Saturday nights. For more intimate Latino jazzy jams, it is always wise to see if any music's going down at the **Nuyorican Poets Café**.

Anything rootsy can be enjoyed at **Tramps**, from country, soul, blues and rock 'n' roll, to Jamaica's Burning Spear, Benin's Angelique Kidjo and New York individualists like Chasidic Hendrix. In a similar vein, the shabby country house chic of **Nell's** (founded by English expat Nell Carter) succeeds in remaining endlessly in fashion. Open-mic sessions here attract visiting VIPs like Stevie Wonder. London-born Nigerian singer, Wunmi, ex Soul II Soul, plays here too. The legendary **Apollo Theatre** is still going, and is home to the famous Wednesday 'Amateur Night', as well as a steady stream of soul and hip-hop stars. And Harlem's churches, like the **Abyssinian Baptist Church**, are the real deal for a Sunday gospel experience.

Considering NYC gave birth to rap, there's a serious dearth of venues booking rap acts. **Tramps** is one of the few places to serve up regular hip-hop nights. But rap artists like the Roots have begun using a stretch at **Wetlands**

(ordinarily a Grateful Dead-type hangout) to warm up for major tours.

---

festivals

Music festivals are a pressure valve for New York in the summertime and are usually free. **Summerstage** is the musical highlight of summer [→153]. The **Guinness Fleadh** ☎307-7171 is a Celtic fun-fest weekend held in June on Randall's Island and one of the most romantic events is the **Midsummer Swing Series** at the Lincoln Center ☎875-5766 (Jun–Jul). Dance lessons are held an hour before the start of the show, and the outdoor dance floor within the main plaza is inevitably packed. There are also free summer concerts in the **World Trade Center** ☎ 435-4170 by artists like Ryuichi Sakamoto and DJ Spooky, and **Celebrate Brooklyn** ☎1-718-855-7882 is a free weekend concert series held between Jul–Aug in Prospect Park [→91], with African music, soul, and silent movies with the score performed by a full live orchestra.

music

media | venue directory

---

tickets & reviews

You can get tickets from venues in advance, but the main purveyor is the monolithic **Ticketmaster** ☎ 307-7171, which can also be accessed on the internet at http://www.ticketmaster.com. As everywhere, good shows get sold out quickly. The desperate can join the tradition of being ripped off by ticket scalpers outside major events.

⏱ There are gigs every night of the week but many more on Friday and Saturday nights. Most start between 8/9pm. Big names will often have a support band, which will start earlier.

♿ Larger venues tend to be seated and smaller ones seating room only.

💲 Tickets for the big names are around $40–$50 mark but otherwise reckon on paying between $8–$20.

❶ The weekly mags have comprehensive listings[→148]. Web-sites offer invaluable info, too [→148]. Up-to-date scoop can also be gleaned from Funkmaster Flex's radio show on 96 Kiss FM every night of the week. Hip happenings can be discovered by making enquiries at places like Earwax Records, 204 Bedford Ave (bet. N 5th & 6th Sts) ☎ 1-718-218-9608. Or trail the underground scene on the internet at sites like www.houseofouch.

↓ get switched on

television

Americans are a nation of TV junkies and New Yorkers, no matter how cosmopolitan they seem, are no exception. There are 70-odd channels to be had if you have cable and around a dozen if you don't, but for the visitor the novelty soon wears off. Exceptions to the rule are channels 13, 21 and 31, which are given over to public broadcasting and have higher quality programming. To get your fix of the big-name shows, channel 11 screens re-runs of *Friends*, *Seinfeld* and *Cheers* every night, and NBC shows the phenomenally successful *ER*. Channel 21 also shows BBC world news every night at 11.30pm. The main television news slot is 10pm on terrestrial channels, but there are plenty of all-news-all-the-time cable channels: MSNBC (15), CNN (10), Fox News (46) and, for good local info, New York News One (1). MTV deserves a mention if only because of its popularity. Don't forget to have a quick flick past the public access channels for freak-show-style laughs.

radio

New York is equally well endowed with 24-hour radio stations, featuring all manner of music and talk shows. FM stations are your best bet but AM stations can also entertain, if not inform. Hot 97 (WBLS, 97.1 FM) provides the essential hip-hop accompaniment to a New York day, while K-Rock (WXRK, 92.3 FM) is shock-jock Howard Stern's personal soapbox every morning. WBGO (88.3 FM) is a round-the-clock jazz station, and the station of choice for rock 'n' roll classics is WNEW (102.7 FM). What you'll hear in most cabs is WKTU (103.5 FM) – pumped-up versions of mainstream house anthems. College radio stations showcase big name DJs at weekends to

get you in the party spirit. Non-music alternatives are WNYC (820 AM), a member station of National Public Radio or WBAI (99.5 FM), both of which have public-forum type news discussions and good coverage of politics.

the papers

Picking up your preferred local paper from one of the city's many street-side newsstands is a morning ritual in NYC. Perhaps with the exception of *The Washington Post*, the *New York Times* is the most well respected paper in America; it prides itself on its world news analysis and, despite its stuffy tone and appearance, is a comprehensive read. The Sunday version weighs in like a set of encyclopedias (and assuaging shrinking-rainforest guilt). As far as tabloids go, the *Daily News* and the *New York Post* can't touch the down-and-dirty tactics of the British rat-pack but, with Rupert Murdoch at the helm of the *Post*, it can't be long in coming. As for the top financial paper, the *Wall Street Journal*: no *WSJ*...no comment.

An excellent way to check out the press without spending a cent is to try a café that has newspapers and magazines: the Pink Pony on Ludlow Street and the News Café on University Place at Union Square are just a couple. Also Barnes & Noble stores all have cafés where you can read for free after you've paid to sup. For foreign press go to Hudson News (753 Broadway at 8th St), Tower Books (383 Lafayette Street at 4th St) or branches of Universal News.

listings magazines & the free press

Time Out New York has made a comfortable niche for itself in the market of

weekly listings mags, which include the more conservative *New Yorker* and yuppie-ish *New York Magazine*. Supposedly providing the skinny on the scene is *Paper* (monthly), though it's a little old hat nowadays.

Free listings magazines and newspapers can be found all over the place, from the laundromat to the bank foyer, or in boxes on the sidewalk, and combine listings with local and national interest features. The *Village Voice*, a long-standing liberal mouthpiece, has declined recently, partly due to competition from the equally liberal listings mag, the *New York Press*. A rash of free specialty publications such as *NYC*, *NYPress*, *HX*, *Next*, *Flyer*, with up-to-date club gossip, and *Literal Latte*, a café-society rag, have become omnipresent in public spaces.

websites

www.citysearchnyc.com has up-to-the-minute info on events; *www.clubnyc. com* is nightlife oriented; *www.sidewalk.com* is Microsoft's comprehensive listings and information network, covering everything from restaurant reviews to club listings. If these don't help you out, *www.nynetwork. com* has a listing of all New York websites. But if your hotel doesn't have internet access, try the free terminals at the New York Public Library [→77], or one of the city's cyber cafés:

Cyber café
273 Lafayette Street
(at Prince St)
☎ 334-5140

Internet café
82 E 3rd Street (bet. First & Second Aves)
☎ 614-0747

alt. coffee
139 Avenue A (bet. 8th & 9th Sts)
☎ 529-2233

🎭 venue directory

Abyssinian Baptist Church
☎ 862-7474

A Different Light
☎ 989-4850

Adobe
☎ 352-0441

Alice Tully Hall
Lincoln Center
☎ 875-5050

Amato Opera Theater
☎ 288-8200

Angelika Film Center
☎ 995-2000

Anthology Film Archives
☎ 505-5110

Apollo Theatre
☎ 513-5300

Arlene Grocery
☎ 358-1633

Asia Society
☎ 288-6400

Atlantic Theater Co
☎ 645-8015

Avery Fisher Hall
Lincoln Center
☎ 875-5030

BargeMusic
☎ 1-718-624-4061

Beacon Theater
☎ 496-7070

Bessie Schonberg Theater
☎ 924-0077

Birdland
☎ 581-3080

Blue Note
☎ 475-8592

The Bottom Line
☎ 228-7880

Bowery Ballroom
☎ 533-2111

Brooklyn Academy of Music (BAM)
☎ 1-718-636-4100

Brooklyn Moon Café
☎ 1-718-243-0424

Brownies
☎ 420-8392

Café Carlyle
☎ 744-1600

Carnegie Hall
☎ 247-7800

Caroline's on Broadway
☎ 367-9000

CBGB
☎ 982-4052

Chicago BLUES
☎ 924-9755

Cine-Noir Film Society
☎ 253-1922

City Center
☎ 581-1212

Clearview's Ziegfeld
☎ 777-FILM 602

CO Encore Worldwide
☎ 246 1583

Comedy Cellar
☎ 254-3480

Comic Strip Live
☎ 861-9386

Coney Island High
☎ 674-7959

Cooler
☎ 229-0785

Copacabana
☎ 582-2672

Dangerfield's
☎ 593-1650

Demu Café
☎ 1-718-875-8484

Don't Tell Mama
☎ 757-0788

Eighty Eights
☎ 924-0088

Ethel Barrymore
☎ 239-6200

Eugene O'Neill Theatre
☎ 239-6200

Fez
☎ 533-2680

FireBird Café
☎ 586-0244

Film Forum
☎ 727-8110

French Institute
☎ 355-6100

Frick Collection
☎ 288-0700

Goethe House
☎ 439-8700

Golden Theatre
☎ 239-6200

Gotham Comedy Club
☎ 367-9000

Hammerstein Ballroom
☎ 564-4882

Iridium
☎ 582-2121

Irish Rep
☎ 727-2737

Irving Plaza
☎ 777-6800

Japan Society
☎ 832-1155

Jean Cocteau Repertory
☎ 677-0060

Jimmy's Bronx Café
☎ 1-718-329-2000

Joe's Pub
☎ 539-8777

Joyce Theater
☎ 242-0800

Judy's Chelsea
☎ 929-5410

Juilliard Theater
☎ 769-7406

King Juan Carlos I Center
☎ 689-4232

Kitchen
☎ 255-5793

Knitting Factory
☎ 219-3055

Latin Quarter
☎ 864-7600

Living Room
☎ 533-7235

Luna Lounge
☎ 260 2323

Lunt-Fontanne Theatre
☎ 307-4100

Madison Square Garden
☎ 465-6741

Manhattan Theater Club
☎ 399-3000

Mannes College of Music
☎ 580-0210

Max Fish
☎ 253-1922

Meow Mix
☎ 334-7474

Mercury Lounge
☎ 260-4700

Merkin Concert Hall
☎ 501-3330

Metropolitan Museum of Art
☎ 570-3949

Metropolitan Opera House
☎ 362-6000

Mitzi E Newhouse Theater
☎ 239-6200

Museum of Modern Art
☎ 708-9480

National Black Theatre
☎ 360-7609/722-3800

Nederlander Theatre
☎ 921-8000

Nell's
☎ 675-1567

New Amsterdam Theater
☎ 307-4100

New York Public Library
☎ 930-0830

New York State Theater
☎ 870-5570

Nick's Pub
☎ 283-9728

92nd Street Y
☎ 996-1100

Nuyorican Poets Café
☎ 475-6541

NYU Cantor Film Center
☎ 375-8116

The Oak Room
☎ 840-6800

Paris Theater
☎ 688-3800

Performing Garage
☎ 966-3651

Perk's
☎ 666-8500

Playwright's Horizons
☎ 279-4200

Poetry Project at St Mark's
☎ 674-0910

Poets House
☎ 431-7920

PS 122
☎ 255-8800

Public Theater
☎ 598-7150

Quad
☎ 255-8800

Roseland
☎ 249-8870

Royale Theatre
☎ 239-6200

St Ignatius Loyola
☎ 288-3588

St John the Divine
☎ 316-2133

Schubert Theater
☎ 239-6200

Screening Room
☎ 334-2100

Second Stage
☎ 246-4422

Smalls Underground
☎ 929-7565

SOB's
☎ 243-4940

Sony Lincoln Square & IMAX Theatre
☎ 336-5000

Studio 54
☎ 239-6200

Supper Club
☎ 921-1940

Sweet Basil
☎ 242-1785

Symphony Space
☎ 864-5400

Tonic
☎ 358-7503

Torch
☎ 228-5151

Town Hall
☎ 997-6661

Tramps
☎ 727-7788

Tribes Gallery
☎ 674-3778

Trinity Church
☎ 602-0872

Two Boots
☎ 254-1441

Village Vanguard
☎ 255-4037

Void
☎ 941-6492

Walter Reade Theater
Lincoln Center,
☎ 875-5600

Webster Hall
☎ 353-1600

Weill Recital Hall
Lincoln Center
☎ 247-7800

Wetlands
☎ 966-4225

Wilson's
☎ 769-0100

night fever

Despite Mayor Giuliani's 'Quality of Life' laws putting a stranglehold on NY nightlife, club promoters still cook up the new, the retro and the extravagant and dish it out at venues all over the city. The club beat goes on, even if at some of the city's lounges, dancing isn't strictly allowed...

↓ top venues

clubs

Baktun

Music comes first at this sleek, cosy and truly unique lounge, with staple nights providing different types of dance or electronic music. Creative party promotions, video projections, reasonable bar prices and friendly staff make this a diamond in the rough. ✿ Bang The Party deep house night (first and third Friday of the month).

418 W 14th St (bet. 9th & 10th Aves), Chelsea ☎ 206-1590 **w** www.baktun.com 🚇 A•C•E to 14th St; L to 8th Ave 💷 $5–$10 ◑ 10pm–4am Wed–Sun. 🖰 AE/MC/V ❏ 👕 casual.

Limelight

The controversy surrounding owner Peter Gatien's involvement with drug rings and murder has made his club a must-see for the curious. As if the impressive church location weren't enough, artists like HG Geiger have been commissioned to design art installations. By day, Limelight presents art shows and theatre; by night, it's home to themed parties. Hard house is usually featured on the main floor while hip-hop and pop styles can be found in the chapel and elsewhere. Some events are private celebrity-studded bashes, but the huge, bright, thumping open-to-all fiestas allow you to appreciate how they can charge top whack admission.

660 6th Ave (bet. 20th & 21st Sts), Chelsea ☎ 807-7780 🚇 F•N•R to 23rd St 💷 $15–$20 ◑ 10pm–5am daily. 🖰 MC/V ❏ 👕 dress up.

Mother

The creators of the long-running Jackie 60 night – known for eccentric themes, performances and funky house music – transformed this club into one of the most enigmatic in NYC. It's bursting with organized confusion, fetish, sleaze and creativity. Phone to find out themes as dress codes are always enforced. High on novelty factor are the Clit Club (Friday's lesbian dance music party) and Click + Drag (Saturday's cyber fetish night). ✿ Jackie 60 (Tue).

432 W 14th St (at Washington St), Chelsea ☎ 366-5680 🚇 A•C•E to 14th St 💷 $10–$15 ◑ 10.30pm–4am Tue–Sun. 🖰 none ❏ 👕 varies.

Nell's

Having hit on the recipe for success way back, Nell's has changed little over the years. Regardless of the nightly promotion or concept, it always has the same smooth vibe. Upstairs, a lush, intimate bar has a DJ playing between live R&B band sets, while downstairs pulsates to a classic dance mix. This club is renowned for its picky door policy so come well-dressed (and men come with a woman). A particularly popular party is Voices (Tue) where amateur songbirds and the occasional celeb-birdie perch on the open mic upstairs and sing R&B.

246 W 14th St (bet. 7th & 8th Aves), West Village ☎ 675-1567 🚇 A•C•E to 14th St, L to 8th Ave 💷 $10–$15 ◑ 10pm–4am daily (1am Mon). 🖰 MC/V ❏ 👕 dress up.

Shine

A plain rock 'n' roll venue transformed into a party paradise, Shine radiates good clean (and sometimes not-so-clean) fun. There are cushy couches and a mini-stage hosting everything from dance and drag to burlesque and comedy. Promoters bring in all sorts of special events and weekly parties.
✿ Home Cookin' hip-hop party (Wed).

285 West Broadway (at Canal St), Tribeca ☎ 941-0900 🚇 A•C•E•1•9 to Canal St 💷 $5–$15 ◑ 10pm–4am daily. 🖰 MC/V ❏ 👕 smart casual.

Tunnel

Thousands of people from all walks of life converge at this megaclub. Every area – even the bathroom – has its own bar and sound system, and you can weave in

practical information

Magazines such as *Paper* and *Time Out* feature nightclub listings, as do free publications like *Flyer NYC*, *NYPress*, *HX*, *Next* and *Wipe*, found on street corners and in record and clubby clothes stores.

Nights move from venue to venue frequently, so it's best to call ahead.

👕 Some clubs have specific dress codes. Many have a 'no sneakers or jeans' policy and a few clubs will refuse entry to men not accompanied by a woman.

💷 Most clubs will only accept a credit card for a large bar tab.

◑ The majority of clubs open at 10pm and fill up around 1am. According to NYC law, all clubs must stop serving alcohol at 4am, so most of them close down at that time.

and out though hard house, 80's pop, hip hop and deep house. Admission is expensive, but there is more than enough bang for the buck with smash hit nights as well as many special events. Dress up, and men – come with a woman.
✧ Saturday night 'Kurfew' hard house.

220 12th Ave (at 27th St), Chelsea ☎ 695-4682 🎦 C•E to 23rd St 🚇 $15–$25 🌓 10pm–6am Thu–Sun. 🖃 MC/V 🔲 🕾 smart casual.

Twilo

The huge dancefloor dominates this magnet for an energetic gay crowd. Large psychedelic globes hang from the ceiling and movies are screened on the walls, giving this club a rich, yet frivolous atmosphere. ✧ Ultimate Twilo (Fri) and Twilo & Junior Vasquez Presents (Sat).

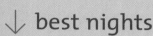

↓ best nights

monday

Konkrete Jungle @ Coney Island High

One of NY's few long-running jungle parties continues to progress. A mixed crowd comes to this traditionally rock 'n' roll venue to experience the hard-edged jungle. Downstairs, in the small lounge is a more mellow mix of dub and trip hop.

15 St Mark's Pl (at 2nd Ave), East Village ☎ 674-7959 🎦 N•R to 8th St; 6 to Astor Pl 🚇 $8–$10 🌓 11pm–4am. 🔲 🖃 AE 🕾 very casual.

tuesday

Beige @ B Bar

Credit is due to the promoters for sustaining the glamour and seduction of this effervescent event. A wide array of tunes play while you watch the tales unfold at this upper-crust yet funky downtown restaurant-cum-lounge. Dress to impress – it's a 'private party' if you aren't up to scratch.

338 Bowery (at 4th St), Noho ☎ 475-2220 🎦 6 to Bleecker St 🚇 free 🌓 11pm–4am. 🔲 🖃 MC/V 🕾 smart casual.

Sweet Thing @ Rebar

A long-running hip-hop party with celeb DJ Mark Ronson spinning hip-hop hits and hard-hitting R&B for a devoted, enthusiastic (if testosterone-heavy) straight crowd.

127 8th Ave (at 16th St), Chelsea ☎ 627-1680 🎦 L to 8th Ave; A•C•E•1•2•3•9 to 14th St-Union Sq 🚇 $15 🌓 10.30pm–4am. 🖃AE/MC/V 🔲 🕾 casual.

wednesday

Clubhouse @ Planet 28

Banjee boys vogue at these 'mini-balls' – all for the honour of being the best in

530 W 27th St (bet.10th & 11th Aves), Chelsea ☎ 268-1600 🆆 www.twiloclub.com 🎦 C•E to 23rd St; 1•9 to 28th St 🚇 $15–$25 🌓 10pm–8am Fri, 10pm–noon Sat. 🖃 MC/V 🔲 🕾 casual.

Vinyl

This hallowed patch of land is the birthplace of the legendary clubs of old: Area, Quick and Shelter. Now known as Vinyl, it's dance heaven, still carving out a giant reputation. Usually closed in the week, weekends see lines wrapping around the corner. No alcohol is served.
✧ Body & Soul deep and underground house music tea party (Sun all day long).

6 Hubert St (at Hudson St), Tribeca ☎ 343-1379 🎦 A•C•E to Canal St; 1•9 to Franklin St 🚇 $10–$15 🌓 vary. 🖃 none 🔲 🕾 very casual.

their category. This night now draws a mixed youngish crowd anxious for a peep at a scene thought to have disappeared a decade ago. Music is varied house.

215 W 28th St (bet.7th & 8th Aves), Chelsea ☎ 643-1179 🎦 C•E to 23rd St; 1•9 to 28th St 🚇 $10 🌓 10pm–4am. 🖃 none 🔲 🕾 casual.

Lust for Life/Legends @ Life

Lust for Life has a cast of rock 'n' rollers hanging out in the glare bouncing off the bare go-go boys and girls. Round the back, the soulful Legends offers deep and underground house for those unafraid to get down and get dirty.

158 Bleecker St (at Thompson St), West Village ☎ 420-1999 🎦 A•B•C•D•E•F•Q to W 4th St 🚇 $15 🌓 10pm–5am. 🖃 MC/V 🔲 🕾 smart casual.

Popstitute @ Vanity

Something fresh with this camp night of retro/modern pop tunes spun by Krista the topless DJ. Vanity's fabulous sound system and cool decor add to the vibe.

28 E 23rd St (bet. 5th Ave & Broadway), Flatiron District ☎ 254-6117 🎦 N•R•6 to 23rd St 🚇 $8 🌓 10pm–4am. 🖃 MC/V 🔲 🕾 smart casual.

Salon @ Flamingo East

Fashionable gents come out in droves for this long-running gay night. DJs rock this lurid lounge with deep house music.
✧ Singing divas at special events.

219 2nd Ave (bet. 13th & 14th Sts), E Village ☎ 533-2860 🎦 L to 3rd Ave 🚇 $5 🌓 10.30pm–4am. 🖃 AE/MC/V 🔲 🕾 smart casual.

thursday

Squeezebox @ Don Hills

A night of fun and frolics at this long-established punk (as in Sex Pistols) party palace. Experience Downtown's decadence with a room full of limber go-go dancers and daring drunkards. Come early to catch live rock 'n' roll every week.

511 Greenwich St (at Spring St), West Village ☎ 334-1390 🚇 C•E to Spring St 💲 $10 ◐ 9pm–4am. 🍴 AE/MC/V ❑ 👕 funky casual.

Susia @ Beer Hall

Susia is ablaze with retro-Latin vibes – mambo, Latin jazz, cha cha, salsa – plus a few house tunes thrown in. A cool space with affordable drinks and a friendly crowd.

29 Second Ave (bet. 1st & 2nd St), LES ☎ 375-1449 🚇 F to 2nd Ave 💲 $5 ◐ 10pm–4am. 🍴 none ❑ 👕 casual.

Trannie Chaser @ NowBar

NY's only transexual promoter Glorya Wholsome has created a place where bodacious Trannies and their Chasers can meet and cavort. Men of all shapes and sizes move to dance beats and woo the 'ladies' downstairs, while in the upstairs 'lap dance' lounge, they go a little bit further.

22 Seventh Ave S (at Leroy St), West Village ☎ 293-0323 🚇 1•9 to Houston St 💲 $15 ($10 for women, TV's and TS's) ◐ 10pm–4am. 🍴 MC/V ❑ 👕 casual.

Vampyros Lesbos @ XVI

In the style of the movie this place was named after, you'll hear 60's French pop, lounge tunes and movie soundtracks in a cosy, couch-filled setting. Beneath the soft-porn projections on the wall, go-go girls in a cage dance for a mostly straight crowd.

16 First Ave (bet. 1st & 2nd St), East Village ☎ 260-1549 🚇 F to 2nd Ave 💲 $7 ◐ 11pm–4am. 🍴 MC/V ❑ 👕 casual.

friday

Indie 5000 @ NowBar

DJs spin independent and underground hip hop... and nothing else in this dark, cavernous hide-away. Strictly old skool.

22 Seventh Ave S (at Leroy St), West Village ☎ 293-0323 🚇 1•9 to Houston St 💲 $5 ◐ 10pm–4am. 🍴 MC/V ❑ 👕 casual.

100% Pure @ El Flamingo

A hugely popular night full of celebs and those who want to rub shoulders with them. Favourite DJ Stretch Armstrong spins a mix of hip-hop, reggae and soul that pumps through the big main floor and VIP rooms. Expect weekly musical performances and/or fashion shows too.

547 W 21st St (bet. 10th & 11th Aves), Chelsea ☎ 243-2121 🚇 C•E to 23rd St 💲 $15–$25 ◐ 10pm–4am. 🍴 MC/V ❑ 👕 dress up. •

saturday

Foxy @ The Cock

A quirky night where between dancing and drinking, patrons are invited to strut

their stuff on stage – and win $100. Judged by the crowd, contestants do dastardly deeds ranging from acrobatics to anal probing and much, much more.

188 Ave A (at 12th St), East Village ☎ 777-6254 🚇 L to 1st Ave 💲 $5 ◐ 11pm–4am. 🍴 none ❑ 👕 casual.

Key to Success @ The Key Club

Myriad well-known promoters get the young to get down here every week. The hip-hop scene to be seen at, it's crammed full of big-willies as well as big-wanna-bes. DJ Stretch Armstrong spins hip-hop with a dash of R&B for this jumping, jam-packed night.

76 E 13th St (bet. 4th Ave & Broadway), East Village ☎ 388-1060 🚇 L•N•R•4•5•6 to 14th St-Union Sq 💲 $20 ◐ 10pm–4am. 🍴 none ❑ 👕 dress up.

Lovely @ 2i's

An urban hang-suite for the soulful. Upstairs, superb DJs make their mark with hip-hop, soul and reggae for the mix of twenty-something hipsters and homeboys. Downstairs, artists paint murals and show slides to the deep-house beat.

248 W 14th St (bet. 7th & 8th Aves), West Village ☎ 807-1775 🚇 A•C•E•1•2•3•9 to 14th St; L to 8th Ave 💲 $10–$15 ◐ 10pm–4am. 🍴 AE/MC/V ❑ 👕 smart casual.

sunday

Café Con Leche @ Creation

Legendary diva Willy Ninja greets the guests at the velvet rope for NY's longest-running Latin house party. The fun keeps the truly diverse dance crowd coming back for more. DJs spin a mix of everything from tribal house to Latin pop at Café's current five-floor home.

20 W 39th St (bet. 5th & 6th Aves), Midtown ☎ 719-9867 🚇 B•D•F•Q to 42nd St; 7 to 5th Ave 💲 $10 ◐ 10pm–4am. 🍴 MC/V ❑ 👕 dress up.

Shout @ 13

Anglophiles congregate in sleek yet comfortable surroundings to listen to Brit-pop through the night. 13's cool, low-key atmosphere makes it a good place to wind down your weekend, especially in summer when the roof-deck is open.

35 E 13th St (at University Pl), East Village ☎ 979-6677 🚇 L•N•R•4•5•6 to 14th St-Union Sq 💲 free ◐ 10pm–4am. 🍴 MC/V ❑ 👕 smart casual.

Sticky Mikes @ 2i's

An excellent night of ready reggae vibes. Roots and rockers enthuse the upstairs crowd, while downstairs, DJ Soulfinger Sam plays soul, funk and hip-hop.

248 W 14th St (bet. 7th & 8th Aves), West Village ☎ 807-1775 🚇 A•C•E•1•2•3•9 to 14th St; L to 8th Ave 💲 $10 ◐ 10pm–4am. 🍴 AE/MC/V ❑ 👕 dress up.

new york agenda

A year's worth of events and happenings in and around the big apple.....

summer

Puerto Rican Day Parade

The parade honours the 2 million plus Puerto Rican residents of New York, but all over town cars beep their horns and sport the flags and banners of their owners' native island.

❶ June
Fifth Avenue from 44th to 79th Street ☎ 1-718-665-4009 ⓜ B·D·F·Q to 47th-50th Sts-Rockefeller Center; any stops on 4·5·6 from Grand Central - 42nd St to 77th St ⚑ free

Gay and Lesbian Pride Day

Body-beautiful, bare-chested men (and women) take to the streets to celebrate Gay Pride and show off their pecs.

❶ end June
Fifth Avenue from 80th Street to Greenwich Village; street party along Christopher Street to West Side Piers ☎ 620-7310 ⓜ 6 to 77th St (start); 1·9 to Christopher St (finish) ⚑ free

Central Park Summerstage

Weekend afternoon concerts feature big name music acts such as Roy Ayres and James Brown. Spoken word and dance recitals on week nights – see listings mags for details [→148].

❶ June–August
Rumsey Field, mid-park ☎ 360-2777 ⓜ 6 to 68th St-Hunter College or 77th St; 1·2·3·9 to 72nd St ⚑ free

New York Philharmonic & Metropolitan Opera in the Park

Humid summer evenings are best spent in the park with the strains of classical music wafting over one's picnic – see listings mags for details [→148].

❶ June–August
Rumsey Field, mid-park ☎ 875-5709 ⓜ 6 to 68th St-Hunter College or 77th St; 1·2·3·9 to 72nd St ⚑ free

Shakespeare in the Park

Every season the Delacorte Theater in Central Park shows two plays: one by Shakespeare and one American classic.

❶ late June–late August
Delacorte Theater, mid-park ☎ 539-8500 ⓜ 6 to 68th St-Hunter College or 77th St; 1·2·3·9 to 72nd St ⚑ free

Mermaid Day Parade

King Neptune chomping on a hot dog while dozens of mermaids and other fairy-tale creatures cavort on the boardwalk at Coney Island make for a real off-beat experience.

❶ end June
From Steeplechase Park to Boardwalk (at 8th St), Coney Island ☎ 1-718-372-5159 ⓜ B·D·F·N to Stillwell Ave-Coney Island ⚑ free

Washington Square Music Festival

Continuing a long-running Greenwich Village tradition of a civilized night out, this festival provides chamber music for an appreciative audience.

❶ July–August
West Village ☎ 431-1088 ⓜ A·B·C·D·E·F·Q to W 4th St-Washington Sq ⚑ free

Macy's Fourth of July Fireworks

14,000 aerial shells and special effects explode over the East River. The hour-long extravaganza ends with a rousing rendition of 'Star Spangled Banner'.

❶ Independence Day
East River; for the best view get down to FDR Drive (bet. 14th & 51st Sts) ☎ 494-4495 ⓜ L to 1st Ave; or 4·5·6·7 to Grand Central-42nd St; 6 to 51st St ⚑ free

Harlem Week

The highlight of this uptown extravaganza is the street festival on Fifth Avenue between 125th and 135th Streets with live jazz, gospel and R&B.

❶ early–mid August
Throughout Harlem ☎ 862-8477 ⓜ 2·3 to 125th St or 135th St ⚑ free

autumn

US Open Tennis Tournament

Pete Sampras, Stefi Graf and Monica Seles have all strutted their stuff here, at one of the most demanding tennis tournaments on the world circuit.

❶ end August–early September
USTA Tennis Center, Flushing, Queens ☎ 1-718-760-6200 ⓜ 7 to Willets Point-Shea Stadium ⚑ approx $30–$65

Feast of San Gennaro

Spicy Italian sausages, fairground games and pumping house music. Crowds flock in from the outer boroughs for this 10-day street party.

❶ mid September
Mulberry Street from Houston Street to Canal Street, Nolita ☎ 764-6330 ⓜ B·D·F·Q to Broadway-Lafayette St; 6 to Bleecker St; N·R to Prince St; J·M·Z·6 to Canal St ⚑ free

Wigstock

As the name implies, it's all about hair – and stilettos and frocks, with a salubrious stage show hosted by the reigning drag-queen of the moment.

❶ Labor Day weekend
Pier 54, West Side Highway, West Village ☎ 774-7470 ⓜ 1·9 to Christopher St ⚑ free

West Indian-American Day Carnival

Not on the scale of London's Notting Hill but excellent beef patties, jerk chicken and many sound systems make for a carnival spirit nonetheless.

❶ Labor Day
Eastern Parkway, Brooklyn ☎ 1-718-77-4052 ⓜ 2·3 to Grand Army Plaza ⚑ free

New York Film Festival

A wide range of new films from established directors debut before a critical audience. Tickets sell out fast in this film-crazed community.

❶ end September–mid October
Alice Tully Hall, Lincoln Center, Columbus Avenue (bet. 62nd & 66th Sts), UWS ☎ 875-5610 ⓜ 1·9 to 66th St-Lincoln Center ⚑ approx $15 per screening

Hispanic Day Parade

Thousands of flag-waving New Yorkers line Fifth Avenue to salute a parade of floats and dancers representing the Hispanic nations.

❶ early October
Fifth Avenue from 44th to 72nd Street ☎ 864-0715 ⓜ B·D·F·Q to 47th-50th Sts-Rockefeller Center; any stops on 4·5·6 from 42nd St-Grand Central to 77th St ⚑ free

Columbus Day Parade

The official celebration of Columbus's so-called 'discovery' of America with a largely Italian-oriented show of floats and military marching bands.

❶ early October
Fifth Avenue from 44th to 72nd Street ☎ 249-9923 ⓜ B·D·F·Q to 47th-50th Sts-Rockefeller Center; any stops on 4·5·6 from Grand Central-42nd St to 77th St ⚑ free

Rangers Ice Hockey Season

NYC is big on local sports – the Rangers are home grown heroes and have a huge following.

❶ October–April
Madison Square Garden, W 33rd St & Seventh Ave, Midtown ☎ 465-6741 ⓜ A·C·E·1·2·3·9 to 34th St-Penn Station ⚑ varies

events

more events

Greenwich Village Halloween Parade

An orgy of freaks, ghouls and outlandish costumes. Gay New Yorkers guarantee a totally un-inhibited, high-spirited affair.

◐ *31 October*
Sixth Avenue from Spring Street to 21st Street
☎ 1-914-758-5519 Ⓜ C·E to Spring St; A·B·C·D·E·F·Q to W 4th St-Washington Sq; 1·9 to 18th St ☒ free

winter

New York City Marathon

Cheering on the stragglers can be combined with a beautiful day in the park – or, if it's your thing, sign up! Best views are usually from within Central Park.

◐ *end October/early November*
Verazzano Bridge on Staten Island (start); Tavern on the Green, W 67th Street (finish)
☎ 860-4455 (for details of route) ☒ free

'Knicks' Basketball Season

New Yorkers are a loyal bunch and despite the ongoing losing streak of the Knicks, diehard fans like Spike Lee and Woody Allen, who are at every home game, keep on cheering and hoping.

◐ *November–April*
Madison Square Garden, W33rd St & Seventh Ave, Midtown
☎ 465-6741 Ⓜ A·C·E·1·2·3·9 to 34th St-Penn Station ☒ varies (tickets are hard to get hold of)

Macy's Thanksgiving Day Parade

Balloons of suitably skyscraper proportions are inflated in Central Park the day before and paraded on Thanksgiving Day – this pre-turkey spectacular is unmissable.

◐ *Thanksgiving Day*
From Central Park W (at 77th St), down Broadway and finishing at Herald Square
☎ 494-4495
Ⓜ 1·2·3·9 to 72nd St (start); B·D·F·N·Q·R to 34th St-Herald Sq (finish) ☒ free

Lighting the Rockefeller Center Christmas Tree

Traditional and kitschy with twinkling lights, Christmas carollers and throngs of shopping-bag-toting tourists.

◐ *early December*
47th to 50th Street (at Sixth Ave), Midtown ☎ 632-3975
Ⓜ B·D·F·Q to 47th-50th Sts-Rockefeller Center ☒ free

'Dropping the Ball'

You thought the subway at rush hour was crowded? A generally well-mannered crowd counts down to the New Year.

◐ *New Year's Eve*
Times Square, Midtown

☎ 922-9393 Ⓜ N·R·1·2·3·7·9 to 42nd St-Times Sq ☒ free

Midnight Footrace in Central Park

A festive race around the park, and plenty of champagne when you make it to the finishing line. Good healthy fun.

◐ *New Year's Eve*
Tavern on the Green, Central Park ☎ 860-4455 Ⓜ 1·2·3·9 to 72nd St ☒ free

Tax Free Week!

No tax on retail items twice a year – takes the sting out of shopping.

◐ *mid January & September*
☎ 788-3000 (mayor's office) for details

Martin Luther King Jr Day

A solemn tribute to Dr King, the parade also serves as a memorial to all black soldiers who have fought for America.

◐ *late January*
Fifth Avenue (bet. 60th & 68th Sts), UES ☎ 374-5176 Ⓜ 4·5·6 to 59th St (start); 6 to 68th St-Hunter College (finish) ☒ free

Chinese New Year

Strict enforcement of the fire-cracker ban has dampened this manic celebration, but dragons still dance around Chinatown.

◐ *February*
Chinatown ☎ J·M·N·R·Z·6 to Canal St ☎ 373-1800 ☒ free

spring

St Patrick's Day Parade

The city's Irish contingent turns out to parade (but mainly drink) in celebration of their cultural heritage: a rowdy day-out.

◐ *17 March*
Fifth Avenue from 44th to 86th Streets, then east to Third Avenue ☎ 1-718-357-7532
Ⓜ 7 to 5th Ave; any stop on Sixth from 51st to 86th Sts ☒ free

New York Underground Film Festival

A young, downtown audience critiques over 120 new movies. Brit films also showcased since 1999.

◐ *March*
Anthology Film Archives, Second Avenue (at 3rd St), LES

☎ 925-3440 ᴡ www.nyuff.com Ⓜ F to 2nd Ave ☒ $7.50

Easter Sunday Parade

Pet dogs dressed up as Easter bunnies, kiddies in bonnets – and eggs galore.

◐ *Easter Sunday*
Fifth Avenue (bet. 49th & 57th Sts), Midtown ☎ 484-1222
Ⓜ B·D·F·Q to 47th-50th Sts-Rockefeller Center; E·F to 5th Ave ☒ free

Yankees & Mets Baseball Season

Tickets are easy to come by, unlike basketball games. The Yankees are team winners and have a huge home following.

◐ *April–October*
Mets: Shea Stadium, 126th St (at Roosevelt Ave), Queens
☎ 1-718-507-8499
Ⓜ 7 to Willets Point-Shea Stadium ☒ $9–$23
Yankees: Yankee Stadium, 161st St & River Ave, Bronx ☎ 1-718-293-6000 Ⓜ C·D·4 to 161st St-Yankee Stadium ☒ $12–$23

Spring Festival

Stalls selling home-baked goods rub shoulders with carnival games and bouncy castles. Sound systems get everyone dancing in the streets.

◐ *April*
Broadway (bet. 110th & 118th Sts), Morningside Heights
☎ 764-6330 Ⓜ 1·9 to Cathedral Pkwy (110th St) ☒ free

Bike New York: The Great Five Boro Bike Tour

The largest mass bike ride passes through Manhattan, the Bronx, Queens, Brooklyn and Staten Island, covering 42 miles in a single day.

◐ *early May*
Starts Battery Park; finishes Staten Island ☎ 932-2453 (for details of route) ☒ free

Memorial Day Parade

Old soldiers are remembered by their comrades in arms. The city is eerily quiet when the minute of silence is observed.

◐ *end May*
Fifth Avenue from 44th to 72nd Street ☎ 374-5176
Ⓜ B·D·F·Q to 47th-50th Sts-Rockefeller Center; any stops on 4·5·6 from Grand Central-42nd St to 77th St ☒ free

events for the millennium

All sorts of millennium events are in the pipeline for NYC. For up-to-date details send a $20 money order to the Communications Department, NYCVB (New York Convention & Visitors Bureau). You'll become a Millennium Club member and receive regular newsletters about the celebrations: Times Square will broadcast images from other countries and cultures, and will have the New Year's Eve tradition of dropping the ball at midnight.

NYCVB, 810 Seventh Avenue, NY 10019 ☎ 484-1222

New York has some of the trendiest, coolest hotels in the world, from the super smooth Time to the thoroughly modern, touch-of-a-button Peninsula. But there is also plenty of trad chintzy and more elegant old-world comfort too. Bedrooms tend to be larger than in European city hotels; they also tend to cost more. Find your niche in the following selections – from no-expense-spared to budget – in all areas of the big apple.

sleep easy
what's where

↓ brooklyn

Bed & Breakfast On The Park | $250 [→161]

↓ chelsea

Chelsea | $185 [→156]

Chelsea International Hostel | $50 [→162]

Leo House | $78 [→163]

↓ gramercy park

Carlton Arms | $73 [→162]

Hotel 17 | $75 [→163]

Inn at Irving Place | $295 [→161]

↓ lower east side (LES)

Off Soho Suites | $179 [→161]

↓ midtown east

Avalon | $270 [→158]

Box Tree | $230 [→159]

Fitzpatrick | $325 [→160]

Four Seasons | $565 [→156]

Gershwin | $129 [→162]

Gramercy Park Hotel | $170 [→162]

Kitano New York | $315 [→160]

Morgans | $320 [→157]

New York Palace | $425 [→157]

Omni Berkshire Place | $389 [→160]

Peninsula | $535 [→157]

Plaza | $425 [→156]

St Regis | $520 [→157]

Shelburne Murray Hill | $306 [→162]

Waldorf Astoria | $250 [→156]

W Hotel New York| $279 [→158]

↓ midtown west

Algonquin | $329 [→156]

Broadway Inn | $115 [→161]

Casablanca | $265 [→160]

Edison Hotel | $140 [→162]

Mansfield | $209 [→159]

Paramount | $300 [→158]

Southgate Tower Suite Hotel | $200 [→162]

Royalton | $365 [→158]

Time | $285 [→158]

↓ soho

Mercer Hotel | $375 [→157]

Soho Grand | $419 [→158]

↓ upper east side (UES)

Carlyle | $375 [→156]

Hotel Elysée | $325 [→159]

Hotel Wales | $219 [→159]

Franklin | $249 [→159]

Lowell | $445 [→160]

Pierre | $480 [→157]

Plaza Athénée | $410 [→159]

↓ upper west side (UWS)

Country Inn The City | $150 [→161]

Hotel Beacon | $170 [→161]

Hostelling International New York | $75 [→163]

Malibu | $79 [→163]

Pickwick Arms Hotel | $115 [→163]

↓ west village

Abingdon | $165 [→160]

Larchmont Hotel | $90 [→162]

Washington Square Hotel | $129 [→163]

→ more hotels

prices – lowest quoted, excluding taxes, for double room in peak season 99 (unless otherwise stated)

↓ dead famous

Algonquin 59 W 44th St (bet. 5th & 6th Aves) | Midtown | 10036

The personality of this literary landmark oozes from the fabulously restored public spaces. This was where Dorothy Parker headed up the Round Table, and the *New Yorker* cartoon wallpaper in the hall is a nod to the local magazine whose staff famously used the Algonquin as their watering hole [→137]. The rooms are a decent size, in soft colours, and carry wonderful examples of old black-and-white photos of 50's New York.

singles from $329
doubles from $329

Ⓜ 7 to 5th Ave

☎ 840-6800
F 944-1419
w camberleyhotels.com

◆165 ☐ ☐ all 📖 ↔
𝄞 ♨ ☐ ♿

Chelsea 222 W 23rd St (bet. 7th & 8th Aves) | Chelsea | 10011

Check out the pinnacle of kitsch in the Chelsea's Room 822, where Madonna and Drew Barrymore have both staged photoshoots. Artists and creatives of all kinds love this place – crushed velvet chaises longues are tucked into light-filled bay windows, rooms may have leopard print curtains, hot pink 70's-style couches with lime green pillows and ornate fireplaces. No two rooms are alike. The lobby is famous for its paintings by artists who've lived here, like Julian Schnabel.

singles from $165
doubles from $185

Ⓜ 1·9 to 23rd St

☎ 243-3700
F 675-5531
w chelseahotel.com

◆250 ☐ ☐ all 📖 🌐 ♨
☐ ℗

Plaza Fifth Ave (at 59th St) | Midtown | 10019

Arguably NYC's most famous hotel: site of Truman Capote's legendary Black and White Ball, and once home to Scott and Zelda (who frolicked in the hotel's fountain), and Marlene Dietrich (who was better behaved). A New York sight in itself, the Plaza was built in 1907 in the style of a French château. Bedrooms feel sparsely furnished only because of their generous size. Decorative fireplaces, crystal chandeliers and elaborate ceilings embellish every grand and conservatively elegant room.

singles from $335
doubles from $425

Ⓜ N·R to 5th Ave

☎ 759-3000
F 759-3167
w fairmont.com

◆808 ☐ ☐ all 📖 🌐 ↔
𝄞 ♨ ☐ ℗ ♿

Waldorf Astoria 301 Park Ave (bet. 49th & 50th Sts) | Midtown | 10022

Every President since Hoover has stayed here when in town. Sure, the presidential four-bedroom suite with dining room is roomy, but you'd be away from the fun if you missed out on people-watching in the enormous lobby (Cole Porter's piano is here). Public rooms exemplify tasteful American excess and standard bedrooms are large with classic decor. With nearly 1400 of them, plus restaurants and shops, it is like a mini-city.

singles from $210
doubles from $250

Ⓜ 6 to 51st St

☎ 355-3000
F 872-0204
w hilton.com

◆1385 ☐ ☐ all 📖 🌐 ↔
𝄞 ♨ ☐ ℗ ♿

↓ last word in luxury

Carlyle 35 E 76th St (bet. Madison & Park Aves) | UES | 10021

With 65 permanent residents, the Carlyle feels like a club but is glad to consider new 'members'. World-famous rooms like Bemelmans' Bar, with murals by the children's book illustrator, and Café Carlyle [→140] where Bobby Short has tinkled the ivories for patrons for 30 years, are all part of New York history. Many of the large rooms have baby grand pianos, are decorated in restrained yellows and greens, and dotted with elegant antiques.

singles & doubles from $375

Ⓜ 6 to 77th St

☎ 744-1600
F 717-4682

◆180 ☐ ☐ all 📖 🌐 ↔
𝄞 ♨ ☐ ℗ ♿

Four Seasons 57 E 57th St (bet. 5th & Park Aves) | Midtown | 10022

'Monumental' best describes the theatrical entrance and lobby of this IM Pei-designed building. The Four Seasons boasts the largest (and most expensive) rooms in town. Decor is updated art deco in muted colours with plenty of warm wood. Luxuriate in the sheer space – walk-in dressing rooms, and opulent marble bathrooms with deep baths which fill in 60 seconds. The view of the Chrysler building from the jacuzzi on the 51st floor is drop-dead amazing.

singles from $515
doubles from $565

Ⓜ N·R to 5th Ave

☎ 758-5700
F 758-5711
w fourseasons.com

◆370 ☐ ☐ all 📖 🌐 ↔
𝄞 ♨ ☐ ℗ ♿

New York Palace 455 Madison Ave (bet. 50th & 51st Sts) | Midtown | 10022

The historical exterior to this 1882 landmark building is intact, making the hip reception area a surprising contrast. A team of French designers revamped the place to include high-back modern couches in the lobby with a Moroccan carpet and quirky gold lamps. Bedrooms come in a choice of two styles; Empire furnishings or updated art deco, inspired by the buildings of the Rockefeller Center.

singles & doubles from $425

Ⓜ 6 to 51st St
☎ 888-7000
F 303-6000
w newyorkpalace.com
🛏 897 ▤ all 📖 🔞 ↔
✐ ⚲ 🖳 🅿 ⅋

157

Peninsula 700 Fifth Ave (at 55th St) | Midtown | 10019

Located in a turn-of-the-century beaux-arts building, the Peninsula has been reopened after renovation. It is now totally high-tech with stereos in the bathrooms (automatically muted if your hands-free phone rings...), built-in TVs, control of humidity and warmth and, of course, mood lighting. Technology aside, wallow in comfy velvet chairs, or dine at gold-leaf tables. Matisse prints and oversized fireplaces all contribute to a surprisingly unfussy, modern look.

singles & doubles from $535

Ⓜ E•F to 5th Ave
☎ 956-2888
F 903-3949
e pny@peninsula.com
w peninsula.com

🛏 241 ▤ all 📖 🔞 ≋
↔ ✐ ⚲ ⚲ 🖳 🅿 ⅋

hotels

Pierre 2 E 61st St (at 5th Ave) | UES | 10021-5402

A hotel within an apartment building for the elite, the Pierre makes you feel that you too are living an upper crust existence. It's a social hub for the NY elite; you can rub elbows with distinguished residents at afternoon tea (the in thing) in the muralled Rotunda Room. Rooms are individual; some French in style with navy toile bedcovers, matching curtains, and botanical prints. Amazing views of Central Park help to keep the elegant, largely European clientele coming back time after time.

singles from $430
doubles from $480

Ⓜ N•R to 5th Ave
☎ 838-8000
F 826-0319
w fourseasons.com

🛏 202 ▤ all 📖 🔞 ↔
✐ ⚲ 🖳 🅿 ⅋

St Regis 2 E 55th St (bet. 5th & Park Aves) | Midtown | 10022

The St Regis, doyenne of Fifth Avenue hotels, harks back to a glamour-filled era. Cherubs draped in roses recline on the ceiling, while baroque gold and Louis XVI furniture fills a lobby which invites you into a gentle 'old money' existence. Feel like a pearl in an oyster shell of a bedroom in shades of green and grey. Pampering the Gucci and Prada shopping-laden clientele seems to be the life-mission of the solicitous staff.

singles & doubles from $520

Ⓜ E•F to 5th Ave
☎ 753-4500
F 787-3447
e reso81_stregisnyc@ittsheraton.com

🛏 314 ▤ all 📖 🔞 ↔
✐ ⚲ 🖳 🅿 ⅋

↓ designer label

Mercer Hotel 147 Mercer St (at Prince St) | Soho | 10012

For the madly hip who have to stay Downtown, the hotel of the moment is the Mercer. Smack dab in the heart of Soho, it's the new place to be seen for a drink or lunch [→121] and music and entertainment industry-types hang out with flip-phones clamped to their ears. Deep, comfy chairs and couches in the lobby are seductively inviting. Rooms are minimal, clean, spare: shades of white on white with fun marble bathrooms, whose walls fold out to expose the big tubs to the room.

singles from $350
doubles from $375

Ⓜ N•R to Prince St
☎ 966-6060
F 965-3838
w themercer.com

🛏 75 ▤ all 📖 🔞 ✐ ⚲
🖳 ⅋

more hotels

Morgans 237 Madison Ave (at 37th St) | Midtown | 10016

Ian Schrager's first NY hotel continues to be the place of choice for the fashion industry. Refurbishment has lightened up the rooms: cream, buff and soft greys with contrasting textures of soft corduroy, silks, maple wood and an ultra-suede window seat to warm up the space. Wide, low-slung beds make the smallish bedrooms appear larger. The lobby is Eastern in feel with a carpet of Escher cubes and large brown leather chairs.

singles from $295
doubles from $320

Ⓜ 6 to 33rd St
☎ 686-0300
F 779-8352

🛏 113 🖵 ▤ all 📖 🔞
⚲ 🖳 🅿 ⅋

158

Paramount 235 W 46th St (bet. 7th & 8th Aves) | Midtown | 10036

singles from $175
doubles from $300

Ⓜ N•R to 49th St

☎ 764-5500
F 354-5237

◆600 ⏻ 🖥all 📋 ↔✦🖉
🖥📺🅿🛗

Billed as Schrager's 'cheap chic' hotel, there is still plenty of style and attitude in the Paramount. Though small, any feeling of claustrophobia is ruled out by ingenious room layouts and decor: large Vermeer prints as headboards, white bedlinen, white leather furniture and you gotta love the hip black and white tiled bathrooms with cool stainless steel sinks. The foyer's intimate seating arrangements encourage lobby socializing. Shades are warmed-up green and orange.

Royalton 44 W 44th St (bet. 5th & 6th Aves) | Midtown | 10036

singles from $350
doubles from $365

Ⓜ B•D•F•Q to 42nd St

☎ 768-5100
F 768-5191

◆169 ⏻ 🖥all 📋 ↔㉔
🖉🖥📺🅿🛗

Ian Schrager's Midtown hotel is a cool-yet-fun Philippe Starck tribute to modernism. A long lobby of poured concrete is softened with cartoonish wing chairs and eccentric tables. Practical things like elevators and lobby desks are tucked out of sight. The large, minimal-decor rooms with real fireplaces reflect the tastes of the cool, trendy clientele – largely media and fashion folk. Splash in the large round tubs after a day's tough shopping.

Soho Grand 310 W Broadway (bet. Grand & Canal Sts) | Soho | 10013

singles from $399
doubles from $419

Ⓜ A•C•E to Canal St

☎ 965-3000
F 965-3200
w sohogrand.com

◆369 🖥all 📋 ㉔↔
🖉🖥📺🅿🛗

Located in chic Soho, this hotel pays homage to the loft-style industrial buildings of the area, and the art community on its doorstep. A dramatic iron stairwell leads to the upper lobby area. The modern decor, complete with drafting table desks and mock sculptures as nightstands, reflects an artistic theme, and there's an added bonus for pet owners: Soho Grand is owned by the family who run Hartz (pet products) and there are cat and dog menus, and even a pick-up dog washing service.

Time 224 W 48th St (at Broadway) | Midtown | 10019

singles from $265
doubles from $285

Ⓜ N•R to 49th St

☎ 320-2925
F 320-2926

◆192 ⏻ 🖥all 📋 ↔✦🖉
🖥📺🅿🛗

Restaurant designer Adam Tihany's first venture into hotels was much anticipated. In the lobby designed around a sculpture by Richard Serra – known for massive minimalist pieces which challenge your sense of space – you start to get an idea of Tihany's mission. The stylish rooms have soft furnishings in a choice of primary colours like red and blue, and you can choose one to suit when you book.

W Hotel New York 541 Lexington Ave (at 49th St) | Midtown | 10022

singles & doubles from $279

Ⓜ 6 to 51st St

☎ 755-1200
F 319-8344
w starwoodlodging.com

◆717 🖥all 📋 ㉔↔
🖉🖥📺🅿🛗

You can't shake the feeling that you're worshipping at the temple of a kinder, gentler chic at the new W Hotel. Maybe it's the huge Mondrian-style stained glass windows dominating the lobby area. These David Rockwell-designed masterpieces cast a warm glow with their earthy colours. Guest rooms are small but beautifully designed and packed with fun luxury touches like feather-top mattresses and the finest quality sheets embroidered with soothing phrases like 'Sleep With Angels'.

↓ chic boutiques

Avalon 16 E 32nd St (bet. 5th & Madison Aves) | Midtown | 10016

singles from $215
doubles from $270

Ⓜ 6 to 33rd St

☎ 299-7000
F 299-7001
e rooms@theavalonny.com

◆100 ⏻ 🖥AE ↔
🖥📺🅿🛗

This is New York's newest privately owned, one-off hotel. Located on lower Madison Avenue, a white-hot area of new restaurants and shops, the hotel manages to feel both grand and cosy. The lobby is definitely grand, with Veronese marble and opulent centre rotunda with black marble columns. At night, snuggle up with the hotel's unique, full-size body pillows. Green-and-cream bedrooms feature luxurious details like Frette bathrobes, Irish cotton towels and marble bathrooms.

Hotel Elysée 60 E 54th St (at Park Ave) | UES | 10022

An impressive list of famous people have called this place home in its days of housing longer term residents. Both Joe DiMaggio and Marlon Brando have lived here, Tallulah Bankhead had public tantrums, Tennessee Williams wrote and died here, and Vladimir Horowitz left his piano behind. The public spaces are large with cheerful bright furnishings. Quirky oil paintings are everywhere, and the large bedrooms contain some lovely antiques. The Monkey Bar is a very happening, packed bar scene, with a sexy red dining room next door.

singles & doubles
from $325

Ⓜ E•F to Lexington
Ave-3rd Ave

☎ 753-1066
F 980-9278
e elysee99@aol.com

◆99 ☐ 🖵 ⊟all 📖 ✐
♨ 🗋 🄿 ♿

Hotel Wales 1295 Madison Ave (at 92nd St) | UES | 10128

Staying a block away from Museum Mile makes sense if art grazing is the plan. Conveniently located in the schmoozy Carnegie neighbourhood, this grand old dame of Madison Avenue is having a facelift (due for completion in summer 99), designed to recreate the civilized New York of a bygone era. Its collection of children's book illustrations graces the public spaces, a touch of whimsy in the classically European rooms. The large tea room, where guests take breakfast, afternoon tea and light desserts, has a plush library feel. Sarabeth's restaurant downstairs also provides the hotel's room service.

singles from $205
doubles from $219

Ⓜ 6 to 96th St

☎ 876-6000
F 860-7000
e hotelwales@mind-spring.com

◆87 🖵 ⊟all 📖 ↔
✐ ♨ ♿

Franklin 164 E 87th St (bet. Lexington & 3rd Aves) | UES | 10128

Diminutive in size, but big on style, pretty much describes this hotel, from the cherrywood lobby to the elegant breakfast room and café-style lounge. Compact, chic rooms in soft neutral colours are offset by black-and-white photos of contemporary NYC, and filmy fabric headboards extend overhead in a modern canopy effect. The CD and video library is for all.

singles from $229
doubles from $249

Ⓜ 4•5•6 to 86th St

☎ 369-1000
F 369-8000

◆47 🖵 ⊟all 📖

Mansfield 12 W 44th St (bet. 5th & 6th Aves) | Midtown | 10036

The clean, modern entranceway leads on to a lobby of polished marble floors, dark woodwork and hip 30's furniture. Original features of the building have been restored, like the elaborate wrought-iron spiral stairwell. Rooms (on the small size) have modern sleigh beds with mesh headboards, and contemporary black and white prints. Laze around in comfy chairs in the lounge where you can sip free espressos 24 hours a day.

singles & doubles
from $209

Ⓜ B•D•F•Q to 42nd St

☎ 944-6050
F 764-4477
w mansfieldhotel.com

◆124 🖵 ⊟all 📖 ✐
🄿

Plaza Athénée 37 E 64th (at Park Ave) | UES | 10021

Once upon a time Lady Di's choice of hotel when in town, this jewel has the look of a French château. Hand-painted wallpaper and dark green leather chairs lend style to the marble-floored lobby. Smart French decor in the rooms includes original antique oil paintings, grey silk moiré-covered walls and elegant blue and green fabrics for bedcovers and curtains. Lovers of luxury will adore the rose-coloured marble bathrooms, flowers and Italian Frette bathrobes. Some rooms have terraces.

singles & doubles
from $410

Ⓜ N•R to Lexington
Ave

☎ 734-9100
F 772-0958
w plaza-athenee.com

◆153 ⊟all 🆚 ↔ ✐
♨ 🗋 🄿 ♿

more hotels

↓ themes & variations

Box Tree 250 E 49th St (bet. 2nd & 3rd Aves) | Midtown | 10019

Tucked into two fabulous side-by-side townhouses, the Box Tree is for romantics. Design references range from a Versailles-style private dining room to another with a table for 12 and a fireplace big enough to roast a wild boar. The main dining room is reminiscent of an art deco Swiss chalet. The lobby, with chairs around a fireplace, could have come straight from *Wuthering Heights*. Individual bedrooms like the Fabergé Room have hand-painted murals, French canopied beds and real fires.

singles & doubles
from $230

Ⓜ 6 to 51st St

☎ 758-8320
F 308-3899

◆13 🖵 🖵 ⊟all ♨ 🗋

hotels

Casablanca 147 W 43rd St (bet. 6th Ave & Broadway) | Midtown | 10036

This Moroccan theme hotel in Times Square provides a touch of the theatrical. The original wrought-iron staircase transports you up to Rick's Café, furnished with a beautiful Moroccan tiled fireplace, Moorish arches, wicker chairs, ceiling fans, and of course, a piano. Potted palms and antique weavings add to the exotic mood. Decent-sized rooms have carved headboards and prints of Moroccan villages. Here's looking at you as you curl up to watch the famous film – every room has a copy.

singles from $245
doubles from $265

Ⓜ N·R·1·2·3·7·9 to
Times Sq–42nd St

☎ 869-1212
F 391-7585
e casahotel@aol.com

✦48 ⌨🖥⏹all 🛗 ✎ ✎
🅿♿

Fitzpatrick 687 Lexington Ave (bet. 56th & 57th Sts) | Midtown | 10022

If peacock blue walls and the Celtic-patterned emerald green carpet of the lobby aren't clues enough, then the enormous photo of the President of Ireland, Mary MacAleese, should do it. The Fitzpatrick is a corner of Ireland set slap bang in the middle of New York. Bedrooms are of fair size with dark furnishings and crystal chandeliers. The towels are thick and the soaps are Irish. There is also a good selection of Irish mags as well as all the practicals such as hairdryers and coffee machines.

singles from $295
doubles from $325

Ⓜ 4·5·6 to 59th St

☎ 355-0100
F 355-1371
e fitzusa@aol.com
w fitzpatrickhotels.
  com

✦96 ⏹all 🛗 ✎ ✎📱🖥
🅿♿

Kitano New York 66 Park Ave (at 38th St) | Midtown | 10016

The Kitano attracts a largely Asian clientele and caters for them with a wonderful kaiseki restaurant, as well as providing clean, minimal rooms painted in soothingly muted tones. Authentic Japanese bedroom suites offer deep soaking tubs, roll-out futon beds and a tea ceremony room. The lobby is streamlined mahogany and marble, with a large Botero bronze. Owner Mr Kitano is an avid art collector and his large collection of works appears in the halls and rooms.

singles & doubles
from $315

Ⓜ 4·5·6·7 to Grand
Central–42nd St

☎ 885-7000
F 885-7100
e reservations@
  kitano.com

✦149 ⏹all 🛗 ✎ ✎📱🖥
♿

Lowell 28 E 63rd St (bet. Park & Madison Aves) | UES | 10021

This hotel confirms that good things come in small packages. Immaculately groomed women sit in the bijou lobby on dainty love seats. Neo-Classical fixtures, trompe-l'oeil marble walls, real marble floors and exquisite Empire-style furniture surround them. Luxurious bedrooms are impeccably furnished with tapestry bedcovers and real fires. For a themed stay, try the Garden Suite, where breakfast can be taken on the terrace.

singles from $345
doubles from $445

Ⓜ N·R to Lexington Ave

☎ 838-1400
F 319-4230
e lowellhtl@aol.com

✦65 ⏹all 🛗 😎 ↔
📱🖥🅿

Omni Berkshire Place 21 E 52nd St (bet. 5th & Madison Aves) | Midtown | 10022

Behind the walls of this 1926 landmark hotel, you'll find a modern oasis of streamlined serenity. A 70 million-dollar renovation created an enormous lobby with honey-toned wood and peach-coloured marble floors. Large, modern rooms have Giacometti-style lamps and silk fabrics galore. Prints hang above velvet couches; the touch of a button controls lights, TV, and music. In a literary mood? Ask for the Author's Suite, where novelists have stayed and left signed copies of their books.

singles from $199
doubles from $389

Ⓜ E·F to 5th Ave

☎ 753-5800
F 754-5018
w omnihotels.com

✦396 ⏹all 🛗 ↔✎
📱🖥🅿♿

↓ city b & b's

Abingdon 13 Eighth Ave (at 12th St) | West Village | 10014

A rare city find in the West Village, the Abingdon is a New England-style charmer. Each bedroom has its own distinct personality, displaying bits and pieces gathered by the owner on his global wanderings. The Ambassador room could be renamed 'Out of Africa', with its rattan mats, African masks on paprika-red walls and an enormous four-poster bed. Definitely for those who appreciate a quiet stay.

singles from $155
doubles from $165

Ⓜ A·C·E to 14th St

☎ 243-5384
F 807-7473
w abingdonguest-
  house.com

✦396 ⏹all 🛗 ↔✎
📱🖥🅿♿

. On The Park 113 Prospect Park West (bet. 7th & ...pe) | Brooklyn | 11215

...abulous period brown-... the 20-minute subway ...anhattan. Owner Liana ...was in the antiques business ...kept the good stuff for herself'. The best of her furniture is exquisitely arranged in every room. The Brooklyn Museum of Art and the Botanical Garden [Y91] are minutes away.

singles from $110
doubles from $250

Ⓜ F to 7th Ave

☎ 718-499-6115
F 718-499-1385
w bbnyc.com

♦7 ⌨ 🖥 AE/MC/V 📖
♨

Broadway Inn 264 W 46th St (bet. 8th & 9th Aves) | Midtown | 10036

The lobby is full of antique charm with a fire and book-lined shelves, where you can read the papers over your continental breakfast. Bedrooms are modern and snug and triple-glazed windows provide a soundless night's sleep in one of the liveliest blocks on the planet. Larger 'suite' rooms are ideal for families or groups, but be warned, there's no elevator up from the lobby. The staff are friendly and happy to help.

singles from $85
doubles from $115

Ⓜ A•C•E• to 42nd St-Port Authority

☎ 997-9200
F 768-2807
e broadwayinn@att.net
w broadwayinn.com

♦41 ⌨ 🖥 all 📖 ↔ 🅿

Country Inn The City 270 W 77th St (bet. Central Park W & Columbus Ave) | UWS | 10024

Reserve early to stay in one of four of the homiest rooms in the city. Owners Larry and Fergus describe these large apartments as being non-chaperoned, meaning; you check in, get your own front door key, and you're on your own. You make your own breakfast with ingredients found in your kitchenette. Rooms have antique four-poster or sleigh beds with decorative fireplaces, oil paintings and fresh roses. Room 6 even has its own terrace with wisteria-covered arbour. Minimum stay three nights.

singles & doubles from $150

Ⓜ 1•9 to 79th St

☎ 580-4183
F 501-9647
e ctryinn@aol.com
w countryinnthecity.com

♦4 ⌨ 📖

The Inn at Irving Place 56 Irving Pl (bet. 17th & 18th Sts) | Gramercy Park | 10003

These adjoining 1830 townhouses are located in the historic Gramercy Park area, and ooze the charm of a bygone era. Both have been immaculately restored with an astonishing array of antique pianos, chandeliers, hand-painted beds and elaborate ceiling roses. The staff are model-beautiful if a little temperamental. Plop down post-shopping and wallow in pillow-piled couches as you take afternoon tea by the fire.

singles & doubles from $295

Ⓜ L•N•R•4•5•6 to 14th St-Union Sq

☎ 533-4600
F 533-4611
e inn@irvingplace.com

♦12 ⌨ 🖥 all 🛗

↓ home from home

Hotel Beacon 2130 Broadway (at 75th St) | UWS | 10023

This lovely, privately-owned hotel is a bargain considering the high quality of the accommodation. Make the most of large, light-filled rooms with classical decor, city and Hudson River views, and pristine bathrooms. Cook in your own fully-equipped kitchen, picking up ingredients at local stores, or grab a takeout from one of the area's ethnic restaurants. Convenient for the Met, so you may catch a glimpse of sweeping dresses and black ties zipping out for some culture.

singles from $145
doubles from $170

Ⓜ 1•2•3•9 to 72nd St

☎ 787-1100
F 724-0839
e info@beaconhotel.com

♦220 🖥 all 📖 ♨ 🅿 ♿

→ more hotels

Off Soho Suites 11 Rivington St (at Bowery) | Lower East Side | 10002

Location, location, location should be the mantra of guests of Soho Suites. You'll be minutes only from Soho, Little Italy and Chinatown with all those ethnic food shops and restaurants. Rooms are basic motel fare with faintly Eastern decor. If you're travelling with friends and gotta stay downtown, this spot is a good money-saving option – rooms have double beds as well as a separate living room with sofabed.

singles from $97.50
doubles from $179

Ⓜ J•M to Bowery

☎ 979-9808
F 979-9801
e info@offsoho.com

♦35 🖥 AE/MC/V 📖 ↔ ♨ ♿

Shelburne Murray Hill 303 Lexington Ave (at 37th St) | Midtown | 10016-3104

Located in the 19th-century brownstone area of Murray Hill, the Shelburne has a genteel lobby belying all its wonderful practicality. Pretty, generously proportioned rooms have fully equipped kitchens, and washers and dryers in the basement. Or just relax and check out the views from the rooftop terrace.

single⬛
doubl⬛

Ⓜ 6 t⬛
☎ 689⬛
F 779-7⬛
⬢ 258 ⬛ a⬛
⬛⬛⬛Ⓟ⬛

hotels

Southgate Tower Suite Hotel 371 Seventh Ave (at 31st St) | Midtown | 10001-3984

This place is ideal if you're in town for a Madison Square Garden event. Rooms are beautifully furnished, considering the reasonable price. Just renovated bedrooms are classical in style with chintz spreads and matching curtains. Suites with two double beds and sofabeds are a boon to families. All the rooms have well-equipped kitchenettes and even better, someone who comes in each day to do your dishes.

singles from $160
doubles from $200

Ⓜ 1·2·3·9 to 34th
Street-Penn Station

☎ 563-1800
F 643-8028
w mesuite.com

⬢ 522 ⬛ all 📖 ↔ ✐
⬛ Ⓟ Ⓟ ⬛

↓ budget beds

Carlton Arms 160 E 25th St (at 3rd Ave) | Gramercy Pk | 10010

This hotel is perfect for art students. There are cartoons in the stairwells, and fourth floor corridors have 3D models. Every room has its own theme with murals and collages, and you may find owner John hands you several sets of keys so you can pick your favourite. Bathrooms (if you get one in your room) are bare bones, but you pay for what you get, and this place is fun.

singles from $57
doubles from $73

Ⓜ 6 to 23rd St

☎ 679-0680

⬢ 54 ⬛ MC/V

Chelsea International Hostel 251 W 20th St (bet. 7th & 8th Aves) | Chelsea | 10011

Centrally located in Chelsea, this hotel is opposite a police precinct, which may put the city-timid at ease. Rooms are very small and simple with bunk beds, lockers and a sink, but the public rooms (TV, billiards and two kitchens) are full of a young, beautiful and budget-challenged clientele. Making friends is easy here, and the garden set-up with picnic tables and barbecue grills sets the scene for impromptu summer parties.

singles from $23
doubles from $50

Ⓜ 1·9 to 18th St

☎ 647-0010
F 727-7289
e email@
chelseahostel.com

⬢ 255 ⬛ AE/MC/V ⬛

Edison Hotel 228 W 47th St (bet. Broadway & 8th Ave) | Midtown | 10036

This large, 900-room, pre-war building, just one block away from Times Square, is a tribute to the art deco era. The busy, gargantuan lobby has lovely high ceilings and elaborate mouldings in pale peach, turquoise and pink with murals of the Radio City Rockettes and the Cotton Club. The bedrooms, although lacking authentic 20's details, are attractive and newly furnished. Guests are a varied bunch, though generally on the younger side, and all are out to have fun.

singles from $125
doubles from $140

Ⓜ N·R to 49th St

☎ 840-5000
F 596-6850
e edisonnyc@aol.com

⬢ 900 ⬛ all ⬛ ⬛
Ⓟ ⬛

Gershwin 7 E 27th St (bet. 5th & Madison Aves) | Midtown | 10016

The Gershwin looks like a Chinese theatre run amok. Step in and the wackiness is confirmed by murals everywhere and hip Euro-type travellers buzzing by. An art collector is a co-owner and you can see his booty everywhere, including a real Lichten-stein artworks in every room. Private rooms have TVs and voice-mail, dorms are cheaper and much more basic.

singles from $89
doubles from $129

Ⓜ N·R to 28th St

☎ 545-8000
F 684-5546
e reservations@
gershwinhotel.com

⬢ 106 ⬛ AE/MC/V

Gramercy Park Hotel 2 Lexington Ave (at 21st St) | Midtown | 10010

International and unpretentious is the order of the day. The halls and rooms have a boarding-house feel to them, and the doors still require old-fashioned keys. All rooms are spacious with minty green walls and darkwood furniture. Some suites have fridges, others kitchenettes; in-room phones have voice-mail. Guests also have access to Gramercy, a rare private park.

singles from $155
doubles from $170

Ⓜ 6 to 23rd St

☎ 475-4320
F 505-0535

⬢ 509 ⬛ all 📖 ⬛ ⬛

All web addresses should be preceeded by www.

Hostelling International New York
891 Amsterdam Ave (bet. 103rd & 104th Sts) | UWS | 10025

singles from $22
family rooms from $75

Ⓜ 1•9 to 103rd St

☎ 932-2300
f 932-2574
e reserve@
  hinewyork.org

◆624 ▣ MC/V/JCB ✎
🖉 ✆ ♿

This landmark Victorian Gothic building is just a couple of blocks from Central Park. The rooms are pristinely clean, large and light-filled. You have your own room key, and keep your gear in lockers. The best deal comes in the form of large family rooms with private bathrooms and bunk beds for two kids for an unbeatable $100. Public areas include a library with web-linked computers, a café, kitchen facilities and a garden.

Hotel 17
225 E 17th St (bet. 2nd & 3rd Aves) | Gramercy Park | 10003

singles from $64
doubles from $75

Ⓜ L•N•R•4•5•6 to 14th St-Union Sq

☎ 475-2845
F 677-8178
e hotel31@
  worldnet.att.net

◆120 ▣

This place is straight out of a 40's film noir. You make your way down narrow, dimly-lit hallways to open darkwood doors with old-fashioned keys. The highly atmospheric, charged mood continues inside with funky fake wood wallpaper, wine and forest green bedcovers and upholstery. Some rooms have original, decorative wooden fireplaces and shutters. Hotel 17 is character-filled enough for Woody Allen to have shot scenes from Manhattan Murder Mystery here.

Larchmont Hotel
27 W 11th St (bet. 5th & 6th Aves) | West Village | 10011

singles from $70
doubles from $90

Ⓜ L to 6th Ave

☎ 989-9333
F 989-9496
w citysearch.com

◆55 ▭ ▤ all ▦ ♿

Behind the bright red door on this quiet street, you'll find a pleasant, cosy brownstone hotel. Rooms are large, with pretty rattan furnishings, and floral bedcovers. No en-suite bathrooms, but the shared baths and showers are sparkling clean and all the rooms have their own sinks. Balducci's [p114], the famous gourmet food grocery store, is just around the corner.

Leo House
332 W 23rd St (bet. 8th & 9th Aves) | Chelsea | 10011

singles from $72
doubles from $78

Ⓜ C•E to 23rd St

☎ 929-1010
F 366-6801

◆58 ▤ MC/V 🖉

An unusual not-for-profit hotel, run by a Catholic organization, though everyone, whatever their belief, is welcome. Non-standard facilities include a chapel and a priest on 24-hour call. Bedrooms are clean and basic. The dining room overlooking a garden offers an all-you-can-eat breakfast for a bargain $5.

Malibu
2688 Broadway (at 103rd St) | UWS | 10025

singles & doubles from $79

Ⓜ 1•9 to 103rd St

☎ 222-2954
F 678-6842

◆150 ▭ ▤ MC/V ▦

A particular favourite with Europeans, this Upper West Side, newly-renovated hotel is a great choice for the budget-conscious. Clean, modern, good-sized rooms, most with their own bathrooms, are in minimal black and white. At $79 a night, including breakfast, it's hard to beat.

Pickwick Arms Hotel
230 E 51st St (bet. 2nd & 3rd Aves) | UWS | 10022

singles from $60
doubles from $115

Ⓜ 6 to 51st St

☎ 355-0300
F 755-5029

◆350 ▤ all ▦ 🖉 ▯

This is one of the best-priced hotels in town. A modern lobby with a beautiful fireplace welcomes you, as do the friendly staff. Rooms are on the small side, but they're pretty and very clean. There's a wine bar, Le Bateau Ivre, on the ground floor and the large roof garden is open to everyone staying.

Washington Square Hotel
103 Waverly Place (at MacDougal St) | West Village | 10011

singles from $110
doubles from $129

Ⓜ A•B•C•E•F•Q to W 4th St-Washington Sq

☎ 777-9515
F 979-8373

◆170 ▭ ▤ AE/MC/V
▦ ↔ ✆ ▯

Smack bang in West Village is this family-owned hotel, which pays tribute to the lovely Washington Square park outside with a lobby of beautiful antique wrought-iron garden furniture. Rooms are comfortable and decked out in pastel colours. For the full effect of staying here, ask for a room with a park view.

hotels

a–z essentials

admission charges

Charges for museums and sights vary; it's always worth checking if there are any concessions. The larger museums have one evening a week when admission is cheaper.

banks

New York's major banks are the Bank of New York, Chase Manhattan, Citibank and Fleet. Opening hours are usually 9am–3pm on weekdays (and often 4pm Thu & Fri), with limited service at most branches on Saturday (10am–2pm). Fleet (318 Grand St bet. Allen & Orchard Sts & 50 Bayard St at Bowery), and Chase Manhattan (180 Canal St at Mott St) are open on Sundays (10am–2pm) for foreign currency exchange only. Bank rates are slightly less competitive than bureaux de change [→bureaux de change; credit & debit cards]. To transfer money from abroad call:
American Express Moneygram
☎ 1-800-543-4080
Western Union ☎ 1-800-325-6000

bars

Most bars open from around 5pm–4am, but bartenders will close earlier when the tips aren't up to much [→tipping]. Carry picture ID (eg passport) to prove you are of drinking age (ie over 21 years) – they can 'card' anyone! If you're told not to dance in a bar, don't laugh – they're serious. Dancing licences are hard to come by and unauthorized boogying incurs fines for the bar owner. NB: it is illegal to drink a can or bottle of anything alcoholic in the street – even if it is in a brown paper bag.

bureaux de change

Rates can be slightly more competitive than the banks'.
AmEx charges $3 commission.
200 Vesey Street (at West St) ☎ 640-5998
◑ 10am–8pm Mon–Fri; 12–8pm Sat–Sun.
Avis charges $4 minimum or 1% commission, whichever is higher.
1451 Broadway (bet. 41st & 42nd Sts)
☎ 944-7600 ◑ 10am–8pm Mon–Fri; 12–8pm Sat–Sun.
Chequepoint USA charges 9¢ on every $1.
22 5th Street (bet. Fifth & Sixth Aves)
☎ 750-2400 ◑ 8am–9.30pm daily.
Thomas Cook charges $5 minimum or 1% commission, whichever is higher.
1590 Broadway (at 48th St) ☎ 265-6049
◑ 9am–7pm Mon–Sat; 9am–5pm Sun.

children

Activities: there are lots of magazines with kid-orientated listings; see also kids' sections of New York Magazine; Time Out; Village Voice; the Friday edition of the New York Times and NY Family Calendar and Resource Book. Or try the
Big Apple Parents' Paper ☎ 533-2277
Parent Guide ☎ 213-8840
Babysitting:
The Babysitters' Guild ☎ 682-0227
Frances Stewart Agency ☎ 439-9222
Hotels: most allow young children to stay in their parents' room at no extra charge. Age limits vary.
Restaurants & bars: It's not illegal for kids to go into bars but on the whole they're not places for family outings (many bars are shut during the day anyway). On the whole cheap and cheerful restaurants and cafés welcome kids but upscale places tend to be more formal and less well equipped.

consulates

Australia: 150 E 42nd Street ☎ 351-6500
Canada: 1251 Sixth Avenue ☎ 596-1600
Ireland: 345 Park Avenue ☎ 319-2555
New Zealand: suite 1904, 780 Third Avenue ☎ 832-4038
UK: 845 Third Avenue ☎ 745-0200

conversions

Women's Clothing

American	6	10	14	16
British	8	12	16	18
Continental	36	40	44	46

Men's Clothing

American	36	40	44	46
British	36	40	44	46
Continental	46	50	54	56

courier services

For services within Manhattan:
Breakaway ☎ 219-8500
CD&L (for a pick-up or delivery) ☎ 337-1460 (for prices and administration) ☎ 337-1450.
National and international services:
DHL ☎ 1-800-225-5345
FedEx ☎ 1-800-247-4747
UPS ☎ 1-800-742-5877

credit & debit cards

Automated Teller Machines (ATMs) are on almost every street corner in Manhattan, in delis, supermarkets, and even some bars. Internationally recognized debit cards can be used to withdraw cash at any ATM displaying the appropriate card sign; normal bank charges apply. Or you can use your credit card if you have a PIN number. Cash advances are also available with your credit or debit card with appropriate picture ID (eg passport). Again, normal bank charges apply.
To report lost cards:
American Express ☎ 1-800-528-4800
Diners Club ☎ 1-800-234-6377
MasterCard ☎ 1-800-826-2181
Visa ☎ 1-800-336-8472

currency

The dollar is made up of 100¢. Coins are 1¢ (pennies); 5¢ (nickels); 10¢ (dimes) and 25¢ (quarters) – the most useful change for buses, vending machines and public telephones. Occasionally you might come across a JFK half-dollar (50¢) or $1 coins, which are annoyingly oversized and often rejected in stores. Dollar bills are uniformly green and of one size; they come in denominations of $1; $5; $10; $20; $50 and $100. Commemorative issues include extremely rare $2 bills.

customs

All passengers arriving in the US are given a customs declaration form to fill out on the airplane. Don't bring in anything from 'unfriendly' countries (Cuban cigars are a no-no) and, while we are on the subject, drugs are not only illegal but you risk being denied entry to the US ever again.

dates

Abbreviated dates are usually given as month/day/year in the USA.

dentists

Although there is no free dental care in the US, the dental schools offer the most cost-effective treatments.

The New York University Dental Center charges a fee of $75 to cover the cost of pain relief and emergency treatment.
345 E 24th Street (at First Ave) ☎ *998-9800*
◐ *8am–9pm Mon–Thu; 9am–7.30pm Fri.*

Columbia University School of Dental Surgery has a walk-in clinic for emergencies only; the $65 fee covers pain relief and emergency treatment.
Vanderbilt Clinic (7th floor), 622 W 168th Street (at Broadway) ☎ *305-6726* ◐ *8.30am–2pm Mon–Fri.*

Private Practise offers a 24-hour call-out service *3 E 74th Street (at Fifth Ave)* ☎ *737-1212*

disabled visitors

Access For All is a guide to disabled access to NYC's cultural institutions. To obtain a copy, send $5 to Hospital Audiences Inc, 220 W 42nd Street, New York, NY 10036 (for all general enquiries call ☎ *1-888-424-4685*).

I Love New York Travel Guide, available from tourist information points and some hotels, also includes accessibility ratings.
For information on transport [→8].

duty free

When entering the US, the allowance on duty-free goods is: one litre of alcohol, 50 cigars and 200 cigarettes. The duty (per extra litre) on wine is $1.07 and a pricey $13.50 on spirits (for 40% proof; the higher the alcohol content the more you pay!). There is a limit of $100 allowed for gifts and souvenirs. Money over $10,000 must be declared. For more information call the US Duty Office at JFK ☎ *1-718-553-1643*

electricity

Electrical supply is 110 volts AC with mainly two-pronged plugs, although the newest sockets and appliances are now made for three prongs. British appliances need an adaptor.

email & internet

Public libraries offer free internet access with time restrictions and inevitably long waits. For information call ☎ *930–0800*. There are a few internet cafés; prices are around $10 per hour [→148].

emergencies

For emergency police, ambulance and fire services, dial ☎ **911**.

In a medical emergency, get yourself to one of the 24-hour emergency rooms at one of these hospitals:

Bellevue Hospital, *First Avenue (at E 27th St)* ☎ *562-4141*

Mount Sinai Hospital, *100 Madison Avenue (bet. 99th & 100th Streets)* ☎ *241–7171*

New York Hospital, *510 E 70th St (at York Ave)* ☎ *746–5050*

St Vincent's Hospital, *Seventh Avenue (bet. 11th & 12th Sts)* ☎ *604–7997*

More often than not (depending on the cost of treatment), you must pay the bill, then reclaim the expense from your insurance provider.

help & advice lines

AIDS Hotline ☎ *447-8200*
Lesbian & Gay Community Center ☎ *620-7310*
Missing Persons Bureau ☎ *374-6913*
Travelers' Aid/Victim Services ☎ *577-7777*

hotels

Book early, especially in December when hotels are usually full to capacity. Apart from the room price (and NY hotels don't come cheap!), you'll have to pay a sales tax (13.25%) and an occupancy tax ($2 per night). NB some hotels take a fraction of the room cost for a late cancellation (the amount varies from hotel to hotel).

You could consider choosing a small b&b [→147–148], or an unhosted apartment (if you're staying more than seven days – you won't have to pay sales tax). For information call the **Bed & Breakfast Network** ☎ *645-8134*.

Most hotels offer discount rates, especially for weekend stays in non-peak season. Or, there are agencies who buy blocks of rooms and offer as much as 50% off regular rates.

Central Reservations Service, *11420 North Kendall Drive, Miami, Florida, FL 33176* ☎ *1-305-274-6832*

Accommodations Express, *801 Asbury Avenue 6th floor, Ocean City, New Jersey, NJ 08226* ☎ *1-609-391-2100*

Quikbook *381 Park Avenue South, New York, NY 10016* ☎ *779-7666*

For general information on room availability call the **Visitors' Bureau** ☎ *484-1205*

immigration

US immigration control has become increasingly strict. If you are entering as a student or to work, make sure you have the appropriate visa and that your papers are in order. For enquiries while in the country, contact the **Immigration and Naturalization Service (INS)** *26 Federal Plaza* ☎ *206-6500* ◐ *7.30am–3pm Mon–Fri.* No vaccinations are needed.

insurance

It is foolhardy to travel in the US without medical insurance. Without it, you will just about be treated in an emergency, but you will spend the rest of your working days paying off the debt. It is wise to have your personal effects covered as well. Keep all receipts (including medical bills) to substantiate a claim.

left luggage

The only place to leave luggage in the city ($2 per item per day) is at Grand Central Station. ☎ *340-2555* ◐ *7am–11pm Mon–Fri; 10am–11pm Sat–Sun.*

lost property

Report the loss to the police and get an incident report to present to your insurance agency. The Police Property Clerk's office is where all lost articles may eventually end up. Call them only after all else fails (and not before one week). ☎ *374-5084*

measurements

As a rule, imperial measures are used.

imperial : metric	metric : imperial
1 inch = 2.5 cm	1 mm = 0.04 inch
1 foot = 30 cm	1 cm = 0.4 inch
1 mile = 1.6 km	1 m = 3.3 ft
1 ounce = 28 g	1 km = 0.6 mile
1 pound = 454 g	1 g = 0.04 oz
1 pint = 0.6 l	1 l = 0.6 (US) gallon
1 (US) gallon = 3.8 l	

practical information

more practical information

medical matters

There is no national healthcare service. Look under 'physicians and surgeons' or 'clinics' in the Yellow Pages. Ask at your hotel or contact your consulate for more advice.
[→emergencies & insurance]

medicines

Most delis carry your vital pharmaceutical needs, and many are open all night. The official line on filling foreign prescriptions is that it can't be done, but try any drugstore (many are open 24 hours – some even deliver), or go to a doctor's office or an emergency room [→emergencies]. The chain drugstore Duane Reade (others include Rite Aid, McKays and CVS) has three stores that are open 24 hours:
224 W 57th Street (at Broadway) ☎ *541-9708*
2465 Broadway (at 91st Street) ☎ *799-3172*
485 Lexington Avenue (at 47th St) ☎ *682-5338*

office & business

Most upscale hotels operate 24-hour business centres, though usually for guests only. Computer terminals, photocopiers, fax machines and printing facilities are available at Kinco's 14 branches around the city (including Brooklyn) – all open 24 hours. For general enquiries ☎ *316-3390*
Mail Boxes etc ☎ *964-5528* will accept deliveries like dry-cleaning and parcels on your behalf, and have cheap mailboxes to rent. For stationery try Staples ☎ *929-6323*. Mobile phones can be hired from:
AT & T Wireless ☎ *333-3150* (charge $7.99 per day and 69¢ per min).
Robert's ☎ *734-6344* (charge $5 per day and $1.25 per min).

opticians

A walk-in eye examination will probably set you back around $50. With a prescription, the chainstore Lenscrafters, open daily (including most evenings), can make glasses up in less than an hour and have contact lenses available over the counter. For locations call ☎ *967-4166* or see 'opticians' in the Yellow Pages.

photography

Camera Repair does just that at *37th W 47th St (bet. Fifth & Sixth Aves)* ☎ *382–0550*
CLIK for a one-hour service.
23rd St (bet. Fifth & Sixth Aves) ☎ *302-4460*
Spectra, pricier than the average one-hour place, produces professional quality prints.
293 E 10th Street (at Avenue A) ☎ *529-3636*

police

For emergencies only, call ☎ *911*. To find your nearest police precinct, dial ☎ *374-5000*.
Crime Victims Hotline ☎ *577-7777* will give you advice on making a report.
For any troubles on public transport call the Transit Police on ☎ *1-718-330-3330*.
Don't antagonize the NYPD's officers in blue; jay walking, for example, incurs tickets and fines.

postal services

Post office lines at peak hours (early mornings and lunchtime) can stretch out the door; allow extra time to avoid stressing out. For any enquiries or to find your nearest branch call ☎ *1-800-725-2161*. Stamps can also be bought from most delis (although they sell domestic 32¢ stamps only). For postcards outside the US, use one 50¢ stamp. The international letter rate starts at 60¢. Letters can be posted in rail and bus terminals, post offices and the rather scarce

blue mail boxes (pull the handle to use).
To receive mail it should be addressed to you *c/o General Delivery, General Post Office, 421 Eighth Avenue, New York, NY 10001.*

public holidays

While banks, offices and museums close on national holidays, most convenience stores remain open for business year round.
Independence Day – 4th Jul 99
Labor Day – 6th Sep 99
Columbus Day – 11th Oct 99
Election Day – 2nd Nov 99
Veterans' Day – 11th Nov 99
Thanksgiving – 25th Nov 99
Christmas Day – 25th Dec 99
New Year's Day – 1st Jan 2000
Martin Luther King Day – 17th Jan 2000
Presidents' Day – 21 Feb 2000
Memorial Day – 29 May 2000

religion

Avodah Jewish Services Corp ☎ *545-7759*
Ba'hai Center ☎ *330-9309*; Baptist ☎ *283-6517*
Buddhist ☎ *406-5109*; Catholic ☎ *1-516-333-6470*; Evangelical ☎ *867-2066*; Jehovah's Witnesses ☎ *862-0945*; Mormon ☎ *928-0714*
Muslim ☎ *481-5244*; Quakers ☎ *682-2745*

restaurants & cafés

Hours: Double-check closing times – restaurants with slow service tend to close the kitchen up to an hour earlier than stated. Best to call before you jump in a cab.
Payment: The majority of restaurants accept credit cards and dollar travellers' cheques with picture ID (eg passport).
Reservations: Always book ahead: the same day is fine for neighbourhood restaurants but for upscale eateries, call as far ahead as you can.
❶ You can eat at the bar if you want to check out a great place but can't spend a lot (or just aren't that hungry).
❶ Pricey restaurants have slightly cheaper menus at lunchtime (set hours), and neighbourhood restaurants often offer special lunch deals (usually served all day).
❶ Be wary of 'upselling', that is waiters subtly suggesting you choose pricier drinks and dishes.
❶ If you don't like something, send it back – but complain nicely: it pays to be friendly to NY waiters. Portions are often massive – no-one will mind if you ask for a doggie bag [→tipping].

safety

NY is now the safest big city in the US. However, precautions should be taken: it is inadvisable for women to walk alone late at night (carrying whistles, CS gas or pepper spray can give extra confidence and is legal); and certain areas are dodgier than others.
Out of hours, wait for subway trains in the designated area on the platform, where there's video surveillance, or by the ticket booth.

sales tax

NY sales tax is 8.25% and it is added at the cash register on top of the price of goods or services purchased [→hotels & shopping].

shopping

Export: tourists do not get a refund on sales tax when leaving the country.
Opening times: in Manhattan, shops generally stay open late until around 7pm. Downtown shops often open until midnight. Nearly all stores are open on Sundays.

Payment: even small shops take the major credit cards. Dollar travellers' cheques with picture ID are widely accepted too.

Returns: keep the receipt and you will be able to return your purchase, although most stores only offer exchange or store credit. Your rights as a shopper include having the right to know the store's refund policy before you buy: if there is none displayed, then you are entitled to a full refund if you return the item within 20 days. If you feel you have been ripped off, call **Consumer Affairs** ☎ 487-4444.

Sales: twice a year (usually mid-January & mid-September) during 'no tax week' the state forgoes the sales tax on items and shopping mayhem ensues. There are also summer and winter sales in May–Jun & Jan–Feb respectively.

smoking

Strictly speaking, it is illegal to smoke in hotel lobbies, banks, public restrooms, taxis, playgrounds, sports stadiums, and in restaurants with seating for over 36 people. Smoking is permitted in all bars, and restaurants with bars if the bar is at least two yards from the nearest table.

students

STA Travel (10 Downing Street ☎ 1-800-777-0112) and **Council Travel** (205 E 42nd Street ☎ 1-800-226-8624) offer discounted travel. They also issue the International Student Identity Card (ISIC), which entitles full-time students to travel discounts and reduced entrance fees. In the US, the card costs $23: it could be worth getting one before you leave home (eg in the UK it's only £6.50).

telephoning

Phone sounds: steady 'brrrrrr' = go ahead and dial; long low-pitched tone with short gaps = ringing tone; repeated short beeps = busy tone; single high-pitched tone = unobtainable.

Calling collect (reverse charge): dial 0 then ☎ 1-800-265-5328 or 1-800-225-5288. The surcharge on Bell Atlantic payphones is $1.58.

International calls: for direct calls overseas dial 011 plus the country code: **Australia**: 61; **Ireland**: 353; **New Zealand**: 64; **UK**: 44. For operator assistance dial 01 plus city code.

Local codes: Manhattan uses 212. Omit the code when dialling from within Manhattan. In this guide, all telephone numbers without a code are Manhattan numbers. For Brooklyn, Bronx and Staten Island the code is 718; for Queens it's 917. When dialling another borough put '1' in front of the area code – the same goes for dialling a number outside the city, and toll-free 800 numbers.

Directory enquiries: call ☎ 411 (addresses are given too). These calls are free from payphones.

Operator: ☎ 0. From here you can also ask for international operator or enquiries.

Payphones: street phone booths are plentiful – stick to the Bell Atlantic ones as the rates are steadier. Payphones take 25¢, 10¢ and 5¢ coins. Local calls cost 25¢ for the first three minutes. The cheapest way to call long distance at a public phone is to buy a prepaid 'charge card', or phone card in varying denominations (dial number on card for instructions), widely available from delis and news stands.

Phone directories: the *White Pages* lists private phone numbers and businesses, the *Yellow Pages* details every consumer-oriented business and service.

Private phone rates: local calls cost 10.6¢ no matter how long you talk, with discounts for certain times of the day and all weekend.

Toll-free numbers: all numbers preceded by 1-800 are free (standard rate applies when calling a 1-800 number from overseas).

time

The US has seven different time zones – Eastern (including New York) is five hours behind GMT. Clocks go forward by one hour in spring and back one hour in the fall. Speaking clock: ☎ 976-0001.

tipping

Tipping is a vital part of America's service-industry culture.

Bars: leave 'good' tips (around a dollar a drink) for your first two or three rounds, and the bartender will often buy you a round back known as a 'buy-back'.

Restaurants: a minimum of 15% is the bottom line – anything less is considered an insult. And at the finer establishments, it's more like 18–20%. For easy maths, double the sales tax at the bottom of the check.

Taxis: cab drivers expect a 15% tip and are not shy about voicing their dissatisfaction if you offer them any less.

tourist information

New York Convention and Visitors' Bureau (NYCVB) 810 Seventh Ave (bet. 52nd & 53rd Sts) ☎ 484-1200.
◑ 8.30am–6pm Mon–Fri; 9am–5pm Sat–Sun. (London office: 33–34 Carnaby St, London W1 ☎ 0171–437 8300 ◑ 10am–4pm Mon–Fri)
New York by Phone call ☎ 484-1222 for the NYCVB's voice-activated information service.
Times Square Visitor Information Center 229 W 42nd Street (bet. Fifth & Sixth Aves) ☎ 869-1890 ◑ 8am–8pm daily.
on the internet: www.nycvisit.com, www.citysearch.com, www.sidewalk.com and www.nyctourist.com give comprehensive listings of where to go, eat, stay and shop.

travellers' cheques (US 'checks')

These are still the safest way to carry your money, with instant refunds if lost or stolen. American Express and Visa are the most widely recognized, with Thomas Cook not far behind. Buy your cheques in US dollars – it's easier than dealing with fluctuating exchange rates, and they are more versatile [→shopping & restaurants]. If you lose your cheques call:

American Express ☎ 1-800-221-7282
MasterCard ☎ 1-800-223-9920
Thomas Cook ☎ 1-800-287-7362
Visa ☎ 1-800-227-6811

visas & entry requirements

For visitors from Australia, New Zealand, the UK, Ireland and most European countries, a passport valid for at least six months after entry is all that is needed. A 'visa waiver' allows a short-stay visit of up to 90 days: the visa waiver form, to be filled out on the incoming plane, must have the address of where you will be staying on your first night in the country. All other nationals must check visa requirements at their local US embassy.

weather

Spring and fall are ideal times to visit. In the winter, the cold can be ferocious, and in summer, it's often too hot. For weather updates call ☎ 976-8463

practical information

↓ index

A

A Détacher 27
A Different Light 44, **112**
  films 142
A Photographer's Place **112**
ABC Carpet & Home 49, **110**
ABC Parlour 50
Abingdon **160**
Abyssinian Baptist Church 147
Academy Books & Records 49, **113**
accessory shops **108**
accommodation agencies 165
Ace Gallery 24
Accuario 29, **132**
Ad-Hoc Software 23, **110**
Adams, Mary 14
Adler, Jonathan 23, **110**
admission charges 164
Adobe 140
Africa 66
African Paradise 66
Air Market 33
airports 164
Alberta Ferretti 22
Algonquin Hotel **156**
Alice Tully Hall 143
Alison on Dominick Street 24, **129**
Allan & Suzi 62
Alley's End 45
Alpana Bawa 22
Alphabet City 13
Alphaville 39
alternative therapies 144
Altogether Different Dance Festival 145
Alvin Ailey American Dance Theater 144
Amalgamated Hardware 39
Amalgamated Home 39
Amaranth 18
Amato Opera Theater 145
American Craft Museum 73, **85**
American Express 164, 167
  moneygram 164
American Fine Arts 24
American football **89**
American Museum of the Moving Image (AMMI) 73, **81**
American Museum of Natural History 73, **79**
American Park 73
AMS Chelsea Bowl 96
Amtrak 9
Amy Downs 14, **108**
Anandmali 19
And Bob's Your Uncle 44
Anderson, Jill 33
Angelica Kitchen 35, **131**
Angelika Film Center 142
Angel's Share 36, **137**
Anna 33
Anna Sui 22, **101**
Annex Flea Market 44, **115**
Anthology Film Archives 142
Antik 18
Antique Boutique 27, **104**
Apartment 48 44
Apartment 141 33
APC **101**
Apollo Theatre 147
Aquagrill 24
aquarium **92**
Aquavit 55, **122**
Arlene Grocery 146
art *see* galleries
Arthur Ashe Stadium 89
Asia de Cuba 54
Asia Society 142
Astor Restaurant & Lounge 29
Astor Wines & Spirits **114**
Astroland Amusement Park 96
Astroturf 70
Atlantic Theater Company 140
Atsuro Tayama 22
Audubon Bar & Grill 67
Australian consulate 164
Avalon Hotel **158**
Aveda 23, **109**
Avenue 63
Avenue A, shopping 99
Avenue A Sushi 35
Avery Fisher Hall 143

Avis 164
Avodah Jewish Services Corp 166
Avon Center 94

B

B & H Photo-Video **113**
B-Bar 29, 36, **120**, **134**, 151
Babbo 40, **120**
Baby Jupiter 16, **134**
babysitting 164
Bagels by the Park 70
bags **108**
Bahá'i Center 166
Baktun **150**
Balducci's 40, **114**
ballet **144–145**
Ballet Tech 145
Balthazar 29, **120**
Bamboozle Studio 66
Banana Republic 49, **105**
banks 164
Bar d'O 41, **135**
Bar 89 25, 135
Bar Pitti 40, **132**
Bar Six 40
Baraza 36, **134**
Barbara Gladstone 45
BargeMusic 144
Barmacy 36, **137**
Barnes & Noble 49, 112, **145**
Barney Greengrass 63, **149**
Barneys New York 58, **100**
bars **134–138**, 164
  Chelsea & the Meatpacking District 46
  children in 164
  Carroll Gardens 70
  Coney Island & Brighton Beach 71
  East Village **35–36**
  Gramercy Park & the Flatiron District 51
  Fort Greene 69
  Harlem & the Heights 66–67
  Lower East Side & Chinatown 16–17
  Midtown 56
  Nolita & Noho 30
  Soho 25
  sports bars **136**
  tipping 167
  Tribeca 20
  Upper East Side 60–61
  Upper West Side 64
  West Village 41
  Williamsburg 69
baseball 89
basketball 89
Battery Park 73, **91**
Bawa, Alpana 22
Bayard's **122**
Beacon Theater 146
Beau Geste 39
Beauty Bar 36
beauty treatments **95**
beauty stores **109**
Bebe 49
Bed & Breakfast Network 165
Bed & Breakfast On The Park **161**
Bed Bath Beyond **110**
Beer Hall 152
Behrle 19
Beige @ B-Bar **151**
Bemelman's Bar 61
Bereket **133**
Bergdorf Goodman 52–53, **100**
Bessie Schonberg Theater 145
Best Cellars **114**
Betsey Johnson 21, **104**
bicycles 11
Big Apple Greeter 73
Big Cup 46
Big Drop 22
Big Nick's Burger 62, **130**
Big Onion Walking Tours 73
Bigelow Pharmacy 39, **109**
Bike New York: The Great Five Boro Bike Ride 154
Birdland 147
Bistro at Candy Bar 46
Blahnik, Manolo 53, **106**
Bleecker Bob's Golden

Oldies 113
Bleecker Street, shopping 99
Bliss **94**
Bliss Spa 23, **109**
Bloomingdales 58, **100**
Blue 33
Blue Bar 56 **137**
Blue Note 147
Blue Ribbon 24, **132**
Blue Water Grill 49–50
boat tours 73
Bodega 19
Body Adorned **95**
body & soul 95
body art **95**
Bond, Veronica 39
Bond 07 28, **108**
Bond St 29, 30, **120**
book shops **112**
Boone, Mary 54
Borden, Janet 24
Borders **112**
Botanica 30, **134**
Bottino 45
The Bottom Line 146
Bouley Bakery 19, **122**
Bowery Ballroom 146
bowling **96**
Bowlmor Lanes 96
The Box Tree **159**
boxing **89**
Bread & Butter 30
Bright Food Shop 46
Brighton Beach 71, **91**, 117
Brisas del Caribe 25
Broadway, shopping 99
Broadway Inn **161**
Bronx 13
Bronx Zoo 73, **92**
Brooklyn **68–71**
Brooklyn Academy of Music (BAM) 143, 144
  dance **145**
Brooklyn Ale House 69
Brooklyn Botanical Gardens 73, **91**
Brooklyn Brewery 69
Brooklyn Bridge 73, **84**
Brooklyn Heights 13
Brooklyn Heights Promenade 73
Brooklyn Mod 70
Brooklyn Moon Café 69, 146
Brooklyn Museum of Art 73, **86**
Brooklyn Philharmonic **143**
Brooks Bros 105
Brownie's 146
Bryant Park 73, **91**, 142
Bryant Park Grill & Café 54
Bubble Lounge 20, **136**
Buddhism 166
Buffa's Delicatessen 30
Built By Wendy/Cake 28
bureaux de change 164
Burberry 53
buses 8, **10**
  airport 6, 7, 8
  long-distance 9
  tours 73

C

C & M Gallery 60
cabaret **140–141**
cabs 6, 7, 8, **10–11**
Café Boulud 60, **122**
Café Carlyle 61, **135**, 140
Café con Leche 63
Café con Leche @ Creation 152
Café des Artistes 63, **124**
Café Gitane 30
Café Habana 30
Café Lalo 63
Café Largo 66
Café Noir 25
Café Restaurant Volna 71
Café Spice 41
cafés & diners 166
  Chelsea & the Meatpacking District 46
  Coney Island & Brighton Beach 71
  cyber cafés **148**
  East Village 35
  Fort Greene 69
  Gramercy Park & the Flatiron District 50
  Harlem & the Heights 66
  Lower East Side & Chinatown 16

Midtown 55
Nolita & Noho 30
Soho 25
Tribeca 19
Upper East Side 60
Upper West Side 63
West Village 41
Williamsburg 69
Cafeteria 45, **121**, **133**
Calle Ocho 63, **127**
Calvin Klein 59, **101**
Calypso St Barths 28, **104**
Camera Repair 166
Campagna Home 49
Canadian consulate 164
Canal Jeans 23, **107**
Canal Street, shopping 99
Candela 50
Capsouto Frères 19, **129**
car services 11
Carapan **94**
Carino 60
The Carlton Arms **162**
The Carlyle Hotel **156**
Carnegie Hall 143
Caroline's on Broadway 141
Carroll Gardens 70
cars, driving in New York 11
cars *see* cabs
Cartier 53
Casa 40
Casa La Femme 24
Casablanca Hotel **160**
Casimir 34
Casio Baby G-Shock 23
Catherine 22, **104**
Catholic Church 166
CBGB 146
CDs, records & tapes **113–114**
Celebrate Brooklyn 147
Center for the Dull 107
Central Park 73, **90**
  for children **93**
Central Park Summerstage 153
Central Park Wildlife Center 73, 90, **92**
Century 21 **107**
chain stores 105
Chanel 53
Chanterelle 19
Charles A Dana Discovery Center 90
Chelsea & the Meatpacking District 43–47, 117
Chelsea Garden Store 44
Chelsea Hotel **156**
Chelsea International Hostel 47
Chelsea Market 44, **115**
Cherry 15, 106
chess **96**
Chess Forum 96
Chez Brigitte 41
Chez Es Saada 34
Chicago BLUES 147
children **92–93**, 164
  on subways and buses 8
Children's Museum of the Arts 73, **92**
Children's Museum of Manhattan 73, **92–93**
Chinatown *see* Lower East Side & Chinatown
Chinatown Ice Cream Factory 16
Chinese emporiums 15
Chinese New Year **154**
Chloë 59
Cho Dang Gol 55, **127**
Choo, Jimmy 53, 106
Christian Dior 53
Christie, Kelly **108**
Christopher Street, shopping 99
Chrome Hearts 59
Chrysler Building 73, **84**
Chumley's 41, **136**
Ciel Rouge 46, 135
Cine-Noir Film Society 142
cinema **142**
  for children **93**
Circa Tabac **135**
Circle Line 73
Circuit City 49
City Bakery 50
City Center **140**, 145
City Hall 73, **84**
Citypass 73
Claremont Riding

index

Academy 90
Clay 29
Clearview's Zeigfeld 142
Clementine 41
CLIK 166
The Cloisters 73, **85**
clothes, size conversions 164
Club Macanudo **135**
Club Monaco 49, **105**
Clubhouse @ Planet 28 **151**
clubs 150–152
  Coney Island & Brighton
    Beach **71**
  East Village **35–36**
  Lower East Side &
    Chinatown **16–17**
  Soho **25**
  Tribeca **20**
  West Village **41**
Cobblestones 53
The Cock 36, **138**, 152
Coffee Shop 50
Cole, Kenneth 49, **106**
Coliseum Books 53
Colony Records **113**
Columbus Avenue,
  shopping 99
Columbus Circle Market **115**
Columbus Day Parade **153**
Columbus Flea Market **115**
comedy **141**
Comedy Cellar 141
Comfort Diner 60, **126**
Comic Strip Live 141
Commes des Garçons 43, **101**
Coney Island & Brighton
  Beach 71, **91**
Coney Island High 146, **151**
consulates 166
conversions 164
Coogan's 67, **136**
Cookie's Fine Foods 46
The Cooler 151
Cooper, Paula 44
Cooper-Hewitt, National
  Design Museum 73, **82**
  museum store 111
Copacabana 147
Copeland's 66, **124**
Corner Bistro 41, **129**
Costume National 22, **101**
Country Café 44
Country Inn the City **161**
courier services 164
Courtney Washington 69
Cowgirl Hall of Fame **92**
Cox, Patrick 59
Crate & Barrel 53
Creation 152
credit cards 164
Crime Victims Hotline 166
Crunch **94**
CulturePass 73
Cunningham, Merce 144
currency 164
Curry in a Hurry 50
customs & excise 164
cyber cafés **148**
Cynthia Rowley 21–22, **104**

D
D/L Cerney 19, **101**
Daffy's 49, **107**
Dakota Building 73, **75**
Dallas, Stella 39, **107**
Dàñal 34
dance **96**
  ballet **144–145**
  dance studios **94**
Dance Theater of Harlem **145**
Dance Theater Workshop **145**
Dancetracks 34, **113**
Dangerfield's 141
Daniel 60, **122**
Darrow 7, 49, **107**
Daryl K 28, 33, **104**
dates 165
Dave's 44
DDC Lab 15
Dean & Deluca 23, **114**
debit cards 164
Decibel 36, **137**
Deitch Projects 24
Delta Water Shuttle 8
Demu Café 146
Denial 25
dentists 165
department stores **100**
Devachan **95**
Dia Center for the Arts 73,
  86–87
Dick's Bar 36, **138**
Diesel 50, **101**
Diner 69
diners *see cafés & diners*

Diners Club 164
Dior, Christian 53
disabled visitors 165
  on subways and buses 8
Disco Rama **113**
discount stores **107**
Disney Store 53, **108**
Dive Bar 64
DKNY 59, **102**
Dojo's 35
Dok Suni's 34
Dolce & Gabbana 59,
  101–102
Dom 23
Domsey's Warehouse
  Outlet 68
Don Giovanni 54
Don Hills 151
Don't Tell Mama 141
Dosa 22
Double Happiness 30
Downs, Amy 14, **108**
Drag 56
Dressing Room 28
Drinkland 36
Drip Café 64, **138**
driving in New York **11**
'Dropping the Ball' **154**
Drovers Tap Room 40
drugstores 166
DT-UT 60
Duane Reade 166
DUMBO **13**
duty free 165

E
E 7th Street, shopping 99
Ear Wax 68
East Village **32–37**, 117
Easter Sunday Parade **154**
Eclectic Home 44
Eddie Bauer **105**
Edison Hotel **163**
8 Ball Records **113**
8th Street, shopping 99
Eighty Eights 141
Eileen Fisher 33
Eisenberg Sandwich Shop
  50
El Cid 45
El Museo del Barrio 73, **84**
El Rey del Sol 45
El Sombrero 16
Elaine's 60, **136**
The Elephant 34
Eleven Madison Park 49, **121**
Eli's Bread at the Vinegar
  Factory **115**
Ellen's Stardust Diner **92**
Ellis Island 73, **77**
email 165
emergencies 165
Emilio Pucci 59
Empire Diner 46, **126**
Empire State Building 73,
  74, **78**
  views from 76
Emporio Armani 48, 59, **102**
Enchanted Forest **93**
entertainment **139–149**
Ess-a-Bagel 55, **123**
Ethel Barrymore 139
Etherea 34
Etro 59
Eugene O'Neill Theatre 139
Evangelical Church 166
events **153–154**
Exodus Industrial Sport 69
Express **105**
eyewear **108**

F
Fab 208 33
Face Stockholm 63, **109**
Fairways 63
Fall Café 70
The Fan Club 49
Fanelli 24
FAO Schwarz 53, **93**
Farhi, Nicole 59
fashion shops **101–105**
  Chelsea & the
    Meatpacking District
    43–44
  East Village **33**
  Gramercy Park & the
    Flatiron District 48–49
  Harlem & the Heights
    65–66
  Lower East Side &
    Chinatown 14–15
  Nolita & Noho 27–28
  Soho 21–23

Tribeca **19**
  Upper East Side **58–59**
  Upper West Side **62–63**
  West Village **38–39**
Fat Beats 40, **113**
Fat Cat Billiards 97
Feast of San Gennaro **153**
Feith, Tracey 28, **105**
Fekkai, Frédéric 59
Felissimo 53, **111**
Fendi 53, **104**
Ferretti, Alberta 22
ferries 8
festivals
  dance **145**
  film **143**
  music **144**, **147**
  theatre **140**
Fez 30, **145**, **147**
Field, Patricia 38–39
Fifth Avenue, shopping 99
57th Street, shopping 99
film *see cinema*
Film Forum 142
Filthmart 33
Finyl Vinyl 36
FireBird Café 140
Firefighter's Friend 28
First 34, **132**
First Wok 60
Fisher, Eileen 33
Fishs Eddy 49, **110**
fitness studios **94**
The Fitzpatrick Hotel **160**
flagship stores **108**
Flatiron Building 73, **74**
Flatiron District *see*
  Gramercy Park & the
  Flatiron District
Flamingo East 151
Flavors 50
Flor de Sol 19
Florent 45, **124**
food stores **114–115**
Foot Locker 108
Footlight Records 34, **113**
Forbidden Planet 34, **112**
Ford, Tom 53
Fort Greene **69–70**, 117
Four Seasons Hotel 156
4W Circle of Art 69
Foxy @ The Cock **152**
Fragments **108**
The Franklin Hotel **159**
Franklin Street, shopping 99
Fred Astaire Dance Studio
  94
Frédéric Fekkai 59
Freelance **106**
French Connection **105**
French Institute 142
French Roast 40, **133**
Fresh 59
Frick Collection 73, **82**
  concerts 144
Frida's Closet 70
The Front 20

G
G 46
Gabriela's 63
Gagosian, Larry 24
Gagosian Gallery 60
The Galaxy 51
galleries **86–88**
  see also museums
  Chelsea & the
    Meatpacking District **45**
  Midtown 54
  Soho 24
  Upper East Side **60**
games & activities **96–97**
Gap 53, **105**
garages, *see gas stations*
Garb 33
Garden of Eden **114**
Garment District **13**
gas stations 11
Gay and Lesbian Film
  Festival **143**
Gay and Lesbian Pride Day
  153
Generation Records **113**
Genesis Center **95**
The Gershwin **159**
gift & museum stores
  111–112
Givenchy 59
Gladstone, Barbara 45
Godiva Chocolatier 53
Goethe House 142
Golden Theater 139
Gotham Bar & Grill 41, **123**
Gotham Book Mart 112
Gotham Comedy Club 141

Gourmet Garage 23, **114**
Gracious Home 59, **110**
Graham, Martha 144
Gramercy Park & the
  Flatiron District **48–51**
Gramercy Park Hotel **163**
Gramercy Tavern 49, **125**
Grand Bar 25, **136**
Grand Central Station 73,
  74, 78, 165
Grand Sichuan 16
Grand Street, shopping 99
Grange Hall 40, **132**
Gray Line (bus tours) 73
Gray Line Airport Shuttle
  6, 7
Great Jones Café 30
Great Shanghai 16
The Greatest Bar on Earth
  136
Greenwich Village *see*
  West Village
Greenwich Village
  Halloween Parade **154**
Greg Wolf 33
Grimaldi's **126**
Grove Street Playhouse 93
Gucci 53, **102**
Guess **105**
Guggenheim Museum
  Soho 73, **80–81**
  see also Solomon R
  Guggenheim Museum
Guinness Fleadh 147

H
H 33
Habib's Place 35
Hackers, Hitters & Hoops
  96–97
hair care **95**
Hamilton Heights *see*
  Harlem & the Heights
Hammerstein Ballroom 146
Hangawi 55
Harlem & the Heights
  65–67, 117
The Harlem Collective
  65–66
Harlem Spirituals 73
Harlem Week 153
Harmony 24
Harry Cipriani 60–61, **136**
Hassidic New York 73
hats 108
Haveli 35
Hearn, Pat 45
Helen's Place 70
helicopter tours 73
Hell 46, **134**
Hell's Kitchen 46
Helmut Lang 22, **102**
help & advice lines 165
Henri Bendel 53
Henrietta Hudson 41
Herban Kitchen 25
Here 93
Hermès 53
Hirschl & Adler 60
Hispanic Day Parade **153**
HMV 53, **113**
Hogs & Heifers 46
Hold Everything 44
holidays, public 166
Holy Basil 35
Home 40
home furnishing shops
  see interiors shops
Hong Kong Egg Cake Co 16
Honmura An 24
Horn 33
hospitals 165
Hostelling International
  New York 165
Hotel Beacon 161
Hotel Elysée **159**
Hotel of the Rising Star 28
Hotel 17 **163**
Hotel Venus 22–23, **102**
Hotel Wales **159**
hotels **155–163**, 165
  children in 164
Housing Works Thrift Shop
  44, **107**
Howard Kaplan Antiques 39
Hudson Bar & Books **135**
Hungarian Pastry Shop 66

I
I Trulli 50
ice hockey **89**
ice-skating **97**
Ideya 24–25
Idlewild 17
If Boutique **102**

more index

Il Bagatto 34, **121**
Il Buco 29, **121**
IMAX 93
immigration 165
Ina **107**
The Independent 19
Indie 5000 @ Nowbar **152**
Indigo 42
Indochine 19
The Inn at Irving Place **161**
'Ino 41, **126**
insurance 165
interiors shops **110–111**
Intermix 48–49
International Center of Photography (ICP) 73, **87**
Internet 148, 165
Intrepid Sea Air Space Museum 73, **93**
Iridium 147
Irish consulate 164
Irish Rep 140
Irving Plaza 146
Isabel Toledo Lab 48
Isamu Noguchi Garden Museum 73, **87**
Isay's Leather 71
Island Burgers & Shakes 55, **119**
Issey Miyake Pleats Please 22, **104**
It's a Mod, Mod World 33

J
J & R Music & Computer World **113**
J Crew 49, **105**
J Morgan Puett Studio 19
J Sisters **95**
Jackson Hole 60, **129**
Jacobs, Marc 22, **104**
Jamin Puech 28, **108**
Janet Borden 24
Japan Society 142
Japas 55 56
Japonica 41, **127**
jazz 146–147
Jazz at Lincoln Center **147**
Jazz Record Center 44, **113**
Jean Claude 25
Jean Cocteau Repertory 140
Jean Georges 63, **123**
Jeffrey 44, **100**
Jehovah's Witnesses 166
Jerry's 25, **124**
Jerry's Men's Hair Styling Salon **95**
jewellery shops **108**
Jewish Museum 73, **83**
Jill Anderson 33
Jimmy Choo 53, **106**
Jimmy's Bronx Café 147
Jing Fong 16
Jivamukti **95**
Joan & David **108**
Joanie's 50
Joe Jr's 41, **126**
Joe's Bar 36
Joe's Pub 30, **135**
  cabaret 141
Joe's Shanghai 16, **128**
John F Kennedy airport (JFK) **6–7**
John Weber 45
Johnson, Betsey 21, **104**
JoJo 60
Jonathan Adler 23, **110**
Jones Beach **91**
Jones Diner 30
Joseph 59
Josie's 51
Joyce Theater 145
Juan Anon 15
Judy's Chelsea 141
Juilliard Theater 143
Jules 34
Junk 69
Junno's 41
Juno's **106**
Jutta Neumann 32–33, **106**

K
Kaarta Imports 66
Kasia's 69
Kate Spade 23, **108**
Kate's Paperie 39
Keens Steakhouse 54
Kélian, Stephane 59, **106**
Kelley & Ping 25
Kelly Christie **108**
Kennedy Galleries 54
Kenneth Cole 49, **106**
Keur 'n' Dye 69

The Key Club 152
Key to Success @ The Key Club **152**
KGB 36, **138**
Kiehl's 32, **109**
Kim's Video & Music 34, **113**
Kind, Phyllis 24
King Cole Bar **135**
King Juan Carlos I Center 142
Kitano New York **160**
Kitchen 144
Kitchen Arts & Letters **112**
Kitchen Club 29
Kitchenette 19
Klein, Calvin 59, **101**
Kmart **105**
'Knicks' **154**
Knitting Factory 20, **146**
Knoedler & Company 60
Konkrete Jungle @ Coney Island High **151**
Krispy Kreme's 66
Kush 16, **138**

L
L Café 69
La Bonne Soupe 54, **129**
La Guardia airport 8
La Lunchonette 45
Lafayette Street, shopping 99
Lakeside Lounge 36, **135**
Lakruwana 55
Lang, Helmut 22, **102**
Language 28
Lansky Lounge 16, **134**
Larchmont Hotel **162**
Larry Gagosian 24
Las Venus 15, **110**
Latin Quarter 147
Lauren, Ralph 59, **102**
Layla 19
Le Bernardin 55, **123**
Le Corset 23
Le Gamin 46
Le Jardin Bistro 29, **130**
Le Petit Peton 39, **106**
Le Tableau 34
Lee's Mardi Gras 44
left luggage 165
Lei Bar 36, **138**
Lenox Lounge 66
Lenox Room 60
Lenscrafters 166
Leo House **163**
Lespinasse 55, **123**
Lexington Avenue, shopping 99
Liam 41
Liberty Helicopters 73
Liberty Science Center 73, 93
Life 19
Lighting the Rockefeller Center Christmas Tree **154**
Limelight 6–7, **150**
limos 6, 7, **97**
L'Impasse 39
Lincoln Center nightlife 117
Lincoln Center Festival **140**, 144, 145
Ling **95**
Lips **97**
Liquid Sky 28
Liquor Store 20
listings magazines **148**
Little Italy **13**
Lively Set 39
Living Room 146
Loeb boathouse 90
Loehmann's 44, **107**
Lola 50
Lombardi's 29, **126**
Long Island Rail Road (LIRR) 9
Los Dos Rancheros Mexicanos 55
lost property 165
Lot 61 46
lottery 97
Lotus Club 16
Louie 22
Louis Vuitton 23
Lovely's @ 2i's **152**
The Lowell Hotel **160**
Lower East Side & Chinatown **14–17**, 117
Lower East Side Gardens 91
Lower East Side Tenement Museum 73, **82–83**
Lower Manhattan **13**
Lucien 34
Lucien Blue 70
Lucien Pellat-Finet 28
Lucky Cheng's 35, **97**
Lucky Strike 24

Lucky Wang 15
Ludlow Street, shopping 99
Luna Lounge **141**
  music 146
Lunt-Fontanne Theatre 139
Lush 20
Lust for Life/Legends @ Life **151**

M
M&I 71
M&R 30
M.A.C. 23, **109**
Macy's 53, **106**
Macy's Fourth of July Fireworks **153**
Macy's Thanksgiving Day Parade **154**
Madden, Steve 23, **106**
Madison Avenue, shopping 99
Madison Square Gardens 89, 146
magazines, listings **148**
Magnum 25, **136**
Main Street Ephemera/ Paper Collectibles 70
Maison Moderne 44
Malachy's Donegal Inn 64
Malcolm Shabazz Harlem Market 66, **115**
Malia Mills 28
The Malibu **163**
Malkovich, Mark 33
Manhattan **13**
  landmarks **74–76**
Manhattan Portage **108**
Manhattan Theater Club 140
Manic Panic 15
Mannes College of Music 143
Manolo Blahnik 53, **106**
The Mansfield Hotel **159**
Marc, Robert **108**
Marc Jacobs 22, **104**
Mare Chiaro 30, **137**
Margie Tsai 28
Mark Garrison Salon **95**
Mark Montana 33
markets **115**
  Chelsea & the Meatpacking District 44
  Harlem & the Heights 66
Markt 46
Marlborough Gallery 54
Mars 35
Mart 125 66
Martin Luther King Jr Day **154**
Mary Adams 14
Mary Boone 54
Marylou's 41
Mastercard 164, 167
Matthew Marks Gallery 45
Max & Roebling 68
Max Fish 16, **137**
Maxilla & Mandible 63
Mayrose 60
Meadowlands Sports Complex 89
measurements 165
Meatpacking District see Chelsea & the Meatpacking District
media **148**
medical matters 166
medicines 166
Mekka 35
MeKong 29
Memorial Day Parade **154**
men's fashion shops **101–104**
Meow Mix 17, **135**
  music 146
Merc Bar 25
Mercer Hotel **157**
Mercer Kitchen 24, **121**
Mercury Lounge 146
Merkin Concert Hall 143
Mermaid Parade **153**
Mesa Grill 49, **128**, 131
MetLife Building 73, **75**
Metro-North Railroad 9
Metro Pictures 45
MetroCards 8
Metropolis 33
Metropolitan Museum of Art 73, **79–80**
  concerts 143
  museum store **111**
  Rooftop Sculpture Garden 79
Metropolitan Opera House 143, 144
Mexican Radio 29
Mezze 55

Michael Jordan's The Steakhouse NYC 54
Midnight Footrace in Central Park **154**
Midsummer Swing Series 147
Midtown **52–57**, 117
MIKS 15
Milano's 30
Millennium events **154**
Miller, Robert 54
Mills, Malia 28
Min Lee 15
minicabs see cabs
Miss Ann's 69
Miss Saigon 60
Missoni 59
Mrs Stahl's Knishery 71
Mitzi E Newhouse Theater 140
Miu Miu 22, **105**
Modell's **108**
MoMA's New Directors/ New Films Festival 143
Montana, Mark 33
Monteleone 70
Montrachet 19
Moomba 41, **134**
Moondance Diner 25
Morgan Le Fay 22, **105**
Morgans Hotel **157**
Mormons 166
Morningside Heights see Harlem & the Heights
Morris-Jumel Mansion Museum 73, **83**
Moschino 59
Moshood 69
Moss 23, 110
Mostly Mozart Festival 144
Mother 150
Moustache 41
MUNY (Music under New York) 9
Murder Ink 112
Murray Hill 13
Murray's Cheese Shop 114
Museum for African Art 73, 84
Museum of American Folk Art 73, **85–86**
Museum of Immigration 73, **77**
Museum Mile 13
Museum of Modern Art (MoMA) 73, **80**
  films 142
  museum store **111**
Museum of Television & Radio 97
museums **79–88**
  for children **92–93**
  Citypass 73
  CulturePass 73
  museum stores **111–112**
music **146–147**
  ballet **144–145**
  CDs, records & tapes **113–114**
  opera & classical music **143–144**
Muslims 166
Mustang Sally's Saloon **136**
Mxyplyzyk 44

N
Nancy Whiskey Pub 20, **137**
Nassau Coliseum 89
Nathan's Famous Restaurant 71
National Black Theatre 146
National Museum of the American Indian 73, **84**
Naturemax (IMAX) 93
Navy Yard 93
NBA store 53
Nederlander Theatre 139
Negril 46
Nell's 147, 150
Neumann, Jutta 32–33, **106**
Nevada Smith's **136**
New Amsterdam Theater 139
New City Café 69
New Jersey Transit 9
New Museum of Contemporary Art 73, **87–88**
New Victory Theater 93
New Wonton Garden 16
New York Airport Express Connection 8
New York Airport Service 6, 8

New York Aquarium **92**
New York Botanical
  Garden 73, **81**
New York by Phone 167
New York City Ballet **144**
New York City Marathon **154**
New York City Opera **143**
New York Convention and
  Visitors' Bureau 167
New York Double-Decker
  Tours 73
New York Film Festival 143,
  153
New York Hall of Science
  73, **81**
New-York Historical
  Society 73, **86**
New York Noodle Town 16
New York Palace Hotel **157**
New York Philharmonic **143**
New York Philharmonic &
  Metropolitan Opera in
  the Park **153**
New York Public Library 73,
  77, 145
New York State Lottery 97
New York State Theater
  143, 144
New York Underground
  Film Festival 143, **154**
New York Youth Theater 93
New Zealand consulate
  164
Newark airport 7
newspapers 167
Next Door Nobu 19
Nha Trang 16
Nicole Farhi 59
Night Café 64
nightlife, getting your
  bearings 116–117
Niketown 53, **108**
9 & Co 106
Nine West 106
92nd Street Y **143, 145**
Nobody Beats the Wiz **113**
Nobu 19, **104**
Nocturne 59
Noho see Nolita & Noho
Nolita & Noho **27–31**, 117
Nova 15, **103**
NowBar 41, 152
Nylon Squid 27
Nyonya 29
NYU Cantor Film Center 142

O _____
O Padeiro 46, **132**
The Oak Room 140
Obaa Koryoe 66
Odeon 19, **125, 131**
Odessa (bar) 36
Odessa (food shop) 31
Off Soho Suites **163**
office & business centres
  166
Old Devil Moon 35, **126**
Old Navy 44, **105**
Olive & Bette 62, **105**
Olympia Trails Bus
  Company 7
Omni Berkshire Place **160**
Once upon a Tart 25
100% Pure @ El Flamingo
  152
125th Street, shopping 99
Only Hearts 62
Open Center **95**
opera **143, 153**
Opera Orchestra of New
  York 143
opticians 166
Orange Chicken 19
Orchard Bar 16, **134**
Orchard Street, shopping 99
Orchard Street Market **115**
O'Reilley's Pub 56
Oriental Dress Company 15
Oriental Gifts 15
Original Levi's Store **108**
Origins Feel Good Day Spa
  94
Osaka Health Center **95**
Oscar Wilde Memorial
  Bookstore 40
Oser 18–19
Other Music **113**
Out of the Closet 59, **107**
Oyster Bar 54, **125**
Oznot's Dish 69

P _____
PaceWildenstein 54
Pall Mall Antiques 39
Pampa 63, **127**
Papaya King 60
Paragon 49, **108**
The Paramount Hotel **158**
Paris Theatre 142
Park Avenue Country Club
  136
Park View at the
  Boathouse 90, **130**
parking 11
parks **90–91**
Pat Hearn 45
Patch 155 15
PATH 9
Patois 70
Patria 50, **128**
Patricia Field 38–39
Patrick Cox 59
Paul Smith 48, **103**
Paul Taylor Dance
  Company **144**
Paula Cooper 45
Payard Patisserie & Bistro
  60, **133**
Payless 106
Pearl Oyster Bar 41
Pearl River Mart 15, **111**
Pellat-Finet, Lucien 28
Penang 21
Peninsular Hotel **157**
Penny Whistle Toys **93**
Pepe Rosso 25, **127**
Performing Garage 140
Periyali 50
Perk's 147
Pete's Tavern 51
Petite Abeille 46
Phare 28
Philip's Candy Store 71
Photographer's Place **112**
photography 166
Phyllis Kind 24
Pickwick Arms Hotel **163**
Pierpont Morgan Library
  73, **83**
Pierre Hotel **157**
Pink Pussycat Boutique 39
Pisces 34, **133**
PJ Hanley's 70
The Place 40
Plan Eat Thailand 69
Planet 28 151
Playwrights Horizons 140
Plaza Athénée Hotel **159**
The Plaza Hotel **156**
Pleasure Chest 39
Pó 40, **133**
poetry **145–146**
Poetry Project at St Mark's
  146
Poets House 145
police 166
Polo Sport 59
Pommes Frites 35
Pop Shop 28
Popstitute @ Vanity **151**
Portico Bed & Bath 23
postal services 166
Pottery Barn **110**
Potion Lounge 60
Power Pilates **94**
Prada 53, 59, **102**
Prada Sport 23, **102**
Pravda 30
Primorski 71
Prospect Park 73, **91**
PS1 Museum of
  Contemporary Art 73, **88**
PS 44 Market **115**
PS 122, **140, 145**
PS 183 Market **115**
public holidays 166
Public Theater 140
Pucci, Emilio 59
Puerto Rican Day Parade **153**

Q _____
Quad 142
Quakers 166
Queen's **13**
Queens Museum of Art
  73, **81**
Quilted Corner 33
Quilty's 24, **130**

R _____
R 68–69
radio **148**
Radio City Music Hall 73, **75**
Radio Perfecto 34
Radio Shack **113**
railways 9

Rain 63
The Rainbow Room 76
Ralph Lauren 59, **102**
Rangers Ice Hockey Season
  153
Raoul's 25, **136**
Rasputin 71
Raymond Dragon 44
Rebar 151
Recon 15
Record Explosion **113**
record shops see CDs,
  records & tapes
Red Hook 51
Reebok Concept Store
  63, **108**
Refinery 70
Regents 56, **138**
religion 166
renting
  bicycles 11
  cars 11
  roller blades 11
Republic 50
Restaurant 147 45, 46
restaurants **118–133**, 166
  brunch **131**
  burgers **129**
  Carroll Gardens **70**
  Chelsea & the
    Meatpacking District
    45–46
  for children 92, 164
  Coney Island & Brighton
    Beach **71**
  diners **126**
  East Village **34–35**
  eat-in delis **123**
  Fort Greene **69**
  Gramercy Park & the
    Flatiron District **49–50**
  Harlem & the Heights **66**
  Lower East Side &
    Chinatown **16**
  Midtown **54–55**
  neighbourhood standouts
    132–133
  Nolita & Noho **29**
  Soho **24–25**
  tipping 167
  Tribeca **18–19**
  24-hours **133**
  Upper East Side **60**
  Upper West Side **63**
  West Village **40–41**
  Williamsburg **69**
Resurrection 28, 33, **106**
Revolution **94**
Rialto 29, 30, **129**
Rice 29
Richart 53
Ricky's **109**
Riverside Church
  Observatory 76
Rizzoli's 53, **112**
Robert Marc **106**
Robert Miller 54
Robert Moses State Park **91**
Rockaway Beach 91
Rockefeller Center 73, 75
Rocking Horse Café
  Mexicano 46
Rockport 23, **106**
Rogue Scholars 146
roller blades 11
Rooftop Sculpture Garden
  76
Roosevelt Island **13**
Roosevelt Island Tramway 76
Roseland 146
Rosemarie's 19, **130**
Rosina's 70
Rowley, Cynthia 21–22, **104**
The Roxy 97
Royale Theatre **139**
Royalton Hotel **158**
Ruby's Old Thyme Bar 71
Rudy's Bar & Grill 56
Russ & Daughters 16, **114**
The Russian Samovar 56,
  138

S _____
Sacco **106**
safety 166
St Dymphna's 35
St Ignatius Loyola 144
St John the Divine 73, **75**
  concerts 144
St Mark's Bookshop **112**
St Mark's Place, shopping 99
St Nick's Pub 66, **147**
St Patrick's Cathedral 73, **75**
St Patrick's Day Parade **154**
St Regis Hotel **157**

Saints 64
Saks Fifth Avenue 53, **100**
Salander-O'Reilly 60
sales 167
sales tax 166
Salon @ Flamingo East **151**
salsa 147
Samiloff, Sarah 33
Sapphire 33
Sarah Samiloff 33
Savoia 33
Savoy 26
Scheme 65
Schomburg Center 73, **88**
Schubert Theater 139
Scoop **105**
Screaming Mimi's 28, 107
Screening Room 19, **130**
  films 142
SEA Cambodian 69
Sea Lane Bakery 71
Sean **103**
Searle 59
Sears & Robot 33
Second Avenue Deli 35, **123**
Second Stage 140
Selima Optique 23, **108**
Sephora 23, **109**
Serendipity 3 **92**
The Service Station **95**
Sesso 63
Shabby Chic **110**
Shakespeare & Co **112**
Shakespeare in the Park
  140, 153
Shanghai Tang 58–59, **103**
Sharper Image **113**
Shea Stadium 89
Shelburne Murray Hill **162**
Shi 28, 114
Shine 15, **150**
shoe shops **106**
shopping **98–115**, 166–167
  accessories **108**
  beauty **109**
  books **112**
  Carroll Gardens **70**
  CDs, records & tapes
    113–114
  chain stores **105**
  Chelsea & the Meat
    packing District **43–45**
  children's stores **93**
  Coney Island & Brighton
    Beach **71**
  department stores **100**
  discount stores **107**
  East Village **32–34**
  electronics **113**
  fashion **101–105**
  food stores **114–115**
  Fort Greene **69**
  getting your bearings
    98–99
  gift & museum stores
    111–112
  Gramercy Park & the
    Flatiron District **48–49**
  Harlem & the Heights **65–66**
  interiors **110–111**
  Lower East Side &
    Chinatown **14–15**
  markets **115**
  Midtown **52–54**
  Nolita & Noho **27–28**
  shoes **106**
  Soho **21–24**
  theme stores **108**
  Tribeca **18–19**
  Upper East Side **58–60**
  Upper West Side **62–63**
  vintage & secondhand
    106–107
  West Village **38–40**
  Williamsburg **68–69**
Shout @ 13 **152**
Shu Uemura 23, **109**
Siberia 56, **137**
Sideshows by the Seashore
  96
Siena 46
Sigerson Morrison 28, **106**
sights **72–88**
  getting your bearings
    72–73
Sixth Avenue, shopping 99
SJ South and Sons 20
skating 97
Slice of Harlem 66
Smalls Underground 147
Smith, Paul 48, **103**
smoking 167
Soba-ya 35

index

➔ more index

SOB's 147
Soho 21–26, 117
Soho Antique Fair
  Collectibles Market 115
Soho Grand Hotel 158
Soho New York 22
Soho Sanctuary 94
Soho Steak 25
Solomon R Guggenheim
  Museum 73, 80
  museum store 111
  see also Guggenheim
  Museum Soho
Sony Lincoln Plaza 142
Sony Style 53, 108
Sony Wonder Technology
  Lab 93
Sophie's 35
Soup Kiosk 25
Soup Kitchen International
  55
Soup Pot 19
Southgate Tower Suite
  Hotel 162
Spade, Kate 23, 108
Spanish Harlem 13
Spartina 19, 130
spas 94
Spectra 166
Splash 51
sport
  games & activities 96–97
  spectator sports 89
  sports gear stores 108
Spring Festival 154
Spring Street Lounge 30
Spring Street Market 115
Squeezebox @ Don Hills
  151–152
SSS Nice Price 107
Stacia New York 70
Staples 166
Staten Island 13
Staten Island Ferry 76
Statue of Liberty 73, 75,
  77–78
Stella Dallas 39, 107
Stephane Kélian 59, 106
Steve Alan's Outlet 33
Steve Madden 23, 106
Steven-Alan 22, 103
Sticky Mikes @ zi's 152
The Strand 34, 112
Strawberry Fields 73, 75
Street Smarts 73
Structure 105
students
  travel 167
Studio 54 139
Studio Museum of Harlem
  73, 88
  museum store 66
Stussy 23
Suarez 53
suburban trains 9
Subway 76
Subway Inn 61
subways 8, 9
Sugar Shack 67
Sui, Anna 22, 101
Summermase 147
Super Shuttle 6, 7
Supper Club 96, 147
Supreme 23
Sur 70
Surya 41, 128
Susia @ Beer Hall 152
Sway 25
Swedish Marionette
  Theater 93
Sweet & Vicious 30, 134
Sweet Basil 147
Sweet Melissa 70
Sweet Thing @ Rebar 151
Swine on Nine 56, 148
Swing 46 96
Sylvia's 66, 131
Symphony Space 147

T
Tabla 49, 128
Taka 41
Takahachi 35, 128
Takashimaya 53, 100
Tam, Vivienne 22
Taquería de Mexico 41
Tatiana Café 71
tax, sales 166
Tax Free Week 154
Taxi Limousine
  Commission 11
taxis 10–11
  airports 6, 7
  tipping 167
Tayama, Atsuro 22

Tea & Sympathy 41, 127
The Tea Box 55
Teddy's 69
telephoning 167
television 148
Temple Records 34
tennis 89
Teresa's 35
The Terrace 66
Teuscher 53
TG-170 14–15, 105
Thailand Restaurant 16
Tharp, Twyla 144
Theater District 3, 117
theatre 139–140
  for children 93
theme stores 108
34th Street, shopping 99
13 152
Thomas Cook 164, 167
303 Gallery 45
Three of Cups 35
Three Lives & Company
  40, 112
Throb 34
Tiffany's 53
Tillie's of Brooklyn 69
time 167
Time Café 29
Time Hotel 158
Times Square 73, 76
Times Square Visitor
  Information Center 167
Timtoum 15, 106
tipping 167
Titou 40
Tod's 59, 106
Tokio 7 33, 107
Tokyo Joe 33
Tom of Finland 44
Tom Ford 53
Tompkins Square Books 44
Tom's Restaurant 66, 126
Tonic 16, 45, 135, 146
Tony Shafrazi Gallery 24
Tootsi Plohound 23, 106
Tootsie's Children's Books 49
Top of the Tower 56, 76, 136
Torch 16, 141
Tossed 50
TOTEM 18, 111
tourist information 167
tours 73
Tower Books 112
Tower Flea Market 115
Tower Records 53, 113
Town Hall 147
Toys in Babeland 51
Tracey Feith 28, 105
trains 9
Tramps 147
Trannie Chaser @ NowBar
  152
Transit Police 166
transport 6–11
Trattoria dell'Arte 54, 125
travellers' cheques 167
Tribeca 18–20, 117
Tribeca Grill 19
Trinity Church 144
Troy 23
Trump Tower 73, 76
Tsai, Margie 28
TSE 59
Tunnel 150–151
Tuscan Square 55
'21' Club 54, 125
27 Standard 50
Twilo 151
2888 30
2A 36, 137
zi's 152
Two Boots 34–35, 92
  films 142
2 Seven 7 19

U
Ugly Luggage 68
UK consulate 164
UN Building 73, 76
UN Delegates' Dining
  Room 55
Union Pacific 50, 131
Union Square Café 49, 125
Union Square Market 115
Union Square Mass Blade 97
Untitled 39, 103
Upper East Side 58–61
Upper Manhattan 13
Upper West Side 62–64, 117
Urban Outfitters 105
Urban Park Rangers 90
US Open Tennis
  Tournament 153

V
Valentino 59
Vampyros Lesbos @ XVI 152
Vanity 151
Vegetarian Paradise 3 16
Velvet 30
Veniero's 35
Vera Cruz 69
Verbena 50, 131
Veritas 133
Veronica Bond 39
Versace 59, 103
Veruka 25
The View Lounge 76
views 76
Village Chess Shop 39
Village Idiot 46
Village Jazz Shop 40
Village Vanguard 147
Vinnie's Tampon Case 15
Vinny's of Carroll Gardens 70
vintage clothes 106–107
Vinyl 151
Vinylmania 40
Virgil's Real BBQ 54
Virgin Megastore 53, 113
Visa 164, 167
Vivienne Tam 22
Vivienne Westwood 22, 103
Void 25, 142, 138
Vuitton, Louis 23
Vynl Diner 55

W
W 18th and W 19th Streets,
  shopping 99
W 25th and 26th Streets,
  shopping 99
W 28th Street, shopping 99
W 47th Street, shopping 99
W Hotel 158
Waldorf Astoria 156
Walker's 19
walking tours 73
Walter Reade Theater 142
Warner Bros. Studio Store
  53, 108
Washington Heights
  see Harlem & the Heights
Washington Square Hotel
  163
Washington Square Music
  Festival 153
Waterloo 40, 121
Wearmart 28
weather 167
Weber, John 45
websites 148
  spectator sports 89
Webster Hall 146
Weill Recital Hall 143
Welcome to the Johnson's
  16
West Broadway, shopping
  99
West Indian-American Day
  Carnival 153
West Village 38–42, 117
Western Union 164
Westwood, Vivienne 22, 103
Wetlands 147
Whiskey Blue 56
Whiskey Park 56
Whitney Museum of
  American Art 73, 81
Wigstock 153
Wildenstein & Co 60
Williams-Sonoma 44, 111
Williamsburg 68–69
Wilson's 17
Winnie's 17, 135
Winter Garden 71
Wolf, Greg 33
Wollman Rink 97
Women's Film Festival 143
Wonder Bar 36, 138
Woolworth Building 73, 76
Working Class 19
World Trade Center 73, 76
  Observation Deck 76
Worldwide 142
Wyeth 18, 111

X
X-Large 28
XOXO 20
XS New York 97
Xuly Bet 15
XVI 152

Y
Yaffa Café 35, 133
Yama 50
Yamamoto, Yohji 22, 103
Yankee Stadium 89

Yankees & Mets Baseball
  Season 154
yellow cabs 10
Yohji Yamamoto 22, 103
Yonah Schimmel's
  Knishery 15
Yorkville 13
Yves Saint Laurent Rive
  Gauche 22, 104

Z
Zabar's 63, 115
Zapatas Manoletas 67
Zara 105
Zen Palate 50, 131
Zero 27
Zona 23, 111
zoos 92

where to shop

accessories 108
  see also eyewear; hats;
  jewellery; shoes
Anna Sui 22
Bond 07 28
Chrome Hearts 59
Isay's Leather 71
Lucky Wang 15
Maison Moderne 44
Pop Shop 28
Ugly Luggage 68
Vinnie's Tampon Case 15
antiques
  see also vintage furniture
Annex Flea Market 44, 115
Columbus Circle Market
  115
Howard Kaplan Antiques
  39
Pall Mall Antiques 39
PS 44 Market 115
PS 183 Market 115
Soho Antique Fair
  Collectibles Market 115
art
Ace Gallery 24
American Fine Arts 24
Barbara Gladstone 45
C & M Gallery 60
Deitch Projects 24
Gagosian Gallery 60
Hirschl & Adler 60
Janet Borden 45
John Weber 45
Kennedy Galleries 54
Knoedler & Company 60
Larry Gagosian 60
Marlborough Gallery 54
Mary Boone 54
Matthew Marks Gallery 45
Metro Pictures 45
PaceWildenstein 54
Pat Hearn 45
Paula Cooper 45
Phyllis Kind 24
Robert Miller 60
Salander-O'Reilly 60
303 Gallery 24
Tony Shafrazi Gallery 24
Wildenstein & Co 60
bags 108
Fendi 53
Jamin Puech 28, 108
Jutta Neumann 32–33, 106
Kate Spade 23, 108
Louis Vuitton 23
Manhattan Portage 108
Refinery 70
Suarez 53
Tom Ford 53
beauty supplies 109
Aveda 23, 109
Bigelow Pharmacy 39, 109
Bliss Spa 23, 109
Face Stockholm 63, 109
Frédéric Fekkai 59
Fresh 59
Kiehl's 32, 109
M.A.C. 23, 109
Manic Panic 19
Ricky's 109
Sephora 23, 109
Shu Uemura 23, 109
books 112
A Different Light 44, 112
A Photographer's Place 112
Academy Books &
  Records 49
Barnes & Noble 49, 112
Borders 112
Coliseum Books 53
Forbidden Planet 34, 112

Gotham Book Mart 112
Kitchen Arts & Letters 112
Murder Ink 112
Oscar Wilde Memorial Bookstore 40
Rizzoli's 53, 112
St Mark's Bookshop 112
Shakespeare & Co 112
Three Lives & Company 40, 112
Tompkins Square Books 34
Tootsie's Children's Books 93
Tower Books 112
Virgin Megastore 53
CDs, records & tapes 113–114
A Different Light 44
Academy Books & Records 49, 113
Bleecker Bob's Golden Oldies 113
Colony Records 113
Dancetracks 34, 113
Disco Rama 113
Ear Wax 34
8 Ball Records 113
Etherea 34
Fat Beats 40, 113
Finyl Vinyl 34
Footlight Records 34, 113
Generation Records 113
HMV 53, 113
J & R Music & Computer World 113
Jazz Record Center 44, 113
Kim's Video & Music 34, 113
Other Music 113
Record Explosion 113
Temple Records 34
Throb 34
Tower Records 53, 113
Village Jazz Shop 40
Vinylmania 34
Virgin Megastore 53, 113
chain stores 105
Banana Republic 105
Bebe 49
Brooks Bros 105
Club Monaco 49, 105
Eddie Bauer 105
Express 105
French Connection 105
Gap 105
Guess 105
J Crew 105
Joan & David 106
Juno's 106
Kenneth Cole 106
Kmart 106
9 & Co 106
Nine West 106
Old Navy 44, 105
Payless 106
Sacco 106
Steve Madden 106
Structure 105
Urban Outfitters 105
XOXO 105
Zara 105
Chinese emporiums
Oriental Dress Company 15
Oriental Gifts 15
Pearl River Mart 15
clubwear
Air Market 33
Hotel Venus 102
L'Impasse 39
Liquid Sky 28
Mary Adams 14
Patricia Field 38–39

Antique Boutique 27, 104
APC 101
Atsuro Tayama 22
Behrle 19
Betsey Johnson 21, 104
Big Drop 22
Blue 33
Built By Wendy/Cake 28
Burberry 53
Calvin Klein 59, 101
Calypso St Barths 28, 104
Catherine 22, 104
Chanel 53
Chloé 59
Christian Dior 53
Commes des Garçons 3, 101
Costume National 22, 101
Cynthia Rowley 21–22, 104
D/L Cerney 19
Daryl K 28, 33, 104
DDC Lab 15
Dolce & Gabbana 59, 101–102
Dosa 22
Dressing Room 28
Eileen Fisher 33
Emporio Armani 48, 59, 102
Etro 59
Fendi 104
Frida's Closet 70
Garb 33
Givenchy 59
Gucci 59, 101
Helmut Lang 22, 102
Horn 33
If Boutique 102
Intermix 48–49
Isabel Toledo Lab 48
Issey Miyake Pleats Please 22, 104
J Morgan Puett Studio 19
Jeffrey 44
Jill Anderson 33
Joseph 59
Juan Anon 15
Language 28
Louie 22
Lucien Pellat-Finet 28
Marc Jacobs 22, 104
Margie Tsai 28
Mark Montana 33
Min Lee 15
Missoni 59
Miu Miu 22, 105
Morgan Le Fay 22, 105
Moschino 59
Nicole Farhi 59
Nova 101
Nylon Squid 27
Olive & Bette 62, 105
Patch 155 15
Phare 28
Prada 53, 102
Ralph Lauren 59, 102
Scoop 105
Shanghai Tang 58–59
Soho New York 22
Stacia New York 70
Steve Alan's Outlet 33
Steven-Alan 22, 103
TG-170 14—15, 105
Tracey Feith 28, 105
TSE 59
Untitled 39, 103
Valentino 59
Veronica Bond 39
Versace 59, 103
Vivienne Tam 22
Vivienne Westwood 22, 103
Xuly Bet 15
Yohji Yamamoto 22, 103
Zero 27

eyewear 108
Robert Marc 108
Selima Optique 23, 108
fashion see chain stores;
clubwear; designer clothes;
discount stores; flagship
stores; menswear;
streetwear; vintage clothes
flagship stores
Burberry 53
Chanel 53
Christian Dior 53
Gap 53
Gucci 53
Hermès 53
Prada 53
flowers & plants
Chelsea Garden Store 44
Union Square Market 115
food 114–115
Balducci's 40, 114
Chelsea Market 44, 115
Dean & Deluca 23, 114
Eli's Bread at the Vinegar Factory 115
Fairways 63
Garden of Eden 114
Godiva Chocolatier 53
Gourmet Garage 23, 114
Jefferson Market 40
M&I 71
Mart 125 66
Mrs Stahl's Knishery 71
Murray's Cheese Shop 114
Odessa 71
Philip's Candy Store 71
Richart 53
Russ & Daughters 114
Sea Lane Bakery 71
Teuscher 53
Union Square Market 115
Zabar's 115
furniture
see also antiques; interiors;
vintage furniture
Amalgamated Home 39
Crate & Barrel 53
H 33
Las Venus 110
TOTEM 111
Wyeth 111
Zona 111
gifts 111–112
see also museum stores
Alphaville 39
And Bob's Your Uncle 44
Felissimo 53, 111
Pearl River Mart 111
Sears & Robot 33
Shi 28, 112
Troy 112
hats 108
Amy Downs 14, 108
Kelly Christie 108
Selima Optique 23
health & beauty
see beauty
home furnishings
see furniture; interiors
interiors 110–111
ABC Carpet & Home 49, 110
Ad-Hoc Software 23, 110
African Paradise 66
Amalgamated Hardware 39
Amalgamated Home 39
Amaranth 18
Anandmali 19
Antik 18
Apartment 48 44
Astroturf 70
Bed Bath Beyond 110
Campagna Home 49
Cobblestones 33
Crate & Barrel 53
Dom 23
Eclectic Home 44
Fishs Eddy 49, 110
Gracious Home 59, 110
H 33
Hold Everything 44
It's a Mod, Mod World 33
Jonathan Adler 23, 110
Kaarta Imports 66
Las Venus 110
Main Street Ephemera/ Paper Collectibles 70
Moss 23, 110
Mxyplyzyk 44
Orange Chicken 19
Oser 18–19
Portico Bed & Bath 23
Pottery Barn 110
Quilted Corner 33

Shabby Chic 110
TOTEM 18, 111
Williams-Sonoma 44, 111
Wyeth 18, 111
Zona 23, 111
jewellery 108
Bamboozle Studio 66
Bond 07 108
Cartier 53
Fragments 108
Greg Wolf 33
Sarah Samiloff 33
Tiffany's 53
lingerie
Le Corset 23
Nocturne 59
Only Hearts 62
magazines
Barnes & Noble 148
Forbidden Planet 34
Hudson News 148
News Café 148
Pink Pony 148
Tower Books 148
Universal News 148
makeup see beauty
markets 115
Annex Flea Market 44, 115
Chelsea Flea Market 44, 115
Columbus Circle Market 115
Columbus Flea Market 115
Malcolm Shabazz Harlem Market 66, 115
Mart 125 66
Orchard Street Market 115
PS 44 Market 115
PS 183 Market 115
Soho Antique Fair Collectibles Market 115
Spring Street Market 115
Tower Flea Market 115
Union Square Market 115
menswear 103–104
Alpana Bawa 22
Anna Sui 101
Beau Geste 39
Brooks Bros 105
Calvin Klein 101
The Harlem Collective 65–66
Helmut Lang 22, 102
Hotel of the Rising Star 28
Lee's Mardi Gras 44
Lucien Pellat-Finet 28
Nova 103
Paul Smith 48, 103
Prada 59, 102
Raymond Dragon 44
Recon 15
Savoia 33
Scheme 65
Sean 103
Tom of Finland 44
Tracey Feith 28
Untitled 39
Wearmart 28
YSL Men 23, 104
museum stores 111–112
Cooper-Hewitt National Museum Design Store 111
Guggenheim Museum Store 111
Metropolitan Museum of Art Store 111
Museum of Modern Art Store 111
Studio Museum Gift Shop 66
newspapers 148
Barnes & Noble 148
Hudson News 148
News Café 148
Pink Pony 148
Tower Books 148
Universal News 148
photography see cameras
secondhand clothes
see vintage clothes
shoes 106
Freelance 106
Jamin Puech 28
Jimmy Choo 53, 106
Joan & David 106
Juno's 106
Jutta Neumann 32–33, 106
Kenneth Cole 49, 106
Le Petit Peton 39, 106
Manolo Blahnik 53, 106
9 & Co 106
Nine West 106
Patrick Cox 59
Payless 106
Rockport 106
Sacco 106

consignment stores
Tokio 7 33
Tokyo Joe 33
cosmetics see beauty
department stores 100
Barneys New York 58, 100
Bergdorf Goodman 52–53, 100
Bloomingdales 58, 100
Felissimo 53, 111
Henri Bendel 53
Jeffrey 100
Macy's 53, 100
Saks Fifth Avenue 53, 100
Takashimaya 53, 100
designer clothes 101–102
see also consignment stores
menswear; vintage clothes
A Détacher 27
Alberta Ferretti 22
Alpana Bawa 22
Anna 33
Anna Sui 101

discount stores 107
Century 21 107
Daffy's 107
Loehmann's 44, 107
SSS Nice Price 107
drink
Astor Wines & Spirits 114
Best Cellars 114
electronics 113
B & H Photo-Video 113
J & R Music & Computer World 113
Nobody Beats the Wiz 113
Radio Shack 113
Sharper Image 113
erotica
Naughty & Nice 62
Pink Pussycat Boutique 39
Pleasure Chest 39
Toys in Babeland 15

Sigerson Morrison 28, **106**
Stephane Kélian 59, **106**
Steve Madden 23, **106**
Tod's 59, **106**
Tootsi Plohound 23, **106**
Zara 105
sports equipment 108
Paragon 49
Modell's **108**
sportswear 108
Club Monaco 49
Diesel 53
Foot Locker **108**
Gap 53
Malia Mills 28
Modell's **108**
Paragon **102**
Polo Sport 59
Prada Sport **102**
Reebok Concept Store 63, **108**
Searle 59
Supreme 28
stationery
Kate's Paperie 39
streetwear
see also chain stores
Banana Republic 49
Bebe 49
Canal Jeans 23
Courtney Washington 69
D/L Cerney **101**
Dave's 44
Diesel **101**
Domsey's Warehouse Outlet 68
Emilio Pucci 59
Exodus Industrial Sport 69
4W Circle of Art 69
The Harlem Collective 65–66
Hotel Venus 22–23
J Crew 49
Max & Roebling 68
MIKS 15
Moshood 69
Prada Sport 23
Searle 59
Shanghai Tang **103**
Stussy 23
Urban Outfitters **105**
Working Class 19
X-Large 28
theme stores 108
Disney Store 53, **108**
FAO Schwarz 53
Firefighter's Friend 28
NBA store 53
Niketown **108**
Original Levi's Store **108**
Sony Style 53, **108**
Village Chess Shop 39
Warner Bros Studio Store 53, **108**
thrift
Housing Works Thrift Shop 44, **107**
Out of the Closet 59, **107**
toys
Enchanted Forest **93**
FAO Schwarz 53, **93**
Penny Whistle Toys **93**
vintage clothes 106–107
see also consignment stores
Allan & Suzi 62
Apartment 141 33
Canal Jeans **107**
Center for the Dull **107**
Cherry 15, **106**
Darrow 7 49, **107**
Dressing Room 28
Fab 208 33
The Fan Club 49
Filthmart 33
Ina **107**
Metropolis 33
Phare 28
Resurrection 28, 33, **106**
Screaming Mimi's 28, **107**
Shine 15
Stella Dallas 39, **107**
Timtoum 15, **106**
Tokio 7 **107**
vintage furniture
Junk 69
Las Venus 15
Lively Set 39
R 68–69
watches
Casio Baby G-Shock 23

where to eat

African/Caribbean
Africa 66
Keur 'n' Dye 69
Mekka 35
Negril 46
Obaa Koryoe 66
American
see also burgers; diners; Mexican; soul food; steaks & grills
Alison on Dominick Street 24, **129**
Alley's End 45
Astor Restaurant & Lounge 29
B-Bar 29, **120**
Blue Ribbon 24, **132**
Bouley Bakery 19, **122**
Bryant Park Grill & Café 54
Cafeteria 45
Candela 50
Copeland's 66, **124**
Danal 34
Drover's Tap Room 40
Eleven Madison Park 49, **121**
First 34, **132**
Gotham Bar & Grill 41, **123**
Gramercy Tavern 49, **125**
Grange Hall 40, **132**
Harmony 24
Home 40
The Independent 19
Indigo 41
Jean Georges 63, **123**
Joanie's 50
Lenox Room 60
Liam 41
Lucien Blue 70
Mercer Kitchen 24, **121**
Mesa Grill 49, **128**, **131**
Miss Ann's 69
Old Devil Moon 35, **126**
Park View at the Boathouse **130**
Quilty's 24, **130**
Savoy 7
Screening Room 19, **130**
Sesso 63
Tabla 49, **128**
Time Café 29
The Tonic 45
Torch 16
Tribeca Grill 19
'21' Club 54, **125**
Two Boots 34–35
Union Square Café 49, **125**
Verbena 50, **131**
Veritas **133**
Austrian
Bistro at Candy Bar's 46
bagels
Bagels by the Park 70
Barney Greengrass 63, **123**
Ess-a-Bagel 55, **123**
Russ & Daughters 16
Yonah Schimmel's Knishery 16
bar/restaurants
Audubon Bar & Grill 67
Baby Jupiter 16, **134**
Bond St 30
Café Largo 66
Café Noir 25
Chumley's 41, **136**
Clementine 41
Decibel 36, **137**
The Galaxy 51
Japas 55 56
Joe's Pub 30
Junno's 41
Malachy's Donegal Inn 64
Marylou's 41
Odessa 36
Pete's Tavern 51
PJ Hanley's 70
Raoul's 25, **136**
Regents 56, **138**
Rudy's 45
SJ South and Sons 20
Sugar Shack 67
Tonic 16
Belgian
Markt 46
Petite Abeille 46
Pommes Frites 35
Waterloo 40, **121**
bistros
Alley's End 45
Balthazar 29, **120**
Bistro at Candy Bar 46
Café Spice 41

Casimir 34
Corner Bistro 41
Fanelli 24
Indigo 41
Jules 34
La Bonne Soupe 54, **129**
Le Jardin Bistrot 29, **130**
Le Tableau 34
Lucien 34
Lucky Strike 24
New City Bar & Grill 69
Odeon 19, **125**
Patois 70
Payard Patisserie & Bistro 60, **133**
Rialto 29, **129**
Soho Steak 25
Vinny's of Carroll Gardens 70
breakfast & brunch 131
Buffa's Delicatessen 30
Flavors 50
Grange Hall **132**
Le Gamin 46
Mayrose 50
Mesa Grill **128**, **131**
Odeon 19, **125**
Screening Room **130**
7A 35, **131**
Sylvia's **131**
Tea & Sympathy **127**
Teresa's 35
Three of Cups 35
burgers 129
Big Nick's Burger 61, **129**
Corner Bistro **129**
Island Burgers & Shakes 55, **129**
Jackson Hole 60, **129**
Rialto 29, **129**
cafés & patisseries
see also bistros; diners; teas
ABC Parlour 50
Big Cup 46
Big Nick's Burger 61, **129**
Bright Food Shop 46
Brisas del Caribe 25
Brooklyn Moon Café 69
Bryant Park Grill & Café 54
Buffa's Delicatessen 30
Café con Leche 63
Café Gitane 30
Café Habana 30
Café Lalo 63
Café Restaurant Volna 71
Cafeteria **121**
Chez Brigitte 41
City Bakery 50
Coffee Shop 50
Cookie's Fine Foods 46
Curry in a Hurry 50
Dojo's 35
DT-UT 60
Eisenberg Sandwich Shop 50
Ess-a-Bagel 55, **123**
Fall Café 70
Flavors 50
Great Jones Café 30
Habib's Place 35
Herban Kitchen 25
Hungarian Pastry Shop 66
'Ino 41
Island Burgers & Shakes 55, **133**
Jackson Hole 60, **129**
Kelley & Ping 25
Krispy Kreme's 66
L Café 69
Le Gamin 46
Les Deux Gamins 41
Lotus Club 16
Mayrose 50
Mezze 55
Monteleone's 70
O Padeiro 46, **132**
Once upon a Tart 25
Papaya King 60
Payard Patisserie & Bistro 60, **133**
Pepe Rosso 25
Petite Abeille 46
Pommes Frites 35
Republic 50
Second Avenue Deli 35
Soup Kiosk 35
Soup Kitchen International 55
Sweet Melissa 70
Tatiana Café 71
Tea & Sympathy 41
Tillie's 69
Tossed 50

Tuscan Square 55
Veniero's 35
Yaffa Café 35
Cambodian
SEA Cambodian 69
Chinese
First Wok 60
Grand Sichuan 16
Great Shanghai 16
Hong Kong Egg Cake Co 16
Jing Fong 16
Joe's Shanghai 16, **128**
New Wonton Garden 16
New York Noodle Town 16
delicatessens 123
Barney Greengrass 63, **123**
Bread & Butter 30
Buffa's Delicatessen 30
Ess-a-Bagel 55, **123**
Katz's Deli 16, **123**
Russ & Daughters 16
Second Avenue Deli 35, **123**
Yonah Schimmel's Knishery 16
diners
see also bistros; cafés
Bodega 19
Comfort Diner 60, **126**
Diner 69
Empire Diner 46, **126**
Jerry's 25, **124**
Joe Jr's 41, **126**
Jones Diner 30
Kasia's 69
Kitchenette 19
Moondance Diner 25
Nathan's Famous Restaurant 71
Old Devil Moon 35, **126**
Soup Pot 19
Teresa's 35
Tom's Restaurant 66, **126**
Vynl Diner 55
Walker's 19
East European
Kasia's 69
Teresa's 35
French
Alison on Dominick Street 24, **129**
Avenue 63
Balthazar 29, **120**
Bar Six 40
Bayard's **122**
Café Boulud 60
Café des Artistes 63, **124**
Capsouto Frères 19, **129**
Casimir 34
Chanterelle 19
Country Café 24
Daniel 60, **122**
Eleven Madison Park **121**
Florent 45, **124**
French Roast 40
Jean Claude 25
Jean Georges 63, **123**
JoJo 60
Jules 34
Kitchen Club 29
La Bonne Soupe 54, **129**
La Lunchonette 45
Le Bernardin 55, **123**
Le Jardin Bistro 29, **130**
Lespinasse 55, **123**
Lucien 34
Mercer Kitchen 24
Montrachet 19
New City Bar & Grill 69
Patois 70
Payard Patisserie & Bistro 60, **133**
Restaurant 147 45
The Terrace 19
Titou 40
global
Asia de Cuba 54
Brooklyn Mod 70
Café Boulud 60
Lola 50
Radio Perfecto 34
27 Standard 50
2 Seven 7 19
UN Delegates Dining Room 55
Union Pacific 50
Greek
see also Mediterranean
Periyali 55
ice cream
Chinatown Ice Cream Factory 16
Monteleone's 70
Indian
Café Spice 41
Curry in a Hurry 50

Haveli 35
Surya 41, **128**
Internet cafés **148**
Irish
St Dymphna's 35
Italian
see also pasta; pizza
Acquario **132**
Babbo 40, **120**
Bar Pitti 40, **132**
Bottino 45
Carino 60
Don Giovanni 54
I Trulli 50
Il Bagatto 34, **121**
Il Buco **121**
'Ino 41, **126**
Lombardi's 29, **126**
Po 40, **133**
Restaurant 147 45
Rosemarie's 19, **130**
Sesso 63
Siena 46
Three of Cups 36
Trattoria dell'Arte 54
Tuscan Square 55
Two Boots 34–35
Veniero's 35
Japanese
Avenue A Sushi 35
Bond St 29, **120**
Japonica 41
Next Door Nobu 19
Nobu 19, **121**
Soba-ya 35
Taka 41
Takahachi 35, **128**
Yama 50
Jewish
Barney
Greengrass 63, **123**
Katz's Deli 16
Russ &
Daughters 16
Second Avenue
Deli 35
Yonah Schimmel's
Knishery 16
Korean
Cho Dang Gol 55, **127**
Dok Suni's 34
Hangawi 55

Latin American see
Mexican; South American
Malaysian
Nyonya 29
Penang 24
Mediterranean
see also French; Greek;
Italian; Portuguese, Spanish
Acquario 29
Astor Restaurant &
Lounge 29
Danal 34
Il Buco 29
Mezze 55
The Place 40
Rice 29
Rosina's 70
Spartina 19, **130**
Mexican
El Rey del Sol 45
El Sombrero 16
Gabriela's 63
Los Dos Rancheros
Mexicanos 55
Mexican Radio 29
Rocking Horse Café
Mexicano 46
Taqueria de Mexico 41
Vera Cruz 69
Middle Eastern
Casa
La Femme 24
Layla 19
Moustache 41
Oznot's Dish 69
Moroccan
Bar Six 40
Chez Es Saada 34
Country Café 24
Time Café 29
Oriental
see also Cambodian;
Chinese; Japanese; Korean;
Thai; Vietnamese
Clay 29
The Elephant 34
Honmura An 24
Lucky Cheng's 35
Republic 29
Rice 29
Zen Palate 50

outdoor tables
American Park **129**
Bar Pitti **132**
Bottino 45
Bryant Park Grill & Café 54
Park View at the
Boathouse **130**
7A **131**
Tatiana Café 71
Verbena 50
pasta
Babbo 40
Bottino 45
Don Giovanni 54
Il Bagatto **121**
Il Buco 29
Pepe Rosso **127**
Rialto 29, **129**
Three of Cups 36
Vinny's of Carroll
Gardens 70
pizzas
Don Giovanni 54
Grimaldi's **126**
Lombardi's 29, **126**
Slice of Harlem 66
Spartina **130**
Three of Cups 36
Two Boots 34–35
Portuguese
Acquario **132**
O Padeiro 46, **132**
Scandinavian
Aquavit 55, **122**
seafood
American Park **129**
Aquagrill 24
Blue Water Grill 49–50
Ideya 24–25
Le Bernardin 55
Markt 46
Oyster Bar 54, **125**
Park View at the
Boathouse **130**
Periyali 50
Pisces 34, **133**
Surya 41, **128**
Trattoria dell'Arte **125**
Union Pacific 131
soul food
Copeland's 66
Mekka 35

Sugar Shack 67
Sylvia's 66
South American
see also Mexican
Calle Ocho 63, **127**
Casa 40
Ideya 24–25
Pampa 63, **127**
Patria 50, **128**
Sur 70
Spanish
Acquario **132**
El Cid 45
Flor de Sol 19
Il Buco **121**
Sri Lankan
Lakruwana 55
steaks & grills
Keens Steakhouse 54
Michael Jordan's The
Steakhouse NYC 54
Virgil's Real BBQ 54
teas
Payard Patisserie & Bistro
60, **133**
Tea & Sympathy 41, **127**
The Tea Box 55
Thai
Holy Basil 35
Plan Eat Thailand 69
Rain 63
Thailand Restaurant 16
Turkish
Bereket **133**
24-hour opening **133**
vegan
Josie's 63
Zen Palate 50
vegetarian **131**
Angelica Kitchen 35, **131**
Cho Dang Gol 55
Hangawi 55
Lakruwana 55
Vegetarian Paradise 3 16
Zen Palate **131**
Vietnamese
Indochine 29
MeKong 29
Miss Saigon 60
Nha Trang 16
Rain 63

↓ acknowledgements

No part of this text may be reproduced, stored in a retrival system, or transmitted in any form or by any means, electronic, mechanical, photocopying, recording or otherwise, without the prior written permission of the copyright owner.

This book is sold subject to the condition that it shall not, by way of trade or otherwise, be lent, resold, hired out or otherwise circulated without the publisher's prior written consent in any form of binding or cover other than in that which it is published and without a similar condition, including this condition being imposed upon the subsequent purchaser.

Conceived, edited & designed by
Virgin Publishing Ltd
London w6 9ht
Tel: 0171-386 3300

Project Editor: Naomi Peck
Designer: Lisa Kosky
DTP Designer: Ingrid Vienings
Editorial Assistant: Claire Fogg
Design & editorial assistance: Cooling Brown, Michael Ellis, Sarah Handy (NYCVB, London), Tony Limerick, Irene Lyford, Ella Milroy, Sally Prideaux, Annie Reid, Jane Simmonds, Clare Tomlinson, Fiona Wild, Trond Wilhelmsen, Simon Winstone
Series Editor: Georgina Matthews
Consultant: Eve Claxton
Researcher: Katya Rogers
Proof reader: Stewart Wild | **Index:** Hilary Bird
Jacket concept: Debi Ani

Maps:
Cartographic editor: Dominic Beddow
Cartographer: Jethro Lennox
Draughtsman Ltd, London
0181–960 1602| Email: maps@atlas.co.uk

Photography: Benoit Peverelli

Reproduced by Colourwise
Printed by Jarrold Book Printers

Features in this guide were written and researched by:
Transport: Katya Rogers | **Getting Your Bearings (areas):** Katya Rogers | **Area write-ups:** Eve Claxton (introductions), Eve Claxton, C Leggett (shopping), Angela Tribelli (bars), Julie Besonen (restaurants), Angela Tribelli | **Brooklyn:** Alfred Gingold, Helen Rogan | **Landmarks:** Katya Rogers | **Sights, Museums and Galleries:** Karen Robinovitz, Walter Robinson, Katya Rogers | **Sport and Kids:** Anngel Delaney | **Parks & Beaches:** Katya Rogers | **Body & Soul and Game for a Laugh:** Karen Robinovitz | **Shops:** Julie Besonen, Eve Claxton, C Leggett, Denise Maher, Karen Robinovitz | **Restaurants:** Julie Besonen, Karen Robinovitz, Kate Sekules | **Bars:** Angela Tribelli | **Cinema:** Michael Atkinson (cinema), Dan Bova (comedy), Lorie Caval (clubs), Viven Goldman (music & poetry), Scott Jolley (cabaret), Ann Midgette (dance, opera & classical music, theatre), Katya Rogers (media and events) |
Hotels: Monica Forrestall | **Practical:** Katya Rogers.

Acknowledgements and credits:
Virgin Publishing Ltd would like to thank all galleries, museums, shops, restaurants, bars and other establishments who provided photographs. Photo credits (t=top; b=bottom): Sara Matthews 40; Todd Eberle 43b; Antoine Bootz for Felissimo 53b; Enrico Ferorelli 79t; Fred George 79b; Ellen Labenski 81; Sara Moy 82; John Berens 87; Linda Farwell 92; Laurence Galud 94; Yann Gamblin 122. New York subway and bus maps were reproduced by permission of MTA New York City Transit.

Great care has been taken with this guide to be as accurate and up-to-date as possible, but details such as addresses, telephone numbers, opening hours, prices and travel information are liable to change. The publishers cannot accept responsibility for any consequences arising from the use of this book. We would be delighted to receive any corrections and suggestions for inclusion in the next edition.

Please write to or email:
Virgin Travel Guides
Virgin Publishing Ltd
Thames Wharf Studios
Rainville Road
London w6 9ht
Fax: 0171-386 3360
Email: travel@virgin-pub.co.uk

index

⊙ key to symbols

symbols

☎ telephone number
F fax
e email
w worldwide web
❶ hot tips
⚘ good points
⚘ bad points
◑ opening times
♿ wheelchair access
  (phone to check details)
🏛 shop
☕° restaurant/café or
  food available
🍷 bar/pub
☞ hotel
⌞$⌟ price
◔ frequency/times
► picture arrow

☰ **credit cards**
  AE = American Express
  DC = Diners Club
  MC = Mastercard
  V = Visa
  all = AE/DC/MC/V
  are accepted
★ recommended (featured
  in listings section)

transport

Ⓜ metro
🚌 city bus/coach
🚐 shuttle bus
🚗 cabs
✈ airport
⛴ ferry/cruise boat pier
🅿 parking
↕ uptown/downtown service
↔ crosstown service
⬭ highway
㊻ US interstate

key to area maps

white streets = streets
with lots of shops,
restaurants, bars etc

grey block =
important building

sights, museums, galleries & parks

▶ forthcoming openings
👁 don't miss
🔲 recorded information line
□ small collection/museum
◲ mid-sized collection/museum
◻ large collection/museum
☞ guided tours
🎧 audio guides
🧒 kids' activities/age group
⦿ sports & activities
🛼 roller blading
⛸ ice skating
🐎 horse riding
🚻 restroom

restaurants & cafés, bars & pubs

$ cheap (main courses under
  $10 excluding taxes)
$$ moderate (main courses
  $10–$20 excluding taxes)
$$$ expensive (main courses
  over $20 excluding taxes)
⚑ capacity
Ⓢ set menu
◿ smoking allowed
▤ air conditioning
🌿 outdoor area/garden
Ⓥ good vegetarian selection
🎵 live music
☆ live entertainments
● DJs
◐ satellite/cable TV
◖ open during the day

clubs

□ small venue
◲ mid-sized venue
◻ large venue
👑 dress code

hotels

🛏 number of beds
☕ breakfast included
▤ air conditioning
㉔ 24-hour room service
≋ swimming pool
↔ fitness facilities
🌿 business facilities
🌿 outdoor area/garden

shops

$ cheap
$$ moderate
$$$ expensive